The Usable Past presents a comparative discussion of American literary modes of historical imagining. Taking America in its hemispheric sense, Lois Parkinson Zamora presents a broad-ranging discussion of essential American voices – among them Borges, Hawthorne, Emerson, Williams, Paz, Carpentier, Cather, Fuentes, Cortázar, Rulfo, Cisneros, Puig, Vargas Llosa, Morrison, García Márquez. These writers dramatize the convergences and divergences of history and fiction as they question the nature of both. Zamora argues that they are impelled by a peculiarly American energy – what she calls an "anxiety of origins" – to search for precursors and connect to (or invent) usable traditions and histories. They conceive of originality not as novelty but as a complicated and enriched relation to their cultural traditions. How American writers thematize usable American pasts, and how their work itself becomes part of the usable past, is Zamora's overarching concern.

THE USABLE PAST

Angelus Novus, Paul Klee, 1920. Courtesy of the Israel Museum.

THE USABLE PAST

PAST

The Imagination of History
in Recent Fiction of the
Americas

Lois Parkinson Zamora
University of Houston

CAMBRIDGE
UNIVERSITY PRESS

PUBLISHED BY THE PRESS SYNDICATE OF THE
UNIVERSITY OF CAMBRIDGE
The Pitt Building, Trumpington Street, Cambridge, CB2 1RP, United Kingdom

CAMBRIDGE UNIVERSITY PRESS
The Edinburgh Building, Cambridge CB2 2RU, United Kingdom
40 West 20th Street, New York, NY 10011-4211, USA
10 Stamford Road, Oakleigh, Melbourne 3166, Australia

First published 1997

Printed in the United States of America

Typeset in Trump Medieval

Library of Congress Cataloging-in-Publication Data
Zamora, Lois Parkinson.
The usable past : the imagination of history in recent fiction of the Americas /
Lois Parkinson Zamora.
p. cm.
ISBN 0-521-58253-9 (hb)
1. Spanish American fiction – 20th century – History and criticism.
2. American fiction – 20th century – History and criticism.
3. History in literature. 4. Literature and history – America.
5. Intertextuality. I. Title.
PQ7082.N7Z35 1997
863 – dc21   96-51160

A catalog record for this book is available from
the British Library

ISBN 0 521 58253 9 hardback

For Kathleen Haney
friend and guide

I have realized as I grow older that history,
in the end, has more imagination than oneself.
Gabriel García Márquez

Contents

Preface

THE USABLE PAST began as I was writing a book on apocalyptic historicism in contemporary U.S. and Latin American fiction. As I worked on that project, I found that I was persistently drawn to investigate other attitudes toward history and literary tradition besides the apocalyptic, in part to test my hypotheses about American apocalypticism and in part, no doubt, to counterbalance the peculiar intensities of that mode. As I strayed from Armageddon, I repeatedly encountered a contrasting impulse to create precursors rather than cancel them. This other impulse involved a characteristic historical awareness – what I call an anxiety of origins – with respect to New World cultural histories and traditions. In my introduction I establish connections between this anxiety and the narrative energies that constitute usable histories and traditions. How these energies operate in selected works of U.S. and Latin American fiction is the subject of the chapters that follow.

My title is drawn from Van Wyck Brooks' essay, "On Creating a Usable Past," and signals the ambivalence (often ironic) of history in a "new" world.[1] "Usable" implies the active engagement of a user or users, through whose agency collective and personal histories are constituted. The term thus obviates the possibility of innocent history, but not the possibility of authentic history when it is actively imagined by its user(s). What is deemed usable is valuable; what is valuable is constituted according to specific cultural and personal needs and desires. How such judgments of value are made, and how they operate to form literary texts and traditions in the Americas, are essential features of my discussion.

Still, one might worry that "usable" risks a kind of single-minded functionalism belying the polysemic nature of both history and literature. In which case, I would suggest its more prospective analogue, the "useful" past. What is usable – a culture's available artifacts – will be useful when it corresponds to the desires and directions of users. This dialectic between historical determinations and literary intentions characterizes the fiction that interests me here.

Other metaphors are also woven into my discussion. "Anxiety of (about) origins" is consonant with "the usable past" in referring to the particular tensions of historical awareness in a "new" world. Borges' Aleph, Walter Benjamin's "aura" and his "Angelus Novus" will provide metaphoric access to the American urge to express historical disjunction and/or absence. Roberto González Echevarría incites me to propose a metaphor to complement his own for the motivating force of the Latin American literary tradition: to his Archival impulse, I will add what I feel to be the stronger operations of an Ancestral impulse. Frank Kermode's sense of an ending suggests the complementary American sense of openness and endlessness – hence the sense of a sequel. Borges' "modest history," along with Fuentes' "eccentric history," encode recognizably American forms of resistance to imported historical hierarchies. I conclude my study by proposing that the baroque is a useful (and heretofore under-used) metaphor for these literary imaginings of New World history.

In short, metaphors abound in the following chapters, as they tend to in discussions of historical consciousness. Because what we call history is a complex of interpretive structures, metaphors are inevitable, whether they happen to be spatial (history as linear, circular, spiraling), conceptual (history as eschatological, dialectical, material, mythic), or existential (Borges' Aleph, Benjamin's Angelus Novus, Charles Simic's fat old man in faded overalls). I engage these metaphors and others as I go along, the better to direct my reader toward a comparative consideration of my overarching metaphor, the American historical imagination.

These figural formulations will have, I hope, the collective effect of suggesting that my critical concerns are larger and more various than those usually implied by the term "historical fiction." The writers whom I discuss here *do* write historical fiction, but not in any ordinary sense. Seymour Menton, in a study of the "new historical novel" in Latin America, limits his critical parameters to novels that depict "action . . . in a period previous to the author's."[2] This is, of course, the traditional definition of historical fiction, but I will need to complicate the category considerably in order to discuss the work of Fuentes, Borges, Hawthorne, Goyen, García Márquez, Vargas Llosa, Cisneros, and others. These writers may base their fictions, or parts of them, on the recorded histories of nations and individuals, but not always, or not always explicitly. They recognize that the concept of history must itself be located historically, whether they write in the past tense, the present, the future or, for that matter, the retrospective future – as in García Márquez's *Cien años de soledad* (*One Hundred Years of Solitude*, 1967) and *Crónica de una muerte anunciada* (*Chronicle of a Death Foretold*, 1981). They also recognize that the work of literature is itself a historical agent and artifact, itself a historical event conditioned by historical circumstances and also conditioning them. So the work may become an event in the history it interprets: *One Hundred Years of Solitude* is clearly an additional event in the inordinate Colombian history that unfolds in Macondo. As García Márquez's novel so clearly illustrates, the recuperation of historical events and personages is only one dimension of these novelists' literary enterprise.

I have organized my discussion into two parts. Part I, "Anxiety of Origins," addresses the divergent dimensions of American history *in* selected works of fiction. In Part II, "Intertextuality and Tradition," it is the history *of* literature and literary form that interests me. To the extent that content can be separated from form, I would say that the chapters in Part I deal with history as subject, and the chapters in Part II with formal structures and strategies that are themselves historicizing devices. But both parts are animated by the common conviction that works of literature are privileged bearers of a culture's history.

In Chapters 1 and 3 I explore the uses of European and indigenous conceptions of history in American traditions of literary realism and counter-realism, respectively. Two pairings – Carlos Fuentes and Willa Cather, and Jorge Luis Borges and Nathaniel Hawthorne – allow me to contrast the historiographic traditions impelling literary realism in the first chapter and, in the third chapter, to compare Latin American magical realism and the U.S. romance tradition. Chapter 2 serves as a bridge between these discussions. Here, I analyze texts that juxtapose conceptions of "fact" and "fiction" in order to test the capacity of novelistic narrative to represent historical realities. Using Linda Hutcheon's term, this fiction is "historiographic metafiction" in that it questions the nature of history as such, the capacity (and limitations) of narrative media to represent it, and the processes by which readers interpret textual histories in the midst of their own on-going experience of history.[3] How can we know the past? How can we speak of it in literary forms? Why should we want to?

R. B. Kersher has noted that the historian is oriented toward diachrony, the literary critic toward synchrony.[4] In Part II, I am concerned with writers who themselves dramatize synchronic, decentered, and often conflictual cultural traditions, and who do so in intertextual narrative structures that include multiple mythic and real(istic) temporal orders. Chapters 4 and 5, "Synchronic Structures" and "Fragmentary Fictions," are paired in their discussion of such narrative strategies. Chapter 6, "Clichés and Community," addresses another intertextual element: clichés are already-used but (potentially) still-usable literary and linguistic structures, so their use (or not) provides a telling index of a writer's historical and cultural positioning. In each of the chapters of this second section, my aim is to uncover the historical operations of literary forms and languages, and trace the ways in which selected authors self-consciously participate in the construction of a usable American canon.

The chapters in Part II are more specific in their analysis of narrative techniques than those in Part I, and unequal in their comparative emphases. In them, I pay more attention to contemporary fiction in Spanish than in English for reasons that are themselves historical: contemporary Latin American writers have tended, to a greater extent than contemporary U.S. writers, to flaunt intertextual narrative strategies because they have felt more urgently the need to create their own precursors and traditions, and literature is widely considered a vehicle for doing so. My commitment in these chapters is nonetheless comparative. Even to make the preceding statement is to pose comparative questions: How do Latin American narrative strategies differ from those of U.S. writers in this regard, and why?

The relative scarcity of comparative studies of literature in the Americas suggests the difficulty of establishing appropriate bases for comparison. Literary production in the hemisphere is vast and various; its traditions and forms did not develop in tandem, nor are its political and social purposes parallel. Comparatists are likely to uncover critical grounds that are comparable but not equivalent, different but not symmetrically so. Thus, I will be exploring differences in order to recognize the outlines of identity, and weighing historical and cultural diversity against shared forms of literary expression. Differences, too, bring texts and writers and readers and cultures together, for in recognizing specific differences we also recognize the shared experience of difference as such – of finitude, limitation, locality.

Throughout, then, I use "American" in its broadest geographical and historical sense to refer to the different but related histories of the U.S. and Latin America, to their mutual but uneven influences North to South, and to their diverse literary manifestations. My grounds for comparison, as I have said, are American attitudes toward the past that condition literary modes of historical imagining. In all cases, I am drawn to writers who dramatize the convergences and divergences of history and fiction as they question the nature of both, and who do so in self-consciously American cultural contexts. I return with what may seem disproportionate frequency to certain essential American voices – Borges, Hawthorne, Emerson, Williams, Paz, Carpentier, Fuentes. I do so in order to establish literary contexts for other American writers of comparable historical imagination – Cather, García Márquez, Cortázar, Garro, Goyen, Rulfo, Cisneros, Puig, Sánchez, Vargas Llosa. The works of these writers are located (whether squarely or obliquely) in American time and space, locations that yield insight into American literary visions/versions of history. They engage American historical experiences thematically – colonization and independence, *mestizaje* and melting pot, domination and self-determination – and they also question how these historical experiences have created and fostered American literary forms and traditions. I am interested, then, in how these writers thematize usable American pasts, and how their work becomes part of those usable pasts.

Acknowledgments

PORTIONS OF *The Usable Past* have, indeed, been used in the past. I am grateful to Reynolds Smith for granting me permission to publish parts of two essays that have appeared in Duke University Press publications. An early version of Chapter One appeared in 1989 in *Do the Americas Have a Common Literature?*, edited by Gustavo Pérez Firmat; some of Chapter Three appeared in *Magical Realism: Theory, History, Community*, which I coedited with Wendy B. Faris. *NOVEL: A Forum on Fiction*, *The Journal of Aesthetics and Art Criticism*, and *Comparative Literature Studies* have also granted me permission to range back over my own past and rethink my rethinkings. How could I theorize a usable American critical tradition but by first discovering my own?

PART ONE

ANXIETY OF ORIGINS

If Death and Liberty
Can be personified,
Why not History?

It's got to be a fat old man
In faded overalls
Outside a house trailer
On a muddy road to some place
    called Pittsfield or Babylon.

He draws the magic circle
So the chickens can't get out,
Then he hobbles to the kitchen
For the knife and pail.

Today he's back carrying
A sack of yellow corn.
You can hear the hens cluck,
The young cocks strut their stuff.
    Charles Simic, "Severe Figures"

THAT FAT OLD MAN in faded overalls is well suited to introduce this study of the historical imagination in U.S. and Latin American fiction. History has indeed been one of the severest figures of the America's collective imagination. The barnyard fairly reeks of that familiar historical anxiety, the motivation and theme of so much of our fiction. There he goes now, clutching his instruments, terrorizing those dumb clucks whose collective fate he seals. Then again, he's fickle, so tomorrow we may get corn. But what's this? History hobbles? Or is he hobbled by the writers who created him? After all, they too travel along that apocalyptic road to Pittsfield, Babylon. We might easily mistake Charles Simic's old man for the eighth deadly sin in some medieval morality play, ready to take the stage with the likes of gluttony and lust and avarice. But no. He is, in fact, the first deadly sin of the novel.

So I begin by recalling that the rise of the novel coincided with the impact of the idea of history upon modern consciousness. The reading and writing of history were prominent features of the culture of eighteenth-century Europe. Voltaire's *History of Charles XII* and Gibbon's *Decline and Fall of the Roman Empire* were international best-sellers, as were the forged histories of Macpherson and Chatterton. About England, Hume would declare, "I believe this to be the historical age and this the historical nation," an assertion that might well have been made about France and Germany as well.[1] In London, the Society of Antiquaries was founded in 1718, but the startling innovation that was to become characteristic of all modern philosophies of history did not occur till the last third of the eighteenth century, and departed distinctly from the historical thinking of Voltaire, Gibbon, and Hume. The idea that the meaning of history resides and reveals itself in the historical process itself, rather than in isolated events, has its roots in the historiographic thinking of Hobbes and Vico, but it found its culminating expression in Hegel's philosophy. Hannah Arendt asserts that the central concept in all of Hegel's metaphysics is history: "This alone places it in the sharpest possible opposition to all previous metaphysics, which since Plato had looked for truth and the revelation of eternal Being everywhere except in the realm of human affairs – of which Plato speaks with such contempt precisely because no permanence could be found in it and therefore it could not be expected to disclose truth."[2] The revolutionary idea that the particular occurrence derives its intelligibility from the process of history as a whole strongly influenced the developing genre of the novel. In his classic exposition of the connection, Georg Lukács refers specifically to the Hegelian foundations of the late eighteenth- and early nineteenth-century historical novel, and much of what he says can be related to the development of the genre in general.[3]

Lukács is concerned with novelistic representation that is radically and uniquely historical; he associates the development of the historical novel directly with the first generalized (i.e. modern) European war. If the *idea* of history had been revolutionized in the late eighteenth century, the *experience* of history was soon to change as well. Lukács describes the "mass experience of history" occasioned by the French Revolution and the subsequent Napoleonic wars, when for the first time the individual was confronted with the direct reality of world history. The advent of mass conscriptions and unlimited geographical warfare made people think globally, and historically. They realized that similar upheavals were taking place elsewhere, a realization, Lukács posits, that must have "enormously strengthen[ed] the feeling first that there is such a thing as history, second that it [was] an uninterrupted process of changes and finally that it [had] a direct effect upon the life of every individual." (20) The generalized conflict also awakened national sensibilities in Europe. There were altogether new appeals to national character and national history, to past greatness and past dishonors – in short, to the particularities of ethnic and cultural heritage. Thus, communities as well as individuals were being made aware of their relationship to world history, a relationship in which change was increasingly viewed qualitatively as well as quantitatively. This nascent ideology of progress found expression in Hegel's philosophy, specifically in his vision of the "world spirit" embodied in the dialectics of historical development. Lukács links this Hegelian idea directly to the development of the novel: "According to the new interpretation, the reasonableness of human progress develops ever increasingly out of the inner conflict of social forces in history itself; according to this interpretation history itself is the bearer and realizer of human progress" (25). In a critical discussion too well known to need reiteration here, Lukács makes us aware of the ways in which the basic generic conditions and characteristics of the novel developed alongside the Hegelian concept of the historical character of existence.

If in the mid to late eighteenth century the development of modern historical consciousness and the development of the novel impinge and intersect, I would have to say that they *parallel* the emergence of independent national identities in the Americas. Lukács completely ignores the possible influence of the Americas on European historiography and historical fiction, and Hegel makes of America an exception to his theory of historical dialectics. In his lectures collected in *The Philosophy of History*, Hegel first refers generally to the New World, then contrasts English and Spanish America, and finally returns to generalize about America's lack of a usable past: "It is for America to abandon the ground on which hitherto the History of the World has developed itself. What has taken place in the New World up to the present time is only an echo of the Old World – the expression of a foreign Life; and as the Land of the Future, it has no interest for us here, for . . . our concern must be with that which has been and that which is."[4] To participate in the dialectical movement of history, a nation must assimilate and preserve its past by negating it, a process that allows a nation to free itself of its past while at the same time making it an integral part of the present continuity of existence. For Hegel, America had no assimilated past, hence no possibility of historical continuity or national identity: Does not the very term "New World" contain and confirm this fact? Hegel concludes: "America is therefore the land of the future, where, in the ages that lie before us, the burden of the World's History shall reveal itself – perhaps in a contest between North and South America" (86).

I will overlook Hegel's blindness to America's indigenous cultural past – there were, after all, innumerable historical cultures in America even as Hegel wrote – and observe instead that he correctly foresaw what would become a principal theme of literature in the Americas: the question of historical identity. He also foresaw, however unconsciously, that America's historical anxiety would be intimately related to the New

World's uses of its Old World predecessors, that is, to the historical process-es of colonialism and independence in this hemisphere. For though the European concepts of history and nationality to which I have referred evolved without substantial reference to America, the reverse is certainly not true. America's ideas about history and its own historical identity are, of course, profoundly rooted in European philosophy: Almost two hundred years have been added to the history of the Americas since Hegel's asser-tion, but the relation of American identity to European cultural models continues to be problematic. Indeed, I will suggest presently that Hegel himself has proved one of the most challenging of our European precursors to negate and assimilate.

Still one more relevant idea coincides with the historical developments I have touched on here by way of introduction, namely, the idea of com-parative literature. The growing sense of the relation of historical process to national identity in Europe raised questions about how to define nation-al culture and how to interpret differences among cultures. During the last quarter of the eighteenth century (primarily in Germany), Herder, the Schlegels, and other critics developed influential theories that conceived of literature as the voice of a nation or culture – even as a power that shaped it – and they promoted the comparative discussion of literature by epoch and ethnicity in these terms. A growing appreciation of various folk liter-atures, and the comparative study of ancient, Eastern, and modern foreign literatures contributed to the idea of literature as a privileged expression of a given culture. Although questions of national and cultural identity are now relatively rare in comparative studies of Western European literatures, they are current in areas where national identity is in more formative stages of development, as it is in Latin America, and where it is undergo-ing deep and historic diversification, as in the U.S. In these regions, liter-ary criticism is effectively redefining concepts of canonicity and collective identity; indeed, postcolonial theorists questioning the very possibility of collective identity have repeatedly taken cultural practices in the Ameri-cas as their testing ground.[5]

My own comparative project is to expand the territory of comparative literary inquiry from its original national parameters in Europe to hemi-spheric ones in the Americas. I have said that I will refer to "American" lit-erature is this larger sense; I will use "New World" to specify a particular set of literary attitudes toward American contexts. The newness of the New World is specious, of course, but it is one of our oldest collective tra-ditions The writers whom I discuss are unanimous in rejecting this New World myth that Americans are free of the burdens of history because they are free to create their own. On the contrary, they dramatize the fact that history may be more burdensome – and more meaningful – when one must create it, a circumstance as likely in the New World as inheriting a histo-ry from a known family or community. It is when cultural traditions are disjunctive or destroyed, and the potential for historical projection apparently endless, that history becomes problematic and literature instrumental. What Jorge Luis Borges says about Argentine writers is applicable to many American writers: ". . . he observado que en nuestro país, precisamente por ser un país nuevo, hay un gran sentido del tiempo."[6] ("I have observed that in our country, precisely because it is a new country, we have a great sense of time.")[7] And more specifically, a great sense of *American* time: "la expresión americana" has been thematic in Latin American literature since the colonial period, and has become so in literary criticism in the past two decades.[8] U.S. writers, too, have long engaged in processes of historical self-definition that are consistently distinguishable from those of European writers. In various ways that my comparative approach will illuminate, these writers posit history not only as background and cause, but also as the generative condition of their fiction.

Does the imagination of history in this literature have recognizably American features? Having just proposed that it does, I will be looking at a number of such features in the following chapters. Underlying them all is a shared condition that I call "anxiety of origins," a phrase that echoes Harold Bloom's anxiety of influence. Bloom's formulation signals both a historical process and a cultural attitude toward one's precursors, as does my own, but Bloom's concept is inferred entirely from European sources – Hegelian historicism, Nietzschean philosophy, Freudian psychology – a Eurocentrism the more noticeable given Bloom's initial reference to Borges.[9] Whereas Bloom's argument underscores the modern European writer's resistance to a past increasingly experienced as oppressive and, more specifically, as a block to the singular creativity of the psychologized self, my own phrase signals a countervailing tendency on the part of American writers. I consistently find that an anxiety about origins impels American writers to search *for* precursors (in the name of community) rather than escape *from* them (in the name of individuation); to connect *to* traditions and histories (in the name of a usable past) rather than dissociate *from* them (in the name of originality). Obviously, this anxiety, like Bloom's, also contests earlier narratives: to imagine and include acceptable precursors is often to overturn or supplant less acceptable ones. But the anxiety of origins is contestatory in ways that are dialogical (multiple and coexisting) rather than competitive (singular and successive); its textual symptoms are not caution or constraint, as one might expect, but rather narrative complexity and linguistic exuberance – energies that I will eventually describe in terms of the New World Baroque. This American anxiety generates literary structures that are inclusive, relative, heterogeneous, synchronic. These structures reject the hegemony of the most recent.

Anxiety of origins: by "origins," then, I mean acceptable sources of cultural authority, communal coherence, and individual agency; by "anxiety," I mean the efforts of American writers to establish such sources by various strategies of research, restitution, revaluation, renovation, and resistance. This litany of "re's" is meant to emphasize the obvious: by anxiety of origins, I do not mean some vague longing for originary mythic unity, though the romance dynamics of voyage/return and separation/reunion may accompany it. Nor is anxiety of origins limited to what Djelal Kadir has correctly identified as the "quest for beginnings" in much recent Latin American fiction, because my term implies the displacement of hegemonies and hierarchies that would sustain any singular version of that quest, or those beginnings.[10] The "re's" stand for the intertextual impulse of the American writers I discuss: their sometimes-virtuosic interplay of texts and traditions may create an aura of (originary) myth, but it also encodes the historical interactions of sign systems and social formations. Their intertextual strategies self-consciously propose that origins are multiple and indeterminate, never fixed or fully decided.

This intertextual response to American historical anxiety obviously transcends mere "modernist nostalgia for origins," a formulation used by several European poststructuralists to characterize (and condemn) such efforts of cultural and historical (re)construction; nor does it conform to the other side of the questionable dichotomy proposed by these theorists – the "postmodernist dismissal of any kind of continuity."[11] Though I will recognize a number of narrative strategies and philosophical positions that may tentatively be described as modernist and/or postmodernist, the work of contemporary Latin American writers does not easily fall into such categories. Nor, for that matter, does the work of the contemporary U.S. writers I discuss: like their Latin American counterparts, they also seek to validate American cultural communities. Take, for example, Toni Morrison's historical reconstructions in *Beloved* and *Song of Solomon*, or Sandra Cisneros' interpenetrating cultural traditions in *Woman Hollering Creek*. Surely they are impelled neither by a "modernist nostalgia for origins" nor by a postmodernist dismissal of "any kind of continuity," but by the need to locate usable historical precursors and precedents. Their search for origins may be ironic and at the same time "authentic," simultaneously self-doubting and subversive. What it is *not* is ahistorical: this literature does not reflect "the disappearance of a sense of history," a distinguishing feature of postmodern cultural artifacts, according to Fredric Jameson's influential argument.[12] My point is this: the challenge for the comparatist of American literature is to apply the proliferating taxonomies of modernism and postmodernism sparingly and selectively so as to emphasize the ideological implications of these writers' historicizing activities. Their anxiety of origins corresponds not to generalizing critical categories but to particular cultural imperatives.

At issue, then, are received ideas about the structure of the past and the potential uses of those structures in the present. So Julio Cortázar's narrator in *Rayuela* (*Hopscotch*) celebrates jazz with a litany of "re's," describing a historical process as American as the musician to whom he pays homage, Louis Armstrong: ". . . con su don de ubicuidad . . . es una nube sin fronteras . . . algo de antes, de abajo, que *reconcilia* mexicanos con noruegos y rusos y españoles, los *reincorpora* al oscuro fuego central olvidado, torpe y mal y precariamente los *devuelve a un origen traicionado* . . ." (". . . with his gift of ubiquity. . . . is a cloud without boundaries . . . something from before, from below, that *reconciles* Mexicans with Norwegians and Russians and Spaniards, *reincorporates* them into that obscure and forgotten central flame, clumsily and badly and precariously *returns them to a betrayed origin* . . .").[13] Cortázar describes Satchmo's music and his own literary aims and processes, as well as the inevitable difficulties that attend the American artist's performance of this project ("clumsily and badly and precariously").

Cortázar's homage to Sachmo's techniques of return, reconciliation, and inclusion underscores the difference between Bloom's anxiety of influence and American writers' anxiety of origins. Bloom does not effectively differentiate between writers in *colonized* cultures, whose relation to their cultural fathers is radically different from that of writers working in *colonizing* cultures (these latter in some sense the fathers of the former, whatever filial burdens they may also bear.)[14] Bloom worries about an oppressively continuous Western tradition, a worry that is itself a European tradition going back at least to Shakespeare, who wondered whether repetition implied sterility, and who lamented "the second burden of a former child."[15] But writers in colonized cultures know that former children may as often disappear as return, that their traditions are as likely to be oppressively *dis*continuous as oppressively ongoing. Whereas Bloom's history, grounded in Hegel, is progressive and agonistic, assuming that cultures will actively produce (and privilege) the new, the colonized history of the New World is often otherwise.[16] Though Hegelian assumptions certainly operate in the Americas – their operations are the subject of my first chapter and are touched upon in my second chapter – cultures nonetheless differ from one another in their appreciation of innovation and their understanding of tradition as such. Some cultures are more traditional than others, hence less devoted to originality than the Bloomian model assumes, and certainly less committed to the assumption that the new is preferable to the known. (Indeed, some cultures might find the binary incomprehensible.) In contrast to Bloom's model, the American writers I discuss do not subvert or shun influence but engage and interrogate it; their anxiety is a response not to the danger of inadequate imaginative individuation but rather to the knowledge that legitimate sources of communal identity have been destroyed or are unevenly available.

For my comparative purposes, the Heideggerian distinction between fear and anxiety is relevant. Whereas fear has a specific object, anxiety has none: fear implies fear *of* something, while anxiety is rooted in the perception of absence, of not being. In *Being and Time*, Heidegger writes: "Anxiety is anxious in the face of the 'nothing' of the world."[17] Following this definition, Bloom's construction of anxiety is, in fact, not anxiety but fear. Bloom posits the fear of known precursors and a Freudian/Nietzschean resistance to them, whereas my construction supposes the obscurity or absence of precursors and a historicizing urge to identify and include them. Contemporary Latin American writers are inheritors of imposed cultural and linguistic traditions from which they are variously distanced and skeptical, but their resistance is often motivated less by the desire to abolish what has been imposed than to identify what is originary in both a historical and a mythic sense. This does not mean that they are not fully aware of the ideological mystifications of utopian desire, and fully in command of postcolonial and poststructural strategies to unmask such mystifications. Nonetheless, in contemporary Latin American literature the emphasis is as often on displaced or vanished sources of cultural legitimacy as on inherited illegitimacies. Carlos Fuentes, in his essay on "eccentric writing," proposes that "the role of marginal cultures is that of guardians of memory. A memory of what the West sacrificed in other cultures through imperialist expansion and what it sacrificed within its own culture."[18] Writers from colonized cultures must imagine what has been sacrificed. They must write about what is *not*.

My intention is not to present a systematic revision of Bloom's model of tradition-formation or other similar models,[19] for to do so might say more about the intergenerational strife of academic critics than about attitudes toward origins and influence in American literature. In any case, a number of critics have already challenged Bloom's universalization of European modernity, with its hypervaluation of individuality and originality and its unacknowledged investment in patriarchy.[20] My own point here is more obvious: origins are often distant or occluded or contradictory or contaminated or otherwise unsatisfying or unavailable in America, a fact that has tended to make American writers' anxiety of origins all the more compelling, and their narrative strategies for encompassing multiple origins or imagining absent ones the more inventive.

D. Emily Hicks has recognized this historical anxiety in her metaphor of "border writing," a formulation that refers to literature and literary processes in multicultural contexts. Her examples are drawn primarily from Hispanic America, but she argues that "what makes border writing a world literature with a 'universal' appeal is its emphasis upon the multiplicity of languages within any single language; by choosing a strategy of translation rather than representation, border writers ultimately *undermine* the distinction between original and alien culture."[21] In this statement, Hicks emphasizes the displacement of antinomies ("original and alien culture") by narrative strategies that "translate" multiple cultural and linguistic codes in the work itself. Although her critical project is allied to my own, my emphasis will be on unresolved antinomies. I will argue that many Latin American writers explicitly refuse the historical and cultural integration that "translation" implies, emphasizing instead the coexistence of discrete, contradictory, and equally necessary semiotic systems. These coexisting codes are placed in narrative structures that foreground (rather than undermine) the antinomies of Latin America's multiple histories and traditions. Not the least of these antinomies is that "origins" are themselves oftentimes "alien."

For Fuentes and many other American writers, the problem of origins is linked to the primal gesture of naming, which they see as a profoundly American act. "History," Fuentes argues in an essay on García Márquez, "is most explicitly linked to language in America."[22] But to which language(s)? Turning to his own country – to Mexico – he writes: "The passage of the language of the Aztec nation into a silence resembling death – or nature – and the passage of the Spanish language into a politically victorious yet culturally suspect and tainted condition not only is the foundation of the civilization of the New World: it perpetually questions it as it repeats a history that becomes a myth" (188). Creating one's precursors requires that one (re)create the very language of those precursors so they may speak (to us). The American modernist poet William Carlos Williams shared this perception: "Americans have never recognized themselves. How can they? It is impossible until someone invent the ORIGINAL terms. As long as we are content to be called by somebody else's terms, we are incapable of being anything but our own dupes."[23] Williams' "ORIGINAL terms" can speak of origins, can grasp past cultural meanings and include them in present cultural formations. This is consonant with the argument presented by Fuentes, who goes on to describe the Latin American anxiety of origins as a speechless terror: "Suddenly, here, in the vast reaches of the Amazonian jungle, the Andean heights, or the Patagonian plains, we are again in the very emptiness of terror that Hölderlin spoke of: the terror that strikes us when we feel . . . deprived of speech and identity" (187). Hölderlinian terror replaces Heideggerian anxiety; the metaphor changes but the response does not. Both authors describe their American intuition of deprivation (Fuentes says "emptiness," Williams says "dupes") and the resulting impulse to create or discover usable origins and influences.

In his widely published 1983 Harvard commencement address, Fuentes again insists upon the problematic historical positioning of Latin America with respect to Europe, noting that Latin America "received the legacy of the West in an incomplete fashion" and, worse, embraced it uncritically: "Latin America has tried to find solutions to its old problems by exhausting the successive ideologies of the West: liberalism, positivism, and Marxism. Today we are on the verge of transcending this dilemma by recasting it as an opportunity, at last, to be ourselves – *societies neither new nor old*, but simply, authentically, Latin American, as we sort out . . . the benefits and the disadvantages of a tradition that now seems richer and more acceptable than it did one hundred years of solitude ago . . . ."[24] This statement honors García Márquez, of course, and also echoes Octavio Paz, who made a similar observation almost a half century ago: "The question of origins, then, is the central secret of our anxiety and anguish. It is worth studying the significance of this fact."[25] Paz himself has repeatedly returned to this point: "The history of Mexico is the history of a man seeking his parentage, his origins. He has been influenced at one time or another by France, Spain, the United States and the militant indigenists of his own country, and he crosses history like a jade comet, now and then giving off flashes of lightning. What is he pursuing in his eccentric course?" (20) The writers I treat in the following chapters dramatize the pursuit, without exhausting Paz's question. They, like Paz, signal the digressive and diverted history of influence in Latin America, which Paz has elsewhere called Latin America's "tradición de la ruptura" (tradition of/as rupture.)[26]

These are versions of American historical awareness, and they embody the concomitant impulse to reconstitute America's multiple histories in usable/useful (Fuentes' word is "authentic") ways. Fuentes and Paz are well aware that "authenticity" and "origins" are ideological constructs and that to use them uncritically is to repeat the errors of the European colonizers. But for the U.S. critic to dismiss as naïve the historicizing impulse encoded in these constructs is to risk imposing a poststructuralist position inappropriate to contexts where the historical (re)construction of foundational narratives is still considered by writers to be an urgent and necessary task. It is also to undervalue these writers' self-conscious connection of "authenticity" and "origins" to literary creation.[27]

Because the processes of colonization have been more onerous and obvious in many parts of Latin America than in the U.S., and for a number of other reasons that I will touch upon in the following chapters, the issue of cultural origins and authority has traditionally been more compelling to Latin American writers. But U.S. writers have also had their historical anxieties. Indeed, the U.S. may be unique in having occupied simultaneously a dual and deeply contradictory position as colonizer and colonized during this century. Certainly it has replaced Europe as the primary economic and political colonizer of Latin America, and yet has itself remained deeply colonized by European cultural traditions and forms of expression. Walt Whitman was the first to recognize this double bind, a fact not lost on Latin American writers, for whom Whitman (along with Faulkner) is universally acknowledged as an essential American precursor. In a speech delivered in 1972, a year before his death, Pablo Neruda said of Whitman: "The bard complained of the all-powerful European influence that continued to dominate the literature of his time. In fact, it was he, Walt Whitman, in the persona of a specific geography, who for the first time in history brought honor to an American name."[28] More recently and in quite another register, Donald Barthelme has also recognized the cultural colonization of the U.S. In *The Dead Father*, Barthelme writes: "Dead, but still with us, still with us, but dead. . . . Fathers are like blocks of marble, giant cubes, highly polished, with veins and seams, placed squarely in your path. . . . They cannot be climbed over, neither can they be slithered past."[29] That Barthelme's novel has been read primarily as a psychological parable (anxiety of influence) rather than as an extended metaphor for the problem of establishing meaningful communal identities and traditions (anxiety of origins) suggests the importance of creating comparative American critical contexts in which shared historical anxieties become apparent. Barthelme's universality, like Whitman's, Neruda's, and Borges', depends upon his keen awareness of the paradoxical historical positioning of the New World writer.

I will begin Chapter 1 by noting that historical anxiety has sometimes led U.S. writers to conceive of America as culturally thin with respect to Europe. Henry James, Henry Adams, T. S. Eliot, Ezra Pound, Gertrude Stein, James Baldwin, and Richard Wright reversed Huck Finn's itinerary, lighting out not for uncharted territory but rather for the Old World in order to seek what seemed to them histories more usable than their own. This is American historical anxiety with a vengeance, but these writers' departure for Europe did not mean that they could alleviate or escape it; fortunately, they continued to write out of their anxiety. As it happens, I will focus on U.S. modernists who did not leave: William Carlos Williams, Willa Cather, William Faulkner, and William Goyen, among others. If Williams, Cather, Faulkner and Goyen were exceptions in finding U.S. history a fertile field, such exceptions are now becoming the rule as contemporary U.S. writers challenge hegemonic histories from positions on the periphery. Buried histories – deep and often tragic – are imagined and included by such "guardians of memory" as Toni Morrison, Leslie Marmon Silko, John Edgar Wideman, Denise Chávez, Jamake Highwater, Maxine Hong Kingston, and many others. These "minority" writers are filling in the blank spaces of U.S. history and altering the terms of inclusion. Their project of validating American cultural communities by reconstituting "authentic" American histories makes seemingly improbable comparisons justifiable and necessary: José María Arguedas and James Welch, Rosario Castellanos and Louise Erdrich, Isabel Allende and Toni Morrison, José Donoso and Vladimir Nabokov. I name these comparative possibilities not because I will explore them here but because I hope that other comparatists eventually will.[30] My own consideration of such buried American histories will involve the works of Juan Rulfo, Elena Garro, William Goyen, and Sandra Cisneros, among others.

Many Latin American writers have also left home, of course, preferring Europe or the U.S. This circumstance is still acrimoniously debated in Latin America, where the political and social responsibility of the writer to his or her own culture and country is taken for granted, a responsibility

that continues to be associated with his or her residency. (That the historical anxiety motivating such debate is uniquely American is confirmed, it
seems to me, if one tries to imagine a comparable debate in France or Germany or England.) Nineteenth- and early twentieth-century Latin American writers left for reasons similar to those of U.S. modernists: their sense
(mistaken, we now feel) of America's historical newness and hence its cultural vacuity. The contemporary Latin American writers who have left
have tended to do so for reasons that are political or economic rather than
cultural.[31] Writers no longer feel that their histories are too new to be
usable, in part because they have been the beneficiaries of a historiographic tradition adapted to Latin American purposes over the course of this century. Antipositivism and *indigenista* politics overlapped in Latin America
in the twenties and thirties; philosophers and writers refashioned European historiographic models to fit American historical experience or rejected European models altogether as they looked for ways to include their
own indigenous past.

Here, again, Pablo Neruda's observations are useful. In an entry in his
"Isla Negra" notebooks from the late sixties, this most cosmopolitan of
local poets comments upon a confrontation between the Argentine writer
Julio Cortázar, who lived and wrote in Paris, and José María Arguedas, who
lived in and wrote about the Andean mestizo culture of his native Peru.
Cortázar had been charged with abandoning Latin America and consequently his responsibility as a Latin American writer. But, asks Neruda,
"Why should we cut the bonds of elegance that bind us to [Europe]?"[32]
Neruda knew that "an imperious and tantalizing Europe . . . can divert us
into an unenduring superficiality"; he also knew that "it is easy for the
American, and no less the native American, to immerse himself not in our
ocean but in a mud puddle, and to so limit himself in form as to embrace
the past" (232–33). But, Neruda writes, this second danger is very different
from the first:

> This danger will not sever our roots. It so happens that the more we sink into
> ourselves, the more we renew ourselves, and the more local we become, the more
> likely our universality. I know a great book that concerned itself with only a
> small region of Spain called La Mancha. And it became the most spacious novel
> ever written. (233)

In Neruda's account, the "danger" of embracing the past is, in fact, to be
desired. The historical anxiety that has impelled these writers – note Neruda's generalizing use of "American" in the first quoted passage – is not negative but necessary, and certainly not merely nostalgic. Rather, it is the
tension generated by historical consciousness, communal imperatives, and
literary creation, and it has operated throughout the Americas.[33]

I have asked if the American historical imagination has recognizable
features. I must also ask if *all* American writers, by definition, share these

American historicizing anxieties? Vera Kutzinski says not, and I agree with her. In her book, *Against the American Grain*, she argues that such anxiety is the pre-existing condition of the New World writer, but that *not all* American writers are New World writers in the sense she intends; only those who integrate an awareness of the contradictory historical conditions and consequences of American newness are New World writers.[34] Borges, for example, is not usually treated as a New World writer in Kutzinski's terms, but he is, in fact, obsessed with the nature of time and tradition in particularly American ways. His much-quoted insight that writers create their own precursors is surely a version – perhaps *the* central one – of the anxiety of origins in American literature, for it reconstitutes the nature of originality and thus our understanding of the operations of the past in the present. Whereas European modernity's devotion to originality is essentially hostile to history, Borges' conception of originality consists not in novelty but in a complicated and enriched relation to cultural origins and traditions, a relation that requires a revised understanding of influence as such. Such a conception is appropriate to the historical positioning of American writers; indeed, it is the product of their historical positioning.

Consider Borges' famous statement in "Kafka y sus precursores" ("Kafka and His Precursors"):

En el vocabulario crítico, la palabra *precursor* es indispensable, pero habría que tratar de purificarla de toda conotación de polémica o de rivalidad. El hecho es que cada escritor *crea* a sus precursores. Su labor modifica nuestra concepción del pasado, como ha de modificar el futuro. En esta correlación nada importa la identidad o la pluralidad de los hombres. El primer Kafka de *Betrachtung* es menos precursor del Kafka de los mitos sombríos y de las institutions atroces que Browning o Lord Dunsany.[35]

The word "precursor" is indispensable in the vocabulary of criticism, but one should try to purify it from every connotation of polemic or rivalry. The fact is that each writer *creates* his precursors. His work modifies our conception of the past, as it will modify the future. In this correlation the identity or plurality of men matters not at all. The first Kafka of *Betrachtung* is less a precursor of the Kafka of the shadowy myths and atrocious institutions than is Browning or Lord Dunsany.[36]

Borges returns to this idea in his essay on Nathaniel Hawthorne, which I discuss in Chapter 3. There, as here, literary tradition is historical but not chronological: influence moves backward and forward in time because texts exist simultaneously rather than sequentially in the author's (and reader's) mind, and in synecdochal relation to the tradition as a whole. According to Borges, the individual text contains all texts, and an individual author subsumes an entire tradition. This synchrony is not a pacific embrace of all by all or a totality that homogenizes difference, nor does it

suggest oedipal strife or Hegelian supersession. Rather, Borges' antiposi-
tivist position – his "modest history" – requires that historical contradictions circulate, that literary currents collide, coalesce, and reconfigure.

Borges' story "Pierre Menard, autor del Quijote" ("Pierre Menard,
Author of the Quixote") describes this process. His character reads, forgets
or sublimates, and then writes parts of Cervantes' Don Quixote verbatim.
He accomplishes this feat, we are told, by means of the "new techniques
[of] deliberate anachronism and erroneous attribution," creating "a 'final'
Quixote," "a kind of palimpsest."[37] "Deliberate anachronism and erroneous attribution" are strategic responses to American historical anxiety:
in his "palimpsest" the narrator will demonstrate that divergent histories
and valuations exist in synchronic and eccentric relation. Consider,
Borges' narrator insists, the different significance of Menard's phrase
"truth, whose mother is history" when compared to Cervantes' identical
phrase:

> La historia, madre de la verdad; la idea es asombrosa. Menard, contemporáneo
> de William James, no define la historia como una indagación de la realidad sino
> como su origen. La verdad histórica, para él, no es lo que sucedió; es lo que juz-
> gamos que sucedió.[38]

> History, the mother of truth: the idea is astounding. Menard, a contemporary
> of William James, does not define history as an inquiry into reality but as its ori-
> gin. Historical truth for him, is not what has happened; it is what we judge to
> have happened.[39]

Again, the issue of origins. Despite Pierre Menard's fictive French nationality, he has assumed his American creator's anxiety of origins and his
American need to create a usable past – "what we judge to have happened."

John T. Irwin's discussion of Borges' doubling of Poe's original detective
stories applies as well to Pierre Menard's (and Borges') project of (re)creat-
ing the Quixote, that most daunting of Spanish originals. Irwin writes: "In
a circular, a temporally reflexive, system where the end leads back into the
beginning, the end often comes to seem prior to the beginning, as original
or more original than the origin. . . . The difficulty Borges experienced in
doubling the genre's original story sprang, as we suggested, from the fact
that the origin no longer existed for him in an uncontaminated form."[40]
The Borgesian call to originate one's origins – in essence, to create and
interpret one's cultural meanings – deconstructs mimetic representation
by focusing not on what is represented but on how, by whom, and to
whom: this process insists upon the reader's complicity in the constitution
of cultural authority. Why this Borgesian challenge (with its "new techniques" and "palimpsest" results) should be particularly appealing to
American writers and readers has been suggested in the foregoing pages
and will occupy my attention throughout the following chapters.

CHAPTER ONE

The Usable Past
History as Idea in the Americas

We are worried about redeeming the past.
They are accustomed to acclaiming the future.

. . .

Their past is assimilated; and, too often, it is simply forgotten.
Ours is still battling for our souls.
     Carlos Fuentes, *Latin America: At War with the Past*[1]

IN THESE SCHEMATIC SENTENCES, deployed typographically as I have reproduced them here, Carlos Fuentes places in opposition what he proposes as the current conceptions of history in the U.S. and Latin America. And in what is after more than four decades still the single most influential comparative treatment of the cultures of the Americas, *El laberinto de la soledad* (*The Labyrinth of Solitude*, 1950), Octavio Paz precedes Fuentes in contrasting the historical visions of the U.S. and Mexico. Paz also assigns to the U.S. the historical character that Hegel imputed to the entire hemisphere: a place without a past, with only a future.[2] But if Latin America's view of the past is first presented as starkly opposed to that of the U.S., a second look reveals that the two views share a common characteristic: their lack of resolution. Fuentes follows Hegel strikingly in his assertion that the past is not yet usable anywhere in America: if the U.S. has too completely assimilated its past, rendering it inaccessible, Latin America has incompletely assimilated its history, to the same effect.

Fuentes elaborates history's "battle for our souls" in Latin America by asserting that no stage of its past has yet been fully assimilated. "Each new historical project not only replaces the foregoing, it annihilates, rejects, and obliges it to start again from the beginning. The Conquest tries to wholly deny the existence of the indigenous world, Independence denies the Colonial world, and the Revolution rejects nineteenth century positivism. While yet claiming to be orphaned, each of Mexico's historical projects is open, *nolens wolens*, to the secret contamination of the traditions thus denied."[3] Latin America has not properly negated its past, so cannot fully integrate it into the present to realize what Hegel defined as the continuity of its being. Almost all of Fuentes' novels depict Mexico's past, and Latin America's, as a series of ruptures, of discontinuous fragments. In fact, history has provided the tensions and ironies of much of the best of recent Latin American fiction, for example, Juan Rulfo's *Pedro Páramo* (1955), Elena Garro's *Recuerdos del porvenir* (*Recollections of Things to Come*, 1962), Ernesto Sábato's *Sobre héroes y tumbas* (*On Heroes and Tombs*, 1962), Alejo Carpentier's *Pasos perdidos* (*The Lost Steps*, 1953) and *El siglo de las luces* (translated as *Explosion in a Cathedral*, 1962), Gabriel García Márquez's *Cien años de soledad* (*One Hundred Years of Solitude*, 1967), Reynaldo Arenas' *El mundo alucinante* (translated as *The Ill-Fated Peregrinations of Fray Servando*, 1969), Augusto Roa Bastos' *Yo el supremo* (*I the Supreme*, 1974), José Donoso's *Casa de campo* (*A House in the Country*, 1978), Mario Vargas Llosa's *La guerra del fin del mundo* (*The War of the End of the World*, 1981), and Isabel Allende's *La casa de los espíritus* (*The House of the Spirits*, 1982), among many others. These novelistic explorations of the national and regional past often project expansive mythic histories of their American territory; Fuentes argues that Latin America's unresolved history can only be encompassed by an inclusive mythic vision and its consequent narrative modes.

If Fuentes describes Latin America's historical dilemma in what are undeniably Hegelian terms, he emphatically rejects dialectical idealism as a solution to that dilemma, and looks back past Hegel to Giambattista Vico's *New Science* (1744). Like Hegel, Vico locates historical significance in the process of history as a whole; but unlike Hegel, Vico's historical process is not linear, nor does it privilege a progressive dialectic. In Vico's metaphoric expression of history as a spiral, Fuentes finds a model capable of encompassing the linear time of Western thought and the circular times of indigenous mythology that meet in Mexico. And in Vico's investigation and presentation of the "poetic" origins of human history and his privileging of fictional texts (one entire section of the five of the *New Science* is devoted to Homer and the Greek fables) Fuentes finds support for his belief that history can – and must – be written by novelists. Fuentes uses Vichian historiography explicitly in *Terra nostra* (1975) and *Una familia lejana* (*Distant Relations*, 1980); both are novels about the European historical origins of Mexican and Latin American culture, and both oscillate back and forth between the Old and New Worlds.[4] I will return to *Distant Relations*, but for the purposes of my comparative overview here, it is enough to say that Vico's rejection of the scientific empiricism of his own century and the Cartesian conception that the intellect can apprehend first principles intuitively, without reference to historical experience, coincides with Fuentes' rejection of similar ideas in this century – ideas that he summarizes as the "bastardization of the philosophy of the Enlightenment"[5] and implicitly associates with what he sees as the cancellation of history in the U.S.

But are our historical sensibilities in the Americas really as divergent as Fuentes insists? Do we seriously entertain the schematic opposition that he proposes, or accede to his idea that U.S. history is only the history of forgetting? Are Fuentes, and we, simply fulfilling Hegel's prediction, opposing North and South America for the purposes of historical self-definition?

Fuentes does make an exception to his generalization for Faulkner and southern writers of the U.S. on the grounds that the South shares with Latin America the historical experience of colonial exploitation and political failure as the rest of the United States does not.[6] And he does recognize that the U.S. is not the only place where the past may be subsumed by an illusory future. One of his Mexican characters in *Distant Relations* speaks globally about this century's habit of divorcing the past from the present, "con el propósito de que el pasado sea siempre algo muerto a fin de que nosotros mismos seamos siempre algo nuevo, diferente del pasado despreciable, nuevos y en consecuencia hambrientos de novedades en el arte, la ropa, la diversión, las máquinas. La novedad se ha convertido en el certificado de nuestra felicidad" ("with the proposition that the past must always be something dead and we always something new, something different from that much-to-be-scorned past – new, and consequently thirsting for the latest innovation in art, clothing, entertainment, machines. Novelty has become the blazon our happiness.")[7] In Mexico, as in much of the world, novelty is advertised, packaged, marketed, and consumed, though it was the U.S. that taught the world how. It is also true that the triumph of technology tends to emphasize innovation rather than preservation, and again, the U.S. undeniably leads the way. Didn't Henry Ford, one of the most important U.S. spokesmen for progress, declare that "history is bunk"?

Still, Fuentes is not unaware that the relation of the present to the past is a major theme in U.S. literature and has troubled not just those writers from the South. In the nineteenth century, one need only think of the major writers to recognize a continuous strain of historical anxiety in their fiction: Cooper's outraged defense of America's indigenous history and natural resources; Hawthorne's guilt-ridden explorations of the Puritan past; Twain's nostalgia for the freedom of the untrammeled land (a fiction based on the illusion of America's paradisal past that Twain was himself instrumental in creating and that found its culminating lyrical expression forty years later in Fitzgerald's famous conclusion to *The Great Gatsby*); and Henry James' wistful regret for a European cultural heritage that never fully took in the New World.

In this century, the sense of U.S. history conveyed in literature has shifted in significant ways. The historical uneasiness of many U.S. modernist writers resulted less from the past's multilayered and unresolved presence (this was, after all, Hawthorne's dilemma as much as Faulkner's and Fuentes') than from what was perceived as the thinness of the past, or even its absence. There was an acute sense of missing history among U.S. modernists; I have already suggested that their pattern of voluntary exile may be understood as a manifestation of historical anxiety. Henry James was the first to leave for Europe, and Eliot and Pound followed him, looking for the past that they could not seem to locate in America. Gertrude Stein referred to Oakland but spoke for a whole "lost generation" of U.S. writers when she concluded, "There is no there." Henry Adams, whom Alfred Kazin calls "the Gibbon, the Voltaire, the Proust and the doom-filled Oswald Spengler" of his time, was also impelled to search for U.S. historical origins, which he found in medieval Europe rather than the more recent national history that his own family had been so instrumental in constructing. For many U.S. modernists, their history came to seem like a photographic negative or the reverse side of a tapestry. The outlines revealed what was *not* there but should have been.

In the thirty years or so following World War II, there was a shift in U.S. fiction away from collective historical preoccupations to more interior realms – or more literary ones. Experimental "metafictions" or "surfictions" or "antifictions" emphasized the self-reflexive capacities of literature rather its mimetic and historiographic capacities. But the Civil Rights movement, the Vietnam war, feminism, and a growing awareness of multiculturalism meant that by the seventies U.S. fiction was again responding to historical (and historicizing) imperatives. I will shortly refer to a number of contemporary U.S. writers for whom the imagination of history is a principal project.

Surely, then, it is a mistake to say, as Fuentes and Paz have, that U.S. writers are devoted to the future and largely unconscious of the past. One must wonder why, in the main, critics have been willing to accept their characterizations to this effect. There are, I think, two general explanations for the tendency to agree with Fuentes and Paz despite ample evidence to dispute the simplification of their opposition.

The first lies in the nature of U.S. literary criticism, not its literature. Until the late seventies, prevailing literary critical thought in the U.S. – New Critical, formalist and structuralist – encouraged ahistorical (or *trans*historical) readings of American literature that minimized the complex influences of historical context in and on the literary text. These critical theories foregrounded aesthetic and psychological issues within the work rather than historical or social issues surrounding the work. Influential critics and theorists of U.S. literature during this much of this century have sought to define what Nina Baym calls the "myth of America": "The myth narrates a confrontation of the American individual, the pure American self divorced from specific social circumstances, with the promise offered by the idea of America. This promise is the deeply romantic one that in this new land, untrammeled by history and social accident, a person will be able to achieve complete self-definition. Behind this promise is the assurance that individuals come before society, that they exist in some meaningful sense prior to, and apart from, societies in which they happen to find themselves."[8] Baym is only one of many materially minded critics who have reacted against the "derealization" of U.S. literature and are focusing on its social and historical subjects and contexts.

Surprisingly, though, the impulse to oversimplify or dismiss ("to forget," as Fuentes would have it) the historical imperatives of U.S. literature continues. Thus, a prominent U.S. critic laments "the incommensurability between the sign system and the material base" and "the apparent canyon between history and language" in the U.S. He both reflects and reinforces the modernists' historical anxiety when he writes, "We can remember the beginnings of American civilization. It is recent, datable, relatively simple. It has not been accumulating long enough to be thick on the ground."[9] Current critical discussions of postmodernism in the U.S. have done little to correct this apprehension since postmodernist theory tends to dehistoricize cultural artifacts, to treat them without respect to historical motive or purpose. Latin American literary critics have also noted the historical discontinuities between contemporary Latin American culture and its European and indigenous roots, but they are far less likely than their U.S. counterparts to detach their literature from those histories or assume, as in the above statement, that American culture was created ex nihilo, as a topological gesture rather than a historical process.[10] Nor have critics in Latin America rushed to enter the critical discussion of postmodernism, in part because of its latent ahistoricism, in part because it is seen as an ideology devised elsewhere in response to others' historical needs.

The second and more important explanation for the perceived dichotomy between U.S. and Latin American historical understanding lies in our conceptions and traditions of historical process. The U.S. and Latin America have different philosophical lineages and, particularly in the twentieth century, a different historiographic heritage. It is these differences that I will pursue in the rest of this chapter.

I

German idealism developed during the formative period of U.S. national self-definition, and its essentially progressive dialectics first supported and then supplanted the Puritans' sense of America as the latest stage of a universal historical process.[11] In the U.S. by the mid-nineteenth century, the charting of universal history became the means of explaining its secular destiny, as it had been for the Puritans the means of explaining their divine destiny. Following Hegel, Lessing and Herder applied to history the concept of development, and Friedrich Schlegel and Schiller espoused the idea that humans outgrow forms of belief and seek newer and more adequate expressions of spirit; the process of history itself came to be viewed as possessing an inner and active purpose that made it intelligible and assured its advance toward truth. These thinkers found in past experience the repository of communal wisdom, but it is the future that inevitably receives systematic emphasis in their dialectical historiographies. Their emphasis on the ideal movement of history has been construed as privileging the future by U.S. prophets of progress from the mid-nineteenth century to the present. A blatant example is the following excerpt from an address entitled "The Progress of Mankind," delivered by the U.S. historian George Bancroft at a meeting of the New York Historical Society in 1854: "Everything is in motion, and for the better. The last system of philosophy is always the best . . . . The last political state of the world likewise is ever more excellent than the old."[12] I cite this futuristic bombast to contrast it to what we know to be the complexities of historical consciousness in U.S. literature, and also to acknowledge the undeniable conversion of German idealism into a facile doctrine of progress in the U.S. – in other words, both to contradict and confirm Fuentes' assertion about the extreme orientation toward the future in the U.S.

Willa Cather's fiction also confirms and contradicts this assertion. Geoffrey Hartman reminds us of the dangers of "those picaresque adventures in pseudo-causality that go under the name of literary history," but he would not disagree that there are instances of influence and confluence that comparative literary studies are in the business of noticing.[13] German philosophical idealism was directly imported into British literature by Coleridge and Carlyle, and through Carlyle into American literature by Emerson, who in turn influenced much subsequent U.S. literature both directly and indirectly through his influence on William James' phenomenological psychology.[14] This German import sees history as propelled forward by a progressive and universal force that may be conceived of in religious, biological, psychological or aesthetic terms, or all of them simultaneously: Carlyle fuses history, poetry, and religion; Emerson yokes Lamarckian evolutionary beliefs to his conception of the Oversoul operating in both history and art; William James' "stream of thought" flows forward even as it accumulates in each instant the whole history of the individual. Though Willa Cather was not a systematic or programmatic thinker (as are, say, Fuentes and many contemporary Latin American writers, with their more political imperatives), she nonetheless read, admired and cited Carlyle, Emerson and James, and her novelistic portrayals of U.S. historical reality clearly reflect this lineage of transcendental idealism.[15]

I choose, then, to discuss Cather's work because it allows me to consider the European historiographic heritage of U.S. modernism. Furthermore, Cather's fiction has not, to my knowledge, been placed in a comparative American context, though her southwestern settings are themselves inter-American in their examination of the mixture of indigenous, Hispanic American, and European cultures and characters.[16] Her fiction was very popular at the time of its publication, and it continues to appeal to both popular and scholarly audiences – a dual audience less usual in the case of U.S. literature than of recent Latin American literature. Nonetheless, it seems to me that Cather's work has only recently begun to receive the kind of academic attention it deserves, in part, perhaps, because its profoundly historical character did not easily conform to the criteria of American criticism that I mentioned earlier. In the U.S. Cather has been treated as a regional writer, or a domestic one; in Latin America she has been completely overshadowed by English and American modernists whose themes are more overtly political and/or whose narrative strategies are more experimental than hers. Though this earlier neglect, or relegation, is now being redressed by feminist criticism and by the current critical shift toward historicist and materialist approaches to U.S. literature, it remains a reason for foregrounding Cather's fiction in this broadly comparative discussion of American literature.

Cather wrote twelve novels and several collections of short stories between 1905 and her death in 1947. Most of her fiction is set in the nineteenth century or earlier. Her basic narrative impulse is to look back to the indigenous and the European roots of American culture, and then follow their complex historical branchings over time in a particular character and/or place. In all but two of her novels about the American past, she locates the framing narrative situation in a contemporary setting or brings the story itself into the present; she clearly wished to avoid romanticizing the past by separating it from the present, a tendency of popular historical romance that she recognized and rejected. Among U.S. writers, her only equal in constituting a cultural memory from both native and imported matrices is William Goyen, whose work, like hers, has been underappreciated. (Faulkner, too, creates brilliant fictions from both native and imported sources, but unlike Goyen and Cather, he chronicles the eclipse of indigenous American culture rather that its mythic presence.) And Cather has no equal, in my opinion, in combining the problematics of historical consciousness with those of artistic activity in what was still a relatively young and unformed culture. Her search for a usable past allies her to the major writers of her time, though she never shared the modernist suspicion that the American past was thin or nonexistent. We might consider this difference in the terms suggested by feminist criticism. Those who have not possessed a history – here, the reference is not to Americans, but to women – naturally prefer to recover the past before dismissing it as inadequate. The retrieval of lost history becomes an essential part of the process of liberation, for an unexamined past operates as fate rather than revelation. Though this observation applies not only to women but also to many contemporary postcolonial writers – it is an essential theme running

through contemporary Latin American fiction – it is nonetheless true that
Cather's most fully drawn characters are women, often artists or aspiring
artists, who search with difficulty for a place in the as yet inchoate American historical and social landscape.

Cather's best novels are set in the West and Southwest, but she does not
glorify the westward movement in the nationalistic terms of manifest destiny, as did Whitman and Frederick Jackson Turner,[17] or in the progressive
terms of scientific materialism characteristic of Bancroft and many others.
Rather, she casts it in terms of Carlyle's conception of the hero and the
hero's historical capacities.[18] Her European immigrants are hardly huddled
masses yearning to be free, nor do they incarnate the banality of hurrying
to America to exchange their Old World pasts for New World futures. The
Czech settlers in the Nebraska territory in My Antonia (1918), the Swedes
in O Pioneers! (1913), the French settlers in Quebec in Shadows on the
Rock (1931), and the French missionary priests in the southwestern Mexican territory in Death Comes for the Archbishop (1927) are at once fugi-
tives from and creators of history. They long (in one case, tragically) for the
civilization they left behind, and attempt to transplant it or, in the most
successful instances, adapt it to their American circumstances. Cather
attributes the strength of frontier culture to the special interaction of the
European character and the American land.[19] However, the towns subsequently created and populated by second and third generation immigrants
are deprecated by Cather because their various European heritages have
been squandered, and nothing has arisen to replace them. Cather joins
Hegel and Fuentes in her historical judgment: in these frontier towns the
past has been inadequately negated and hence inadequately assimilated
into a genuinely American culture. But Cather does not stop here: her novels contain individuals – often artists or characters with special aesthetic
sensibilities – who are heroes in a Carlylean sense and are thus capable of
historical assimilation. It is they who participate in what Carlyle (and following him, Emerson) conceived of as the soul of history, they who assure
that "one form passes into another, nothing is lost . . . and the Present is
the living sum-total of the whole Past."[20]

Thea Kronberg, in The Song of the Lark (1915, rev. ed. 1937), is the daughter of second-generation Swedish parents living in the small town of
Moonstone on the western plains of Colorado. The novel recounts Thea's
struggle to free herself from the vacuous (yet encumbering) culture of
Moonstone, and to realize herself as an artist; she manages to do this
through the medium of music and her capacity to intuit and integrate her
cultural past into her own creative performance. She has the good fortune
to find two European music teachers, a German and a Hungarian, who introduce her to the European aesthetic tradition that is already lost to Moonstone.[21] It is during a concert in Chicago (thanks to a ticket given to her by
her Hungarian music teacher) that she experiences her first, almost mystical intuition of the historical nature and imperatives of art. While listening

to Dvorak's Symphony in E Minor, she senses "the amazement of a new soul in a new world; a soul new and yet old, that had dreamed something despairing, something glorious, in the dark before it was born; a soul obsessed by what it did not know, under the cloud of a past it could not recall."[22] She eventually travels to Germany to study voice, begins her operatic career there, and then returns to interpret the great roles of German opera to American audiences in New York, Chicago and San Francisco.

If Thea intuits the historical imperatives of her art in Dvorak's *New World* Symphony, she finds the strength to act upon them – to go to Germany and commit herself fully to her art – in the ruins of an ancient city of Indian cliff dwellers in Arizona. The short middle section of the novel, "The Ancient People," contains the account of Thea's stay in Panther Canyon (actually Walnut Canyon, the site of the ancient city of the Sinagua Indians, near Flagstaff). In the majestic architectural ruins, she finds shards of beautifully wrought pottery, the "fragments of desire" of this vanished civilization; in these fragments she recognizes a continuity, an "older and higher obligation" than any she has ever experienced. She intuits her origins mystically in the dreams and whispers of "the night of ages" that surrounds her, in visions of an Indian youth and an eagle. Then she enters imaginatively into that history. While bathing in the stream at the bottom of the canyon, she joins "a continuity of life that reached back into the old time. The glittering thread of current had a kind of lightly worn, loosely knit personality, graceful and laughing. Thea's bath came to have a ceremonial gravity. The atmosphere of the cañon was ritualistic" (378). Thea recognizes that "under the human world there was a geological world, conducting its silent, immense operations which were indifferent to man" (388–9). The "silent, immense operations" of historical process, recorded in the archeological imprint of Panther Canyon, transcend individual consciousness and provide the continuity that neither individuals nor civilizations can sustain.

Clearly Cather is doing far more in this section than simply introducing a historical background for her character. She is dramatizing a concept of American history as unconscious memory or racial unconscious, a temporal mode that she embodies and makes visible in an unmistakably American space (as she does in *The Professor's House* [1925], where she uses the site of the Mesa Verde cliff dwellings in Colorado as the crucial space for her historian-protagonist). Cather's description of Thea's experience in Panther Canyon explicitly echoes William James' theory of the unconscious as it was presented in *Principles of Psychology* (1890), particularly in the chapter entitled "The Stream of Thought." James' ideas and imagery are explicitly present in Cather's descriptions of Thea's experiences in Panther Canyon.

For William James, the past is unrepeatable but always present in the unconscious: "Experience is remoulding us every moment, and our mental reaction on every given thing is really a resultant of our experience of the

whole world up to that date."[23] Thea experiences the sensation of having
been in the canyon before. James discusses and rejects such sensations on
the grounds that psychic experience is temporally continuous: psychic history is not static but is constantly being modified by its integration into the
present stream of thought. Each "brain-state" is therefore a record of the
entire history of its owner: it is out of the question, James asserts, that a
"total brain-state" should recur identically. James was arguing against the
functional psychology of his day, which divided perceptions into discrete
units, and it is in this disciplinary context that he gives his now famous definition of the stream of thought as flowing, as constantly in motion. Thea
bathes in the stream at the bottom of Panther Canyon, where she intuits,
in Jamesian fashion, that the past is not discontinuous or fragmented but a
continuous stream that flows in the present of mental experience. She is
able to imagine the presence of the ancient civilization of cliff dwellers and
make them a part of her own cumulative psychic history. Intuition and
imagination are the bases of her historical understanding, the means by
which "the Cliff-Dwellers had lengthened her past" (383). The American
cultural heritage provides Thea with a mystical antithesis to European
rationalism. Thus Cather dramatizes Thea's artistic synthesis of cosmic
and collective history (Carlyle, on the one hand), and individual phenomenological and psychic time (James, on the other), a synthesis that can only
occur for her on the terra firma of America's own cultural territory.

It is not enough, then, for the American artist to discover the European
past and master its artistic and cultural legacy; he or she must also come
to terms with the American past (as Cather's aspiring artist in *Lucy Gay-
heart* [1935] is tragically unable to do). Because Thea has left the impoverished present of Moonstone and gone back to the rich communal and
mythic roots of America, she is able to rejoin contemporary American culture and enrich it. We are told that while she is in Panther Canyon, she
clings to "whatever was left of Moonstone in her mind"; she ultimately
does return to Moonstone – not in person, but in the town's communal
memory. The novel concludes with news of Thea that has reached Moonstone through her aunt:

> Her stories give them something to talk about and to conjecture about, cut off
> as they are from the restless currents of the world. The many naked little sand-
> bars which lie between Venice and the mainland, in the seemingly stagnant water
> of the lagoons, are made habitable and wholesome only because, every night, a
> foot and a half of tide creeps in from the sea and sends its fresh brine up through
> all the network of shining waterways. So, into all the little settlements of quiet
> people, tidings of what their boys and girls are doing in the world bring refresh-
> ment; bring to the old, memories, and to the young, dreams. (581)

This final geographical and topographical metaphor places in a communal
context the dialectic between past and present, and between Europe and

America, that we have followed in the individual character's life and art. The renewing tidal waters reiterate Thea's own experience of the past's regenerative force, and recall the daily struggle of a community (consisting neither of artists nor heroes) to assimilate America's divergent and often buried pasts into their own ongoing present.

In Cather's willingness to posit for Thea in Panther Canyon a kind of Hegelian "absolute knowledge" – a union of subject and object, individual and collective consciousness – Cather reflects the end of the nineteenth century rather than the first decades of the twentieth, despite the fact that she was writing contemporaneously with Faulkner, Fitzgerald, Hemingway, and Dos Passos. It is true that she still believed in the possibility of finding a historical center that would hold, a possibility dismissed by most European and U.S. modernists. It is also true that her fiction is untouched by the physics of relativity, or by the mechanics of entropy, a scientific metaphor for historical process introduced into U.S. literature in 1907 by Henry Adams in *The Education of Henry Adams*. And though subtle narrative ambiguities and ironies abound, her fiction does not self-consciously or self-reflexively call into question the mimetic capacities of language, as the work of her contemporaries often did. Nonetheless, Cather's work *does* contain and exemplify the European historiographic heritage of U.S. literary modernism, and it *does* suggest the ways in which that heritage has been – must be – assimilated in order to be useful in America. It suggests, furthermore, the essential historical and historiographic concerns of many of her successors. Flannery O'Connor, Saul Bellow, Walker Percy, Robert Coover, and others have continued to work both through and against the tradition that Cather's fiction so clearly embodies; in their work, as in Cather's, philosophical thinking inevitably becomes historical thinking. It is relevant that the same European philosophical heritage has served as the basis for an important historicist reorientation in U.S. literary criticism. The "dialectical criticism" of Fredric Jameson is, of course, deeply rooted in Hegelian historicism as modified by Marx and interpreted by Lukács, Adorno, Benjamin, and Marcuse.

II

The U.S. tradition of historical idealism I have just traced may seem to differ considerably from the vision of history impelling recent novelistic practice in Latin America. For example, contrast Cather's acceptance of Carlyle's transcendental historicism to Augusto Roa Bastos' explicit rejection of it in *Yo el Supremo* (*I the Supreme*, 1974). Roa Bastos makes ironic use of Carlyle's 1843 "Essay on Dr. Francia" to undermine the Carlylean conception of epic and prophetic history; Latin American history is portrayed as having produced few heroes, much less a dialectical progression toward truth. Nonetheless, Roa Bastos consistently treats history not as a record of civilization but as the process of civilization itself, with art as its necessary embodiment. These are undeniably the intuitions at the heart of Carlylean and German historical idealism, as is the conviction that the past is always present, that history is necessarily cumulative. In fact, I have already observed that modern Latin American writers often engage history as a primary and primal force. So we find that Roa Bastos is influenced by historical idealism, his dismissal of Carlyle notwithstanding. But before going further, I want to trace the broad outlines of modern Latin America's European historiographic lineage, as I have just traced those of modern U.S. literature.

Nineteenth-century sources of Latin American historiography are well documented. European positivism was adopted repeatedly, as Leopoldo Zea has shown, to suggest more rationalistic and democratic models of government and education than those provided by the Spanish tradition of centralized power and culture.[24] The overarching transcendental idealism of German historiography was generally rejected in favor of the more scientific modes of French positivism. Nonetheless, the progressive character of German historiography was also attractive to nineteenth-century political leaders throughout Latin America because it allowed the errors of past governments to be discounted, new orders to be justified, and reforms to be submitted to empirical criteria. Angel Rama, in his study of Latin American literary culture entitled *La ciudad letrada*, describes the differences between these French and German imports. He is concerned less with differences in their historiographic patterns than with their attitudes toward individual and collective identity. In Latin America, "we did not have the idealistic and individualistic German romanticism, but rather the socialistic French romanticism which made of Victor Hugo an American hero, in the same way that positivistic sociology engrained itself with enormous success in the Latin American mind, making of Comte and Spencer thinkers to whom obeisance was paid, not only for their clear explicative virtues but also because that doctrine adapted itself to the collectivized patterns of regional culture, permitting interpretations based on groups and classes as had always been done . . ." (78).

Rama's focus is on the collective and empirical orientation of French positivism, but he does not wholly dismiss German historicism as an influence in Latin America. Comte was no less convinced than the German idealists that phenomena could be understood philosophically only if they were first understood historically through a demonstration of their temporal derivations and destinations, that is, through their relative positions in the whole course of history. Furthermore, like his predecessors, Condorcet, Turgot, Saint-Simon, Comte was a social evolutionist with a strong secular faith in progress and human perfectability.[25] The same is true of Spencer, whose statements about the future's superiority to the past are in the same vein as the futuristic bombast of the U.S. historian, Bancroft.[26] In fact, it was Spencer rather than Marx who inspired the working class in Argentina late in the nineteenth century: socialism, not communism, was their goal. Marxist historiography was considered abstract and philosophical in comparison to Spencerian empiricism, despite Marx's repeated rejection of the intellectual abstraction of Hegelian idealism in favor of dialectical materialism. (Marx became an important historiographic source for Latin American literature only during the twenties and thirties of this century as Latin American artists and writers involved themselves in the international Communist movement, among them Pablo Neruda and Diego Rivera.) There are, then, more similarities than differences in the nineteenth-century European historiographic imports into the Americas, despite the sociological orientation of Latin America's choices. It is only during this century that positivism has been self-consciously challenged and systematically rejected by Latin American philosophers and writers. It is in this relatively recent negation and assimilation that one may find (pace Hegel) a genuine American historiography.

In the early decades of this century, Latin America ceased to be Europe's monologue (as Leopoldo Zea has put it) and entered into a dialogue, then an argument, with imported concepts of progressive history. The most visible of the arguers were Alejandro Korn in Argentina, Carlos Vaz Ferreira in Uruguay, Alejandro Deústua in Peru, Enrique Molina in Chile, and Antonio Caso, José Vasconcelos, and Octavio Paz in Mexico. Mexicans had more cause than most Latin Americans to reject positivism, for though it had been the basis for educational reforms under Benito Juárez in the mid nineteenth century, it also provided the philosophical justification for the subsequent dictatorship of Porfirio Díaz, with its accompanying racial and social theories of intellectual and political domination.[27] Furthermore, the model of the U.S. was often invoked in nineteenth-century Mexico to suggest the advantages of scientific positivism and a forward-looking mentality, a fact that no doubt gave impetus to the subsequent rejection of positivism as such, and to Paz's and Fuentes' proposition that the historical attitudes in the U.S. and Latin America are diametrically opposed. During the first half of this century, establishing and maintaining a distance from imported and imposed histories came to be considered essential to the process of national self-definition throughout Latin America.

In the U.S. during this period, there was also a reaction against empirical positivism, variously referred to as "mechanism," "rationalism," and "materialism." Unlike the reaction in Latin America, however, the U.S. reaction was not based on a specific sense of national historical necessity. Nor did it result in a coherent shift in historiographic attitudes based on evolving national identity, a failure that may explain the feeling of so many U.S. modernist writers that they were lacking a usable history in America. What they may have been lacking was a usable historiography.[28]

By contrast, the positivism imported into Latin America in the nineteenth century encountered widespread resistance in the twentieth. The philosophical and humanistic reaction against positivism has been discussed by Michael Weinstein, who has grouped the most influential Mexican antipositivists and explored their related philosophies of history.[29] He argues that they rejected existing positivist attitudes that focused on the efficient use of means to attain material and social ends, and instead developed a doctrine of human action that privileged the realization of intrinsic human values:

> The evolutionary philosophies of history propounded by such thinkers as Comte, Marx, and Spencer all had as their focus the progressive and self-conscious control of human beings over their material circumstances. The principle for conquering nature is the rule of economy, embodied in technologies resulting from applied natural science. . . . The Mexican finalists were well schooled in nineteenth-century evolutionary philosophies, since the doctrines of Comte and Spencer had provided the foundation for public education during the Díaz era, and Marxism was used to legitimize many of the actions of post-Revolutionary governments. Their antipositivism was based on their observation that the public situation in the twentieth century was not evolving in the directions of love, justice, and peace, but was marked by the emergence of more refined techniques of domination. The perfection of science, the socialization of production, and economic development (industrialization) seemed to result in the appropriation of human beings-as-instruments by elites rather than in the liberation of humanity, the proletariat, or the individual. (4–5)

The Mexican antipositivists also rejected concepts that posited human history as unfolding in accordance with an immanent or predetermined norm, whether the mechanism for the unfolding was metaphysical (Hegel) or sociological (Comte). They sought to create a national philosophy by analyzing the Mexican personality in its historical context, and by invoking humanistic and ethical precepts that would condition that context. But even this specifically American project was not carried out without the intermingling of European philosophical currents.

Weinstein names the Spanish philosopher José Ortega y Gasset and the French philosopher Henri Bergson as two of the most important European influences on Mexican and Latin American historiographic thinking in this century. Via a brief discussion of their philosophies of time, I will approach more specifically the nature of Latin American antipositivism. Furthermore, because I am comparing European sources of historical consciousness in the Americas, I will entertain for a moment the idea that Ortega and Bergson have served *functions* in contemporary Latin American literary culture analogous to those served by Carlyle and James in modernist U.S. literary culture, though the substance of their historiographic conceptions differs considerably. It also seems possible, in this comparative context, to juxtapose the essayists and poets, Paz and Emerson: Paz has adapted a European historiographic tradition to suit the Latin American literary imagination of this century, as Emerson did in the United States in the last century.

III

Ortega's influence on Latin American literature and philosophy has remained a controversial question, in part because of his conservative political and cultural ideas, in part because of his condescending (or, perhaps more accurately, his paternalistic) attitude toward Latin America.[30] Paz and the Cuban novelist Alejo Carpentier have proclaimed Ortega an essential influence on their entire generation, but my interest here is in his function as a mediator among cultures.[31] Ortega acted as the essential conduit for German philosophy into Spanish and Latin American culture in this century, as did Carlyle (whom Ortega greatly admired) into British and American culture in the previous century. As editor of the *Revista de Occidente*, which he founded in 1923, Ortega introduced philosophers (English as well as German) and also writers (Valéry, Kafka, Huxley, Lawrence, Proust, Joyce) into Spain and, more important, into Spanish.[32] His own views were conveyed to Latin America in his voluminous writings – particularly *Meditaciones del Quijote* (*Meditations on Quixote*, 1913), *El tema de nuestro tiempo* (*The Modern Theme*, 1923), *La rebelión de las masas* (*The Revolt of the Masses*, 1930), *En torno a Galileo* (translated as *Man and Crisis*, 1933) – and also in the migration of Spanish intellectuals to Latin American universities during the Spanish civil war. All of them would have known Ortega's work, and many of them had been his students. If the specific nature of Ortega's influence remains open to question, his widespread presence in modern Latin American culture does not.

Ortega was not a systematic philosopher but an essayist whose profound interest in the nature of Hispanic culture he persistently couched in historiographic terms. In his essay "History as a System" (1935), he summarizes the concept of history that runs throughout his work. He writes, "Man is what has happened to him, what he has done. . . . *Man, in a word, has no nature; what he has is . . . history.* Expressed differently: what nature is to things, history, *res gestae*, is to man."[33] To attribute to human history an intrinsic or necessary character is an error: every man is "a drama": "each one in his turn is nothing but happening" (200). Like Vico, Ortega insists upon the primacy of historical research and experience, explicitly rejecting Descartes' identification of truth with subjective certainty; and, like Heidegger (with whom he associated his work), Ortega rejects the culmination of the Cartesian tradition, Hegel's identification of the subject and object in an all-inclusive knowledge. Instead he proposes a phenomenological "disintellectualization of the real": his theory of the *razón vital* (vital reason or rational vitalism) of history depends upon an understanding of social and historical context. Ortega displaces Hegelian (and Carlylean) idealism and adopts instead a view that resembles the Husserlian (and Bergsonian) phenomenological insistence on the existence of the object world as well as the subject's perception of it. This view is epitomized in Ortega's famous slogan, "Yo soy yo y mi circunstancia" ("I am myself and my circumstances.")[34] For Ortega, historical process is not ideal but phenomenological, not metaphysical but specifically located in geographical and political space.

For the Mexican antipositivists engaged in the attempt to create a genuinely American history and historiography, this idea of the specificity of historical experience provided an essential impetus. Octavio Paz writes that for Latin American intellectuals, Ortega inserted ideas into a lived and living context, thus changing them from abstractions into "instruments, weapons, mental objects which we use and live. . . . His lesson consisted in showing us what ideas were used for and how to use them: not for the purpose of knowing ourselves or contemplating essences, but to clear a way though our circumstances, to dialogue with the world, with our past and our fellow men."[35] Paz's own contribution can, of course, be understood in exactly these terms. Furthermore, multiperspectival narratives like Rulfo's *Pedro Páramo* (1955) or García Márquez's *Crónica de una muerte anunciada* (*Chronicle of a Death Foretold*, 1981) or Vargas Llosa's *La guerra del fin del mundo* (*The War of the End of the World*, 1981) are Ortegan in their sense of circumstantial history. As I will show in subsequent chapters, these novels filter history though the divergent understanding of groups or representative individuals, dramatizing how historical circumstance conditions lives and nations. Despite Paz's reference to dialogue, Ortega's historiography forcefully conjures up the idea of monologue; individuals and groups are inevitably encased and isolated by their own historical circumstances, in their own labyrinths of solitude. This idea, current in contemporary Latin American fiction, may also contribute to dichotomies such as those proposed by Paz and Fuentes, which oppose U.S. and Latin American cultural attitudes without entertaining the possibility of a third and synthesizing term. Paz summarizes Ortega's historical vision, and in his statement we again sees his own historical vision and that of many contemporary Latin American writers, "a Promethean vision and also a tragic one. . . . History is our condition and our freedom: it is where we find ourselves and what we have made" (104).

Along with Ortega's concept of circumstantial history, the Mexican antipositivists found the philosopher's rejection of linear, progressive history congenial. Ortega conceived of history as a series of epochs – and within them generations – that reiterate certain basic civilizational patterns, a model of recurrence akin to those of Vico, Spengler or Nietzsche in its cyclical conception of human civilization and its description of periods of historical plenitude and crisis.[36] Ortega refused to posit an intrinsic movement of history, but he nonetheless observed an recurrent nature of human activity. Each generation both argues and collaborates with the generations that precede and follow it; each generation is both a continuation and a beginning. The past is active in the present ("The past is I – by which I mean my life" [223]) in ways that are not so much progressive as cumulative – one might almost say rhythmic, as in his reference to the "vital pulse" of human history. Ortega's *razón vital* is not dialectical in a Hegelian or Carlylean sense, and he carefully differentiates between his own concept and "the facile anticipations of logical dialectic": "The idea of progress, placing truth in a vague tomorrow, has proved a dulling opiate to humanity. Truth is what is true now and not what remains to be discovered in a undetermined future" (182).

Ortega's oblique reference to Marx in this statement is revealing, for though he was not a Marxist and rejected the historical discontinuity implied by the revolutionary utopianism of Marxism, he nonetheless coincided with Marx in challenging Hegelian idealism on materialist grounds. Ortega follows Marx, who praises Hegel ("that mighty thinker") and then negates and assimilates Hegelian idealism in order to "discover the rational kernel within the mystical shell."[37] Ortega and Marx coincide, furthermore, in their essentially Hegelian understanding of alienation as a function of historical and material circumstance; Ortega repeatedly insists that historical circumstance may be the source of social and political alienation, as well as the cause of eventual social and political integration. Indeed, Paz cites Ortega on just this point to conclude the essays in *The Labyrinth of Solitude*: "The sterility of the bourgeois world will end in suicide or in a new form of creative participation. This is the 'theme of our times,' in Ortega y Gasset's phrase; it is the substance of our dreams and the meaning of our acts" (212). Ortega's conception of history clearly complements and reinforces other historiographic conceptions in modern Latin American literature and culture; not only Paz, but also Carpentier and García Márquez and Cortázar may profitably be examined in terms of Ortegan ideas of historical alienation and cyclical recurrence. In the case of Fuentes, I would argue that Ortega's presence in Latin American historiographic thinking generally, and in Paz's work particularly, creates the intellectual medium by and in which Fuentes can reject progressive, dialectical historical models in favor of Vico's spiraling history.

If Ortega's *razón vital* has been assimilated into contemporary Latin American literary versions of *communal* history, Bergson's creative vitalism has been assimilated into contemporary Latin American literary versions of *individual*, subjective time. Both philosophers conceive of history in vitalistic terms. Bergson's theory of *la durée* proposes a continuous temporal current of psychic experience that is both different from and yet conditioned by communal historical experience. While Bergson's ideas do not need detailed exposition here, the issue of Bergson's cultural *function* in Latin America may. Weinstein states simply: "Henri Bergson was the leader of the revolt against nineteenth-century absolutism in the West. His notion of spontaneous and imprevisible creative evolution freed the concept of becoming from subordination to static truth systems."[38] Bergson's vitalism, like Ortega's *razón vital*, provided an essential source of European philosophical support for the Latin American critique of the linear and normative structures of nineteenth-century positivistic historiography.[39] Just as William James' phenomenological psychology complements the larger Carlylean and Hegelian patterns of universal history in Willa Cather's fiction, so Bergson's theory of the individual temporal experience accompanies and conditions the Ortegan and Vichian patterns of collective historical experience embodied in Carlos Fuentes' fiction. Fuentes' *Distant Relations* implicitly reflects this European historiographic lineage of Latin American literature as Willa Cather's *The Song of the Lark* reflects the different yet related lineage of U.S. literature. Like *The Song of the Lark*, *Distant Relations* dramatizes the ways in which America's own indigenous cultural heritage modifies and conditions its received European tradition.

IV

In *Distant Relations*, American culture contains (and is also in some sense contained by) the European past. If German arias resound magisterially and symbolically in *The Song of the Lark*, it is a French air that provides the leitmotif for *Distant Relations*: "A la claire fontaine, en m'allant promener, j'ai trouvé l'eau si belle, que je m'y suis baigné. Il y a longtemps que je t'aime, jamais je ne t'oublierai." ("In the clear fountain, as I walked, the water was so beautiful that I bathed there. I have loved you for a long time and will never forget you.") The fountain of the children's song suggests symbolically the French *sources* (literally, the wellsprings) of Latin American literary culture that the novel details, and the renewing American sources for French literature as well. For Fuentes illustrates (as Cather, writing seventy years earlier, did not) that the intellectual current now flows strongly from west to east as well. *Distant Relations* alludes centrally to nineteenth- and twentieth-century Latin American writers who were influenced by French literature and who also went to France to add their Hispanic voices to the French literary tradition. Isidore Ducasse, Comte de Lautréamont ("el francés de Montevideo"; "Frenchman from Montevideo"), José María de Heredia ("el francés de La Habana, el conquistador entristecido que regresa al viejo mundo . . . ebrio del sueño del continente nuevo, la pesadilla del continente viejo" [121]; "Frenchman from Havana, the disconsolate conquistador who returns to the Old World . . . drunk with . . . the dream of the new continent, the nightmare of the old" [124]), Alexandre Dumas (whose father went to France from Haiti), Jules Laforgue (who went to France "a apresurar el paso de su 'juventud trieste y hambrienta' junto al Plata a esa trama temprana de la ilusión universal que se llama la muerte junto al Sena" [120–21]; who "exchanged the passage of a 'sad and insatiable youth' beside the River Plate for the speedier universal illusion called death beside the Seine" [123–24]). A poem by Jules Supervielle, another "Frenchman from Montevideo," serves as the epigraph to the novel's English translation. The relation of Europe and America comes full circle: the Latin American poets reach out to Europe and then back again; new worlds grow old and old worlds are renewed in Fuentes' spiraling history.

Fuentes' characters live not on the new and sparsely settled frontier but in the largest city in the world, and one of the oldest. The Heredias, a Mexican family, have roots and branches in France and Spain, and they know the history of French and Spanish exploitation in the Caribbean, a history in which their forebears participated profitably. They themselves travel to Europe frequently and know it intimately if not comfortably; like cultural influences, tourism now moves in both directions across the Atlantic, a fact that only increases the difficulty of historical assimilation for Hugo, the father of the Mexican Heredias. Hugo Heredia is an archeologist, and as he speaks about Mexico's pre-Cortesian past, a Frenchman who is listening thinks (not condescendingly but admiringly) that Heredia has

esa característica de los latinoamericanos cultos: sentirse obligado a saberlo todo, leerlo todo, no darle al europeo cuartel ni pretexto, conocer igualmente bien lo que el europeo ignora y lo que considera propio, el Popol Vuh y Descartes. Sobre todo, demostrarle que no hay excusa para desconocer a los demás. (15)

that quality so characteristic of cultured Latin Americans: the passion to know everything, to read everything, to give no quarter, no pretext, to the European, but also to know well what the European does not know and what he considers his own, the Popol Vuh *and* Descartes. And, above all, to demonstrate to the European that there is no excuse not to know other cultures. (9–10)

Hugo is burdened by the irony of his own Spanish heritage in Mexico: he believes that the foundations of the land and its greatest cultural achievements are to be found in the very monuments buried or destroyed by the Spanish invaders, the monuments of the cultures indigenous to Mexico. Heredia laments the expulsion of the ancient gods from the modern city and the replacement of mythic time by mere chronological sequence; there is no longer an accreting present that would recuperate and revitalize the mythic Mexican past. Nonetheless, he insists that the ruins of ancient civilizations in Mexico testify to the fact that "las civilizaciones no mueren del todo; perduran, pero sólo si no progresan" (12; "civilizations do not die completely; they endure, but only when they do not progress" 6). Unfortunately Hugo, like other Mexicans, has not adequately assimilated this past; in attempting to educate his son to revere the past, he sacrifices the present, teaching him to scorn his contemporaries. Hugo's attempt to find a satisfactory position between the colonizer and the colonized fails. It is not an antiquarian devotion to monuments of stone that should determine one's relation to cultural history, Fuentes suggests, but rather the conviction that the present will remain incomprehensible and incomplete *except* in the context of the past.

There is in Fuentes' novel, as in Cather's, a particular ancient site that the characters must recognize and internalize if they are to participate fully and consciously in American historical reality. The site is Xochical-co, the ruins of a city of pyramids near Cuernavaca. In a country of hundreds of excavated sites, Fuentes' choice of Xochicalco is revealing. Xochicalco reflects a late mixture of cultures: in a *cámara de ofrendas* (room of sacrifices) objects have been found that attest the presence of elements from the Mayan, Teotihuacán, Mezcal, Totonaca, Zapoteca, and Nahua cultures. Furthermore, Xochicalco is known to have been an important center for astronomical and hence historiographic research; congregations of astronomers are believed to have met there to determine the fifty-two-year Aztec "century." A cave with a hexagonal perforation through the top of the mountain was used to calculate solar cycles; on the twenty-second of September the sun's rays penetrate perpendicularly, totally illuminating the subterranean room. What strikes the contemporary visitor to this site are not just the vestiges of its astronomical genius and cultural diversity but also the quantity of artifacts and edifices that still lie buried under the sediment of centuries. Architectural forms are softened, rounded, disguised by the accretion of dirt, vegetation, and stones extraneous to the original constructions. The past literally seems to await recuperation and assimilation into the present, as Fuentes' novel continually suggests.

So we understand that if the French and German cultures are *sources* of the American worlds depicted by Fuentes and Cather, the ancient cultures of Xochicalco and Panther Canyon are their *genesis*. If their European sources can be visited and studied, their American origins must be dreamed; the former are a question of education, the latter a question of psychic energy. Without an imaginative re-creation of the native substratum, no European culture can be fruitfully assimilated in America, nor can the process work in the other direction either.

That Fuentes portrays Mexico's contemporary national identity as embedded in its indigenous past reflects the Ortegan idea of the utter specificity of historical circumstance, an idea also consistently engaged, as I have said, in the essays of Octavio Paz. Paz has written that "every history is a geography and every geography is a geometry of symbols"; Mexico's ancient pyramids represent the cyclical time of myth, "the end and the beginning of motion. An immobility in which the dance of the cosmos ends and begins again."[40] More specifically than Cather in *The Song of the Lark*, in *Distant Relations* Fuentes dramatizes this translation of time into space. In his own essay, Fuentes, like Paz, describes the particular chronotopic configuration of Mexico as round and recurring: ". . . ancient Mexican art consists precisely in creating a great area, space and time, which may contain the implacable *circle* of the subsistence of the cosmos, as well as the *circularity* of a perpetual return to one's origins, and the *circulation* of all those mysteries that cannot be limited by rationalization. . . . Mexico's ancient art contains a secret tension that cannot be admitted by positivistic thinking. . . ."[41]

To this vision of the communal and racial past, Fuentes joins a Bergsonian theory of personal memory to suggest the complexity of historical remembering. Bergsonian philosophy is integrated into *Distant Relations* by means of references to Bergson's closest literary kin, Marcel Proust, and also through references to the multiple narrators who will tell and retell the history that the novel contains. In *Creative Evolution* (1907), Bergson's seminal work on subjective temporal apprehension, time is defined as "the continuous progress of the past which gnaws into the future and which swells as it advances. And as the past grows without ceasing, so also there is no limit to its preservation."[42] In *Distant Relations*, there is a metaphor that self-consciously reflects this definition and (despite Fuentes' rejection of linear temporality) reflects as well Bergson's description of duration as "a stream against which we cannot go." One character tells another, whose name is Fuentes, to retell the history that he has just heard, for each version is

un río más de esta carta hidrográfica que estamos dibujando, desde hace varias horas, usted y yo; sí, usted también, usted lo sabe, no puede echarse para atrás ahora, usted es ya otro río de esta cuenca cuyos verdaderos orígenes aún desconocemos, como ignoramos la multiplicidad de sus afluentes y el destino final al cual desemboca. (157)

another river in the hydrograph we have been tracing for the past few hours, you and I. Yes, you as well, you know it; you cannot turn back now. You, too, have become a river in this watershed whose true source we still do not know, as we do not know the multiplicity of its tributaries or the final destiny toward which it flows. (162)

Fuentes' image adds narrative renewal to the topographical and cultural renewal contained in Cather's image of the canals of Venice at the end of *The Song of the Lark*. The past is the sum of the narrative modifications and transformations of present consciousness, a sum that never decreases, that perpetually increases. If an Ortegan sense of the circumstantial specificity of historical experience contributes to the solitude that afflicts the Heredias in *Distant Relations*, then the Bergsonian telling and retelling of that experience is the antidote to their solitude. One character says that narration is "un desesperado intento por restablecer la analogía sin sacrificar la diferenciación" (191; "a desperate attempt to re-establish analogy without sacrificing differentiation" 200). Fuentes' novel dramatizes the ways in which the regenerative process of narrative remembering makes distant relations less so.

It is clear that my own comparative study also attempts to "re-establish analogy without sacrificing differentiation." I will state explicitly what I have already implied: the visions of history in the U.S. and Latin America seem to me to be less distant than Fuentes' and Paz's oppositions allow. Despite their different heritages and contexts, and their different political purposes, the novelistic engagements of American history by Cather and Fuentes are surprisingly congruent. Cather's final image of the canals of Venice, like Fuentes' fluvial image, suggests the ebb and flow (not the progress) of culture, the intermingling of various cultural currents (not a single, impelling source), and the expansive flow of individual and communal historical experience in expressive forms (both narrative and musical). Cather and Fuentes are united in their conscious reaction against the tenacious idea, first made explicit by Hegel and still held in America in obvious and manifold ways, that our American pasts have been little more than an unrequited love affair with the European past. Their novels do not deny this love affair – indeed, they acknowledge and incorporate it in the ways I have suggested and in others that I haven't – but they also know that American historical experience moves along more than just a transatlantic axis. Precisely because they share a Hegelian awareness of the interrupted history of the New World, they understand the consequent need to discover or invent a usable past from both European and native materials. Their novels posit art as the means of recuperating and assimilating the sundered pasts of America, and are themselves examples of that process. They contradict Fuentes' assertion that the past is unusable in America; in their form and their content, the historical anxiety so typical of American self-definition is confronted, negated, assimilated. Such works as these, set in a comparative context, may themselves serve as the third, synthesizing term of the necessary dialectic between U.S. and Latin American historical consciousness.

V

In the novels I have discussed, neither Cather nor Fuentes insists on the equation of history to its narrated versions. On the contrary, both posit external histories that precede narration and that must be discovered by the characters *before* they can be narrated. However, in a considerable number of recent Latin American and U.S. works, that order has been reversed. As I will show in the next chapter, critical terms like "documentary fiction," "nonfiction novel," and "metahistory" are frequently used, and useful, to describe literature in which textual definition precedes historical definition. Such literature clearly responds to the historical anxiety I am positing, but its emphasis is on narrative assimilation rather than cultural constitution. Its authors entertain the generic conflation of "history" and "fiction" on the premise that there is only narrative, only constructed versions of the world. This realization may be presented as disillusioning because it undermines historical agency or, on the contrary, it may be presented as liberating. The coherence that narrative provides (as events rarely do) may serve as consolation in the face of an impenetrable history (or "destiny," as García Márquez often calls historical exigency). History-as-narrative may suggest both continuance and continuity – essential to cultures where indigenous traditions have been disrupted and European traditions interrupted.

The blurring of historical and fictional narratives, and the blurring of generic distinctions, are hardly recent ("postmodernist") developments.[43] Melville's *Moby Dick* (1851), Domingo Faustino Sarmiento's *Facundo o Civilización y barbarie* (*Facundo, or Civilization and Barbarism*, 1845), Euclides da Cunha's *Os Sertões* (translated as *Rebellion in the Backlands*, 1902), John Dos Passos' trilogy, *U.S.A.* (1938), or James Agee's *Let Us Now Praise Famous Men* (1941) would belie such a suggestion. What I *do* wish to suggest here is that the shift in emphasis from historical to narrative issues may be an indication that Hegel's question about the nature of America's past has been superseded by Barthesian and Derridean questions about the nature of language per se. This shift implies that the concept of universal historical process, which Lukács believed fundamental to the novel, has been replaced by processes that are linguistic and literary rather than historical in the sense that Lukács intended. This shift has been foregrounded in recent theories of postmodernism, though I repeat that the phenomenon itself is not at all recent; novels self-consciously engaging these issues date back to the origins of the novel, when Cervantes set the conventions of the chivalric romance against more realistic assumptions and conventions not yet named. Jorge Luis Borges will allow me to entertain these generalizations and conclude my own discussion.

Borges' work presents an assiduous investigation of America's cultural origins. "El escritor argentino y la tradición" ("The Argentine Writer and Tradition") is his best-known and most explicit essay on the subject, but it is not his only one to explore the historical and cultural traditions inherited by the American writer.[44] I will return to this essay in Chapter 3. For now, let me reiterate the assertion of my introduction: Borges' work consistently and brilliantly embodies a New World historical imagination. Not that he ordinarily describes such specifically geographical locations as those of Cather and Fuentes, or such localized ideological and cultural oppositions as those proposed by Fuentes and Paz. Rather, his approach to historical definition is suggested in the oxymorons of his titles *Historia de la eternidad* (*History of Eternity*, 1953) and "Nueva refutación del tiempo" ("New Refutation of Time," 1952). These titles (and the works themselves) signal Borges' characteristic oscillation between the poles of phenomenological particularity and philosophical abstraction, between the finite and the infinite; they underscore the sense we so often have, when reading

Borges, that we are entering into a discussion that is simultaneously about America and the cosmos. Borges entertains ideas, texts, events and settings that are localized in time and place and also operate on a universal plane. In the introduction to his 1932 collection, *Discusión*, Borges states that his essays are *"resignados ejercicios de anacronismo: no restituyen el difícil pasado – operan y divagan con él"* (*"resigned exercises in anachronism: they do not restore the difficult past – they work and wander with it."*)[45] His imaginative historiography, which I will call philosophical anachronism, rejects overarching European paradigms of world-historical process, and instead modestly universalizes the fragments of felt history.

Borges' 1952 essay, "El pudor de la historia" ("The Modesty of History"), begins with Goethe. On September 20, 1792, after witnessing a battle in which a handful of French militiamen improbably defeated the German army, Goethe is reported to have observed, "En este lugar y el día de hoy, se abre una época en la historia del mundo y podemos decir que hemos asistido a su origen."[46] ("In this place and on this day, a new epoch in the history of the world is beginning, and we shall be able to say that we have been present at its origin."[47]) By quoting Goethe's statement, which is anything but modest, Borges acknowledges the late-eighteenth-century German positivist historiography so basic to American modernism and also amends it, stating that such historic events are now fabricated regularly by governments, newspapers, and Cecil B. DeMille. "Real history," according to Borges, is more modest and is principally textual. A phrase from the *Poetics*, another from the *Tusculanea*, yet another from the *Seven Pillars of Wisdom*, suggest that history is a matter of linguistic use rather than empirical data. And heroism is a matter of heroic *fictions*: the *Poema del Cid*, the *Aeneid*, the *Chanson de Roland*, Whitman, Hugo, Faulkner, and Housman convey to the author "el elemental sabor de lo heroico" (133; "the fundamental flavor of the heroic" 169). Carlyle appears here too, but this writer who provided Emerson's and Cather's literary archetype of historical heroism is relegated by Borges to a footnote that documents Carlyle's inadequate translation of a phrase from the Icelandic saga *Heimskringla*. So Borges modestly sets to one side the Hegelian mainstream of universalizing historical order that Carlyle represents.

Borges' central example of history's modesty is from the *Heimskringla*. He cites a passage that details an exchange of words before a skirmish in 1225 between Saxon and Norse armies, a skirmish that the Norsemen subsequently lost. It is not the skirmish, however, with its preceding verbal exchange that Borges takes to be significant, but the fact that it was recorded at all, for the author of the account was an Icelander – "un hombre de la sangre de los vencidos" (134; "a man of the lineage of the vanquished" 170). Snorri Sturlason recorded the defeat of his own people, a gesture that Borges treats as prophetic of a time when the distinction between nations will be effaced, when "la solidaridad del género humano" (134; "the solidarity of all mankind" 170) will be established. Having undermined Hegelian historiography, Borges nonetheless concludes by observing a Hegelian dialectic of negation and assimilation that Snorri's text embodies. The skirmish between the Saxons and the Norsemen attests to nationalistic self-interest; the *recording* of the event attests to the transcendence of that self-interest: "Snorri, por el hecho de referirla, lo supera y trasciende" (134; "by relating it, Snorri surmounts and transcends that concept." 170) It is the text itself that exists in dialectical relation to history, incorporating it, transforming it, renewing it. History is advanced not by history but by narrative, which "surmounts and transcends" the events it describes. The writer's language does not so much represent history as signify it.

In accordance with the Latin American antipositivism that I have discussed here, Borges' history is circumstantial rather than ideal, subject to many minor adjustments and many readings: The loci of culture are numerous and widespread. Borges' history operates by means of small shifts in a world where historical interactions are eccentric, not progressive or causal; such history can be understood in terms of Borges' philosophical anachronism, and narrated by means of the "new techniques" of "deliberate anachronism, and erroneous attribution." This is not cause for disillusion but for imaginative recuperation and revitalization. Like Charles Simic's personification of history, the fat old man in faded overalls, Borges' modest history is also clad in workclothes, but he is less severe; instead of a knife and pail, he carries books, and his magic circle limns infinity, not apocalypse. His distracted gaze only sharpens his historical vision, for he knows that history is mythic and malleable and that narrative form is responsive and responsible to such history. In his creative decentering of historical process and his insistence on the historicity of all narrative, Borges' figure may signal the most usable American past of all.

CHAPTER TWO

For the Record

Novels, Newspapers, Narration

Even if all the reports that have come down to us concerning the past, up to our own time, were true and were known by some person, it would be less than nothing in comparison to what is unknown. . . .
Michel de Montaigne, "On Vehicles"[1]

La imposibilidad de penetrar el esquema divino del universo no puede, sin embargo, disuadirnos de planear esquemas humanos, aunque nos conste que éstos son provisorios.
Jorge Luis Borges, "El idioma analítico de John Wilkins"[2]

But the impossibility of penetrating the divine scheme of the universe cannot dissuade us from outlining human schemes, even though we are aware that they are provisional.
Jorge Luis Borges, "The Analytic Language of John Wilkins"[3]

I REFERRED IN MY INTRODUCTION to Georg Lukács' observation concerning the parallel development in the eighteenth century of the novel and the modern conception of history. Hegelian historicism found its appropriate literary form (or, rather, produced it) in the realistic novel. The Borgesian "modest history" that concluded the previous chapter and the magical realist ghosts that will appear in the next one are mitigating circumstances – disruptions of linear, causal, Hegelian ("realistic") narrative structures.[4] In this chapter, I consider a number of realistic novels as well as other "provisional" schemes, to use Borges' term cited in my epigraph, that purport to record history: newspapers and photojournalism. The interactions of novelistic narration with these nonfiction narrative modes (verbal and visual) are my critical concern. I begin with *Gringo viejo* (*The Old Gringo*, 1985), by Carlos Fuentes, focusing first on Fuentes' fictionalization of Ambrose Bierce and then on his narrative and thematic uses of Agustín Victor Casasola's famous photographs of the Mexican Revolution. García Marquez's *Crónica de una muerte anunciada* (*Chronicle of a Death Foretold*, 1981) and Vargas Llosa's *La guerra del fin del mundo*

(*The War of the End of the World*, 1981) provide concluding instances of the relations between novels and newspapers in American literary culture.

Carlos Fuentes' novel centers on a U.S. journalist and fiction writer in Mexico and I, too, will be crossing territorial borders to entertain some broad historical comparisons (and contrasts) between U.S and Latin American literary attitudes toward journalism. My comparative discussion is based on the hypothesis that the explicit integration of journalistic discourse into literary narration raises pointed questions about narrative referentiality, and foregrounds what aesthetician Nelson Goodman calls the truth-claims of the work.[5] We are accustomed to the current critical conflation of "factual" and "fictional" narrative, and to the related idea that the past is the sum of its narrated (or otherwise recorded) versions. Reasons for the willingness to suspend the distinction between the narrative claims of history and fiction move along a continuum whose poles exist in obverse relation. One pole is the modernist privileging of autonomous consciousness and thus the individual's version of the past, true by definition because reality exists as it is *perceived* to exist. The other pole is the post-structuralist privileging of the ideological and material effects of discourses as they operate collectively, conditioning (obviating) individual versions. At this pole, reality exists as it is *conceived* to exist: history is a commodity produced by language and other controlling systems of power, no matter whether it is presented as history or fiction or journalism or myth. The first pole takes historical understanding as inevitably singular, the second as inevitably not; the first is phenomenological and constructivist, the second political and deconstructivist. At both extremes, history and fiction collapse into each other.

The works that I discuss here operate between these poles, recognize both, and maintain a tension between them; the variable relations of historical truth and narrative truth is their theme, a primary source of their narrative energy, and the basis for their critique of narrative as such. By establishing an explicit dialectic between journalistic and novelistic discursive modes, they acknowledge and often embody multiple, simultaneous, and conflicting versions of the world and ask their readers to make distinctions among those versions. We will see that these distinctions, like attitudes toward journalism, vary considerably in the Americas from North to South. Let's begin with Latin America.

Angel Rama argues that newspapers have played an indispensable role in the development of modern Latin America's literary culture.[6] He credits the popular press both with heralding and hastening the profound social and political changes on the horizon of the twentieth century in Latin America. In Mexico during the last two decades of the nineteenth century and the first decade of this century, besides newspapers there were the *gacetas populares*, tabloids and broadsheets such as those published by Antonio Vanegas Arroyo and illustrated by José Guadalupe Posada. The Díaz dictatorship, in power during this period, recognized the subversive potential of the Mexican press and systematically subsidized various newspapers and *gacetas* in an attempt to neutralize their oppositional character. In Argentina, the *revistas gauchescas* and large dailies like *La Nación* and *Crítica* in Buenos Aires were also reaching newly literate portions of the population as no other print medium could. The extension of educational systems in the last decades of the nineteenth century and the first decades of the twentieth was producing not just increasing numbers of readers but increasing numbers of writers as well, for whom newspapers and periodicals were providing an important market. By 1900, groups that had recently been given access to education, and hence to the structures of social and political power, were challenging those very structures. The press, in its various and often picturesque forms, was an important vehicle for this challenge and subsequent processes of modernization in Latin America.

Until this time, according to Rama, the literate segment of Latin American society had been almost exclusively at the service of the existing power structures of the ecclesiastical and bureaucratic establishments, first as colonial administrators and then as functionaries in the independent, centralized national governments. Rama is surely right in emphasizing the democratizing role of the popular press in the late nineteenth century, but his emphasis should not minimize our recognition of the crucial function of earlier journalistic writing during and after the independence movements in the early nineteenth century. The Venezuelan Andrés Bello is perhaps the best example of a literary intellectual whose journalism helped shape the political and cultural identity of newly-independent Latin America.[7] From the mid 1830s to the mid 1850s in Santiago de Chile, Bello wrote articles that unabashedly bear the stamp of their writer, both rhetorically and ideologically. Far from the objectivity and reportorial emphasis of U.S. journalists, Bello and many other leaders in Latin America took positions on political and cultural issues and debated them in self-consciously literary fashion in the pages of newspapers. Their journalistic essays and articles were instrumental in establishing national institutions, and also in establishing the literary, polemical journalism that continues to this day in Latin America.[8]

The participation of contemporary writers in public debate is expected now as before, though their political positions are as often oppositional as official. Almost all of Latin America's first-rank novelists are also journalists, if not by training then by constant and passionate practice. Gabriel García Márquez and Mario Vargas Llosa, whose "journalism novels" I'll discuss shortly, have specifically linked their novelistic and journalistic writings to the political responsibility of the intellectual in Latin America.[9] These writers suggest that journalism and fiction may be less clearly separated in Latin America than elsewhere, and imply that the novel, like the newspaper, must address political and social issues if it is to serve as an instrument of knowledge, and hence as an instrument of social change.

Indeed, in recent years Latin American literature has often responded when the press has failed to address (or has been prevented from addressing) actual political and social conditions. The novels of Brazilian journalists Márcio Souza (*The Emperor of the Amazon*, 1980) and Ivan Angelo (*The Celebration*, 1976) are examples of fiction written to disseminate information that was being suppressed by an authoritarian regime. If government censors create fictions by distorting actual events, writers like Souza and Angelo invert that process, writing fictions that document actual events even as they disguise those events in vivid, elliptical satires. Where newspapers cannot publish all the news that's fit to print, fiction may become the medium to fulfill that function. For various reasons and in various ways, contemporary Latin American writers are taking into account the crucial importance of the press, however doubtful they may be about its efficacy to redress the political and social abuses it must constantly confront.

Given the importance of the press in the literary and political culture of Latin America, it is no wonder that a number of recent Latin American novels are *about* journalists and/or journalism and may, moreover, be narrated by journalists. Besides García Márquez's *Chronicle of a Death Foretold* and Vargas Llosa's *The War of the End of the World*, there are Vargas Llosa's *Conversación en La Catedral* (*Conversation in The Cathedral*, 1969), to which I'll return in Chapter 4, and *Historia de Mayta* (translated into English by Alfred MacAdam as *The Real Life of Alejandro Mayta*, 1984). Further examples are Julio Cortázar's *Libro de Manuel* (translated by Gregory Rabassa as *Manual for Manuel*, 1974), Isabel Allende's *De amor y de sombra* (*Of Love and Shadows*, 1984), Hector Aguilar Camín's *Morir en el golfo* (1987), as well as Elena Poniatowska's creative journalism in *Noche de Tlatelolco* (translated by Helen R. Lane as *Massacre in Mexico*, 1971). These works engage the strategies of realistic narration yet challenge the assumptions of realism.[10] In this sense, they are situated between the narrative realism I discussed in the previous chapter and the magical realism that I will discuss in the following chapter, for they share with magical realist fiction an essential concern with the nature of reality and its representation. Though journalistic narrative would seem to be the antithesis of the mythic plots and fantastic/phantasmagoric settings associated with magical realism, it is not always so. In fact, García Márquez has linked his journalist writing to magical realism, referring to ". . . the tricks you need to transform something which appears fantastic, unbelievable into something plausible, credible, those I learned from journalism. The key is to tell it straight. It is done by reporters and country folk."[11] Journalistic fiction integrates into its narrative structures the reportorial assumptions and interviewing techniques of newspapers, the better to challenge the mimetic assumptions of the realistic novel.[12]

The various strategies for integrating nonfictional and fictional genres makes the relationship between "facts" and language both the thematic and the structural core of these novels. Nelson Goodman's distinction between "truth" and "rightness of rendering" is relevant here because it privileges not the text's supposed factualness (its "truth") but rather its "cogency and compactness and comprehensiveness, the informativeness and organizing power of the whole system," that is, its "rightness" (19). Taking examples from the history of science, Goodman shows that "truth" is often rooted in cultural "belief," and that what is held as true (in the sense that it is taken to report verifiable aspects of a verifiable world) may not conform to basic criteria of "rightness." Conversely, "right" versions are not necessarily "true." Goodman proposes that instead of conceiving of factual and fictional versions of the world, we should concern ourselves with the relative "rightness of rendering" of those worlds. Goodman's kind of "rightness" clearly motivates the Latin American novels I have just named, and impels their authors to explore in innovative ways the shifting borders between fictional and nonfictional narration. It is in terms of these borders that I want to discuss *The Old Gringo*, and then place it in the larger American comparative context that the novel itself proposes.

I

Fuentes' novel is about Ambrose Bierce, a U.S. writer and journalist born in 1842, who in 1914 went to Mexico as an old man to see Pancho Villa's revolution for himself. He died there, though the circumstances of his death are not known. Fuentes has said that his novel was inspired by an epigrammatic comment attributed to Bierce at the outbreak of the Mexican Revolution: "To be a gringo in Mexico: ah, that is euthanasia." Indeed, the novel replays Bierce's flair for death, depicting him as too self-conscious – and too conscious of history – to concede the final point without a flourish. Because the embittered old gringo is willing to meet death more than halfway, he quickly gains a reputation for courage, though the reader knows it is not courage but despair that impels him. Inevitably, Bierce tempts death once too often. He burns the papers that supposedly legitimate the revolutionaries' claim to the lands they have worked for generations, papers they do not know how to read. But if the revolutionaries don't know how to read, they *do* know that the written word has always been the basis of institutional legitimacy in the Spanish New World. They refuse to tolerate Bierce's gesture, even though they are themselves enthusiastically engaged in just such incendiary activities. They shoot him in the back, though a few days later, in a marvelously mock-heroic moment, Villa himself disinters Bierce's corpse and has it decently shot from the front by a firing squad.

Fuentes' fictional projection of a historical figure's unknown fate makes this novel a candidate for the label of documentary fiction. Documentary fiction incorporates historical material in its fictional structure, actively engaging it in the service of the fiction rather than making it merely a backdrop for the fictional action, as realistic fiction (what Barbara Foley calls "pseudofactual" fiction) has always done.[13] By foregrounding actual people and events from the world *outside* the fictional world, and simultaneously integrating them into the structure of the fictional world in ways that suggest a multiplicity of narrative possibilities for those people and events, documentary fiction calls the conventions of realism into question. The conceptual adjustment of the relation between historical truth and narrative truth that documentary fiction requires is reflected in E. L. Doctorow's insistence that there is no fiction or nonfiction, only narrative, only constructed versions of the world.[14] While this idea is the obvious premise of documentary fiction, I refuse to dismiss essential distinctions among the various narrative means of enacting that premise, and the aesthetic and ethical implications of the enactments. Nelson Goodman argues convincingly that our acceptance of many "right" versions of the world does not obviate our obligation to distinguish among "versions that do and those that do not refer, and to talk about the things and worlds, if any, referred to" (96). The reader must not accept generic conflations summarily or simplistically.

In *The Old Gringo*, the problematic border between cultural and geographical territories figures thematically the ambiguous border between narrative truth and historical truth. The fictional Bierce crosses the border at El Paso, which the novel proposes as the dividing line between reason and passion, order and chaos, between a code of law and a code of honor – and between fact and fiction. Before his death, the old gringo is described as "aturdido por el quebradizo planeta que separa a la realidad de la ficción" ("dazed by the fragility of the planet that separates reality from fiction") and aware that he will have to "optar entre la *noticia* dirigida a Hearst y sus lectores, o la *ficción* dirigida al padre y a la mujer" ("choose between the *news* directed to Hearst and his readers and the *fiction* directed to the father and the woman.")[15]

Norman Mailer, referring to his own practice in his "nonfiction novel" *The Armies of the Night* (1968), comments that "to write an intimate history of an event which places its focus on a central figure who is not central to the event is to inspire immediate questions about the competence of the historian. Or, indeed, his honorable motives. The figure he has selected may be convenient to him rather than critical to the history."[16] *The Old Gringo* is about nothing if not the competence of the historian and the nature of historical narrative, so we may well ask how Bierce – a main character in the novel and a very minor one in the Mexican Revolution – is "convenient" for Fuentes. Bierce is dramatized in the novel as a reporter, and in fact he did exert an enormous influence on American journalism through H. L. Mencken and others. Bierce also wrote fiction, and his best stories are set during the Civil War, U.S. history's analogue to the fratricidal (and parricidal) Mexican conflict that concerns Fuentes in *The Old Gringo*. He fought for the Union army, was severely wounded, and deeply affected by the tragic experience of the slaughter, as his battle pieces, including his remarkable account of Shiloh, attest.[17] Several of his war stories are examples of magical realism *avant la lettre*, and it is tempting to entertain the paradox that, like García Márquez, Bierce's journalism inspired him to write fantastical fictions. "An Occurrence at Owl Creek Bridge" suspends the death of a young Civil War soldier until his story can be imagined and finished, a narrative strategy that precedes Borges' similar suspensions of history in "The Secret Miracle." Bierce's "A Horseman in the Sky" is repeatedly invoked in *The Old Gringo*; the story describes a Confederate soldier who fires at an airy vision and kills his own father. Again the journalist/fiction writer's concern is the nature of reality and imagination, and the ways in which the two impinge and overlap—sometimes fatally, as in this story.

Bierce's satiric spirit also suits Fuentes' novelistic purposes. Bierce detested the bombast and corruption of the post-Civil War decades and continually opposed political and social abuses in print. This spirit is epitomized in *The Devil's Dictionary*, a work that once again seems to predict Borges in its dependence on apocryphal sources and imaginary ancients, as well as in its supposed academic and annotative format. Begun in 1881 as a series of definitions in a San Francisco periodical called "The Wasp" ("born to sting") and published as an entity only in 1906, the dictionary allowed Bierce to provide in alphabetical order the "true" meanings of social practice and institutions. His entry for "Historian" is "A broadgauge gossip"; and for "History" it is "An account mostly false, of events mostly unimportant, which are brought about by rulers mostly knaves, and soldiers mostly fools." He adds to his definition of history the following doggerel by the unknown authority Salder Bupp:

> Of Roman history, great Niebuhr's shown
> 'Tis nine-tenths lying. Faith, I wish 'twere known
> Ere we accept great Niebuhr as a guide,
> Wherein he blundered and how much he lied.[18]

Bierce cast doubt upon history and historian alike and was himself apparently cast into doubt in his own lifetime. His biographer states that "Ambrose Bierce was so often discovered only to be forgotten that some doubt arose as to whether a man of this name really existed."[19] His mysterious disappearance in Mexico put the final eerie mark on the question, and makes him a poignantly appropriate person/*personaje* for Fuentes' documentary fiction of the revolution.

The historical Bierce worked for several California newspapers, including the San Francisco *Sunday Examiner*, which was a part of the newspaper empire of Randolph Hearst, and then as a Washington correspondent for the *American*. He was hardly alone among U.S. journalists and other self-interested U.S. media men who descended upon Mexico to scoop the revolution. Fuentes' fictionalized Bierce fully expects "un enjambre de periodistas como él, venidos de ambas costas, revoloteando alrededor del ejército de Pancho Villa" (28; "swarms of newspapermen like him, from both coasts, prowling around Pancho Villa's army" 21), and several scenes in the novel depict groups of reporters shouting questions to which they appear to have the answers already. The refrain "News. National news" punctuates their interviews. There is also a scene in the novel that shows Raoul Walsh, a cameraman and actor in D. W. Griffith's *The Life of General Villa* (1914), the movie that made Villa a Hollywood star. We see Walsh matter-of-factly asking Villa to postpone the daily executions until the light of dawn so that he can film the firing squad at work. His request is magnanimously granted. And if Villa is pleased to be mythologized by the media, Porfirio Díaz, the dictator whom the revolution overthrew, is no less cooperative. He is described by Fuentes as "el deleite de los periodistas, un viejo tirano con genio para las frases publicables" (27; "the delight of newspapermen, an aged tyrant with a genius for publishable phrases" 20). The example given is his rueful statement, "Pobre México, tan lejos de Dios y tan cerca de los Estados Unidos." ("Poor Mexico, so far from God, so close to the United States"). We are meant to recall that Díaz and Villa were among the first political leaders to recognize the power of the news media, a power that was not *systematically* exploited until twenty years later by Adolph Hitler and Franklin Delano Roosevelt.

Fuentes is pointed in his condemnation of the American press' involvement in the Mexican Revolution. In one scene in *The Old Gringo*, the newsroom of the San Francisco *Chronicle* is conjured up and described metonymically by means of an accumulation of headlines full of "instant stereotypes" for easy mass consumption: ". . . en México unos bandidos llamados Carranza, Obregón, Villa y Zapata se habían levantado en armas . . . con el propósito principal de robarle sus tierras al señor Hearst. Wilson habló de la Nueva Libertad y dijo que les enseñaría la democracia a los mexicanos. Hearst exigía: Intervención, Guerra, Indemnización (27–28; ". . . in Mexico, bandits named Carranza, Obregón, Villa, and Zapata had taken up arms . . . with the principal aim of stealing Hearst's land. Wilson spoke of the New Freedom and said he would teach the Mexicans democracy. Hearst demanded: Intervention, War, Indemnification" 20). The jingoistic juxtapositions indict the role of Hearst's papers in determining U.S. interventionist policy in Mexico; furthermore, the novel's repeated references to the Spanish-American War, which most historians agree was declared and directed by the U.S. press, emphatically reinforce Fuentes' point.

The U.S. novelist Gore Vidal makes explicit novelistic use of Hearst's role in hemispheric politics in his historical novel, *Empire* (1987). In fact, Vidal encompasses the same geographical and narrative borders as Fuentes, borders held in place by the relations of power. The final scene of *Empire* is set in the White House, where Vidal pits Hearst against Teddy Roosevelt. They are vain and powerful men who aim to extend their own empires, both journalistic and national; their purposes coincide, but their judgments of who is to be emperor do not. Hearst brags of making war with Spain and winning, then of writing the whole American story. Roosevelt demurs:

> Roosevelt produced his dazzling smile. "I may be a hypocrite, Mr. Hearst, but I'm not a scoundrel."
> "I know," said Hearst, with mock sadness. "After all, I made you up, didn't I?"
> "Mr. Hearst," said the president, "History invented me, not you."
> . . .
> "True history," said Hearst, with a smile that was, for once, almost charming, "is the final fiction. I thought even you knew that."[20]

Vidal treats the borders between history and fiction thematically, but unlike Fuentes he never succeeds in making them structurally problematic. *Empire* never unsettles its own referential status by playing different representations of historical reality against a posited reality beyond those representations. Most traditional realistic novels present fiction as if it were history; historical novels such as Vidal's reverse the referential model and present history as if it were fiction. The result is the same. *Empire* offers its version of history as the only one, the real one; the reader is given no narrative or structural grounds to think that it could be otherwise.

To the extent that *The Old Gringo* is a serious critique of the Hearst empire and U.S. imperialist policies in Latin America (rather than merely a wry dramatization of them, as is Vidal's novel), it stands in close relation to an earlier generation of fiction in the United States that also made the unethical practices of U.S. journalism the subject of its satire. During the first two decades of this century, a number of U.S. writers were active journalists as well as novelists, publishing articles and novels on specific social and economic injustices, with the aim – and often the result – of effecting political and social reforms. Upton Sinclair and Theodore Dreiser knew the abuses of the newspaper world from the inside and wrote novels indicting those abuses, as had William Dean Howells in the 1880s.[21] John Dos Passos, in the "newsreel" sections of his 1930s trilogy, *U.S.A.*, uses the format of the newspapers for the purposes of his satire, juxtaposing headlines and snatches of fatuous reporting and advertising to suggest the incoherence – the sheer wrongheadedness – of contemporary definitions of "news."[22] During the early decades of this century, then, socially committed writers combined careers in journalism and fiction, and used journalistic structures and narrative strategies in their fiction, a practice continued in the U.S. into the forties by James Agee. These literary activities were first consistently conjoined in the U.S. by Ambrose Bierce.

Fuentes' character Bierce is an amalgam of his journalism, his fiction, and his biography. Considered in his time a conservative for opposing the "democratic" cause of nascent U.S. imperialism, we now see him in the bright light of historical hindsight as an astute critic of the sort of rhetoric that has continued to inspire and justify U.S. expansionist activities during this century. Fuentes' Bierce travels to Mexico with a copy of *Don Quixote*, and is himself regarded by others in the novel as the aging Quixote. The project of political self-definition may be as quixotic when one crosses the border from north to south as when crosses from the other direction; clearly, Bierce's opposition to the self-interested policies of the U.S. in Mexico are meant to be understood as quixotic – and necessary. Bierce wrote against U.S. expansionism in Hearst's newspapers, the very bastion and vehicle of that policy, and in Fuentes' novel he reluctantly acknowledges his complicity with the colonizer even as he emphatically rejects colonialism. This dialectic between the desire of the colonizer and the resistance of the colonized is present in much of Fuentes' writing; given Fuentes' tendency to self-dramatization, it is not unreasonable to sense that the author may even have inscribed some version of himself in his characterization of Bierce.

Such authorial inscription is speculative and not to be insisted upon, but I *will* insist upon the cultural and political implications of Fuentes' fictionalization of the historical Bierce. I have said that historical hindsight allows us to view Bierce in a new light, but in fact I know of only one critical revaluation of Bierce's work.[23] Despite the frequency with which two or three of his Civil War stories are anthologized, Bierce is rarely considered a fiction writer of the first rank, nor is his nonfiction much discussed in academic forums. In nineteenth-century U.S. literature, his work is almost fully eclipsed by writers who were more concerned with overarching psychological and metaphysical questions than with specific political policy. While I would not deny the greater genius of Hawthorne, Emerson, Thoreau, and James when compared to Bierce, I *would* propose that Bierce's relative obscurity reflects U.S. attitudes toward the social and political function of the writer and hence toward journalistic writing. Fuentes' revivification of Bierce's writings attests to the different attitudes toward journalistic discourse in Latin America and, by extension, to the different political imperatives of writers in that region. A brief expedition into U.S. literary history is necessary to properly explore this premise.

II

Sinclair, Dreiser, and Dos Passos, like Bierce, resemble contemporary Latin American writers in using the discourse and practice of journalism for social and political purposes. But it would be an oversight (given my comparative project) not to observe that they also resemble many of their own U.S. literary precursors and contemporaries in their mistrust or deprecation of the press. Until recently most U.S. writers who have treated journalistic discourse in their fiction have treated it satirically. Canonized nineteenth-century U.S. writers – Melville, Hawthorne, Emerson, James – were less concerned with current political events than with more general definitions of the human condition, and it may follow from this (as well as from a certain carefully constructed provincialism) that they were not particularly interested in journalism. It is not that they were suspicious of journalism's political agenda; on the contrary, they were more likely to be condescending toward what they saw as its ephemeral vulgarity. In his own inimitable jingoistic style, H. D. Thoreau enjoins us to read not the *Times* but eternity, exclaiming "What news! How much more important to know what that is which was never old!"[24] James never ceased to find in newspapers the locus of linguistic decay; clearly he understood the power of the press not in political terms but aesthetic ones. His fulminations against newspapers in "The Question of Our Speech" are worth quoting at length:

> From the mere noisy vision of their ubiquitous page, bristling with rude effigies and images, with vociferous "headings," with letterings, with black eruptions of print, that we seem to measure by feet rather than by inches that affect as positively as the roar of a myriad faced monster – as the grimaces, the shouts, shrieks and yells, ranging over the whole gamut of ugliness, irrelevance, dissonance, of a mighty maniac who has broken loose and who is running amuck through spheres alike of sense and sound. So it is, surely, that our wonderful daily press most vividly reads us the lesson of values, of just proportion and appreciation.[25]

That the word "cliché" comes from the ready-made unit of type in standard use in newspaper printing and is a variant of *cliquer*, the onomatopoetic French verb meaning "to click," suggests the clatter of typesetting machines, printing presses, and (figuratively) the noise of the newspaper language that James so abhorred.

These writers' comments may accurately reflect mid to late nineteenth-century U.S. reporting: James reacts against jingoismo and yellow journalism, on the one hand, and Thoreau against the developing ethic of unmediated objectivity, on the other. In either case, educated opinion was being segregated from and made secondary to reporting – a practice that has continued in this century and done much to standardize journalistic language and rhetorical structures. The ideal of objectivity (however unattainable) is widely held in the U.S. – and for good reason – but it is a journalistic ethic and aesthetic that has effectively limited intellectual argument and literary creativity to the editorial pages of U.S. newspapers, or displaced them to literary magazines, quarterlies, and reviews. As I have said, the journalistic tradition in Latin America differed notably in this regard in the nineteenth century and still does in the late twentieth.

Thoreau's and James' reactions would also seem to be part of a larger project to preserve for the novel a domain apart from the encroachments of popular language and media. (In Chapter 6, I show that this project still conditions U.S. fiction.) Among nineteenth-century U.S. prose writers,

besides Bierce, only Edgar Allen Poe and Mark Twain found it unnecessary
to draw an emphatic line between newspapers and novels. Poe established
his reputation as a critic by publishing essays on literary aesthetics in periodicals; Twain participated in the home-grown tradition of humor that
used periodicals to communicate measured doses of daily life and common sense. Beginning with Benjamin Franklin and his *Poor Richard's
Almanack* and including Twain and Ambrose Bierce, American humorists
reached large audiences by publishing in newspapers their moralizing tales
about the attitudes and activities of entire classes and regions of the country.[26] The popularity and influence of writers like Art Buchwald and Calvin
Trillin and Erma Bombeck may be understood as an extension of this particularly American mode of social commentary.

The pragmatic view of newspapers by humorists, though, is unusual, for
serious writers in the U.S. have generally been reluctant to associate their
literary forms with journalistic media. Willa Cather left her position at
McClure's magazine when she began to write fiction, stating that journalism was incompatible with her fiction writing.[27] Fitzgerald and Faulkner
did not object to popular media but they preferred Hollywood to Hearst,
where they could still be writers rather than reporters. And Hemingway,
despite his terse "journalistic" style, does not engage the metafictional
issues that are generated by the explicit inclusion of journalism's different
referential status. The writers we have placed in positions of greatest pres-
tige among U.S. modernists (following the lead of canonized nineteenth-
century U.S. writers) have generally preferred not to mix fictional and nonfictional media, but rather to distinguish their own novelistic enterprise
from what have been considered the more public, impersonal, conventional and hence lesser forms of journalism.

More recently, purveyors of the idea of the "nonfiction novel" – Truman
Capote, Norman Mailer, Hunter S. Thompson – and "new journalism"
– Joan Didion, Tom Wolfe, Joyce Carol Oates – *do* seem to have adopted a
journalistic stance. Their generic experiments have raised many of the
same questions as documentary fiction, questions that are foregrounded in
the two section headings of Mailer's *The Armies of the Night* (1968): "History as a Novel" and the considerably longer "The Novel as History."
These writers do coincide with current Latin American literary practice in
using journalist reporting to question how reality may be represented. But
they are far less apt than contemporary Latin American writers to address
public or political issues, a telling difference because it suggests that they
write less journalistically than autobiographically. Even when they are
"reporting" events or occasions, their tone is essentially that of the extended personal essay. They often describe historical events and settings not so
much to elucidate them as to structure and focus the persona that they
wish to convey, a narrative strategy typical of the personal essay. Consider, for example, the centrality and subjectivity of the authorial voice in

Capote's *Music for Chameleons* (1980), Thompson's *Fear and Loathing in Las Vegas* (1971), Didion's *Miami* (1987), or Oates' *On Boxing* (1986). Even as acute a political and social observer as Mailer writes from a self-consciously ironic perspective, and whatever political indignation he may have wished to express is ultimately subsumed by his own personal flamboyance. Mailer leaves his readers only vestiges of his initial claims to social and political engagement.

So I return to my comparative assertion. The writer's sense of political and social responsibility will affect his or her use of journalistic discourse. Clearly, U.S. writers have engaged the political and literary potential of journalistic writing less than Latin American writers. I have already mentioned the public role assumed by many contemporary Latin American writers and the ways in which fiction and journalism become less clearly separated when channels of public expression are subverted or silenced. My argument for a contemporary reevaluation of Bierce's work is inspired by contemporary Latin American writers who refuse to separate their journalistic activities from literature, and who understand journalistic writing as an ideological rather than a reportorial (or autobiographical) mode. Although I have also mentioned several U.S. writers who, like Latin American writers, *have* responded to political and social imperatives by combining journalistic and novelistic modes and practices, my point here is that in U.S. culture, where literature is not generally conceived as having a political function, these combinations are the exception rather than the rule. Having made this comparative generalization, I want to return to Fuentes' *The Old Gringo* and link it to what is, in my opinion, the most important of such exceptions in U.S. literature: James Agee's *Let Us Now Praise Famous Men* (1941). Both writers use photojournalism as a final test of their literary "rightness of rendering," Fuentes implicitly, Agee explicitly and emphatically.

The Mexican Revolution was "covered" by more than just Hearst's reporters.[28] Besides Bierce's journalistic past and perspective, *The Old Gringo* incorporates into its descriptive structure the documentation of the Mexican photojournalist Agustín Victor Casasola. Casasola has been called the Mathew Brady of the Mexican Revolution, but the similarity exists more in the fact that they both covered civil wars than in their photographic achievements. In fact, Casasola's work is more aptly compared to the brilliant social documentary photography of his American contemporary Lewis Hine or the later work of Dorothea Lange and Walker Evans. Furthermore, Casasola not only took photos but also commissioned and collected the photographs of other photojournalists, thereby leaving a visual record of the Mexican Revolution that is an irreplaceable artistic and documentary achievement. His career followed the times: from 1900, he worked as a writer and photographer for one of the official newspapers of the Díaz dictatorship; when opposition to Díaz crystallized around the

1910 presidential elections, Casasola went to work for Díaz's main chal-
lenger, Francisco Madero; and in 1911, as revolution swept the country, he
formed a press agency. After the revolution, Casasola was employed by
agencies of the newly democratic government to photograph factories,
jails, hospitals, courts, popular entertainers. After his death in 1938, his
photographic collection passed to his son. His family still has a shop in
Mexico City where they make and sell photographs from Casasola's original glass negatives.[29]

It is arguable that Casasola's photos conditioned the course of the Mexican Revolution, and undeniable that they have permanently conditioned
the ways in which historians, and everyone else for that matter, regard it.
They influenced José Guadalupe Posada, the illustrator of the Mexican
Revolution, who often copied Casasola's images for his engravings in the
popular press; decades later, they served as models (sometimes by way of
Posada's engravings) for Diego Rivera's and José Clemente Orozco's murals
depicting Mexican history. And it seems certain that they condition both
the form and content of Fuentes' novel (which was originally published in
Mexico with a photograph by Casasola on the cover). The events of the
novel are filtered through the consciousness of an American woman who
found herself in Mexico during the upheaval. The character's memories,
like Casasola's photos, freeze time and space in dramatic still shots; for her,
the past is sepia-toned and soft-edged, its static images reflecting the same
haunting irony that pervades Casasola's photographs. We see in Harriet
Winslow's memory the visual images of the revolution that we all
carry – the images caught by Casasola's camera: the revolutionary leaders
with cartridge belts crisscrossing their chests, their peasant troops and
camp followers, the *soldaderas* and the children unnaturally encumbered
by steel and leather trappings against backgrounds of trains and dusty roads
suggesting the continual displacements of war. (Figs. 1 and 2) So a typical
Casasola photograph shows a young Indian soldier awaiting deployment,
sitting beside the railroad tracks with his wife and baby, a rifle vertically
dividing them and the picture. They are posed/composed in timeless, ceremonial fashion, their bodies describing soft, flesh-and-fabric circles
against the steel rails of war.

In Fuentes' verbal images, as in Casasola's visual images, we perceive
behind the youthful innocence of the revolutionaries the shadows of bat-
tles, firing squads, and assassinations. In their depictions of the young revolutionaries, we are reminded of Cyril Connolly's dictum that nothing so
dates a person as his ignorance of the horrors in store. Their images seem
like tombs, beautiful monuments to the remote mechanisms of history,
savored by the survivors, not yet foreseen by the departed. An early scene
in Fuentes' novel describes Bierce asking directions to Villa's camp of a
group of soldiers sitting in a boxcar. In reply to his inquiry, they shout in
chorus: "Villa! Villa! Viva Villa!" And a soldier, whose narrative descrip-

Figure 1. Emiliano Zapata with rifle and sabre. Photo by Víctor Agustín Casasola.

Figure 2. Federal soldier with his wife and child. Photo by Víctor Agustín Casasola.

tion makes him appear to have just walked out of a Casasola photograph, yells, "We are all Villa!" But the defiant optimism of this phrase, like the defiance so often embodied in Casasola's photos, is undercut by subsequent events: the postrevolutionary perversion of ideals is made explicit in an earlier novel by Fuentes, *The Death of Artemio Cruz* (1962), where not coincidentally, his character's most effective instrument of political corruption is the newspaper that he owns and edits. When Villa himself does eventually make an appearance in *The Old Gringo*, it is a cameo appearance in a literal sense: the narrator describes his head as we remember it from Casasola's photographs. Casasola's presence in Fuentes' iconography of revolution remains implicit in this novel but is made explicit in the novel that follows it. In *Cristóbal Nonato* (1987), Fuentes describes a character with "eyes of a guerrilla from a photo by Casasola."[30]

The use of still shots to structure the moving medium of verbal narration is hardly new in Latin American fiction, nor, as I have said, is the mixing of fictional and nonfictional modes.[31] However, Fuentes' use of preexisting and well-known photodocumentary images *is* unique and may begin to explain some of the weaknesses of his novel as well as its considerable strengths. The tendency of its language to romantic excess may stem, in part, from the temptation (inadequately resisted) to reiterate Casasola's photographic lyricism in prose narration. Furthermore, the temporal segmentation of the novel also appears to be conceptually conditioned by the photographic images. Photographs, however telling, can only be cross-sections of history, and in the case of this novel the narrative analogy to them may engender the static quality of the characters and the action that we sometimes sense. For a novel concerned with historical events and their potential consequences, there is surprisingly little development through time: Harriet Winslow's relations with Bierce and the revolutionaries proceed abruptly, often without sufficient psychological continuity or causality, as if we were following their histories in an old family album, looking first at one photograph and then another.

The interaction of Fuentes' historical narration and Casasola's photographs may be compared to the interaction between the prose of James Agee and the photographs of Walker Evans in *Let Us Now Praise Famous Men*. Agee and Evans were commissioned by *Fortune* magazine to do a series of illustrated articles on the situation of white sharecroppers in Alabama during the Great Depression. When *Fortune* rejected their work, they published it in the form we now know it.[32]

The book begins with Walker Evans' 62 classic photographs of three share-croppers and their families, houses, the land. No title page precedes the photos, nor are they labeled or their pages numbered, as if to insist that they be allowed to speak their own visual language before the identifying signs of the printed medium intrude. Following the photos are James Agee's 471 pages of almost obsessively detailed descriptions of objects, rooms, faces – even the assiduously catalogued contents of drawers – descriptions that attest to his desire to equal in prose the documentary capacities of Evans' photographs. In his "preamble," Agee writes, "If I could do it, I'd do no writing at all here. It would be photographs; the rest would be fragments of cloth, bits of cotton, lumps of earth, records of speech, pieces of wood and iron, phials of odors, plates of food and of excrement. Booksellers would consider it quite a novelty; critics would murmur, yes, but is it art; and I could trust a majority of you to use it as you would a parlor game."[33] Here the nature and adequacy (or inadequacy) of his written medium is obviously at issue; Agee believed the camera to be, "next to unassisted and weaponless consciousness, the central instrument of our time" (11). He implies throughout his narrative that the camera can do what words never can, that the lens is a transparent and hence truthful window on the world as words never are. Though he (and we) know that the camera *does* mediate between objects and their expression, he nonetheless insists that words, because of their symbolic (conceptual) relation to their objects, can never attain the expressive immediacy of photographic images, which exist in iconic (sensory) relation to their objects. In Goodman's terms, Agee considered the certain "truth" of the photograph preferable to the potential but elusive "rightness" of words. Indeed, Evans' images of the Great Depression in the U.S.

have stamped our communal memory of history in ways that no written document of the period, including Agee's, has.

The gulf between verbal narration and photographic images is not the only one that frustrates Agee. He also opposes the novel to nonfiction, and Art (with a capital A) to his own journalistic enterprise. If for Agee, the photograph has greater expressive immediacy than narration, nonfiction has greater expressive immediacy than the novel. He writes:

> In a novel, a house or person has his meaning, his existence, entirely through the writer. Here, a house or a person has only the most limited of his meaning through me: his true meaning is much huger. It is that he *exists*, in actual being, as you do and I do, and as no character of the imagination can possibly exist. His great weight, mystery, and dignity are in this fact. As for me, I can tell you of him only what I saw, only so accurately as in my terms I know how: and this in turn has its chief stature not in any ability of mine but in the fact that I too exist, not as a work of fiction, but as a human being. Because of his immeasurable weight in actual existence, and because of mine, every word I tell of him has inevitably a kind of immediacy, a kind of meaning, not at all necessarily "superior" to that of imagination, but a kind so different that a work of the imagination (however intensely it may draw on "life") can at best only faintly imitate the least of it. (12; Agee's emphasis)

Here Agee's argument for nonfiction is clearly political rather than epistemological. Because nonfiction is based on the historical existence of its object, it can engage social and economic realities as fiction cannot. When Agee says about *Let Us Now Praise Famous Men*, "Above all else: in God's name don't think of it as Art" (15), he expresses his fear that the political effect of his work will be neutralized if it is accorded the official acceptance and homage conferred upon "Art." This fate, he implies, is less likely to befall nonfiction than the novel. To report what the "senses take: in as great and perfect and exact particularity as we can name them" (110) is Agee's journalistic program. It hardly needs saying that despite his desire for the "artless" anonymity and hence the politicized communality of nonfiction, Agee's lyrical prose is a constructed (i.e. artistic) version of the world.

The centrality of journalistic writing to Agee's political agenda recalls the journalistic engagement of contemporary Latin American writers, though I doubt that any of those writers would agree to Agee's hierarchy of forms, which places the novel at the bottom. Nor would they agree to Agee's absolute separation of fiction and nonfiction, an idea that now seems to us naïve. There is, however, a major contemporary writer who *does* agree with Agee, namely Elie Wiesel. Though Wiesel is not an American writer in the usual sense, his immigration to the U.S. after the Second World War and his consequent consideration of the writer's historical relevance make his literary practice germane to my theoretical and comparative concerns.

Wiesel's literary purpose, like Agee's, is explicitly political, and like Agee he addresses the potential of narrative to recuperate and communicate social and political injustice. Wiesel's subject is the Holocaust, a historical horror that does not depend upon but rather defies the literary imagination. He is not, therefore, concerned with the metahistorical questions of documentary fiction but with the most basic of journalistic questions: how to report what actually happened. In Holocaust literature, reality so grotesquely outstrips any believable proportion that it replaces fiction, makes it irrelevant.[34] So Wiesel insists that "a novel about Auschwitz is either not a novel or not about Auschwitz," and proposes "testimonial literature" as the most important generic form of our century.[35] His autobiographical work *Night* provides a primary example of this genre and fully engages the etymological resonances of the word "testimonial": it bears witness to events not only in the sense of observing and documenting them but also in the juridical and religious senses.

Agee and Wiesel agree on the mimetic function of narration, but they disagree on the capacity of words to fulfill that function. Both are moved by the urgent desire to let events speak for themselves, without mediation, but they differ on how to achieve that immediacy. Agee mistrusts words and credits the camera with the capacity to render present reality, whereas Wiesel clearly believes that language can recapture the past without falsifying it and make it available in the present. Despite this difference, they share the implicit belief that whatever the medium, it is a historical luxury to equate fiction and nonfiction; one can afford such equations only during periods of prosperity and social justice, but certainly not in extreme situations such as those they hope to document. Both insist that the writer must respond to historical crisis by attempting to separate the reality of events from the mode of their telling, even as they recognize that such a separation contradicts prevailing epistemological and narrative theory and practice and is, furthermore, impossible to achieve.

If the conceptual conflation of historical and imaginative narrative categories is a luxury, then one must concede that the nonfiction novels of Capote and Mailer and Thompson use luxury to advantage, as does Fuentes' novel *The Old Gringo*. That is as it should be. Besides, we have seen examples of recent Latin American literature in which the mixing of narrative modes is *not* a luxury born of political and social stability, as Agee and Wiesel imply, but rather a reaction to instability and injustice.

At the outset of this chapter, I posited a continuum of conceptual relations between historical truth and narrative truth, the poles being extreme ideologies of collective history, on the one hand, and extreme ideologies of individual autonomy, on the other. Wiesel would have been aware of the errors of both extremes. As a Jew, he had suffered the madness of the Nazi ideology of collective historical destiny, which excluded the very possibility of individual versions; as a survivor of that madness, he wishes to confirm the collective historical experience of the Holocaust not as a novelist but as a witness. Hence his rejection of fictional accounts of the Holocaust in the face of his obvious awareness of the value of such accounts. Wiesel would, I think, agree that history is an interpretive structure – a narrative – but he would insist that history must be consensual as fiction need not be, for history is not without facts and artifacts. Fact from *factum*: that which is *made* (not, in this case, made up); that which is *done*. For Wiesel, the profound task of the writer and/or the historian is to decipher a shared locus of events – never objective but never totally subjective either – and assign significance that itself participates in the making of the shared present.

I would not argue that either Wiesel or Agee is representative of U.S. writers, but they do serve to remind us of the very current idea that reality is amenable to any construction placed upon it, an idea that may easily seduce novelists (and critics), in part because it implies that reality is itself a fiction, a text, a linguistic construct. While this idea has the virtue of underscoring the fact that all encoding of knowledge is ideological and that narrative modes, whether historical or fictional, verbal or visual, necessarily infiltrate the realities they describe, it is an idea that has unduly obscured and sometimes even erased necessary and valid distinctions among different modes of cognition and representational procedures. It is in this context that Fuentes' fiction, Agee's nonfiction, and the associated photographic expressions of the histories they treat are so interesting. Like Wiesel's testimonial literature, they teach us a great deal about how different artists and art forms construe and contain reality, and they also teach us (should I say it?) about reality itself.

III

"Reality itself" is the aim of the journalist/narrator in García Márquez's *Chronicle of a Death Foretold* and the journalist/character in Mario Vargas Llosa's *The War of the End of the World*. This phrase – reality itself – may be narrowly used to imply a positivist historiography unacceptable to anyone not naively devoted to the myth of realism, but it is precisely their characters' devotion to this myth that these authors wish to test. Far from conflating narrative categories, these works foreground their different mimetic desires and possibilities. García Márquez and Vargas Llosa dramatize the ideological and narrative issues that I have discussed in the first part of my chapter – issues raised whenever journalistic and novelistic forms compete for the reader's attention between the covers of a single book. I'll look first at García Márquez's novel, then at Vargas Llosa's.

The subject of *Chronicle of a Death Foretold* is the problem of knowing and narrating the past, whether in the supposedly factual mode of journalism or the supposedly fictional mode of the novel. Can one ever know what really happened, or why? If so, can one's knowledge ever be satisfactorily told, or shown? What is one's potential for discovery and disclosure in any medium? These are the questions that García Márquez's journalist/narrator asks obsessively. After exerting great effort, he is obliged to accept an ambivalent answer: he finds that he can neither fully know nor adequately narrate the past, but he also feels that the attempt is necessary and worthwhile. The problematic equation of history with its narrated versions is, then, both subverted and celebrated by García Márquez in this novel. The past cannot be recuperated, but the process of its narrative reconstruction provides the consolations of conclusion *and* continuance that events often withhold.

It is in *Chronicle of a Death Foretold* that García Márquez's journalistic training calls itself most clearly to our attention.[36] García Márquez has never stopped writing for periodicals, and has often expressed his fascination with the relationship between journalism and literature, between reality and its written versions, between facts and their narration and, most important, between reportorial detachment and creative participation. The paradoxical title of the novel announces not only the hindsight of the narrator but also the problematic relation between journalism and literature and the narrator's ambivalent stance between (or in) both realms. "Chronicle" is, after all, a word that more frequently describes newspapers than novels; it suggests an unmediated, sequential account of events rather than an order determined by narrative intent. Indeed, a part of García Márquez's journalism is anthologized under the title *Crónicas y reportajes* (*Chronicles and Reports*, 1987).[37]

In an essay on the nature of historical narration, Hayden White discusses the medieval chronicle, which typically lists in two parallel vertical columns the year and the events of that year. If no events are deemed of sufficient importance to merit chronicling in a given year, the space opposite that year testifies to that fact by its blankness. The chronicle, White states, "possesses none of the attributes which we normally think of as story; no central subject, no well-marked beginning, middle, and end, no peripeteia. . . ."[38] It is, above all, the lack of an ending that characterizes the chronicle; time is represented as paratactical and endless. The list of years in the chronicle that White analyzes continues beyond the list of events, suggesting "a continuation of the series *ad infinitum*, or rather, until the Second Coming. But there is no story conclusion" (p. 12). For White, the difference between story and chronicle – the sine qua non of "narrativizing" events – is the constitution of an ending that confers meaning on events that have already occurred, or have yet to do so. Of course, the temporal and spatial linearity of the chronicle, as White describes it, is very far from the lay-out of the modern newspaper. Marshall McLuhan argues that the development of the newspaper, with its mosaic effect of a dozen stories on one page, significantly increased the reader's sense of the synchronic complexity of history during the early nineteenth century. And presumably it still does. García Márquez's narrator is a journalist, and the "chronicle" he ultimately creates is indeed a synchronic mosaic of times, voices, and documents.

The narrator returns to narrate a crime twenty-seven years after it occurred, hoping to understand his friend's death and the nature of historical inevitability by imposing a long overdue conclusion – the narration itself – on the events he describes. His sense of his friend's interrupted life moves him to attempt to complete in words the life that history refused to finish. The narrator intentionally assumes the stance of "chronicler," but his narration attempts to accomplish precisely what, according to White, the chronicle typically lacks, a narrative ending that confers meaning and coherence upon unpunctuated diachronicity. The impossibility of his aim – the necessary partiality of both experience and narrative – makes his "chronicle" and his effort almost unbearably ironic.

The death that the novel treats actually occurred in the Colombian *departamento* (state) of Sucre on January 22, 1951; the victim was, in fact, an acquaintance of the author's when he was a young newspaperman in the city of Barranquilla, on the Caribbean coast. The explicitly autobiographical narrator of this novel is an investigative journalist who records the senseless death of Santiago Nasar. He hides his own passionate engagement with the moral and ethical issues of the murder behind the mask of the reporter. He is methodical, detached, and rarely states a personal opinion. His only subjective observation about the murder is that he believes Santiago died without understanding his own death. This is hardly an idiosyncratic opinion, since the whole town believes that Santiago was innocent of the crime of honor for which he was killed, a crime of which he was unaware until only moments before his death. The narrator's observation could be applied far more generally than just to Santiago. He names several "victims" of the circumstances he recounts, implying an aspect of interchangeability in Santiago's fate and that of the community at large. In fact, his observation also applies to himself, for he does not understand Santiago's death either in any philosophical or moral sense. That the narrator is twice mistaken for Santiago suggests his identification with the victim, despite his tone of journalistic detachment: his lack of understanding applies to his own death and to ours, also foretold and unsearchable.

In his self-conscious role as impartial reporter, the narrator meticulously documents his sources. He willfully minimizes the apparent control he exercises over the structure of his narration by constantly citing his informants and quoting directly from myriad interviews: "he said," "she said," "he said that she said," "according to them," and so on. As a journalist, he both listens and records, casting himself as the medium, the mere vehicle of the story. His obsessive attention to the precise time of the occurrences leading to the catastrophe serves as a reminder of his preferred role as chronicler. We know minute by minute who does what during the hour before Santiago's murder, as if sequence alone will somehow reveal cause and confer meaning. The narrator explicitly disavows any special insight, and thus the Latin American journalistic practice of editorializing. It is as if by refusing to acknowledge his role as *creator* of a verbal order he can force events to speak for themselves, to yield their own objective truth. Here he shares with James Agee the longing for a transparent medium, one that does not require the *imposition* of linguistic or narrative structure.

There is in the novel a precedent for the narrator's effort. Referring to an earlier chronicle written by another investigator immediately after the murder, the narrator indirectly describes his own intent: "El juez instructor que vino de Riohacha debió sentir [tantas coincidencias funestas] sin atreverse a admitirlas, pues su interés de darles una explicación racional era evidente en el sumario."[39] ("The investigating judge who came from Riohacha must have sensed [the fatal coincidences] without daring to admit it, for his impulse to give them rational explanation was obvious in his report."[40]) Furthermore, the judge is "un hombre abrasado por la fiebre de la literatura. Sin duda había leído a los clásicos españoles, y algunos latinos, y conocía muy bien a Nietzsche" (103–4; "a man burning with the fever of literature. He had doubtless read the Spanish classics and a few Latin ones, and was quite familiar with Nietzsche" 98). So he reflects García Márquez's own stated literary and philosophical preferences. In this foretold world, even the narrator and his narrative account are prefigured.

The explanation of Santiago's death is *not* contained in the minute details that the journalist (or the investigating judge) presents, as the narrator knows only too well. Despite the journalistic conventions to which he carefully adheres, the structure of his narrative is hardly a chronicle in the original sense given by Hayden White. Interviews and the actual events they treat overlap as the narrator shifts his focus frequently and without warning back and forth through time, from the day of the murder to its subsequent verbal versions. The time of the narration becomes a temporal layer superimposed upon the events that occurred twenty-seven years earlier: diachronicity becomes synchronicity as the survivors' memories subsume historical eventuality. Narration, García Márquez insists, is always an appropriation of events, even as he dramatizes its powerlessness to possess or undo them.

Chronicle of a Death Foretold, like much of García Márquez's work, engages the problematic relation of historical inevitability to its narration – that is, the relation of the foreordained to the foretold. In *One Hundred Years of Solitude*, Macondo's foretold future remains unstated until the final pages of the novel, when we learn that Melquíades has written the community's history one hundred years ahead of time. In *The Autumn of the Patriarch*, premature descriptions of the patriarch's death initiate and conclude several of the chapters, dramatizing the dictator's power and treachery; he is able, it seems, to escape his fate forever. In *Chronicle of a*

Death Foretold, however, the future foretold in its title and its opening sentence is not revoked: "El día que lo iban a matar, Santiago Nasar se levantó a las 5:30 de la mañana para esperar el buque en que llegaba el obispo" (7; "On the day they were going to kill him Santiago Nasar got up at five-thirty in the morning to wait for the boat the bishop was coming in" 3). Unlike Aureliano Buendía, whose imminent death before a firing squad is described in the first sentence of *One Hundred Years of Solitude*, and unlike the Patriarch, who can substitute subordinates' deaths for his own, Santiago is given no reprieve. Before they act, one of the murderers says to the other, "Esto no tiene remedio: es como si ya nos hubiera sucedido" (66; "There's no way out of this. It's as if it had already happened" 61). It is this irrevocability that most concerns the journalist/narrator; precisely *because* Santiago's death is foretold, *because* everyone shares the foreknowledge of his end, the narrator is moved to undertake his investigation. Why did no one prevent his death? Could no one intercede in the "announced" scenario of events leading to catastrophe? Does announcement imply irrevocability? And will the narrator's written account (the death "aftertold") modify the future, even if it cannot undo the past?

The narrator is unwilling to acknowledge his role as creator, but he does recognize that the "astillas dispersas" ("scattered shards") of memory with which he works are dangerously slippery, and that the backward movement of the mind through time is far less certain than the forward movement of clock and calendar toward the foretold death he wishes both to chronicle and cancel. It is precisely the disjunction between the patterns of time and those of narration that occasions the definitive crack in the narrator's journalistic facade. The final chapter begins with the reference to the narrative impulse that the whole town shares:

> Durante años no pudimos hablar de otra cosa. Nuestra conducta diaria, dominada hasta entonces por tantos hábitos lineales, había empezado a girar de golpe en torno de una misma ansiedad común. Nos sorprendían los gallos del amanecer tratando de ordenar las numerosas casualidades encadenadas que habían hecho posible el absurdo, y era evidente que no lo hacíamos por un anhelo de esclarecer misterios, sino porque ninguno de nosotros podía seguir viviendo sin saber con exactitud cuál era el sitio y la misión que le había asignado la fatalidad. (101)

> For years we couldn't talk about anything else. Our daily conduct, dominated then by so many linear habits, had suddenly begun to spin around a single common anxiety. The cocks of dawn would catch us trying to give order to the chain of many chance events that had made absurdity possible, and it was obvious that we weren't doing it from an urge to clear up mysteries but because none of us could go on living without an exact knowledge of the place and the mission assigned to us by fate. (96)

Not only the narrator but the entire town wants to use Santiago's death to foretell their own – "the place and mission assigned to us by fate." They, like the narrator, are moved by the need to reconcile the contradiction between their "linear habits" and "spinning" events, though the towns-people will do so by telling rather than writing their histories. This passage recalls the metaphoric description of the Buendías' history as "una rueda giratoria que hubiera seguido dando vueltas hasta la eternidad, de no haber sido por el desgaste progresivo e irremediable del eje."[41] ("a turning wheel that would have gone on spilling into eternity were it not for the progressive and irremediable wearing of the axle."[42]) Both metaphors evoke García Márquez's central theme: the nature and relation of historical and narrative patterns, and the inevitability of both.

In a long paragraph immediately following the one I have just cited, the narrator of *Chronicle* provides his reader with the knowledge the towns-people seek. He describes "the fated place and mission" of one character after another from his vantage point beyond their "assigned" ends. This privileged position is due to the twenty-seven years that have elapsed since the murder. Unlike the omniscient Melquíades, this narrator's hindsight is personal rather than cosmic; his knowledge of their individual fate is the product of mere survival. The narrator then describes his own fate: the painstaking research required to write the text we are reading. Clearly the narrative itself is "the place and mission" of the narrator, and of the victim as well, for the narrator understands that his written account is the only historical event that can imbue Santiago's "senseless" death with meaning. If Melquíades' narration survives the end of Macondo and miti-gates its tragic finality, *Chronicle of a Death Foretold* is the extenuating circumstance of Santiago's murder, the end that confers meaning on the succession of events it recounts. Through the process of returning, researching, ordering, and telling Santiago's history, the narrator under-stands what he has suspected all along, that the murder *was* inevitable and that it *cannot* be justified – only accepted. The meaning of Santiago's death lies in this acceptance, an acceptance reflected in the narrator's final, pow-erful description of the murder. So he concludes Santiago's history with his own narration; to repeat Hayden White's definitions, his "chronicle" gives way to "story" as he imposes meaning on history by creating an order that ends. The novel itself is the product and the emblem of this process.

Following upon the magical happenings and sinuous syntax of *One Hundred Years of Solitude* and the surreal imagery and baroque style of *The Autumn of the Patriarch*, the spare realism of *Chronicle of a Death Foretold* comes as something of a surprise. The style emphasizes the jour-nalistic impulse behind the novel, of course, and also serves to foreground the conflict between facts and their narration that burdens the journal-ist/narrator. Twice the narrator directly addresses this conflict. The first instance occurs in his description of his encounter with Angela Vicario in a remote Indian village in the Guajira: "Al verla así, dentro del marco idílico de la ventana, no quise creer que aquella mujer fuera la que yo creía, porque me resistía a admitir que la vida terminara por parecerse tanto a la mala literatura" (93; "When I saw her like that in the idyllic frame of the window, I refused to believe that the woman there was who I thought it was, because I couldn't bring myself to admit that life might end up resembling bad literature so much" 88–89). His second reference concerns the investigative judge who, like himself, does not think it legitimate that "la vida se sirviera de tantas casualidades prohibidas a la literatura" (104; "life should make use of so many coincidences forbidden literature . . . " 99). In both instances, the usual relation of the terms is reversed. It is *history* that demands our suspension of disbelief; only "bad literature," the journalist/narrator says, would so ignore the laws of probability and causality.

We imagine the *novelist* García Márquez with tongue in cheek as he gives such comments to his journalist/narrator, and we also recognize their resemblance to comments made by the *journalist* García Márquez in the introduction to his series of newspaper articles, *Relato de un naúfrago* (*Story of a Castaway*, 1955). He writes there that the castaway's account of his ten days at sea was so detailed and fascinating that "my sole literary problem was to find a reader who would believe it."[43] I have already cited his assertion that he learned from journalism "the tricks . . . to transform something which appears fantastic, unbelievable into something plausible, credible. . . ."[44]

I want to return to a point I made earlier in this chapter. In comparing the uses of journalism in U.S. and Latin American literary traditions, I said that the writer's sense of political and social responsibility will affect his or her literary uses of journalistic discourse. The extent to which a community confers upon literature a role in defining communal structures and values is in direct proportion to the involvement of novelists and poets in journalism, whether in periodicals of cultural and political commentary such as *Vuelta* and *nexos* in Mexico, the *New Republic* and *Commentary* in the U.S., or in daily newspapers. The journalist has a public voice and an audience that the novelist rarely does, and novelists engage in journalism because they can perform a communal function distinct from that of belles lettres.[45] García Márquez wrote a novel, of course, when he wrote *Chronicle of a Death Foretold*, but one that thematizes the role of journalistic effort in the arduous process of communal self-definition. It is a process that he and most other novelists currently writing in Latin America know first hand.

The journalist/narrator in *Chronicle of a Death Foretold* reports on events about the community to the community. He is aware that his narrative activity reveals the community to itself, that it in some sense constitutes the community, because Santiago Nasar's death is more that the death of an individual. It is, as he tells us, a communal obsession. The extravagant fiesta that sets the scene for the murder allows García Márquez to dramatize the connection between individual destiny and communal responsibility, and the role of the narrator in creating that connection.

The communal celebration that is both wedding and wake resounds throughout the novel (except during the final description of the murder, when the town falls ominously silent). The delirium of the fiesta is the necessary prelude to Santiago's death, which might best be construed in terms of the culminating ritual sacrifice of the festivals of ancient Greece. Or of modern Mexico. Octavio Paz finds in the Latin American fiesta elements of the Dionysian festivals, relating the energy of their collective frenzy to death, their beauty to brutality. This communal function is based in its temporal nature. In an essay entitled "Todos santos, día de muertos" ("The Day of the Dead"), Paz asserts that in the ecstatic present of the fiesta, past and future are integrated into ". . . un presente redondo y perfecto, de danza y juerga, de comunión y comilona con lo más antiguo de México. El tiempo deja de ser sucesión y vuelve a ser lo que fue, y es, originariamente: un presente en donde pasado y futuro al fin se reconcilian."[46] (". . . a complete and perfect today of dancing and revelry, of communion with the most ancient and secret Mexico. Time is no longer succession, and becomes what it originally was and is: the present, in which past and future are reconciled."[47]) The fiesta, like the account that the narrator hopes to construct, converts temporal succession into a synchronic whole.

The motive for the murder, the protection of the honor of the bride and her family, also stems from communal practice. The code of honor is traditional, inflexible and, in this case, irrationally acceded to by the entire town. Though condemned by the narrator, we are told that the court finds it a legitimate motive for murder; those who did not intervene to prevent the murder later console themselves with "el pretexto de que los asuntos de honor son estancos sagrados" (101; "the pretext that affairs of honor are sacred monopolies" 97). The engagement of the townsfolk with the communal myth of honor gives to their ceaseless commentary the resonance of the chorus in Greek tragedy: the future of the hero is abruptly truncated because he transgresses a law understood by all as divinely sanctioned. García Márquez's journalist/narrator, like the Greek chorus, fully understands his communal function. He must construct for and with the community an understanding of a catastrophic event that will otherwise remain a mere irrational moment in a succession of isolated moments.

As in *Chronicle of a Death Foretold*, it is the irrationality with which fate selects its victims that impels Truman Capote and Norman Mailer to narrate other such crimes (Capote in "Handcarved Coffins" and *In Cold Blood*, Mailer in *The Executioner's Song*). Perhaps, like the journalist/narrator of García Márquez's novel, these U.S. writers wish to write the ending that the facts won't concede, to conclude the mystery with the text itself. In the introduction to his collection *Music for Chameleons* (1980), Capote states that his integration of the techniques of journalism and fiction "altered my entire comprehension of writing, my attitude toward art and life and the balance between the two, and my understanding of the difference between what is true and what is *really true*."[48] Capote's distinction recalls Nelson Goodman's between "truth" and "rightness of rendering." It is this same struggle to balance historical experience and its creative expression in the service of communal self-definition that compels the journalist/narrator of *Chronicle of a Death Foretold* and (I feel certain) its journalist/author as well.

The interaction between journalistic and novelistic narration in the works I have discussed foregrounds the relation of what-is-taken-for-real with what-is-given-as-its-description – that is, the tension inherent in the term "literary realism." These authors (and narrators) are aware of the impossibility of journalistic and novelistic comprehensiveness even as they strive to create it. Their efforts are by definition ironic as they aim for conclusive wholes and instead create accounts that are partial (in both senses of the word), whether they write chronicles or novels or newspaper articles, or a combination of these forms. Although I agree with Hayden White's assertion that fictional narration may confer meaningful conclusions as experience rarely does – this is the point of the narrator's struggle in *Chronicle*, and his sole satisfaction – I also recognize that literature may be most lifelike in its partiality, that historical experience may be most realistically narrated when it is narrated incompletely, indecisively, conditionally. The aesthetic satisfactions of literary realism – the reader's experience of identifying with the text – depends upon this paradox. In *Chronicle of a Death Foretold*, the narrator strives to put an end to the murder, even as he adds one more telling to the narrative chain. It is less the Kermodian sense of an ending that consoles the narrator (and the reader) than the sense of a sequel – the sense that an open-ended narrative tradition is being engaged and extended. In this model, narrative energy is rekindled rather than released: meanings are added rather than resolved; history is cumulative; knowledge accretes; versions multiply. Like Pierre Menard's *Quixote*, the narrator's *Chronicle* does not repeat but reconstitutes the literary tradition and increases the meaning[s] of both literature and history.

IV

Finally I turn to Mario Vargas Llosa, whose fiction routinely encodes historical and narrative suspension – what I have just called the sense of a sequel. Like García Márquez, Vargas Llosa directs his characters to the parallel activities of action and confession, experience and explanation. They, too, search for (re)solution even as they acknowledge the impossibility of certainty; they, too, content themselves with continuations rather than conclusions. Consider the following passages, from three of Vargas Llosa's novels.

> El acusado, conmovido por alguna rememoración secreta, suspiró hondo.
> – La verdad, la verdad – murmuró con tristeza – .¿Cuál, señor juez?
>
> Mario Vargas Llosa, *Tía Julia y el escribidor*[49]

> The accused, moved by some secret memory, heaved a deep sigh.
> "The truth, the truth," he murmured sadly, "Which truth, Your Honor?"
>
> Mario Vargas Llosa, *Aunt Julia and the Scriptwriter*[50]

> Fabulaciones. No hay en Quero rastro de insurgentes o soldados. Tampoco me sorprende este nuevo desmentido de la realidad a los rumores: la información, en el país, ha dejado de ser algo objetivo y se ha vuelto fantasía, tanto en los diarios, la radio y la televisión como en la boca de las personas. "Informar" es ahora, entre nosotros, interpretar la realidad de acuerdo a los deseos, temores o conveniencias, algo que aspira a sustituir un desconocimiento sobre lo que pasa, que, en nuestro fuero íntimo, aceptamos como irremediable y definitivo. Puesto que es imposible saber lo que de veras sucede, los peruanos mienten, inventan, sueñan, se refugian en la ilusión. Por el camino más inesperado, la vida del Perú, en el que tan poco gente lee, se ha vuelto literaria.
>
> Mario Vargas Llosa, *Historia de Mayta*[51]

> Tales. In Quero, there's no sign of either insurgents or soldiers. I'm not surprised that reality contradicts these rumors. Information in this country has ceased to be objective and has become pure fantasy – in newspapers, radio, television, and ordinary conversation. "To report" among us now means either to interpret reality according to our desires or fears, or to say simply what is convenient. It's an attempt to make up for our ignorance of what's going on – which in our heart of hearts we understand is irremediable and definitive. Since it is impossible to know what's really happening, we Peruvians lie, invent, dream, and take refuge in illusion. Because of these strange circumstances, Peruvian life, a life in which so few actually do read, has become literary.
>
> Mario Vargas Llosa, *The Real Life of Alejandro Mayta*[52]

> Las verdades que parecen más verdades, si les das muchas vueltas, si las miras de cerquita, lo son sólo a medias o dejan de serlo.
>
> Mario Vargas Llosa, *¿Quién mató a Palomino Molero?*[53]

> The truths that seem most truthful, if you look at them from all sides, if you look at them close up, turn out either to be half truths or lies.
>
> Mario Vargas Llosa, *Who Killed Palomino Molero?*[54]

Walter Benjamin observed that the history of things "as they really are" was the strongest narcotic of his time.[55] Of the authors I discuss in this chapter, Mario Vargas Llosa is perhaps most compelled by such an intuition. I cite several passages from his fiction to show that his work is centrally concerned with the truth-claims of received narrative structures and conventions. In virtually all of his novels, he dramatizes multiple and conflicting understandings of the historical past by engaging multiple and conflicting narrative forms and media. An avowed realist ("I write all of my novels in a realistic way"[56]) Vargas Llosa in his essays and journalism, also returns obsessively to the nature (and very possibility) of narrative truth.[57] We are reminded by this writer that if the illusion of things "as they really are" were simple to dispel, the problem would be less pervasive, and less provocative, in his work.

Like Fuentes and García Márquez, Vargas Llosa is a committed journalist. Three of his novels (*Conversation in The Cathedral*, *The War of the End of the World* and *The Real Life of Alejandro Mayta*) are narrated by journalists who search for historical truth (and social justice.)[58] Following a discussion of *Chronicle of a Death Foretold*, however, it is tempting to ignore these novels in favor of another one by Vargas Llosa, *Who Killed Palomino Molero?*, because it so closely parallels García Márquez's novel in both plot and narrative structure. *Who Killed Palomino Molero?* also details a senseless murder in a small town, investigated by a character who is deeply involved emotionally in the outcome of his investigation. It is a policeman (rather than a journalist) who interrogates the inhabitants of the town, only to discover that truth is elusive, justice impossible, and the past no more than the shifting sum of people's self-interested versions. The character's disillusioning discoveries are both political and psychological, and include a case of remembered sexual abuse (or false-memory syndrome – he never knows which). The questions raised by this small-town cop are analogous to those raised by García Márquez's journalist/narrator: the nature of historical experience, the possibility of expressing that experience, and the value of doing so. But since I am tracing the relations of novels and newspapers, I will focus instead on Vargas Llosa's *The War of the End of the World*.

The War of the End of the World deals with a historical event, a rebellion incited by a messianic figure called "el Conselheiro" (the Counselor); the rebellion occurred in 1897 and 1898 in Canudos, Brazil, in the backland regions of the northeast province of Bahia. Understanding the historical events in Canudos depends upon understanding the languages of the participants – what the author has called their "reciprocal fanaticisms."[59] A number of languages collide on the pages of the novel (here I use the word "language" in a broad semiotic sense, to mean a coherent system of signs that encodes a set of cultural beliefs and practices). The languages in *The War of the End of the World* include the odd combination of imperialism, militarism, and positivism of the newly established Brazilian republic; the mystical languages of a messianic leader and his band of fanatical followers; the pseudoscience of the anarchist/phrenologist observer, Galileo Gall; the supposed positivistic realism of an unnamed myopic journalist modeled on the Brazilian engineer/journalist Euclides da Cunha, author of the classic account of the Canudos war, *Os sertões* (1902). Da Cunha's account, which was translated into English in 1944 by Samuel Putnam under the title of *Rebellion in the Backlands*, includes political, military, geographic, and ethnographic information, and has been called "the Bible of Brazilian nationality."[60]

Vargas Llosa expressed his "amazement, enthusiasm, and passion" for da Cunha's book when he first discovered it: "Euclides da Cunha's book *Os sertões* is the explanation he gives himself, his country, and posterity of what Canudos was, how Canudos was possible, and how the civil war was possible. . . . By trying to understand what Canudos was, what this rebellion was, I think da Cunha discovered what Latin America is, what a Latin American country is and . . . what a Latin American country is not."[61] What a Latin American country is *not* involves the positivism imported to Brazil from France. Vargas Llosa continues: "It became an official philosophy of the government and society. . . . In Brazil, positivism had much more influence than in France itself. I think that Brazil was the only place in the world where these temples of reason that Comte suggested were actually built, temples that should be oriented toward Paris as mosques are oriented toward Mecca" (126). Vargas Llosa explains that like all Brazilian progressive intellectuals of his time, da Cunha was convinced that positivism was the key to the future, the means, as Vargas Llosa puts it, to "transform Brazil into something similar to the United States of America" (127). But Vargas Llosa also explains that da Cunha recognized the disastrous consequences of imposing positivism on Canudos, that is, of assuming a continuous cultural tradition from Europe to Latin America. *Os sertões*, Vargas Llosa concludes, is both "a personal and a national self-criticism. . . . What [da Cunha] showed in his book is that importing institutions, ideas, values, and even aesthetic tendencies from Europe to Latin America is something that can have very different consequences, something that can produce unexpected results" (131).

Not surprisingly, Vargas Llosa specifically notes da Cunha's role as a journalist in recording Latin American historical reality: "It is a pedagogical experience to read what he wrote in the articles he sent to his São Paulo newspaper from the front" (130). About other contemporary newspaper accounts of the Canudos uprising he writes: "It is fascinating . . . because you can see how journalism and history at a given moment can become a branch of fiction, exactly like poetry or the novel" (130). Clearly Vargas Llosa identifies with da Cunha's argument that European traditions are not automatically continuous with Latin American realities and should be resisted rather than imposed uncritically. He also identifies with the use of journalism to address this ongoing cultural and political dialectic.

Like *Os sertões*, Vargas Llosa's novel dramatizes the unfolding of events in Canudos. The rebellion occurred for a number of political and socioeconomic reasons, including the indiscriminate imposition of European rationalist ideologies like positivism, which result in the utter lack of communication or, as I will suggest, the utter excess of languages spoken by the various groups involved.[62] Referring to the events of the Canudos war, the journalist in the novel comments:

Desde que pude sacarme de encima a los impertinentes y a los curiosos, he estado yendo al Gabinete de Lectura de la Academia Histórica. . . . A revisar los periódicos, todas las noticias de Canudos. El *Jornal de Notícias*, el *Diário de Bahia*, el *Republicano*. He leído todo lo que se escribió, lo que escribí. Es algo. . . difícil de expresar. Demasiado irreal, ¿ve usted? Parece una conspiración de la que todo el mundo participara, un malentendido generalizado, total.[63]

As soon as I was able to get rid of the cheeky and curious strangers who besieged me, I started going to the Reading Room of the Academy of History. . . . To look through the papers, all the news items about Canudos. The *Jornal da Notícias*, the *Diário de Bahia*, *O Republicano*. I've read everything written about it, everything I wrote. It's something . . . difficult to put into words. Too unreal, do you follow me? It seems like a conspiracy in which everyone played a role, a total misunderstanding on the part of all concerned, from beginning to end.[64]

The conflicting accounts reflect a basic condition of events in this novel. Each of the groups involved in the war has its own language that defines its members and excludes outsiders; these languages often have less to do with communication than with concealment. Vargas Llosa exploits this irony, dramatizing how the reality of each group is modeled according to its own idiosyncratic language, and how events in Canudos are a result of this central, semiological fact. So Vargas Llosa moves beyond da Cunha's exploration of the motivating forces behind the Canudos disaster in *Os sertões* to create a metahistorical perspective on those events. It is the interaction between the rhetorical and realistic levels of the novel – that is, between the various ideological formulations and the historical events of Canudos – that generates the aesthetic and political significance of *The War of the End of the World*.

Vargas Llosa presents this historical process as a process of communication in which new information is constantly eliciting different (and conflicting) responses from various social groups. The semiotician Boris Uspensky proposes just such a conception of history, arguing that the "language" of a social group (again, the word "language" is to be understood in its broadest cultural sense) determines the perception of events.[65] So a "text" of events is "read" by a social group in its own language; the process of history is conceived as generating new "sentences" in the language of a given group in a given cultural and historical context. Uspensky proposes that it is this semiotic process that provides the very mechanism for the unfolding of events in the historical process.

As Uspensky points out in his essay, and Vargas Llosa dramatizes in his novel, it is in situations of cultural conflict that the competing languages of a given historical context are most clearly heard. In periods of cultural homogeneity, different cultural languages may be few and mutually understandable, whereas in periods of cultural heterogeneity, the reverse is true. Uspensky notes that in the latter case it is possible that the sender of a message and its receiver may speak essentially different "languages" that nonetheless have the same external means of expression.

This is, of course, the situation depicted in *The War of the End of the World*. The tenor of the times is eschatological and the events in Canudos are conceived by everyone in apocalyptic terms, but these events yield wildly divergent interpretations. The apocalyptic message of the Counselor is received by his followers in a context akin to medieval, Joachimite millenarianism, as a promise of an impending third age in which God will reward them, and – no less important – punish their enemies. For Galileo Gall, another recipient of the Counselor's apocalyptic message, it is a gloss on the social theories of Marx, Engels, and Bakunin, and promises cathartic social change. For the politicians and military men of the new Brazilian republic, the Counselor's apocalypticism is sedition of the most dangerous sort. Thus, to his various audiences, the Counselor is simultaneously the Christ and the Antichrist, the creator of society and its destroyer, inspired and insane, modern and medieval, charismatic and cataclysmic. Vargas Llosa presents these various readings of the Counselor without authorial evaluation, his character thus becoming, in the semiotic system that is the novel itself, an empty signifier surrounded by a constantly shifting complex of signifieds. The emptying out of the interiority of this signifier, the exhaustion of content by form, is the necessary culminating point of the historical process dramatized in this novel – and it is also the point at which history becomes myth. As the situation intensifies in Canudos, historical understanding of events gives way to mythic understanding. As social and political chaos increases, each group raises its voice, so to speak, to impose its cultural language, and thus its own normative understanding on events.

If history is conceived as a text of events and actions whose information is read in the language of a particular social group, then we see in Vargas Llosa's novel that myth must be considered as an extreme enactment of this process, an extension and intensification of historical understanding. Myth shapes the surrounding world in the minds of individuals belonging to the group, generating a behavioral model that projects the group's ideas about its existence back onto the world.[66] The narrative patterns and projections of myth condition historical understanding in the same way that other cultural or political projections do, though the intensity and irrationality of historical desire as it is embodied in myth often outstrips more rational readings of the same events. Thus, historical and mythic understanding differ more in degree than in kind. Vargas Llosa is concerned with the points of overlap on this continuum, and with the shift in emphasis from the former to the latter as the stakes begin to escalate in Canudos.

As its title announces, the prevailing myth in this novel is the myth of apocalypse. *The War of the End of the World* constantly refers to biblical apocalypse, to popular apocalyptic legends and folk traditions going back to medieval European millenarianism, particularly to the Portuguese legend of the imminent return of King Sebastian and also to the Brazilian indigenous mythology of the Tupi-Guaraní.[67] Like the biblical apocalyptist, the Counselor presents himself, and is understood by his followers, as both decipherer of God's veiled truths and creator of his own veiled text, as both observer and participant in the historical drama that God has enjoined him to translate into mythic truth. Like the novelist, the historian, and the journalist, the mythmaker "reads" events, deduces meaning from the concretions of historical reality, and translates that meaning into his own mythic text. What separates him from the novelist, journalist, and historian is that his version of events is presented as divinely inspired, and is received by its audience as definitive. Furthermore, the mythmaker, to the extent that he is viewed by nonbelievers as a fanatic, attends first to the supposed correctness of his language and only second to its actual impact upon his followers, that is, to its actual historical consequences.[68] Such mythic construction of history collides with the rationalist paradigms of positivism in Canudos, and in the multiple perspectives that structure Vargas Llosa's novel as well.

The mythologizing of history by positivist and apocalyptist alike may be related once again to Hayden White's discussion of narrativity and historical understanding. Each of the groups in *The War of the End of the World* narrativizes history in its own cultural language, but only the myopic journalist in the novel does so consciously, that is, *historiographically*. Because he has broken his glasses and has no way to replace them in the besieged backlands, he cannot see to record events as they happen, and is therefore forced to abandon the journalist's pretensions to the unmediated recording of reality. He will have to *recreate* events from his memory, and because he can see only blurred shapes without his glasses, he will recreate it from his imagination as well. In short, he will have to become a novelist. As I have said, Vargas Llosa's novel is an homage to the work that the narrator will write; the journalist, modeled on da Cunha, will exit from Vargas Llosa's text to write his own text, which will, in turn, inspire Vargas Llosa's novel.[69]

This dizzyingly circular intertextuality suggests the perception at the heart of this novel, that events never speak for themselves, that journalism, myth and history – like fiction – will always balance various orders of truth. It is the struggle to understand the distinction among these orders and their ideological embodiments – among the various languages spoken in Canudos – that impels the myopic journalist to write his account and Vargas Llosa to write his novel. *The War of the End of the World* explores the relation of history to myth and the different ways in which the journalist and the novelist both record and create them in Canudos. The novel is itself offered as the most recent instance of this process.

Though *The War of the End of the World* dramatizes a particular historical moment in Brazil, Vargas Llosa has stated his more general historical and ideological intent with respect to this novel: "I felt that if I wrote a persuasive novel using Canudos as a setting for that story, I would perhaps be able to present in fiction the description of a continental phenomenon, something that every Latin American could recognize as part of his own past and in some cases his own present because in contemporary Latin America you still have Canudos in many countries. In Peru, for instance, we have a living Canudos in the Andes."[70] This familiar "continental phenomenon" is the imposition of European ideologies upon Latin American realities, and the tendency of intellectuals to accept European ideologies without questioning whether they are usable in Latin America.

For Vargas Llosa, uncritical transculturation is also a matter of literary form. The novel developed alongside positivism in Europe, a fact that makes the generic experimentations of contemporary Latin American writers not merely a literary gesture but also a political position. No one is more aware than Vargas Llosa that Latin American novelists must amplify the possibilities of their genre to suit the expressive requirements of their historical experience. His generic mixings in *The War of the End of the World*, like da Cunha's in *Os sertões*, become a means of contesting the linear rationalism of positivistic history that fostered the novel in the first place.

Vargas Llosa thus foregrounds the fact that in the novel, historical insights, theoretical positions, and narrative techniques are interdependent and debatable. The particular capacity of the novel to chart historical contingencies over time is epitomized by what John Burt Foster calls the "felt history" in the work of fiction. Foster defines felt history as "the eloquent gestures and images with which a character or lyric persona registers the direct pressures of events . . . ."[71] These pressures and their subjective interpretations are the shared meanings of a given culture and are expressed in its various narrative forms. Vargas Llosa shows that these forms are symbiotic and synergistic, and that felt history cannot be expressed in the novel without their multiple and shifting interactions.

Borges foresees this necessity in his speculation that the novel includes all other narrative forms:

No es imposible (y sin duda es inofensivo) asimilar todos los géneros literarios a la novela. El cuento es un capítulo virtual, cuando no es un resumen; la historia es una antigua variedad de la novela histórica: la fábula, una forma rudimental de la novela de tesis; el poema lírico, la novela de un solo personaje, que es el poeta.[72]

It is not impossible (and no doubt it is inoffensive) to assimilate all literary forms in the novel. The short story is, in effect, a chapter, if not a summary; history is an ancient form of the historical novel; the fable is a rudimentary form of the novel of ideas; the lyric poem is a novel about a single character, the poet.

Borges' parenthetical comment is disingenuous: the assimilation of all literary genres by the novel is not an innocent matter. As we have seen, historical truth is subject to its modes of expression, and the narrators of the past – especially the collective past – are always in some sense mythmakers, whether they call themselves journalists, historians, novelists, or lyric poets. Vargas Llosa, García Márquez, and Fuentes remind us that the past can be easily revised, defaced, and even effaced, as it has been by totalitarian and colonizing regimes in this century and before. Their novels dramatize their conviction that events are never exhausted by singular or absolutist readings, that felt histories must necessarily include multiple forms and perspectives. I will have more to say about this inclusive impulse and its openness to generic experimentation in the chapters of Part Two.

CHAPTER THREE

Ancestral Presences
Magical Romance / Magical Realism

Ghosts can be very fierce and instructive.
Flannery O'Connor, *Mystery and Manners*[1]

I HAVE CONSIDERED the different historiographic heritages of U.S. and Latin American fiction and consequent generic arguments about the nature of realism: how (and whether) historical experience can be remembered, reported, and (re)created in words. I now want to turn to literary works that enlarge these definitions of history by resuscitating figures from the past that the realist novel ordinarily excludes. These figures are ghosts, and I will be conjuring a number of them in order to consider how they are embodied (or not) in particular works of prose fiction; whether they are visible (and if so, to whom and why); and whether they speak, eat, or dream. An investigation of the nature of literary ghosts will tell us a great deal about their authors' philosophy and poetics of history – how they understand and embody the past in literary structures. The frequent appearance of ghosts in magical realism and romance suggests current redefinitions of the self and runs parallel to redefinitions of positivism such as Borges' "modest history," to which I referred earlier. Borges will again play an important role in my comparative discussion, as will Octavio Paz. Borges and Paz are consistently engaged in comparing literatures and cultures in the Americas – our different versions of Western civilization, as Paz puts it in his essay "Mexico and the United States." Their essays will help me to situate magical realism and romance in a hemispheric context and locate some ancestral apparitions as well.

Ghosts in American literature may serve as carriers of metaphysical truths, as visible or audible signs of atemporal, transhistorical Spirit. Or, they may carry historical burdens of tradition and collective memory: ghosts often act as correctives to the insularities of individuality, as links to lost families and communities, or as reminders of communal crimes, crises, and cruelties. They may suggest displacement and alienation or, alternatively, reunion and communion. Still other ghosts are agents of aesthetic effect: *el escalofrío, le frisson,* the fantastical release/relief from the constraints of reason. Ghosts of this sort, whose function on first reading seems primarily affective, are not to be taken lightly. They, too, are often bearers of cultural and historical burdens, for they represent the dangers, anxieties, and passional forces that civilization banishes. They may signal primal and primordial experience, the return of the repressed, or the externalization of internalized terrors. They are always double (here and not) and often duplicitous (where?) They mirror, complement, recover, supplant, cancel, and complete. Which is to say that literary ghosts are deeply metaphoric. They bring absence into presence, maintaining at once the "is" and the "is not" of metaphoric truth.

Ghosts in their many guises abound in magical realist fiction, as we shall see, and they are crucial to any definition of magical realism as a literary mode. Because ghosts make absence present, they foreground magical realism's most basic concern – the nature and limits of the knowable – and they facilitate magical realism's critique of modernity. Their presence in magical realist fiction is inherently oppositional, because they represent an assault on the scientific and materialist assumptions of Western modernity, namely, that reality is knowable, predictable, and controllable. They dissent, furthermore, from modernity's (and the novel's) psychological assumptions about autonomous consciousness and self-constituted identity, proposing instead a model of the self that is collective; subjectivity is not singular but several, not only individual and existential but also mythic, cumulative, and participatory. Magical realist apparitions also unsettle modernity's (and the novel's) basis in progressive, linear history; they float free in time, not just here and now but then and there, eternal and everywhere. Ghosts embody the fundamental magical realist sense that reality always exceeds our capacities to describe or understand or prove, and that the function of literature is to engage this excessive reality, to honor that which we may grasp intuitively but never fully or finally define. Magical realist texts ask us to look beyond the limits of the knowable, and ghosts are often our guides.

My argument, then, is that magical realism is truly postmodern in its rejection of binarisms, rationalisms, and reductive materialisms, and that its counterrealist conventions are particularly well suited to enlarging and enriching Western ontological understanding. I will focus on magical realism's opposition to modern ideologies of individualism: magical realist texts tend to universalize the individual self, a strategy that goes a long way toward explaining the presence of so many ghosts in magical realist texts. I will be looking at a number of literary ghosts in order to see their creators' postmodern revisions and reunions of the modern divorce between matter and nonmatter, past and present, self and other. Ghosts are liminal, metamorphic, and intermediary; they exist in/between/on modernity's boundaries of physical and spiritual, magical and real, and challenge the lines of demarcation.

Literary ghosts take many forms. For my purposes, to qualify as a ghost a literary apparition need not have arms and legs or, for that matter, be limited to two of each. It need only exist as a spiritual force that enters the material world of the fiction and expresses itself as such. The stain on the ceiling in Flannery O'Connor's "Resurrection" is a symbolic repository of religious truth, a holy ghost. Miss Rosa's conjuring of Sutpen, "man-horse-demon" in William Faulkner's *Absalom, Absalom!* is an archetypal embodiment of cultural memory. The fantastical creatures that haunt Isaac Bashevis Singer's world, the manifestations of ancient gods that irrupt into Carlos Fuentes' fictions – Tezcatlipoca, Huitzilopochtli, Quetzalcóatl, Chac-Mool – are also ghosts in the sense I intend here. Such ghosts, as these examples attest, are culturally specific, behaving according to particular cultural patterns of belief and serving particular cultural (and literary) purposes. Indeed, they may be evoked in order to overcome or escape a particular cultural heritage, that is, evoked in order to exorcise themselves. (Just so, Miss Rosa's paradoxical conjuring of Sutpen's ghost: man-horse-demon.) Ghosts have often been cast as dead souls, temporarily returned to, or unable to leave, the living. In their association with death – that most mysterious and extreme condition of the living – ghosts transgress yet other dividing/divisive lines, those between theology, mythology, philosophy, and fiction. In this role, they serve their authors to challenge and enlarge the narrative space of each of these forms of ontological inquiry.

I will be attending to the ghostly presences in works by American writers from a number of countries in the hemisphere. I will not be able to discuss all of the varieties of ghosts I've just mentioned (that would require a far longer study than this one), but perhaps my readers will test these types, and others, in their own considerations of magical realism. My chapter is divided into two distinct sections. I begin by tracing the nineteenth-century U.S. romance tradition with the help of twentieth-century Latin American magical realists in order to show the tendency of both romance and magical realism to archetypalize the self, to move away from the specific historical portrayal to historical existence as such. Whatever the political purposes and cultural contexts of romance and magical realism, their characters move toward mythological levels and universal communities in order to dramatize individual realizations of archetypal human patterns. My first section, then, is primarily concerned with the conditions that favor spectral presences rather than with particular apparitions, though to make my argument I will look through Borges' eyes at a ghostly figure in a story by Nathaniel Hawthorne.

In my second section, I focus on the ghosts who inhabit novels by the Mexican writers Elena Garro and Juan Rulfo and the Texas writer William Goyen. These writers share with Borges and Hawthorne the urge to translate individuals into archetypes, mimesis into myth. But unlike the ethereal specters of Borges and Hawthorne, the ghosts of Garro, Rulfo, and Goyen live underground, in an earth animated by ancestral inhabitants. Their novels are American books of the dead, necrogeographies of the buried traces of indigenous cultural identity in a shared region of America. My aim throughout this chapter (like the magical realists') is to blur boundaries – literary, historical, and national boundaries – in order to speak of traditions of American counterrealism in a hemispheric sense. To enter this vast territory, it will be useful to survey the ontological and formal issues that make spectral presences so common in magical realist texts.

Magical realist texts, like ghosts, subvert "the commonsense dichotomies of the daylight consciousness," dichotomies upon which modern prose fiction depends, according to Northrop Frye in his seminal discussion of fictional modes in *The Anatomy of Criticism*.[2] The subversions of "commonsense dichotomies" in magical realism are, as I have suggested, both ontological and generic. Magical realist texts question the nature of reality *and* the nature of its representation. In this, then, magical realist texts share (and extend) the tradition of narrative realism; they, too, aim to present a credible version of experienced reality. The crucial difference is that magical realist texts amplify the very conception of "experienced reality" by presenting fictional worlds that are multiple, permeable, transformative, and animistic. And (it follows) they create readers whose relations to the fictional world are necessarily ambiguous, and unpredictable. Contemporary magical realist narratives remove the ground upon which the reader of conventional novels and short stories expects to stand – the ground of a fictional world that is stable enough to be knowable. In this way, magical realist texts dramatize the process of knowing (and not knowing); the reader is obliged to wonder how we are to locate the "real" in magical realism. This repositioning of the reader with respect to the truth-claims of the narrative further obliges us to recognize our responsibility for the constitution of *all* meanings in the world, to recall our fundamental and necessary implication in the definition of reality as such.

Magical realism's unsettling of generic and ontological assumptions calls new attention to old questions about narrative form, and to the fictional worlds that narrative forms seek to create. Whereas conventional narrative realism such as I discussed in Chapter 1 constructs the illusion of a fictional world that is continuous with the reader's (and whose ontological status is therefore naturalized, transparent), magical realism foregrounds the illusionary status of its fictional world by requiring that the reader follow its dislocations and permutations. So we arrive at an essential paradox: contemporary magical realists write *against* the illusionism of narrative realism by heightening their own narrative investment in illusion. They undermine the credibility of narrative realism by flaunting their own relative *incredibility*. In short, they point to the literary devices by which "realistic" literary worlds are constructed and constrained, and they dramatize by counterrealistic narrative strategies the ways in which those literary worlds (and their inhabitants) may be liberated. I would, therefore, propose that contemporary magical realism, in flaunting its departures from narrative realism, is self-reflexive and metafictional, even as I recognize that not all self-reflexive fiction is magical realist; Fielding, Sterne, Unamuno, Nabokov, Barth, and many others question the conventions of literary realism without necessarily engaging magical realist modes of narration. My point is that contemporary magical realists are closely allied to writers in other traditions of counterrealism, with whom they share the urge (as Nabokov puts it) to write novels in order to show that the novel does not exist.[3]

In their most distinct departure from the conventions of literary realism, magical realist texts often seem to pulsate with proliferations and conflations of worlds and histories, with appearances and disappearances and multiplications of selves and societies. These magical instabilities depend upon an array of narrative strategies that multiply/blur/superimpose/unify or otherwise transgress the solidity and singularity of realistic fictional events, characters, and settings. In magical realist fiction, individuals, times, and places have a tendency to transform magically into other (or all) individuals, times, places. This slippage from the individual to the collective to the cosmic is often signaled by spectral presences. Consider, for example, Toni Morrison's *Beloved* (1987), where Sethe is haunted by her dead daughter, a symbolic and historical embodiment of both her past and her future; Julio Cortázar's stories in *Final del juego* (*End of the Game*, 1964) and *Todos los fuegos el fuego* (*All the Fires the Fire*, 1974), which shift among times, places, and selves, and brilliantly subvert our analytic efforts to decide which are dreamed and which are not; Isabel Allende's *La casa de los espíritus* (*The House of the Spirits*, 1982), where the women characters' domesticity and spirituality are inseparable, a point made literal by the mundanity of the ghosts, who rattle the cupboards of the family residence and bring messages that forecast rain.[4] In this novel, as in magical realism generally, the cosmic and quotidian are at the ends of a continuum along which characters and readers move.

The temptation is to multiply examples, so rich and varied are the spectral presences in recent American literature: Fuentes' *Aura* (1962), William Kennedy's *Ironweed* (1983), Maxine Hong Kingston's *The Woman Warrior* (1976) Leslie Marmon Silko's *Ceremony* (1977), Louise Erdrich's *Tracks* (1988), José Donoso's *Casa de Campo* (*A House in the Country*, 1978), Paul Bowles' mythic short stories set in Mexico and Morocco, Joyce Carol Oates' collection of ghostly tales, *The Poisoned Kiss and Other Stories from the Portuguese* (1975). I will resist the temptation to enter all of these haunted worlds, trusting that my readers will to do so sooner or later (or already have). Here I want to consider the most influential of American magical realists, Gabriel García Márquez and Jorge Luis Borges, and their possible precursor, the U.S. romancer Nathaniel Hawthorne.

I

In *Cien años de soledad* (*One Hundred Years of Solitude*), García Márquez's fictional world does not pulsate or proliferate into multiple times and spaces, though it does, of course, eventually disappear into thin air. His characters are another matter. García Márquez systematically unsettles discrete, stable identity with his familial repetitions and self-reflections and his integrations of the living and the dead. The repeating José Arcadios and Aurelianos are the successive generations of a family, but not in any realistic sense. Rather, we may think of them, paradoxically, as a simultaneous series, an ongoing progression of ahistorical archetypes. That *One Hundred Years of Solitude* was originally published in Spanish without a genealogy suggests García Márquez's archetypalizing intent: The Buendías are more significantly connected to prior human patterns than to prior individuals. Only when the novel was translated into English, in deference to the expectation of readers for individualized characters, was the genealogy added. With or without the genealogy, one José Arcadio is in some sense all José Arcadios, one Aureliano all the rest; we are told that the Buendía twins, who seem to reverse the archetypal patterns, may have been switched at birth. It is, then, as if the José Arcadios and Aurelianos are their own dead precursors, their own ghosts. This shifting relation of individual to archetype often attends the psychology of magical realist characters, making them the offspring of Jung, not Freud.[5] The Buendías are ciphers of a collective unconscious, related to each other less by family history than by mythic paradigm.

The presence of the dead among/in the living in *One Hundred Years of Solitude* – the simultaneity of the self, as it were – becomes explicit in the case of the matriarch Ursula:

> – Pobre la tatarabuelita – dijo Amaranta Ursula – , se nos murió de vieja.
> Ursula se sobresaltó.
> – ¡Estoy viva! – dijo.
> – Ya ves – dijo Amaranta Ursula, reprimiendo la risa – , ni siquiera respira.
> – ¡Estoy hablando! – gritó.
> – Ni siquiera habla – dijo Aureliano – . Se murió como un grillito.
> Entonces Ursula se rindió a la evidencia. – Dios mío – exclamó en voz baja. – De modo que esto es la muerte.[6]

> "Poor great-great-grandmother," Amaranta Ursula said. "She died of old age."
> Ursula was startled.
> "I'm alive!" she said.
> "You can see," Amaranta Ursula said, suppressing her laughter, "that she's not even breathing."

"I'm talking!" Ursula shouted.

"She can't even talk," Aureliano said. "She died like a little cricket."

Then Ursula gave in to the evidence. "My God," she exclaimed in a low voice. "So this is what it's like to be dead."[7]

Death and the past are present and alive in Macondo, as they are throughout García Marquez's fiction; consider the mythic corpses in *Hojarasca* (*Leaf Storm*, 1955) and "El ahogado más bello-del mundo" ("The Handsomest Drowned Man"), or the mythic almost corpse in *El general en su laberinto* (*The General in His Labyrinth*, 1989). Macondo's timeless paradise ends and its communal history begins when Prudencia Aguilar's ghost arrives. Prudencio brings with him the past and death, that is, time: his apparition incites the clocks to tick in Macondo. Not only the history of Macondo but also its narration depends upon the arrival of a ghost. Melquíades' ghost, returned to Macondo from death by fever on a beach in Singapore, narrates its history and provides a generative instance of the simultaneity of selves and multiplicity of ontological strata characteristic of magical realism.

The Autumn of the Patriarch (1975) also cycles and recycles a character, a nameless dictator who dies and returns from death to impose an endlessly repeating series of political abuses. His status as archetype depends upon this sense of repetition and return as surely as does that of Melquíades and the Buendías. Clearly, García Márquez's phantoms facilitate their creator's account of the vicious circles of Colombian politics. Like Carlos Fuentes' self-replicating characters in *Terra nostra* (1976), García Márquez's characters convey their author's sense that Latin American reality is haunted by what has gone before. History itself is a ghost to be confronted, engaged, exorcised, and overcome.

Jorge Luis Borges' wraiths are situated elsewhere or, it often seems, nowhere. Whereas Prudencio Aguilar, Melquíades, the simultaneous series of José Arcadios and Aurelianos, the Patriarch, and the General are culturally specific ghosts, Borges' wraiths are not. They are embodied ideas, figures of philosophy or dream. The universalizing of the subject in Borges' fiction, and in much magical realism, would seem to undercut the possibility of specific political and cultural critique. After all, archetypes by definition encode dominant cultural stereotypes. And yet it is undeniable that magical realist authors have provided some of the most trenchant contemporary political literature, and with ghosts aplenty. That the most counterrealistic fiction is also the most political fiction results, I think, in large part from the magical realist insistence upon the universality of the subject. By elaborating for the self a transhistorical context, magical realists give added weight to their dramatizations of specific historical abuses. Archetypal conceptions of subjectivity drawn from collective sources provide bases upon which magical realists may construct political positions resistant to the abuses of individualism – exploitative capitalism and messianic nationalism, among others. These authors generalize in order to unsettle absolutes, to clear a space for a larger perspective from which to view the particular histories and cultures they dramatize. Magical realists are what Flannery O'Connor calls "realists of distance."[8]

My argument, then, is that the effectiveness of magical realist political dissent depends upon its prior (unstated, understood) archetypalizing of the subject and its consequent allegorizing of the human condition. Magical realists recognize both the appeal and the cost of their discourse of universality, and they negotiate the telescopings of generality and particularity, the accordion-like contractions and expansions of perspective, in a number of ways. Borges knew well that all experience is necessarily individual, but he also knew that individuals necessarily generalize in order to make sense of their experience. In his essay on Hawthorne, Borges refers to Jung, a reference that I cite below. Though I do not wish to make Borges (merely) a Jungian, I do think that he shares with Jung the desire to bridge the gap between multifaceted human experience and its symbolic expression in literature. In *Mythical Intentions in Modern Literature*, Eric Gould states that Jung's theory of archetypes aims "to objectify psychological processes, even while it satisfies our need to locate somewhere (however mysteriously) the universalizing function of symbols."[9] This seems to me to be true in Borges' and García Márquez's fiction, and in magical realism generally. The universal is indeed located somewhere, but the location is distilled and magically distanced from everyday experience, even as it also refers directly to it.

Ironically, for Borges to write universalizing tales in the nineteen-twenties, thirties, and forties *was* a specifically political act because it meant opposing the then-current Argentine mode of literary realism, *costumbrismo* ("local color" realism), with its philosophical bases in positivism and empiricism and its literary bases in nineteenth-century realism. In his 1932 essay, "El escritor argentino y la tradición" ("The Argentine Writer and Tradition") Borges argues a point that now – in part because of Borges – seems obvious, namely, that the Argentine writer does not have to write about the specific material realities of Argentina in order to represent Argentine reality. Borges describes himself as positioned simultaneously in the mainstream of Western culture and on its colonized margins, arguing that Argentines, like Jews and the Irish, "podemos manejar todos los temas europeos, manejarlos sin supersticiones, con una irreverencia que puede tener, y ya tiene, consecuencias afortunadas. . . . repito que no debemos temar y que debemos pensar que nuestro patrimonio es el universo. . . ."[10] ("can handle all European themes, handle them without superstition, with an irreverence which can have, and already does have, fortunate consequences. . . . I repeat that we should not be alarmed and that we should feel that our patrimony is the universe. . . ."[11]) He describes his early, failed attempts to depict Buenos Aires realistically, and then his inadvertent success:

. . . hará un año, escribí una historia que se llama *La muerte y la brújula* que es una suerte de pesadilla, una pesadilla en que figuran elementos de Buenos Aires deformados por el horror de la pesadilla; pienso allí en el Paseo Colón y lo llamo Rue de Toulon, pienso en las quintas de Adrogué y las llamo Triste-le-Roy; publicada esa historia, mis amigos me dijeron que al fin habían encontrado en lo que yo escribía el sabor de las afueras de Buenos Aires. Precisamente porque no me había propuesto encontrar ese sabor, porque me había abandonado al sueño, pude lograr, al cabo de tantos años lo que antes busqué en vano. (270–71)

. . . about a year ago, I wrote a story called "*La muerte y la brújula*" ("Death and the Compass"), which is a kind of nightmare, a nightmare in which there are elements of Buenos Aires, deformed by the horror of the nightmare. There I think of the Paseo Colón and call it rue de Toulon; I think of the country houses of Adrogué and call them Triste-le-Roy; when this story was published, my friends told me that at last they had found in what I wrote the flavor of the outskirts of Buenos Aires. Precisely because I had not set out to find that flavor, because I had abandoned myself to a dream, I was able to accomplish, after so many years, what I had previously sought in vain. (181–82)

"The Argentine Writer and Tradition" may be partially self-justifying, for Borges had, by the time he wrote it, long been "abandoned to dream." Nonetheless, the essay places in a specific American cultural context the universalizing impulse that makes magic and politics so powerfully synergistic in recent examples of magical realism. It is an impulse that one recognizes in the more overtly oppositional work of García Márquez, Allende, Morrison, Rulfo, Garro, Goyen, and many other American magical realists – and in American romance, as we will see.

In Borges' stories, selves seem to fuse rather than repeat or reappear, as they do in García Márquez's fiction. The cabbalistic ideas that one man is all men and, conversely, that the microcosm contains the macrocosm, animates Borges' magical realism, as does the related idea that the self is a dream of God.[12] A preference for archetype over psychology or sociology consistently marks Borges' fictional creatures. There is no need to search far for instances: "La biblioteca de Babel" ("The Library of Babel"), with its "eternal traveler"; the "gray man" of "Las ruinas circulars" ("The Circular Ruins"). Even the stories with seemingly individualized characters and local settings explicitly dramatize the individual's participation in the universal life. For example, "La otra muerte" ("The Other Death") and "La biografía de Tadeo Isidoro Cruz (1829-1874)" ("The Life of Tadeo Isidoro Cruz [1829-1874]") begin at specific times and places in Argentina, with named agents of the action. I will not say "characters," because the trajectory of both narratives is to undo this specificity, to confuse, then fuse individual identity with archetype. The parenthetical dates in the title of "Tadeo Isidoro Cruz" are highly ironic because the singularity of Cruz's life is eventually revoked and a transindividual mythic identity conferred upon him as he is associated with the archetypal gaucho Martín Fierro.

"The Other Death" also concludes with the turn from individual to arche-type, with a consequent ironic reversal of "fantastic" and "real." Speaking of the "character" Pedro Damián, Borges' narrator says:

He adivinado y registrado un proceso no accesible a los hombres, una suerte de escándolo de la razón. . . . Sospecho que Pedro Damián (si existió) no se llamó Pedro Damián, y que yo lo recuerdo bajo ese nombre para creer algún día que su historia me fue sugerida por los argumentos de Pier Damiani. . . . Hacia 1951 creeré haber fabricado un cuento fantástico y habré historiado un hecho real; también el inocente Virgilio, hará dos mil años, creyó anunciar el nacimiento de un hombre y vaticinaba el de Dios.[13]

I have guessed at and set down a process beyond man's understanding, a kind of exposure of reason. . . . It is my suspicion that Pedro Damián (if he ever existed) was not called Pedro Damián and that I remember him by that name so as to believe someday that the whole story was suggested to me by Pier Damiani's the-sis. . . . A few years from now, I shall believe I made up a fantastic tale, and I will actually have recorded an event that was real, just as some two thousand year ago in all innocence Virgil believed he was setting down the birth of a man and fore-told the birth of Christ.[14]

Borges' rejection of unitary, self-constituting consciousness and his con-sequent refusal to draw characters according to the conventions of literary realism may also take the form of an animistic vision of self and world, in which subject and object are mutually generative and reflexive. In his epi-logue to his collection of philosophical and literary speculations, *El hace-dor* (translated with the title *Dreamtigers*), Borges writes:

Un hombre se propone la tarea de dibujar el mundo. A lo largo de los años puebla un espacio con imágenes de provincias, de reinos, de montañas, de bahías, de naves, de islas, de peces, de habitaciones, de instrumentos, de astros, de caballos y de personas. Poca antes de morir, descubre que ese paciente laberinto de líneas traza la imagen de su cara.[15]

A man sets himself the task of portraying the world. Through the years he peo-ples a space with images of provinces, kingdoms, mountains, bays, ships, islands, fishes, rooms, instruments, stars, horses, and people. Shortly before his death, he discovers that that patient labyrinth of lines traces the image of his face.[16]

Individuals, nature, and culture interpenetrate, overlap, and fuse. Borges reverses the Cartesian priority of autonomous consciousness: the self does not create the world but contains it.

This idea appears frequently in Borges' essays on literature as well, where the mythic fusion is of authors and literary texts. If García Márquez's replicating characters carry within them the ghosts of their own ancestors, Borges' authors are ghosts of other authors and their stories the ghosts of other stories or, rather, of an archetypal story. The narrator of

"The Library of Babel" asserts: "La certidumbre de que todo está escrito nos anula o nos afantasma."[17] ("The certitude that everything has been written negates us or turns us into phantoms."[18]) Here "phantom" must be understood in the context of Borges' subversions of individualism and originality, not (as it is sometimes read) as a statement of literary exhaustion. In his 1945 essay "La flor de Coleridge" ("The Flower of Coleridge"), Borges refers to Valéry's insight that the history of literature is the history not of authors but of the Spirit, and to Shelley's opinion that "todos los poemas del pasado, del presente y del porvenir, son episodios o fragmentos de un solo poema infinito, erigido por todos los poetas del orbe"[19] ("all the poems of the past, present, and future were episodes or fragments of a single infinite poem, written by all the poets on earth."[20]) In this context, Borges also quotes Emerson: "Diríase que una sola persona ha redactado cuantos libros hay en el mundo; tal unidad central hay en ellos que es innegable que son obra de un solo caballero omnisciente" (17; "I am very much struck in literature by the appearance that one person wrote all the books; . . . there is such equality and identity both of judgment and point of view in the narrative that it is plainly the work of one all-seeing, all-hearing gentleman."[21])

From a contemporary feminist perspective, Emerson's and Borges' masculist language seems to undermine their universalizing impulse by excluding women's experience from their generalizations. But we should recall that in their cultural contexts, "man" – even "gentleman" – *was* a universal category and therefore consonant with their transindividualizing intent. From a comparatist's perspective, their obliviousness to cultural difference would seem to obviate the very possibility of cultural critique. But in magical realist fiction, as I have already argued, the self is first a transcendental category, and then a political one. Borges challenges the limits of ideological certainty by refusing the limits of individual identity, both of the self and the literary work. This challenge implies a further challenge: to the ideology of originality. The modern conception of originality assumes a Hegelian history that is linear, progressive, future-oriented, and made by autonomous egos. It is ironic that Borges invokes Emerson in an essay that contests Hegelian historiography, for (as I pointed out in my first chapter) Emerson was a principal conduit of German idealism into nineteenth-century U.S. intellectual culture.[22] But Borges understood correctly that Emersonian Transcendentalism also posits a mythic participation in a "universal history" that is present, available, and communal: "Quizá la historia universal es la historia de la diversa entonación de algunas metáforas."[23] ("It may be that universal history is the history of a handful of metaphors."[24]) This Borgesian dismissal of singularity and originality has generic echoes in the synchronic and intertextual narrative strategies that structure much contemporary Latin American fiction. I will explore these structures in the following chapters; here we glimpse their metaphysical basis. Borges treats the particular as an apparition of the universal: the self contains all others; history is the moving account of timeless moments. This characteristic instability of strata – individual, community, cosmos – inevitably impels magical realism toward allegory.

In "The Flower of Coleridge" Borges cites Coleridge's statement: "Si un hombre atravesara el Paraíso en un sueño, y le dieran una flor como prueba de que había estado allí, y si al despertar encontrara esa flor en su mano . . . ¿entonces, qué?" (17; "If a man could pass through Paradise in a dream, and have a flower presented to him as a pledge that his soul had really been there, and if he found that flower in his hand when he awoke – Ay! – and what then?" 10–11). In Borges' reprise of Coleridge's vision, we hear a nostalgic sigh for the proof ("that flower in his hand") forever lost to the contemporary magical realist. In the final question ("and what then?") we hear an invitation into his own created world of spectral presences, where proof is moot.

Borges' references to Emerson's Transcendentalism, Coleridge's and Shelley's Romanticism, and Valéry's Symbolism, suggest the confluent sources of his magical realism and tie it to the nineteenth-century U.S. romance tradition.[25] In a study of U.S. romance writers, Leon Chai argues that its writers were marked by a deepening awareness of the opposition between spiritualism and materialism. Chai notes in particular that Hawthorne's literary project was driven by a search for the "magical quality of the actual."[26] No wonder Borges felt an affinity for these romance writers, and saw reflections of his own work in theirs.

The hallmark of magical realism that I am tracing here – its rejection of the rugged Cartesian individual – is congruent with romance narrative practice. Northrop Frye's genre and myth criticism is useful in this context. In elaborating his theory of fictional modes in *The Anatomy of Criticism*, he says of romance:

The essential difference between novel and romance lies in the conception of characterization. The romancer does not attempt to create "real people" so much as stylized figures which expand into psychological archetypes. It is in the romance that we find Jung's libido, anima, and shadow reflected in the hero, heroine, and villain respectively. That is why the romance so often radiates a glow of subjective intensity that the novel lacks, and why a suggestion of allegory is constantly creeping in around its fringes. (304)

Frye's observations implicitly link romance to magical realism, and both to Jungian archetypes and allegory. Allegory, like magical realism and romance, is less concerned with individual psychology than with archetypal patterns. Borges, in his 1949 essay "From Allegories to Novels," writes: "The allegory is a fable of abstractions, as the novel is a fable of individuals."[27] And in his essay on Nathaniel Hawthorne, also written in 1949, Borges defends Hawthorne against Poe's charge of allegorizing by recurring to his beloved Chesterton, who, he tells us, "implies that various languages can somehow correspond to the ungraspable reality, and among them are allegories and fables."[28]

Borges' defense of Hawthorne attests to their shared sensibilities: Hawthorne's compelling intuition, like Borges', was to find some "ungraspable" symbolic significance in ordinary experience. Hawthorne was deeply influenced by the Puritan allegorical understanding of the visible world as an embodiment of God's invisible purpose, as well as by the Transcendentalist view of the interpenetration of nature and divinity. He was, in fact, caught between the Puritan pessimism about fallen nature and the Transcendentalist celebration of nature and natural man, and was deeply skeptical of both. But he embraced instinctively (and also self-consciously) the *openness* of both attitudes to the presence of mystery in the commonplace. In a deservedly famous passage from "The Custom-House" introduction to *The Scarlet Letter* (1850), Hawthorne writes of a familiar room in moonlight, of its material contents "so spiritualized by the unusual light that they seem to lose their actual substance [and become] invested with a quality of strangeness and remoteness, though still almost as vividly present as by daylight."[29] The room, writes Hawthorne, becomes

a neutral territory, somewhere between the real world and fairy-land, where the Actual and the Imaginary may meet, and each imbue itself with the nature of the other. Ghosts might enter here, without affrighting us. It would be too much in keeping with the scene to excite surprise, were we to look about us and discover a form, beloved, but gone hence, now sitting quietly in a streak of this magic moonshine, with an aspect that would make us doubt whether it had returned from afar, or had never once stirred from our fireside. (31)

This "neutral territory" where "ghosts may enter without affrighting us" is, of course, the territory of twentieth-century magical realism as well.

Once again, in romance as in magical realism, the question arises as to the relation of literary abstraction to particular cultural and political conditions. Fredric Jameson's observation that postcolonial literatures allegorize for the purpose of national self-definition is debatable, but I do agree with him that allegory (often in conjunction with magical realism, and sometimes indistinguishable from it) has become a frequent device of postcolonial writers.[30] Paul de Man's discussion of allegory as "immediacy and mediation" is also pertinent to this question, as is his understanding of the tensions created in the dialectical field of allegory.[31] For Hawthorne, as for Borges, to abstract *was* to react specifically to his cultural situation as an American writer. Like Borges, Hawthorne concerned himself with American cultural relations to Europe: like him, he was aware of his belated and adoptive status as a New World writer. Because neither Borges nor Hawthorne used indigenous culture to any significant extent in his definition of America (as do the novelists in the second section of this chapter), both felt the lack of a significant American past when compared to that of Europe. And both worried about the present. Hawthorne opposed the prevailing mid-nineteenth-century ideologies of individualism and nationalism, as Borges opposed similar ideologies in Perón's Argentina eight decades later. Borges (made inspector of chickens by Perón) recognized Hawthorne's feelings of invisibility, speculating that Hawthorne recorded thousands of trivialities in his notebooks "to show himself that he was real, to free himself, somehow, from the impression of unreality, of ghostliness, that usually visited him."[32] Hawthorne, too, found that he could describe his American reality only by abandoning himself to dream.

Hawthorne foregrounds America's colonized relationship to Europe by setting many of his works in the colonial past. *The Scarlet Letter* begins with an ironic reference to the failed utopian projects of the European forefathers in the New World, and traces the story of Hester Prynne, doubly marginalized as a sensualist/sinner and a female.[33] In this novel and throughout Hawthorne's work, one senses his ambivalence between past and future ideals, his nostalgia for the lost innocence of the New World, and his wistful desire for the ideal realm that the New World might yet become. This romantic longing, projected both backward and forward in time and space, is also present in contemporary magical realism. Borges' speculations on impossible orders and García Márquez's descriptions of failed utopias parallel the ambivalent idealism of Hawthorne's romance, though there are also points of difference to which I'll return. Hawthorne uses eighteenth-century European gothic conventions to reflect ironically upon his own idealizations and those of mid-nineteenth-century America. His most brilliant piece of American gothic is the haunted ancestral home of the Pyncheons in *The House of the Seven Gables*. The house is an American version of a gothic castle or ruined abbey, a Puritan house of the spirits. In it, gothic ghosts ironize, and then undermine, contemporary ideologies of individualism, science, progress, perfectability and, above all, the notion of America's historical innocence. Hawthorne's ghosts remind the living that their past is inescapable, and their future encumbered.

Because my primary concern here is with the uses of literary form, I am better served for the moment by Northrop Frye's formal analysis of the effects of abstraction in romance than by Jameson's Marxist or de Man's deconstructive analyses. Having noted the archetypal characters in/of romance, Frye observes:

Certain elements of character are released in the romance which make it naturally a more revolutionary form than the novel. The novelist deals with personality, with characters wearing their *personae* or social masks. He needs the framework of a stable society, and many of our best novelists have been conventional to the verge of fussiness. The romancer deals with individuality, with characters *in vacuo* idealized by revery, and, however conservative he may be, something nihilistic and untamable is likely to keep breaking out of his pages. (304–05)

It is precisely the "idealized" nature of romance, Frye suggests, that admits the political, indeed, the "revolutionary." As in magical realism, the romance conception of archetypal subjectivity carries within it dynamic political potential. In both modes the self is politically empowered only when it is mythically connected to communal values and traditions, that is, to the collective unconscious of its culture.

Borges' discussion of Hawthorne's fiction and his survey of the nineteenth-century U.S. literary tradition are useful to my comparative purposes here. Besides his many reviews of U.S. literature for the magazine *El hogar* in the thirties,[34] his essays on Melville and Whitman and his homage to Poe's mystery stories in his own,[35] he collected his lectures on North American literature in *An Introduction to American Literature* (1967).[36] Borges is surely the most idiosyncratic of American literary comparatists. To look over his shoulder as he reads U.S. literature is to see a tradition of fantastic literature that U.S. readers will scarcely recognize, and to find the makings of magical realism everywhere. Borges sees a fantastic tradition flourishing in U.S. literature beginning with the Puritans. In his first chapter, entitled "Origins," he attributes Cotton Mather's *The Wonders of the Invisible World* and especially his discussion of his "diabolical possession" not to theological dementia (as would many contemporary readers) but rather to his fertile fantastic imagination.[37] Of Mather Borges writes: "He thought that the written word should always communicate something but that allusions and citations could increase its efficiency and embellish it 'like the jewels that adorn the garments of a Russian ambassador'"(7). Borges' choice of metaphor immediately attests to what will become the implicit theme of his study: his sense that this fantastic tradition in the U.S. is rich but rarified, in part because of a naturalistic critical practice. It is almost as if Borges set out to redress the imbalance.[38] I want to look at some relevant excerpts from his survey, and then return to Borges' Hawthorne.

About Washington Irving Borges says, "He thought that his country lacked a romantic past and so he Americanized legends of other times and places" (16). About the historian William Prescott, whose *History of the Conquest of Mexico* (1843) he juxtaposes to Irving's *Tales of the Alhambra* (1832) and whose theme, he asserts, was furnished by Irving, Borges writes: ". . . like Irving, [Prescott felt] the peculiar enchantment of the Hispanic world" (16). About Whitman, who demonstrates Borges' own practice of archetypalizing and synthesizing the subject, he states: "In previous epics a single hero was dominant: Achilles, Ulysses, Aeneas, Roland, or the Cid. Whitman, for his part, was determined that his hero should be all men" (32). Borges cites the following lines from section 17 of "Song of Myself," which again demonstrate not only Whitman's philosophy but also his own:

These are the thoughts of all men in all ages and lands – they are not
  original with me;
If they are not yours as much as mine, they are nothing, or next to nothing;
If they are not the riddle, and the untying of the riddle, they are nothing,
If they are not just as close as they are distant they are nothing. (32)

Elsewhere he says of Whitman that he "wrote his rhapsodies in terms of an
imaginary identity, formed partly of himself, partly of each of his readers."[39] Jack London, whom U.S. readers usually consider a naturalist,
becomes in Borges' reading a kind of American Ovid, a contributor to the
tradition of tales of metamorphosis. About *The Call of the Wild* (1903)
Borges writes: "It is the story of a dog that has been a wolf and finally
becomes one again" (38); Jack London's "style is realistic, but he re-creates
and exalts a reality of his own" (39). Borges' final chapter is on the oral
poetry of the Plains Indians. He observes this poetry's "contemplative perception of the visual world, its delicacy, its magic" and notes that its
images "are like the echo of an absent, a distant and almost dead world"
(89–90).

Borges devotes a relatively long chapter (six pages) of *An Introduction to
American Literature* to Transcendentalism.[40] As elliptical as it is, his discussion suggests the principal philosophical affinities of nineteenth-century U.S. romance and his own *ficciones*:

The roots of Transcendentalism were multiple: Hindu pantheism, Neoplatonic
speculations, the Persian mystics, the visionary theology of Swedenborg, German
idealism, and the writing of Coleridge and Carlyle. It also inherited the ethical
preoccupations of the Puritans. Edwards had taught that God can infuse the soul
of the chosen with a supernatural light; Swedenborg and the cabalists, that the
external world is a mirror of the spiritual. Such ideas influenced both the poets
and the prose writers of Concord. (24)

Borges continues, listing the shared beliefs of these writers of Concord,
which reflect his own: the immanence of God in the universe; the identification of the individual soul with the soul of the world, and the soul of God
with both. Borges paraphrases Emerson's Transcendentalist idea: "If God is
in every soul, all external authority disappears. All that each man needs is
his own profound and secret divinity" (25). So, Borges concludes, "pantheism, which leads the Hindus to inaction, led Emerson to preach that there
are no limits to what we can do since divinity is at the center of each of us"
(26). In the irony of his cultural comparison, Borges implies the subsequent
abuses of "divine individualism" in the history of our own century.

In the paragraph that I have just cited, Borges makes the Calvinist the-
ologian Jonathan Edwards a precursor of the Transcendentalists.[41] His
association of Puritanism and Transcendentalism is historically and philosophically accurate, of course. He was well aware that for the Puritans, and
later for the Transcendentalists, reality was always symbolic, experience

an allegory of invisible presence. But as usual, Borges is revisionary. Referring to a beautiful image in Edwards' hell-fire-and-brimstone sermon, "Sin-
ners in the Hands of an Angry God," he comments: "Metaphors of this sort
have led to the supposition that Edwards was fundamentally a poet, frus-
trated by theology" (8). Borges' Edwards is not a ranting moralist but a mys-
tic. He believed, Borges tells us, "that the material universe is but an idea
in the divine mind," and he quotes Edwards' poignant description of God:
"He is everything and he is alone" (9). Borges' subtle appreciation of Puritan mystical poetics takes us back to Nathaniel Hawthorne, about whom
Borges writes, "By his feeling of guilt and his preoccupation with ethics
Hawthorne is grounded in Puritanism; by his love of beauty and his fantastic invention he is related to another great writer, Edgar Allan Poe" (20).
In his characteristic anachronizing of literary history, Borges also connects
the Salem Puritan to a Prague Jew. In Hawthorne's tales, "we have already
entered the world . . . of Kafka – a world of enigmatic punishments and
indecipherable sins. . . . There is the murky background against which
the nightmare is etched. . . . Hawthorne's particular quality has been
created, or determined by Kafka. . . . The debt is mutual; a great writer
creates his precursors."[42]

I now return to Borges' 1949 essay "Nathaniel Hawthorne," from which
I have taken the preceding statement. In it, Borges discusses at unwonted
length (fifteen pages in my edition of the collected works) the writer who
is for him the beginning, and perhaps the culmination, of U.S. literature.

If literature is a dream (a controlled and deliberate dream, but fundamentally a
dream), then . . . a look at Hawthorne, the dreamer, would be a good beginning.
There are other American writers before him – Fenimore Cooper, a sort of Eduardo Gutiérrez infinitely inferior to Eduardo Gutiérrez; Washington Irving, a con-
triver of pleasant Spanish fantasies – but we can skip over them without any con-
sequence. (217–18)

That Nathaniel Hawthorne inaugurates U.S. literature is a point upon
which Borges insists, as he insists upon the fantastical nature of U.S. literature in comparison to the more "rhetorical" nature of Latin American literature. In the course of his discussion of Hawthorne, Borges reverses our
usual sense of U.S. literature as less prone to myth and magic than Latin
American literature. Borges writes:

At the beginning of this essay I mentioned the doctrine of the psychologist Jung,
who compared literary inventions to oneiric inventions, or literature to dreams.
That doctrine does not seem to be applicable to the literatures written in the
Spanish language, which deal in dictionaries and rhetoric, not fantasy. On the
other hand, it does pertain to the literature of North America, which (like the literatures of England or Germany) tends more toward invention than transcription,
more toward creation than observation. Perhaps that is the reason for the curious
veneration North Americans render to realistic works, which induces them to

postulate, for example, that Maupassant is more important than Hugo. It is within the power of a North American writer to be Hugo, but not, without violence,
Maupassant. In comparison with the literature of the United States, which has
produced several men of genius and has had its influence felt in England and
France, our Argentine literature may possibly seem somewhat provincial. Nevertheless, in the nineteenth century we produced some admirable works of realism – by Echeverría, Ascasubi, Hernández, and the forgotten Eduardo Gutiérrez – the North Americans have not surpassed (perhaps have not equaled) them
to this day. Someone will object that Faulkner is no less brutal than our gaucho
writers. True, but his brutality is of the hallucinatory sort – the infernal, not the
terrestrial sort of brutality. It is the kind that issues from dreams, the kind inaugurated by Hawthorne. (229)

Literature in the Spanish language "deals in dictionaries and rhetoric, not
fantasy"; clearly, Borges wrote this essay before the flowering of magical
realism in Latin American literature. It was precisely 1949 in which magical realism was first described as *lo real maravilloso* and designated an
indigenous American phenomenon by Alejo Carpentier.[43] And in that
same year Faulkner, writing in the "hallucinatory" tradition "inaugurated
by Hawthorne," won the Nobel Prize for Literature. Nonetheless, in 1949,
Borges awarded his own private prize for fantastical literature in the Americas to Hawthorne.

   According to Borges, it is Hawthorne's tales and sketches that contain
his greatest gift, for in them, Borges argues, Hawthorne is able to present a
"situation" rather than "the convolutions of the story [or] the psychological portrait of the hero."[44] Borges notes that whereas the novelist must
believe in the reality of his characters, Hawthorne "first conceived a situation, or a series of situations, and then elaborated the people his plan
required. That method can produce, or tolerate, admirable stories because
their brevity makes the plot more visible than the actors, but not
admirable novels" (221). The length of the novel requires detailed specifics,
whereas the brevity of the sketches and the tales allowed Hawthorne to
generalize, and thus to create archetypal characters and allegorical plots.
Borges admits to disliking Hawthorne's novels, despite some "memorable
passages" in *The Scarlet Letter*, and insists upon the sketches: "Hawthorne
liked those contacts of the imaginary and the real, those reflections and
duplications of art; and in the sketches I have mentioned we observe that
he leaned toward the pantheistic notion that one man is the others, that
one man is all men" (221). Borges reads Hawthorne's sketches in the same
terms he intends his own *ficciones*, namely, as challenges to Cartesian
notions of autonomous consciousness, as necessary unsettlings of identity, as desirable diffusions of personality.

   What Borges celebrates in Hawthorne's sketches as "situation" – what
he sees as facilitating "the contact of the imaginary and the real" – is this:
an unstable configuration of circumstance, image, and character that leads

to a metaphor of being. This configuration contains plot, which Borges tells us is the more visible because of its brevity, but not "the convolutions of story." By plot Borges means only the barest outlines of action, indeed, action so pared back that the "situation" may figure a universal pattern. Character is also required, but certainly not any detailed "psychological portrait of the hero." Again, Borges requires only enough psychology to posit an archetypal subjectivity. As for images, from Hawthorne's vast corpus Borges chooses as an example a sketch whose central image is a ghost.

Predictably idiosyncratic, Borges selects "Wakefield," a little-read (rarely anthologized) sketch published in *New England Magazine* in 1835 and collected in *Twice-Told Tales* in 1837. Hawthorne's narrator tells of a man in London who deserts his wife with no warning or reason, surreptitiously takes a room across the street from his home, and for twenty years observes the life he might have lived. The world considers him dead, as Borges explains it: "Without having died, he has renounced his place and his privileges among living men" (223). Then, writes Borges, one afternoon, "an afternoon like other afternoons, like the thousands of previous afternoons," Wakefield decides to return home. "He walks up the steps and opens the door. The crafty smile we already know is hovering, ghostlike, on his face. At last Wakefield has returned. Hawthorne does not tell us of his subsequent fate, but lets us guess that he was already dead, in a sense" (223).

"Already dead, in a sense": Borges' phrase betrays his attraction to this obscure work. It is Hawthorne's "ghostlike" character, who exists midway between the living and the dead, who is both at once. Wakefield is his own ghost, his own twice-told tale. Like all ghosts, he is metaphoric in his status as simultaneously absent and present and in his movement between worlds. Hawthorne repeatedly emphasizes Wakefield's in-between status: ". . . an almost impassable gulf divides his hired apartment from his former home. 'It is but in the next street!' he sometimes says. Fool! it is in another world. . . . The dead have nearly as much chance of re-visiting their earthly homes as the self-banished Wakefield."[45] Hawthorne describes Wakefield as "haunting" his home, "vanishing," ceasing to be among the living "without being admitted among the dead" (42). Wakefield is in between, and also double. If García Márquez's characters proliferate and Borges' characters fuse, Hawthorne's character divides. In each case, psychology merges with ontology, and the literary modes most dependent upon individualized psychologies – novel and short story – are altered accordingly.

At the beginning of Hawthorne's story, the narrator of "Wakefield" expresses the hope that "there will be a pervading spirit and a moral, even should we fail to find them, done up neatly, and condensed into the final sentence" (36). Borges criticizes Hawthorne for sometimes overburdening his sketches with a moral, but in "Wakefield" Borges obviously found the "pervading spirit" that Hawthorne wished, unconstrained by the moralizing that Borges disliked. Hawthorne's conclusion is not "done up neatly, and condensed into the final sentence," though the ending is, of course, a calculated climax. Hawthorne writes:

[Wakefield] has left us much food for thought, a portion of which shall lend its wisdom to moral; and be shaped into a figure. Amid the seeming confusion of our mysterious world, individuals are so nicely adjusted to a system, and systems to one another and to the whole, that, by stepping aside for a moment, a man exposes himself to a fearful risk of losing his place forever. Like Wakefield, he may become, as it were, the Outcast of the Universe. (44)

Wakefield's "situation" becomes a metaphor of being. The story remains inconclusive, "ungraspable" – to repeat Chesterton's term quoted by Borges – because it reconfirms in these last sentences its status as allegory, and Wakefield's status as archetype. Emily Miller Burdick argues Chesterton's point in more contemporary critical terms: romance performs "what we might see as [its] moral function by remaining decentered and continuously deferring restrictive and hence ideologically coercive meaning."[46] Well, yes. Ungraspable. "Wakefield" achieves what Borges most admires: a universal human "situation" unencumbered by specific moral prescription. Kafka is indeed predicted by Hawthorne.

And yet, precisely because "Wakefield" is allegorical, the reader is asked to speculate on its significance, to grasp at the ungraspable. I have said that magical realism heightens the reader's awareness of our intentional relation to the world; the allegorical structure of romance also performs this function. Readers of romance must constitute meaning and at the same time run the risk of arriving at a meaning "done up neatly." I recognize this responsibility and choose to run this risk. I would propose that on its most abstract level, Wakefield configures our human condition as living creatures capable of imagining our own death: we are beings capable of imagining nonbeing. Hawthorne engages this most basic human ambivalence metaphorically and dramatically in the form of the ghostlike Wakefield. And he does so at a distance. Recall my assertion, using Flannery O'Connor's phrase, that magical realists are realists of distance. Borges chooses a story by Hawthorne set in London as a representative example of U.S. romance, when he might have chosen one of Hawthorne's better-known ghost stories explicitly set in New England, such as "The Minister's Black Veil," "The Prophetic Pictures," "Lady Eleanore's Mantle," "Young Goodman Brown," or "The Wives of the Dead." Perhaps Borges felt that the London of "Wakefield" embodied Hawthorne's New England as, he tells us in his essay "The Argentine Writer and Tradition," the French setting of his own story allowed him to capture the reality of Buenos Aires. In that same essay, Borges cites Gibbon's observation that "in the Arabian book *par excellence*, in the Koran, there are no camels" (*Labyrinths*, 181). Absence is not the opposite of presence but its necessary condition.

So, then, are magical realism and romance the same fictional mode? Perhaps nineteenth-century U.S. romance is an early and local flowering of twentieth-century magical realism, if I may permit myself this Borgesian anachronism. Their emphases are different, of course, and here I have treated so few texts that any conclusion is premature. I have elsewhere explored Hawthorne's mythic strategies in "Rappaccini's Daughter," and compared them to those of Carlos Fuentes' in his novella *Aura*.[47] Here, if there were space and time, I would extend my discussion (as Borges suggests) from Hawthorne to Faulkner, add Flannery O'Connor, and compare the grotesque and gothic conventions in their work to analogous conventions in contemporary Latin American magical realism. I would look at the ghost stories of Ambrose Bierce, whom Borges does not mention but whose "Occurrence at Owl Creek Bridge" is strikingly similar to Borges' "El milagro secreto" ("The Secret Miracle") in its dramatization of death's extension of living desire. And I would certainly include the supernatural tales of Edgar Allan Poe, a writer whom Borges most certainly *does* mention. In *An Introduction to American Literature*, Borges writes of Poe: "Poe's tales are divided into two categories which are sometimes intermingled: those of terror and those of the intellect. As for the first, someone accused Poe of imitating certain German romantics; he replied: 'Terror is not of Germany, but of the soul'" (23). Borges' relation to the second type, Poe's tales of the intellect, has been exhaustively discussed by John T. Irwin,[48] but Borges' relation to the first has not. Poe's tales of terror must be central to any comparative consideration of the U.S. romance and Latin American magical realist traditions.

If I were to pursue these comparisons, I would find fairly consistent differences. In tone, for example, the comic ebullience and sheer inventive energy of Latin American magical realism differs markedly from the darker, even lugubrious tone (the "hallucinatory" quality, as Borges puts it) of U.S. romance. Further differences would be found in the narrative conventions of U.S. romance drawn directly from eighteenth- and nineteenth-century European Romantic and gothic sources, in the more explicit political critique of Latin American magical realism against the metaphysical categories of U.S. romance; in the greater emphasis of U.S. romance on natural beauty that may seduce and betray, and so on. Some of these comparative generalizations will be tested in the second section of this chapter. But Borges' appreciation for Hawthorne points to the similarities of magical realism and romance rather than their differences, and to their shared project: the expansion and redefinition of our conceptions of subjectivity against the ideological limitations of Cartesian (and Freudian) consciousness, Hegelian historicism, and scientific rationalism.

Because my ostensible subject is ghosts, I return to Northrop Frye's theory of fictional modes to see if there are generic grounds on which to differentiate magical realism from romance. To conclude his discussion of his five categories of narrative realism, Frye proposes that we "take, as a random example, the use of ghosts in fiction." Frye is disingenuous; the example is hardly random, and it goes as follows:

In a true myth there can obviously be no consistent distinction between ghosts and living beings. In romance we have real human beings, and consequently ghosts are in a separate category, but in a romance a ghost as a rule is merely one more character: he causes little surprise because his appearance is no more marvellous than many other events. In high mimetic [i.e., the epic, tragedy], where we are within the order of nature, a ghost is relatively easy to introduce because the plane of experience is above our own, but when he appears he is an awful and mysterious being from what is perceptibly another world. In low mimetic [i.e., the novel], ghosts have been, ever since Defoe, almost entirely confined to a separate category of "ghost stories." In ordinary low mimetic fiction they are inadmissible, "in complaisance to the scepticism of a reader," as Fielding puts it, a skepticism which extends only to low mimetic conventions. The few exceptions, such as *Wuthering Heights*, go a long way to prove the rule – that is, we recognize a strong influence of romance in *Wuthering Heights*. In some forms of ironic fiction, such as the later works of Henry James, the ghost begins to come back as a fragment of a disintegrating personality. (50)

Frye does not mention "magical realism," of course, since the term was not yet current in literary criticism in 1957, when *The Anatomy of Criticism* was published. Nonetheless, we see immediately that what we now call magical realism corresponds to Frye's second category, romance, where ghosts are expected inhabitants of reality who may (as Hawthorne puts it in "The Custom-House") enter without affrighting us. I might, then, reverse my earlier Borgesian anachronism and propose that twentieth-century magical realism is a recent flowering of the more venerable romance tradition that Frye describes. Viewing the American versions of this European romance tradition from a comparative perspective reminds us that European literary historical categories rarely travel across the Atlantic without need of acclimatization and acculturation upon arrival. So I trace their adaptive capacities in their various New World historical circumstances.

Of course, some American magical realist texts are not adaptations of European traditions at all but, rather, flowerings of indigenous American traditions in which Frye has no interest. But I do. I turn now to three American novels in which the spirits of ancestors are enlivened by indigenous mythologies of "afterlife" (that are *not* after life but present in life) and by popular ritual practices that still reflect those mythologies. Whereas Borges' and Hawthorne's counterrealism may still be situated with respect to European literary and philosophical movements, the writers I discuss in the next section engage systems of belief specific to the American cultural and historical territory. William Goyen, Elena Garro, and Juan Rulfo imagine inhabited undergrounds that recall a time when Texas was Tejas, a state of Los Estados Unidos de México rather than of the United States of America, when the Río Grande/Río Bravo was not a drastic demarcation between vastly different cultures but, on the contrary, a connecting link among indigenous groups and later, among the various colonizers of New Spain. Here, then, I shift my discussion from the philosophy of magical realist subjectivity to its embodiments in three American novels, and to the indigenous American cultures and histories they reflect. My aim is to test my construction of magical realist subjectivity by allowing the spectral presences in these novels to emerge from/in the mythic ground they inhabit. If Borges and Hawthorne are realists of distance, we may think of Goyen, Garro, and Rulfo as realists of depth. So I bring my discussion of ghosts down to earth.

II

William Goyen's *The House of Breath* (1950), Elena Garro's *Recuerdos del porvenir* (translated as *Recollections of Things to Come*, 1963), and Juan Rulfo's *Pedro Páramo* (1955) are comparable in their investigations of the relations of the dead to the living, and the relations of the land to both. These writers create fictional communities that dramatize ironically the inevitability of human solitude, but unlike García Márquez's Macondo, Borges' Triste-le-Roy/Buenos Aires, or Hawthorne's Salem/London, the people in Goyen's, Garro's, and Rulfo's communities are already dead and buried. Goyen's fictional community of Charity, Garro's Ixtepec, and Rulfo's Comala are ghost towns to which narrators make mythic returns to remember, recount, and reconstitute the histories and cultures of their regions. Their theme is our *residencia en la tierra*, a phrase used by Pablo Neruda to title three volumes of his poetry, a phrase whose preposition, *en*, suggests a crucial ambivalence lost in English: our residence *in* and *on* the earth. These writers entertain the possibility of returning home, even though "home" is underground and the land has been sold.

The House of Breath (1950) is a lamentation for the lost. Charity, Texas, is gone and its inhabitants are ghosts, resuscitated by the efforts of a single estranged survivor. The narrator, archetypalized as "Boy," occupies a present time and place from which he is alienated, and he narrates out of an orphic need to enter the world of the dead. He announces his need at the outset: ". . . to find out what we are, we must enter back into the ideas and the dreams of worlds that bore and dreamt us and there find, waiting within worn mouths, the speech that is ours."[49] He descends into a realm where

(. . . faces are unreal, worn blurred stone faces of ancient metopes of kin, caught in soundless shapes of tumult, wrestling with invasion of some haunted demon race, half-animal, half-angel – O agony of faces without features like faces in fogs of dreams of sorrow and horror, worn holes of mouths opened, calling cries that cannot be heard, saying what words, what choked names of breath that must be heard). . . . (9)

During the course of the narrator's visit to this underworld, faces come into focus, as do the features of the land above ground. In the end, Boy is able, like Orpheus, to return to the surface to sing to the rocks, the trees, and to a human community that includes the reader. A picture of a blind girl with a lyre on the kitchen wall in Charity, along with the map ("the world's body") tacked up beside her, images Boy's orphic achievement.

So we understand Boy's problem as the disintegration of the self in a modern U.S. city, and his narrative project as his reintegration into the vanished community of Charity and the natural world that contains it. Repeated images of fog and melting and dissolution remind us of the narrator's need to let go his individual ego, to merge with the community of the dead and with the land. By the end of the novel, Boy has spoken and listened to the inhabitants of Charity, as well as to the voices of the town itself, the river, the well, the shutters, and the cistern wheel. The town of Charity is a principal narrator, as is the River (with a capital R) that runs through it. The narrator's project of reintegration, then, involves not only his family and his regional culture but the natural world as well. Hence the novel's ambiguous subtitle, *Under All the Land Lies the Title*: Goyen's articulate/d earth can and must be repossessed emotionally, despite the bills of sale.

Elena Garro's *Recollections of Things to Come* (1963) is not so sanguine. Her novel contains more of the narrative devices that we associate with magical realism and, predictably for a Latin American writer, more references to specific political events. Garro's story takes place during the Cristero rebellion, a popular uprising against government repression of the Catholic Church that occurred in the aftermath of the Mexican Revolution, primarily in the Mexican states of Jalisco, Michoacán, and Colima during the second half of the 1920s. The story is set in, and narrated by, the town of Ixtepec.[50] Garro devises a dual narrator: a "we" that is the collective voice of the dead town and an "I" that belongs to the stone promontory upon which the town was situated. The novel begins:

> Aquí estoy, sentado sobre esta piedra aparente. Sólo mi memoria sabe lo que encierra. La veo y me recuerdo, y como el agua va al agua, así yo, melancólico, vengo a encontrarme en su imagen cubierta por el polvo, rodeada por las hierbas, encerrada en sí misma y condenada a la memoria y a su variado espejo. La veo, me veo y me transfiguro en multitud de colores y de tiempos. Estoy y estuve en muchos ojos. Yo sólo soy memoria y la memoria que de mí se tenga.[51]

> Here I sit on what looks like a stone. Only my memory knows what it holds. I see it and I remember, and as water flows into water, so I, melancholically, come to find myself in its image, covered with dust, surrounded by grass, self-contained and condemned to memory and its variegated mirror. I see it, I see myself, and I

am transfigured into a multitude of colors and times. I am and I was in many eyes. I am only memory and the memory that one has of me.[52]

Here, too, the title lies under all the land, and history is grounded in more ways than one; people speak from underground, the earth itself speaks, and the story they tell is of a community that has gone nowhere.

Porfirio Díaz, Francisco Madero, Venustiano Carranza, Emiliano Zapata, Pancho Villa, Alvaro Obregón – the great actors in Mexico's now mythic revolutionary drama – provide the backdrop for the fateful occupation of Ixtepec by federal troops, counterrevolutionary ruffians sent to impose the government's ban on Catholic practices. Their commander, General Rosas, has no interest in the liberal reforms that impelled Mexico's postrevolutionary suppression of the Catholic Church. His only interest is to impose his personal will and he instantly becomes absolute dictator in Ixtepec. Rosas brings with him his captive mistress, Julia, a woman set apart by her electrifying beauty and, as Rosas' mistress, her sexual power. She becomes a living legend in the town, an obsessive presence more dangerous to the communal order than General Rosas himself. But such is her mythic energy that she magically escapes from Ixtepec one night, aided by a former lover, a mysterious stranger who arrives to conjure Julia's getaway.

With their disappearance, political realities overwhelm magical resolutions: the mythologized Julia may escape as in a fairy tale, but the town cannot. Isabel Moncada, daughter of an upstanding family in Ixtepec, replaces Julia as General Rosas' lover, but her seduction by abusive power turns her, at the end of the novel, into the very stone that has narrated her story. *Recollections of Things to Come* chronicles not the psychological reintegration of an individual, as does *The House of Breath*, but a community's futile attempt to construct an ongoing history in the face of impossible political obstacles. As my summary suggests, not the least of these obstacles is a social order that defines women solely in terms of the men with whom they sleep.

The third of my American books of the dead, Juan Rulfo's brief masterpiece *Pedro Páramo* (1955), is the most metaphysical. The word *páramo* in Mexican Spanish signifies a high plateau, and carries the connotation of bleak, rugged, abandoned terrain; Pedro/Peter is, of course, related etymologically to *piedra*, stone, rock. In an essay called "Landscape and the Novel in Mexico," Octavio Paz says that Rulfo's landscape "is a symbol and something more than a symbol: a voice entering into the dialogue, and in the end the principal character in the story. . . . [It] never refers only to itself; it always points to something else, to something beyond itself. It is a metaphysic, a religion, an idea of man and the cosmos."[53] Rulfo's ghost town, Comala, is explicitly located in the *páramo* of his native state of Jalisco, but his haunting and poignant images insistently transcend specific location. This is, in part, because Comala is at the intersection of mythic spaces; in it, the necrogeographies of both Mexican Catholic and indigenous afterworlds coverge. More than Goyen's Charity or Garro's Ixtepec, Rulfo's Comala is an archetypal enactment of a culture's conception of the place and performance of the dead.

Pedro Páramo begins with the first person account of the character Juan Preciado:

> Vine a Comala porque me dijeron que acá vivía mi padre, un tal Pedro Páramo. Mi madre me lo dijo. Y yo le prometí que vendría a verlo en cuanto ella muriera. . . .
>
> . . .
>
> Era ese tiempo de la canícula, cuando el aire de agosto sopla caliente, envenenado por el olor podrido de las saponarias.
>
> El camino subía y bajaba: *"Sube o baja según se va o se viene. Para el que va, sube; para el que viene, baja"*.[54]

> I came to Comala because I was told that my father, a certain Pedro Páramo, was living here. My mother told me so, and I promised her that I would come to see him as soon as she died. . . .
>
> . . .
>
> It was in the dog-days, when the hot August wind is poisoned by the rotten smell of the saponaria, and the road went up and down, up and down. They say a road goes up or down depending on whether you're coming or going. If you're going away it's uphill, but it's downhill if you're coming back.[55]

Downhill, indeed. Juan enters an underground community of ghosts who have died because the town boss, Pedro Páramo, has willed it so.

In the first half of *Pedro Páramo*, Juan Preciado's conversations with the dead are interpolated with third-person sections describing the career of rape, murder, and political cunning that has made Pedro Páramo the absolute owner of Comala. Midway through the novel, Juan seems to join the dead once and for all, to die himself, though his conversations with the dead before this point leave open the possibility that he has been dead all along. Here, as in *The House of Breath*, images of melting and dissolving signal the character's integration into earth. Juan lies down beside a woman who becomes the very soil in which they are both buried:

> El calor me hizo despertar al filo de la medianoche. Y el sudor. El cuerpo de aquella mujer hecho de tierra, envuelto en costras de tierra, se desbarataba como si estuviera derritiéndose en un charco de lodo. Yo me sentía nadar entre el sudor que chorreaba de ella y me faltó el aire que se necesita para respirar. . . .
>
> . . .
>
> No había aire. Tuve que sorber el mismo aire que salía de mi boca, deteniéndolo con las manos antes de que se fuera. Lo sentía ir y venir, cada vez menos; hasta que se hizo tan delgado que se filtró entre mis dedos para siempre.
>
> Digo para siempre.
>
> Tengo memoria de haber visto algo como nubes espumosas haciendo remolino sobre mi cabeza y luego enjuagarme con aquella espuma y perderme en su nublazón. Fue lo último que vi. (74)

. . .

The heat made me wake up. It was midnight. The heat and the sweat. Her body was made of earth, was covered with crusts of earth, and now it was melting into a pool of mud. I felt as if I were drowning in the sweat that streamed from her. I couldn't breathe. . . .

. . .

There wasn't any air. I had to swallow the same air I breathed out, holding it back with my hands so it wouldn't escape. I could feel it coming and going, and each time it was less and less, until it got so thin it slipped through my fingers forever.

Forever.

I remember seeing something like a cloud of foam, and washing myself in the foam, and losing myself in the cloud. That was the last thing I saw. (55–56)

Death is dramatized as a metamorphosis from one state of consciousness to another rather than a radical interruption or change of form. So Juan joins the faceless chorus of Comala's *calaveras* (skeletons). The text no longer provides his first-person account; rather, the third person narrator circles back to recount the decline and death of the town that occurred long before the point at which the novel begins.

The voices that tell Comala's history are not so much voices as echoes of voices that float free of faces, bodies, and individual histories. Goyen's description of the forgotten inhabitants of Charity at the beginning of *The House of Breath* (. . . "faces in fogs of dreams of sorrow and horror, worn holes of mouths opened calling cries that cannot be heard. . . ." 9) also describes Rulfo's dead in *Pedro Páramo*. But in *Pedro Páramo*, the faces never come into focus for Juan Preciado (or the reader) as they do for Boy in *The House of Breath*. In Comala, images of blurred sight and muffled sound are everywhere: "the thin sound of weeping," "the echo of the shadows," "voices worn out with use." Juan says, "Y de las paredes parecían destilar los murmullos como si se filtraran de entre las grietas y las descarapeladuras. Yo los oía. Eran voces de gente; pero no voces claras, sino secretas, como si me murmuraran algo al pasar, o como si zumbaran contra mis oídos" (76; "And those murmurs seemed to come from the walls, to seep out of the cracks and broken spots. They were people's voices but they weren't clear, they were almost secret, as if they were whispering something to me as I passed, or were only a buzzing in my ears" 57). At one point, Juan calls an interlocutor by the name of Doroteo, to which the voice replies, "Da lo mismo. Aunque mi nombre sea Dorotea. Pero da lo mismo" (74; "It's all the same. My name is really Dorotea. But it's all the same" 56). Even gender distinctions are blurred, muted, effaced.

Breath is a central image in *Pedro Páramo*, too. In the passage I cited above, Juan's breath is so thin it slips through his fingers forever. This image recalls Boy's final sentence in *The House of Breath*: ". . . it seemed that the house was built of the most fragile web of breath and I had blown it – and that with my breath I could blow it all away" (193–94). Though similar on the surface, these metaphors bode different ends. Whereas Rulfo's image signals the final dissolution of Juan's ego into the community of death and earth, Goyen's image signals Boy's ultimate movement toward individuation. If the voices of the dead in Charity breathe life into those who can hear, Comala's dead sing no such song. "Me mataron los murmullos" (75; "It was the voices that killed me" 57), Juan tells Comala's ghosts, after he has himself become one of them. I will speculate further on these differences in the concluding section of this chapter. Here, my point is to call attention to the fact that though Rulfo's and Garro's Mexican characters are not revitalized by the mythic realities they encounter below the surface of the American land, their narratives of communal disintegration depend upon them as clearly as does Goyen's narrative of individual integration.

What, then, are the shared cultural topographies of these American books of the dead? The ancient Egyptian books of the dead were guides to the underworld containing prayers and spells designed to ward off dangers that the dead were likely to encounter there. Variously called "Book of Coming Forth by Day," "Book of the Underworld," "Book of Breathings," these texts were at once how-to manuals and maps of metaphysical space. Western classical literature also abounds in books of the dead, narratives that describe the negotiations of heroes and gods in the underworld. I have already mentioned Orpheus; one also thinks of Odysseus and Aeneas and their literary offspring in Dante's more elaborate medieval Catholic underworld. The "theme of descent," as Northrop Frye calls this literary archetype, obviously animates the novels of Goyen, Garro, and Rulfo.[56] When, in *The House of Breath*, Boy says, "I will dive down naked and alone into that place and touch what I never had and hold it there" (178–9), he speaks for the narrators of *Pedro Páramo* and *Recollections of Things to Come* as well. The River that runs through Charity speaks, acknowledging the universality of Boy's project: ". . . to drop down into any of us, into depths (in river or self or well or cellar) is to lower into sorrow and truth" (28). Boy is an archetypal descender, and a descendant, too, of this archetypal Western literary tradition.

But Boy, Juan Preciado, and Isabel Moncada also move in other directions, as will I. Orpheus, Odysseus, and Aeneas are far removed in time and space from the American territory I am mapping here. While Goyen's, Garro's, and Rulfo's books of the dead are enriched by resonances of these European literary precursors, their novels seem to me to create different kinds of underworlds and stress other aspects of their characters' descent. Their emphasis is not on their capacity to *free* themselves from the earthbound dead, but rather their capacity to become permanent *residents* of the ghostly communities they enter. They must become integral elements of earth itself. Orpheus and Aeneas care nothing for the landscape of the underworld – indeed, Orpheus is commanded upon pain of great loss *not* to look back at it. The French painter Jean-Baptiste-Camille Corot understood this classical tradition perfectly. In his 1861 masterpiece *Orpheus Leading Eurydice from the Underworld*, he depicts the couple leaving a gray landscape peopled with pale, listless figures, Eurydice still veiled though no longer featureless. Our three American books of the dead, on the contrary, provide remarkably specific evocations of place. Their underworld settings – Charity, Ixtepec, Comala – are not mere backdrops for the action, but agents of the action. The earth is animate and natural phenomena are instrumental, generative. Boy, Juan Preciado, and Isabel Moncada enter the earth and converse with it and its inhabitants. The "world's body" is alive, and these characters know that they must occupy its body before they can fully occupy their own. As I have said, these are not realists of distance, but of depth.

Goyen, Garro, and Rulfo embody earth as a sedimentation of cultures, a stratification of the living remains of ancient peoples. The "New World" in their novels is not new but old: they incorporate belief systems that reflect Amerindian attitudes and ritual practices involving the land as the habitation of both the living and the dead. Boy, Juan Preciado, and Isabel Moncada look back with regret to a time before the land was exploited by careless commercialism or appropriated by corrupt *caudillos* (bosses). They remember a time before the modern Western separation of culture and nature, when the land was not conceived as private property in need of "development." At first glance, these memories seem to contain the "wilderness," "virgin land," "paradise lost," and/or "utopia" motifs so common in American romance literature. But there is something different, something un-Western, about these embodiments of earth.

In fact, Goyen, Garro, and Rulfo reject the Eurocentric conception of the American land as "virgin" in order to dramatize their characters' experience of the earth as alive with ancient peoples and rituals patterns and sacred places. Their characters speak for/from/as the earth: they speak with dirt in their mouths, they eat the earth, they are themselves "figures of dust" (an image from a story by Goyen to which I will return.) And recall García Márquez's character Rebeca in *One Hundred Years of Solitude*, who eats dirt, ". . . rescatando el apetito ancestral, el gusto de los minerales primarios, la satisfacción sin resquicios del alimento original" (61; ". . . getting back her ancestral appetite, the taste of primary minerals, the unbridled satisfaction of what was the original food . . ." 67). But this theme is not developed by García Márquez; *One Hundred Years of Solitude* is not a novel of the animate earth such as those of Rulfo, Garro, or Goyen.

In Rulfo's *Pedro Páramo*, Juan Preciado suffers the muffled voices of the dead and their ironic descriptions of Comala's bygone beauty; he lies with them, and then melts bodily into their earth. Isabel *is* the rock that is Ixtepec in Garro's *Recollections of Things to Come*, a rock that laments the time when its splendor did not fall on ignorance, on "voluntary forgetful-ness": ". . . yo me veía como joya. Las piedras adquirían volúmenes y for-mas diferentes y una sola me hubiera empobrecido con sólo moverse de lugar" (116; ". . . I saw myself as a jewel. The stones acquired different shapes and sizes and I would have been impoverished if a single one had changed its place" 111). In Goyen's *The House of Breath*, phenomena and consciousness merge. Boy's psychic integration depends upon his physical integration into the earth, upon his bodily, sensuous contact with the world, a contact reiterated in his incantatory phrase "I touch you and name you." Boy makes love to the River, and the River to the land. The River summarizes Boy's erotic engagement of earth: "Everything flows into everything and carries with it and within it all lives of its life and others' life and all is a murmuring and whispering of things changing into each other, breeding and searching and reaching and withdrawing and dying" (28). All is in process, intermingling, conjoining: physical and metaphysi-cal, body and mind, self and other, life and death.

The perspectives of Rulfo's and Garro's narrators reflect the cosmology of the Nahuatl-speaking peoples of the central and northern highlands of Mexico. The Nahua peoples conceived of five "world-directions": North, South, East, West, and the Center, the direction of up and down. The human figure representing this direction in the pre-Hispanic Borgia Codices is painted as if propelled by centrifugal force, his body spinning, his feet above his head, his arms below and in motion. Earth is above and below and around him: he hovers within it. So also Garro's narrator circles above and around herself, as it were, in the Center: "Desde esta altura me contemplo: grande, tendido en un valle seco. Me rodean unas montañas espinosas y unas llanuras amarillas pobladas de coyotes. . . . Quisiera no tener memoria o convertirme en el piadoso polvo para escapar a la conde-na de mirarme" (9; "From this height I contemplate myself: vast, lying in a dry valley. I am surrounded by spiny mountains and yellow plains inhab-ited by coyotes. . . . I wish I had no memory, or that I could change myself into pious dust to escape the penalty of seeing myself" 3). The "pious dust" is proposed as the earth's antidote to the abuses of human history – too late, it would seem, since the abuses have already occurred and the community is already dead. But the land is still animate, still contains the communi-ty, still functions as a psychic component of character and a source of nar-rative energy.

Nahua culture posits the integration of human, natural, and cosmic realms: Inga Clendinnen's study confirms its "flesh-and-earth identifica-tions."[57] Garro's characters are repeatedly described in terms of natural phenomena. The eyes of one character are described as "deep and [having] rivers and sheep bleating sadly in their depths." The narrator sympathizes with Julia: "Solitaria, perdida en Ixtepec, ignoraba mis voces, mis calles, mis árboles, mis gentes. En sus ojos oscuros se veían las huellas de ciudades y de torres lejanas y extrañas a nosotros" (76; "Isolated, out of her element, she was cut off from my voices, my streets, my people. Her dark eyes showed traces of cities and towers, distant and strange" 71). Yet another character is described as wishing to find "the comings and goings of the stars and the tides, the luminous time that spins around the sun" (255). Topography, climate, and the products of the land are registered in/as the characters' somatic and psychic terrain. Like Goyen's narrating town, river, and wind, Garro's narrative voices become a kind of spirit-field that penetrates the earth and the population of Ixtepec.

Garro refuses the Western hierarchy that places nature at the service of human beings. Rather, she returns mythically to the pre-Hispanic belief that it was humans who served the earth and nourished it with their blood. Octavio Paz writes about the practice of human sacrifice, without which, it was believed, the sun would not rise: "Without human blood, life would cease to flow and the universe would come to a halt. This view of the world and of mankind is the exact opposite of our modern conception, which sees nature as an enormous reservoir of energy and resources that the human race can dominate and exploit with impunity."[58] Beyond practices of human sacrifice, Paz writes that Mesoamerican cultures projected onto the natural world what he calls a "universal sympathy," a "vital fluid that unites all animate beings – humans, animals, plants – with the elements, the planets, and the stars" (20). Garro's narrator would seem to trace what happens when humans upset this universal sympathy, when neither the earth nor the cosmos can redress their violations. This narrative strategy allows her to reaffirm the agrarian, communitarian, mythic underpinnings of Mexico's indigenous heritage even as she describes their unsettling by European attitudes, and their ultimate demise.

In *Pedro Páramo*, indigenous and Catholic systems of belief intersect to create a syncretic mythic space. Rulfo's underground community of Comala reflects the Catholic concept of purgatory, as critics have frequently noted, but more importantly (and more subtly), it reflects the complex afterworld of pre-Hispanic Mexico. Hugo G. Nutini, in his remarkable book *Todos Santos in Rural Tlaxcala*, states that among Nahuatl-speaking peoples in central Mexcio there was no fundamental distinction between cosmology and theology:

The origins of the gods and the world, the provenance of human beings, their trajectory on earth, their relationship to the gods, and their final destination were basically a single normative system. In this conception of the universe, humans were created by the gods, went through life in intimate ritual and ceremonial contact with their creators, and joined them in their final destination. . . . *The structure and social organization of earthly life were mirrored in the afterlife,* where the dead went to serve their creators. As servants of the gods in the afterlife, the dead were at the same time men and gods.[59]

The realms of the dead and the living reflect one another, are penetrable, permeable, and mutually knowable. Mictlan, literally "the place of the dead," is not like the Catholic concept of purgatory in that it implies no system of reward or punishment. Individuals were accommodated in one of its nine infraworlds or thirteen supraworlds not according to their moral behavior but according to the cause or circumstances of their death. Thus, someone who had died by drowning or in circumstances associated with water would naturally proceed to the region of Tlaloc, the god of water; those who died in battle or in childbirth joined Huitzilopochtli, the god of war and the sun; death by natural causes (disease, death in infancy) also resulted in discrete communities around appropriate deities whom the dead served as intermediaries with the living. Nutini tells us that there were, presumably, "as many celebrations of the dead during the year as there were identifiable ways of dying marked by patron gods" (69). One's place and activity in death follows directly from one's final act or condition in life: death is not a truncation of life but a continuation. If the Catholic concept of purgatory separates the dead from the living by a psychological (as well as theological) abyss, the Nahua afterworld is joined to this world and reiterates its structures and concerns. It offers a bridge to the world of the living, not a radical judgment upon it.

Amerindian mythology is not explicit in *Pedro Páramo*, but indigenous attitudes toward death are nonetheless present as they are currently practiced in Mexico. On November 2, the Day of the Dead (*Día de muertos*), All Souls' Day (*Todos Santos*), food is placed on graves so that the spirits of the dead may eat while they converse with the living. Candles and flowers are arranged on altars (*ofrendas*) to welcome departed friends and family members in homes, restaurants, markets, as well as in cemeteries and churches. To make the dead feel at home, their favorite foods are placed on the *ofrendas*, along with traditional breads and sweets. Objects that were used by the dead during life in their professions and pastimes are also placed on the altars and graves to make their one-night stay familiar.

The most important symbol of the Day of the Dead celebrations are the toy replicas of skeletons (*calaveras*, literally "skulls"). They are everywhere, made of everything – paper, papier maché, wire, wood, sugar – and are historically associated with a satirical verse form also called a *calavera*. *Calaveras* are still published in tabloids sold in the streets at the time of Todos Santos: presumably social criticism can be practiced with impunity only from the grave. These satirical verses are, in turn, visually associated with the engravings of the great Mexican printmaker José Guadalupe Posada (1852-1913), who illustrated them in the popular press at the end of the last century and the beginning of this one. In Posada's engravings, *calaveras* form communal scenes representing social classes and political events; on individual graves, miniature *calaveras* re-enact the favorite activities of the person buried there. *Calaveras* celebrate the pleasures of the living, mock our follies, and remind us that death is a part of life. They laugh at death, domesticate it, socialize it. Rulfo's characters in *Pedro Páramo* may be thought of as *calaveras* in this popular tradition of the living dead; they are satiric go-betweens for whom life and death are indistinguishable, for whom "underworld" and "afterworld" are meaningless spatial and temporal markers.

It is here that Goyen's novel most clearly converges with those of Rulfo and Garro: the necrogeography of *The House of Breath* also subverts the Western separation of life and afterlife, body and soul. In a fashion more Mexican than Texan, Goyen privileges the past by honoring the animate earth and the living spirits it contains. The River is, again, the novel's authority: "And we are to keep turning the wheels we turn, we are wind we are water we are yearning; we are to keep rising and falling, hovering at our own marks, then falling, then rising. (Who can set a mark or measure us? They cannot name my tides or measure me by the marks drawn on a wall; I hover") (28). Goyen, like Garro and Rulfo, challenges the hierarchy upon which Frye's "theme of descent" is based, a hierarchy that places earth below heaven, the world of the dead below that of the living. He recognizes that this metaphoric axis does not fully express his narrator's need, that it belies our *residencia en la tierra*, our complex location *in/on* the world's body. Goyen's earth is circumambient and central; like the turning figure in the Borgia Codices that represents the direction of the Center in the Nahua cosmos, his characters must learn not only to dive, but also to hover.

The photographer Keith Carter has recorded the topography, fauna and flora of East Texas. *The Blue Man* is Carter's collection of photographic images of this region – William Goyen's region and his own. In an interview, Carter refers to the region as Deep East Texas, a term that suggests the mythic depths of place.[60] (The term is also used unmythically by professional and commercial associations to indicate the fifteen county area along the Louisiana border between the Trinity and Sabine rivers.) Carter reminds us that this part of Texas has little in common with the dry, flat terrain of the rest of the state:

East Texas is primarily rural and dotted with forests and lakes. It's culturally and ecologically diverse. The Big Thicket is there. Four of the five carnivorous plants found in North America occur in the thicket. You can find things like orchids growing next to cactus. The last vestiges of the red wolf are thought to be there, and every now and then you hear of the sightings of the supposedly extinct ivory bill woodpecker. It's a real peculiar place, a landscape full of baygalls and titi thickets. (124)

The interviewer asks Carter to describe these natural phenomena.

Well, a baygall is a depression that has been cut off from a river or creek at one time. It's a very swamp-like region with tupelo and cypress. Alligators, beavers, deer, otters will make their homes in a baygall. They're very dark, very mysterious places. A titi thicket is made up of the titi vine, which is something like a grapevine. The region is called the Big Thicket because in some areas it's virtually impenetrable. All kinds of buried treasure is in there, legends, Indian ghosts, unexplainable moving lights. Anyway, it's a landscape that knows how to keep a secret. (124)

A landscape that knows how to keep a secret, and William Goyen grew up hearing the whispers.

In his introduction to his collected stories, Goyen insists upon the ancient voices that animate his Deep East Texas earth: "The landscape of my stories, generally East Texas, is pastoral, river-haunted, tree shaded, mysterious and bewitched. Spirits and ghosts inhabit it: the generations have not doubted their presence, their doings."[61] Goyen's reference to "the generations" suggests the rootedness of Deep East Texas, a relatively poor rural population that does not conform to U.S. patterns of mobility. In *The Blue Man*, Keith Carter refers to a family in one of his photographs that has been on the same land since before Texas became a republic. They have no telephone, no television, so he asks them what they do for entertainment. The mother replies:

"We go down to the creek after it rains," she said. "Arrowheads, spearheads, we have mounds all over this land. We have all these animals." She took me into this little room. They live in the house that Mr. Cutler's great-grandfather built, and there's this whole wall of arrowheads and spearheads that I suspect some museum would dearly love to have. (128)

Deep East Texas is spotted with Caddoan burial mounds, testaments to a past that pervades the present in this region.

I do not know whether Goyen was consciously influenced by Amerindian social structures or cosmogonies, as Rulfo and Garro certainly were. But I do know that Goyen's Deep East Texas retains echoes of non-European cultures, both in his own experience of growing up in the region and in his reader's experience of the region he creates in his fiction. Because my perspective is comparative, I will again cite Octavio Paz. In a useful essay of cultural comparison entitled "Mexico and the United States," Paz writes about modern Mexican culture that there is always a part of the culture that is not Western: "Every Mexican carries within him this continuity, which goes back two thousand years. It doesn't matter that this presence is almost always unconscious and assumes naïve forms of legend and even superstition. It is not something known but something lived."[62] Deep East Texas resembles Mexico in this way, and Goyen, like Rulfo and Garro, *lives* this knowledge. He dramatizes an indigenous part of the collective unconscious of his region, a part that is intuited, imagined, invented.

This assertion will need historical grounding because it does not generally occur to contemporary residents of the U.S. that Amerindian culture might be a living cultural presence. Rather, the "minority" status of Native American cultures is recognized as something that survives separately in New Mexico, Oklahoma, Oregon, Alaska, but does not affect U.S. culture generally. Goyen reflects a different attitude. In his fictional construction of the animate earth and its inhabitants, he resists the accepted American ideology that our indigenous past, because it is no longer visible in most parts of the United States, has been totally erased. He refuses to resign himself to such a loss.

Why should Goyen's attitudes seem so Mexican? And why should he hear indigenous ancestral echoes that most U.S. writers do not? I propose that it is because the culture of Deep East Texas, like that of Mexico, is the product of racial and cultural *mestizaje*, the *mixing* of histories and races and cultures. Of course, Rulfo and Garro, as contemporary Mexican writers, write in and about a mestizo culture created from the encounter of European and indigenous cultures and races in Mesoamerica. Rulfo's state of Jalisco is not populated by indigenous groups to the same extent as Garro's state of Puebla; nonetheless, in the work of both writers we may safely assume the active presence of indigenous cultural beliefs and practices alongside those imported from Europe. But what about William Goyen, writing in and about Deep East Texas in the mid-twentieth century?

Octavio Paz's insights are instructive. Paz makes a strong distinction between the culturally exclusive model, upon which the United States was founded, and the culturally inclusive model of Mexico. In the essay that I just cited, Paz argues that whereas Mexico was settled by Spaniards who justified their military conquest on the grounds of the need (and duty) to convert the conquered, North American Protestant settlers had no such aim. The imperial project of the Spanish Catholics demanded the assimilation of indigenous peoples and their cultures; the idols were baptized and indigenous women impregnated. The Protestant settlers of North America, on the contrary, had little interest in converting Native Americans or intermarrying. In fact, the early Puritan settlers had a horror of such contact, as their name suggests and their written texts amply confirm. They preferred to ignore the indigenous cultures they encountered in America, and their descendants to annihilate them when they could no longer ignore them.

From our historical position, we deplore the destruction of cultures and lives caused by the imperial ideologies of both Spain and England. Certainly Paz's point is not to vindicate the crimes of either empire but to show the cultural consequences of these different policies in New Spain and New England. He argues that the Spanish colonizers were culturally centralist and inclusive, whereas the Anglo colonizers were pluralist and exclusive. By this he means that the Spanish included cultural differences within their single ecclesiastical hierarchy, whereas the English did not because they did not need to. In a pluralist culture, differences can be separated out, tolerated, or ignored. If one group or individual in New England differed from another, that group or individual simply separated and began another cult or colony. Paz notes that this exclusivity worked well in North America, where indigenous groups were nomadic rather than settled, and English settlers did not need to reckon with great cities such as those encountered in Mesoamerica by the Spanish. Thus, unlike modern Mexico, which is a mestizo culture resulting from imperial policies that included and assimilated indigenous cultures, modern U.S. culture is the product of a pluralist model that moved indigenous cultures to the margins, and then off the edge. Paz concludes:

In the United States, the Indian element does not appear. This, in my opinion, is the major difference between our two countries. The Indians who were not exterminated were corralled in "reservations." The Christian horror of "fallen nature" extended to the natives of America: the United States was founded on a land without a past. The historical memory of Americans is European, not American. For this reason, one of the most powerful and persistent themes in American literature, from Whitman to William Carlos Williams and from Melville to Faulkner, has been the search for (or invention of) American roots. We owe some of the major works of the modern era to this desire for incarnation, this obsessive need to be rooted in American soil. (362)

Paz's analysis of the U.S. national ideology of a great "melting pot" implies that the "melting" has corresponded to a national need to homogenize cultural differences rather than respect and understand them. The English colonizers were largely blind to indigenous cultures, a blindness that has continued to afflict U.S. culture to this day.

While Paz's metaphor of rootedness in the American soil might seem to coincide with my metaphor of the animate earth, it does not, for Paz's soil is silent. His argument is historically sound with respect to colonizing patterns in the northeastern and central plains regions of North America, but Deep East Texas and William Goyen's fiction do not conform to Paz's generalizations. After all, Texas was not settled by Anglos until after the first quarter of the nineteenth century, and not in significant numbers until after 1848. It was, of course, a part of the Spanish Empire in the New World, explored by Cabeza de Vaca in 1528 and Hernán de Soto in 1541, and subsequently colonized by Spaniards. After Mexico gained its independence from Spain in 1821, Tejas was a state in the Mexican republic; in 1836, when a group of Anglo settlers declared their independence from Mexico, Mexico sent troops to prevent the secession. Texas' admission to the Union in 1845 was considered by Mexico to be an act of war, but by 1848 Mexico was forced to relinquish Texas and more than half of the rest of its territory as well. The Treaty of Guadalupe Hidalgo legitimized the purchase of Mexican land that was not for sale, land usurped by the U.S. in what Octavio Paz has called "one of the most unjust wars in the history of

imperialist expansion" (124). Until 1848, then, Texas was Hispanic, populated by settlers who operated according to the centralist, inclusive cultural model outlined by Paz.

There were a great number of distinct indigenous groups in Tejas/Texas,
many of which do correspond to Paz's generalization about North American indigenous groups as nomadic hunters rather than settled cultivators.
In the western and northern Tejas plains, there were buffalo-hunting
Apaches and Comanches and Kiowas; in South Texas and Northern Mexico, the Coahuiltecas, hunters of small animals and gatherers of wild
crops.[63] Again, though, East Texas is an exception. The Caddoan-speaking
cultures of East Texas were primarily settled agriculturists rather than
hunters. But before discussing this exception, I should mention the shared
characteristics of the tribal groups in the region.

William W. Newcomb Jr. points out that all groups indigenous to
Tejas/Texas were structured according to bonds of kinship rather than
occupation, class, or wealth; family relationships extended throughout
entire tribal communities.[64] Furthermore, all tribal groups shared a sense
of the natural world; they lived in a direct, personal, and intimate relationship with nature, and invested animals and natural phenomena with
supernatural powers. Newcomb states:

Perhaps the most dramatic differences between Anglo-Americans and Indians are
found in attitudes about the earth. No Indian people in Texas regarded the varied
lands they hunted over or raised corn on as commodities to be bought and sold,
or to be held or owned by individuals. The majority, at least implicitly, regarded
themselves as belonging to or as part of the natural world. Often the earth was
regarded explicitly as Mother. Many consciously sought to live in harmony with
the earth, with the animals it nurtured, and the forces that created it all. (47–48)

Newcomb mentions especially the Caddoan-speaking groups as believing
that the Earth Mother had given birth to everything, and that "people lived
on her and flourished under her guidance; it was unimaginable that individuals might possess her, inconceivable that they could sell her" (48).

The Caddo confederacies, loosely associated tribal groups sharing a
common language, were, as I have said, a settled culture of agriculturists.
East Texas' climate and topography favors agriculture as the rest of Texas
territory does not; it is a subhumid, mild climate, a low-lying land that
slopes gently toward the Gulf of Mexico. The name "Texas" comes from
the Hasinai confederation of Caddoes. Pronounced "Tayshas" or "Taychas," the word means allies or friends and refers to the tribes in the confederation. The Caddoes also used "Taychas" to refer to the Spaniards
(however mistakenly, we now feel), and the Spaniards in turn used it to
refer to the Caddoes and other friendly indigenous groups.[65]

The abundant food supply of the agricultural Caddoes allowed for a
denser population and more complex social institutions than those of the

plains hunters. Large ceremonial centers, including burial and temple mounds, formed the nucleus of Caddoan communities, and their burial practices are well documented by colonizing Spanish clerics. Fray Francisco Casañas described the tribal practices of the Caddoan culture in his record written between 1691 and 1722.[66] For the Caddoes, as for the Nahuatl-speaking cultures of central Mexico, life and death were not separate conditions. The spirit was not thought to leave the body immediately, but needed nourishment for six days after death. Food was brought for the spirit (one thinks of the contemporary Mexican practice of placing food on graves on the Day of the Dead), and personal equipment and artifacts were buried with the body for later use. It was customary for the mourners to touch the corpse and then their own bodies in order to send messages with the corpse to dead relatives. According to Newcomb, just before burial, a holy man would advise the dead person that he or she must now go to "that other house" to join the dead and take up life there (302–3). Caddoan burial mounds began with the subsurface burial of five individuals; over the years, their complex layerings grew to heights of twenty feet or more.[67] There is, in fact, an important Caddoan site near Alto, Texas, about forty miles northeast of Goyen's hometown of Trinity. The site was first noted by archeologists in 1919 and excavated systematically during the 1930s. The residents of the region would surely have been aware of the burial mounds and the ancient communities they represented. Despite the virtual disappearance of the Caddoes by the last quarter of the nineteenth century, their traditions continue to be lived, if not known (to use Paz's formulation), in Goyen's Deep East Texas.[68]

Besides the indigenous underpinnings of *The House of Breath*, we may locate explicit traces of Transcendentalism in Goyen's animate earth. Like Borges, Goyen responds to the Transcendentalist doctrine of the immanence of Spirit in the universe, the interpenetration of the physical and spiritual. In one italicized passage, Goyen's narrator metaphorically becomes the world: "*O I am leaf and I am wind and I am light. Something in the world links faces and leaves and rivers and woods and wind together and makes them a string of medallions with all our faces on them, worn forever round our necks, kin*" (48, Goyen's emphasis). Conversely, as we have seen, nature is humanized and embodied. A voice from the well (a "well-voice") is described "like a speaking mouth filled with wind, opening and closing in the wind. . ." (61). The Emersonian identity of microcosm and macrocosm, individual and archetype, is lyrically presented by (and in) Boy: "Something forms within the world of a tear, shaped by the world that caused it; something takes shape with this uttered breath that builds an image of breath" (43). And Whitman is also echoed here – not Whitman the bombastic individualist but, on the contrary, Borges' Whitman, the poet whose epic hero is everyman. In a direct allusion to Whitman's "As a Child Went Forth," Boy says, "I melted into the world and changed into everything that had ever been created or constructed, buildings, woods, rivers, pomp, love, history; and everything entered into me, all involved in all" (33). In such images, we sense the complementary conceptions of "universal sympathy" in Transcendentalism and pre-Hispanic Mesoamerican mythology.[69] I do not wish to cast Goyen oversimply as a Texas Transcendentalist. Rather, I want to suggest that he adds the fecundity and agency of Romantic nature to the vitality of the spirits of Mesoamerican myth. In *The House of Breath*, the nineteenth-century U.S. romance tradition provides the natural landscape in which Goyen's magical realist ghosts become audible.[70]

It is not just in Goyen's novel that we hear ancestral voices. His collection of short stories entitled *Ghost and Flesh* (1952) is perhaps his most Deep East Texan in its focus on kinship in/on/with the animate earth. Like *The House of Breath*, the stories in *Ghost and Flesh* are influenced by U.S. Romanticism, but here there are few literary allusions – only Goyen's sensitivity to his rural, regional culture, to the East Texas earth and its inhabitants. In these stories, Goyen's ear is pressed to the ground.

In "Ghost and Flesh, Water and Dirt," Goyen's narrator buries her daughter after an accident, and then her husband two weeks later when he kills himself from grief and guilt. Her husband returns to visit her from the dead, and he seems more an embodied *calavera* in Mexican style than a disembodied wraith.

"I'm Raymon Emmons," the steamin voice said, "and I'm here to stay; putt out my things that you've putt away, putt out my oatmeal bowl and putt hot oatmeal in it get out my rubberboots when it rains, iron my clothes and fix my supper. . . I never died and I'm here to stay."[71]

But Raymon Emmons' wife knows he's dead, however hungry and desiring, and she longs to join him underground: "I wish I uz dirt I wish I uz dirt. O I uz vile with grief" (57).

As in Juan Rulfo's Comala, where water is always seeping, steaming, and dripping upon the dead who swelter underground, this narrator's "Texis" (as she pronounces it and Goyen writes it) is hot and wet.

I wish I'd melt – and run down the drains. Wish I uz rain, fallin on the dirt of certain graves I know and seepin down into the dirt, could lie in the dirt with Raymon Emmons on one side and Chitta on the other. Wish I uz dirt. . . . (55)

She visits the graves "carryin potplants and cryin over the mounds" and lamenting "all my life is dirt I've got a famly [sic] of dirt" (53). The story concludes, as does Goyen's fiction so often, by affirming the commingling of the realms of the dead and the living. The narrator tells her listener (who is the reader):

... there's a time for live things and a time for dead, for ghosts and for flesh 'n bones: all life is just a sharin of ghosts and flesh. Us humans are part ghost and part flesh. . . . there's a world both places, a world where there's ghosts and a world where there's flesh. . . . (58)

She concludes that "ghosts can give you over to flesh 'n bones; and that flesh 'n bones, if you go roun when it's time, can send you back to a faithful ghost. One provides the other" (59).

In "The Children of Old Somebody," another of the stories in *Ghost and Flesh*, Goyen again dramatizes the permeability of the worlds of the dead and the living. This time he creates not so much a ghost or *calavera* as a mythological presence, a communal legend called "Old Ancestor" or "Old Somebody."

... he was a shape of dust – and if all things return to dust, fall back into it, dust was his great pile, he the dust grubber, himself formed of the dust of the ground, from which he would find the first things formed out of the ground and bring them to himself and to us all to see what would we call them. Breathed out of dust, he was yet the enemy of dust-eaters; he would save the dust from the appetite, from the blind voracious driving bit of hunger: the grasshopper and the worm. Then, before it all is eaten, he would have his hands in it, on it, to touch it to smut it with his fingermarks – but even more: to shape it, out of its own dust and with the miraculous light of his own dust, and thus set it away, preserved. (76)

Goyen connects the vitalizing activities of eating and touching to the earth, and to lying buried in it. The communal narrator of the story insists: "If we build the bridge of flesh we must cross over, over it, into the land of dust, and burn the bridge of burning flesh behind us: *cross over flesh to reach ghost*" (85, Goyen's emphasis).

This call to heed the voices that inhabit the earth is dramatized in the mythic origins of "Old Somebody." He is the impossible son of an old and barren couple, magically born in the woods and placed in a log, "a little wood animal," "a druid":

This little tree spirit, could you believe it, lay unmolested by the life of the ground or by gypsies, never an ant stung it or snake bit it, there was no hostility between its world and the creatures' world, that hostility is learnt. . . .

. . .

Now in the old histories we can read of such, like of Childe Percival and like of little princes, secret folk, kept in secret woods places by charmers or enchanters. But would you believe it that this child could be put there in our sensible time, so far along later after old fables have faded away into just stories to be told for want of fable, after all the fancies had perished. . . . (82)

The communal narrator laments the loss of mystery "in our sensible time," when all the "fancies" have perished, but he nonetheless insists upon the possibility of recovering them: "See how an old Shape hidden in the depths and folds of the mind can appear, knocked for, when it is time, and show its meaning, salvage the dust of the truth . . ." (85). It is the "old Shape" of buried ancestral cultures that Goyen summons in his fiction, a rescue operation more Tejano than Texan.

Goyen's invocation of Childe Percival, charmers, and enchanters leads me to my concluding question, a variant of the question that concluded the first section of this chapter. Do romance and magical realism respond to essentially the same cultural conditions and purposes? Clearly, all three novels – Goyen's, Garro's, Rulfo's – correspond to Frye's definition of romance and to my own definition of magical realism, but I will not re-trace these correspondences here. Rather, I want to speculate on why these writers – indeed, why any contemporary American writer – chooses romance and/or magical realism to express his or her version of reality. Here, Fredric Jameson's materialist critique will be useful to my speculations.

In "Magical Narratives: Romance as Genre," Jameson writes that romance

expresses a transitional moment, yet one of a very special type: its contemporaries must feel their society torn between past and future in such a way that the alternatives are grasped as hostile but somehow unrelated worlds. . . . this genre expresses a nostalgia for a social order in the process of being undermined and destroyed by nascent capitalism, yet still for the moment coexisting side by side with the latter.[72]

To support his argument, Jameson gives such widely separated examples as Shakespearean romance, *Wuthering Heights*, and the "great art romances of the Romantic period." According to Jameson, all are "only too obviously symbolic attempts to come to terms with the triumph of the bourgeoisie and the new and unglamorous social forms developing out of the market system" (158). This, too, may be said of many contemporary American magical realist texts. In the final passage cited from "Old Somebody," we hear Goyen's narrator "coming to terms" with a culture in which "old fables have faded away into just stories to be told for want of fable. . . ." In both form and content, each of the works that I have discussed dramatizes the transition between modernity's failed conceptions of self and society and more humane alternatives. The ghosts of Goyen, Garro, and Rulfo may be thought of as metaphors for the transitional periods these novelists represent: in between; neither here nor there; both here and there. And the animate earth provides the metaphoric grounds for alternative constructions of community and consciousness.

These novelists write out of their sense of the displacement of traditional communities and the resulting ruin of the land. Each feels his or her community and countryside torn between past and future, between hostile and unrelated worlds (as Jameson describes the conflict). Their ghosts, themselves in-between beings, dramatize the painful economic and social liminality caused by the obliterating forces of modernization. In *The*

House of Breath, Goyen's Charity is destroyed by economic forces (the sawmill closes) and urbanization (members of the community must exile themselves to Houston to find work). The "world's body" becomes "the bare scalp of earth stretched scabrous and feverish under the metallic light," and the underground community stagnates: ". . . all of bone and rock and metal, we could no longer melt together but stood apart hard as bone and rock. What ruined us?" (38–9) Yet the heard voices of ghosts – dead family and friends and the land itself – rescue the ruins for Boy and allow him to establish a viable community above ground.

Rulfo and Garro also present their transitional dramas metaphorically as the conflict between a buried community and abusive activities above ground. Like Goyen, they participate in an essential romance pattern: the struggle between higher and lower realms and values, with the higher values here paradoxically invested in ghosts below ground. In their novels, as I have said, the tension between levels is political rather than personal. The Mexican Revolution is their failed utopian dream, and both project the characteristic ambivalence of traditional romance: nostalgia for a lost innocence and longing for a future ideal. But here, the signs of romance signify differently. "Lost innocence" is construed as actual past indigenous cultural coherence, rather than Hawthorne's and the U.S. Transcendentalists' Eurocentric longing for a unitary "virgin" realm of moral purity. And "future ideal" is construed as a coherent system of revolutionary political and social justice. I stress the ideal of coherence rather than unity here, for when indigenous myths interact with the structures of romance, the idealized vision that results (whether projected backward or forward in time) is of coherence, not unity. Indeed, coherence is conceivable only when cultural differences are asserted; unity results when no "other" is imagined.

In their self-conscious rejection of the binarisms of modern Western culture and their engagement of alternative indigenous cultural models, Rulfo, Garro, and Goyen are magical realists; in their symbolic fusion of the material and the spiritual in a foregrounded natural order, they reflect and amplify the romance tradition. The former category implies a more self-consciously oppositional stance; the latter corresponds to the intuition that there still exists somewhere a center that will hold. Both impulses operate in relative degrees of intensity in all of the U.S. and Latin American literary works that I have discussed, and their differences may be considered in terms of the extent to which the balance ultimately tips toward one impulse or the other. Goyen and Hawthorne still imagine a center that holds, however tenuously – a Texan house of breath, a Salem house of spirits. Even Faulkner, Hawthorne's offspring (according to Borges), predicts the reconciliation of races and families at the end of *Absalom, Absalom!*

Rulfo and Garro share romance patterns with Goyen, but they project a tragic vision as Goyen does not. In Goyen's work, the U.S. Transcendentalist legacy combines with his sensitivity to indigenous cultural currents, allowing his character to integrate the animate underground with the world's body. Boy is able to integrate past with present – ghosts of his family and community with the living self – as Rulfo's, Garro's, García Márquez's and Borges' characters cannot. Dissolution (Comala), petrification (Ixtepec), apocalypse (Macondo), Borges' "elegant hope" of an undiscovered order in his daunting library of Babel, are recognizable conditions of Latin American magical realism. Here, then, I arrive at a crucial difference between U.S. and Latin American traditions of counterrealism.

Most contemporary U.S. magical realists find a way to bring their ghosts above ground and integrate them into contemporary U.S. culture in order to enrich or remedy it. Like Goyen, Isaac Bashevis Singer, Leslie Marmon Silko, Maxine Hong Kingston, Toni Morrison, imagine re-established communities after disruptive cultural transitions and political abuses. The specific cultural conflicts they dramatize make their communal resolutions very different from one another, of course, but communal nonetheless. Most contemporary Latin American magical realists, on the contrary, refuse such consolation; magical resolutions are considered and then canceled by crushing political realities. Elena Garro's *Recollections of Things to Come* is a representative example of this trajectory, Isabel Allende's *The House of the Spirits* an exception that proves the rule. Latin American literature has always had a political function, and Latin American writers a dissenting role, as U.S. writers have not.[73] Contemporary Latin American magical realists repeatedly represent the destruction of communities caught between indigenous and Western cultural models of self and society, between solidarity and solitude. Centers have ceased to hold in Latin American magical realism, the better, it would seem, to envision salutary decenterings.

The different historical remove of romance legacies may explain, in part, the greater subversiveness of Latin American magical realism when compared with U.S. counterrealism. Contemporary Latin American magical realism does not look back to a relatively recent local Romantic flowering analogous to the nineteenth-century U.S. romance tradition but, as Borges argues in his essay on Hawthorne, to a naturalistic tradition of "dictionaries and rhetoric." Borges' fascination with U.S. romance and its Transcendentalist foundations may be taken as evidence of this argument: there is no Latin American Hawthorne with whom Borges may claim kinship, nor is there an Emersonian mainstream in which contemporary Latin Americans must necessarily bathe (as U.S. writers must). Rather, Latin American writers recur to more distant Spanish sources for their romance tradition, to *Don Quixote* and the *Amadís de Gaula*, and to pre-Hispanic indigenous American mythologies for their archetypal patterns, that is, to traditions preceding the disasters of modernity that magical realism opposes. This distance has, I think, liberated contemporary Latin American writers to invent fantastical strategies for political purposes, expend dazzling narrative energy on political entropy, and resist the temptations of resolution that narrative conclusions offer.

Still, both U.S. and Latin American writers share the experience that Jameson describes of being torn between incompatible pasts and futures and, as we have seen, between contradictory conceptions of subjectivity. Traditional (mythic/archetypal) standards of selfhood based on similarity have been eclipsed by modernity's standards of difference: archetypes have been individualized, ghosts have been buried and silenced – or almost. The ghosts who still inhabit magical realist fiction contest the annihilation of the mythic self by the modern self: paradoxically, magical realists are most postmodern in their recuperation of premodern conceptions of subjectivity. They refuse to remain locked in modern categories of individual psychology, insisting instead that the self is actualized by participation in communal and cosmic categories. Even when such participation fails – in Macondo, Comala, Ixtepec – magical realism's essential commitment is to universality rather than uniqueness. Not that magical realists avoid engaging specific historical, cultural, racial, and gender distinctions: the writers I have discussed here are ample proof to the contrary. By means of their galleries of ghosts, magical realists may describe the inhabitants of Argentina and Massachusetts, Mexico and Texas, and at the same time project a human condition free of essentializing stereotypes.

In late twentieth-century Western culture, divided as we are by economic self-interest and competition, injustice among races and classes and nations and violence against women, to write universalizing fictions is a revolutionary act. As each of us risks becoming an embattled community of one, the archetypal strategies of magical realism and its confluent romance traditions may yet remind us of our shared humanity.

Flannery O'Connor was right. Ghosts *can* be fierce and instructive.

III

I have mentioned Gabriel García Márquez several times in the course of my discussion. I want to elaborate briefly my sense of this author's attitudes toward the indigenous past, and his relation to U.S. fiction in this respect. García Márquez has, of course, repeatedly acknowledged his debt to Faulkner and to the writers of the U.S. South.[74] This debt is due, in part, to the parallel histories of Hispanic America and the Deep South: colonization and exploitation of the land; feudal systems of land tenure with their accompanying aristocracies and enslaved or indentured peoples of color; the burden of defeat by invading armies from the North (Yankees/yanquis); belated and abrupt modernization that masked (and sometimes exacerbated) long histories of political, racial, and economic inequity. Southern Protestant and Hispanic Catholic attitudes also run parallel. In their understanding of the irrational forces operating in history, southern writers share with Latin American writers a basic source of magic realism: the Bible. The Bible often gives a framework to the fatalism and the fantasy of the literature from these regions, a point epitomized by García Márquez in *One Hundred Years of Solitude* when he has a character say, "Si se lo creyeron a las Sagradas Escrituras, no veo por qué no han de creérme a mí" (254; "If they believe it in the Bible, I don't see why they shouldn't believe it from me" 277). Southern fundamental Protestantism, too, is characterized by a literal reading of biblical images and events, and by a literal application of biblical prophecies to current history. This biblical tradition underpins the gothic supernaturalist elements of southern fiction as it does the magical realism of much contemporary Latin American fiction. Faulkner and García Márquez are prime examples of my generalizations, and are central to any discussion of American literature as a hemispheric matter. Elsewhere I have discussed the relation between these histories, especially the shared apocalyptic historicism of *Absalom, Absalom!* and *One Hundred Years of Solitude*.[75] But here, I want to differentiate between the baroque tropics of Mississippi and Macondo, and the Mexican/Texan territory of Goyen, Garro and Rulfo.

Both García Márquez and Faulkner follow European models that conceive of the American land as a paradise now lost. Their novels dramatize the irremediable gulf between nature and twentieth-century culture; their earth does not speak, nor do natural phenomena, as they do in Goyen's, Garro's, and Rulfo's fiction. And when a character returns from the dead in *One Hundred Years of Solitude*, he moves back into the family house in Macondo rather than speaking from and through the earth. García Márquez's characters do not hear indigenous ancestral voices. Indeed, it is the Buendías' Indian servants, Cataure and Visitación, who recognize and diagnose the memory plague in Macondo, presumably because they have already experienced it in their own colonized culture. Indigenous cultures in Colombia did not survive to mix with European cultures as they did in other Andean and Mesoamerican countries, as García Márquez implies by giving to Cataure and Visitación their singular insight into oblivion. I do not mean to suggest that García Márquez's magical realism is unaffected by indigenous elements. On the contrary, I have already suggested ways in which his permeable worlds and archetypalized characters depart from European systems of belief and literacry practice. Surely García Márquez's magic histories would be impossible without the mythic temporality – vestigial and vital – in rural, oral Colombian culture. But García Márquez's particular genius is, I think, historiographic rather than topographic: Macondo is enlivened by temporal magic – timeless rain, terminal hurricanes – rather than by the voices from an animate earth.

In *Absalom, Absalom!*, Faulkner's earth is "manured with black blood," a fact that has extinguished Amerindian ancestry and offspring as surely as it has, and will, those of the Sutpens and the Compsons. And yet, in the stories in *Go Down, Moses* (1942), Faulkner clearly *is* aware of a native legacy. He does not dramatize the indigenous substrata of Yoknapatawpha County or conduct his characters into its realm, but he acknowledges its loss and elegizes it. In "The Old People," Sam Fathers, the only remaining Chickasaw Indian in Jefferson, Mississippi, speaks to the young Ike McCaslin

about those old times and those dead and vanished men of *another race from either that the boy knew*, gradually to the boy those old times would cease to be old times and would become a part of the boy's present, not only as if they had happened yesterday but as if they were still happening, the men who walked through them actually walking in breath and air and casting shadow on the earth they had not quitted.[76]

But Faulkner ironizes Sam Fathers' hope. At the end of the story, Ike's cousin tells him that "the earth is shallow: there is not a great deal of it before you come to the rock. And the earth dont want to just keep things, hoard them; it wants to use them again" (179). Though Ike protests, and Faulkner validates his protest, it is Ike's cousin who is given the final word. In Faulkner's Mississippi, as in García Márquez's Colombia, races remain separate ("another race from either that the boy knew"). The earth is not animate, but exhausted.

In this respect, Faulkner is more representative of U.S. literature than Goyen, for few U.S. writers give the earth voice, and fewer still hear indigenous ancestral voices buried within it. Nonetheless, there are writers (labelled "minority") who do dramatize the confluences and disjunctions of Native American and imported cultures in the U.S. Leslie Marmon Silko's novel *Ceremony* (1977), for example, is a mythic evocation of the conflict between Laguna Pueblo mythology and U.S. mainstream culture. Silko, herself a member of the Laguna Pueblo tribe, interpolates traditional Pueblo narratives about the earth and its gods into her Western narrative form, thus suggesting the potential revitalization of contemporary culture by means of indigenous mythic sources and practices. Ubiquitous ancestral presences in a contemporary U.S. setting also characterize Susan Power's first novel *The Grass Dancer* (1994). Power, whose heritage is Sioux, dramatizes a moment in which a contemporary Sioux paints his face for a ritual dance and hears the "dead grandfathers' voices scratching the house with hoarse whispers, rasping like static from the radio. *We are rising, we are rising*, the voices hummed."[77]

Louise Erdrich's fictional world also admits ancestral apparitions who may act capriciously to avenge or to console but who are consistent in their close association with the land, animals, and natural phenomena. Her novel *Tracks* (1988), set in North Dakota among the Ojibway between 1912 and 1924, begins, "We started dying before the snow, and like the snow, we continued to fall."[78] An old Ojibway man, who remembers the last buffalo hunt and the last beaver with a pelt of more than two years' growth, narrates the scene: "I was not prepared to think of the people I had lost, or to speak of them, although we did, carefully, without letting their names loose in the wind. . . . We feared that they would hear us and never rest, come back out of pity for the loneliness we felt. They would sit in the snow outside the door, waiting until from longing we joined them" (4–5). Like Silko and Power, Erdrich engages the ironic disjunctions of indigenous ancestral presences in a contemporary U.S. cultural context: "They say the unrest and curse of trouble that struck our people. . . was the doing of dissatisfied spirits. I know what's fact, and have never been afraid of talking. Our trouble came from living, from liquor and the dollar bill. We stumbled toward the government bait, never looking down, never noticing how the land was snatched from under us at every step" (4). Indigenous groups have been dispossessed, but if they'd "looked down," the narrator implies, they'd have noticed not just that the property that was being pulled out from under them but also that spirits still reside under the land. In Erdrich's *Tracks*, as in Silko's *Ceremony*, we understand that indigenous cultural sources may yet offer a historical perspective to balance contemporary consumer culture in the U.S.

If Silko, Power, and Erdrich are considered "minority" writers in the U.S., there are others who are not but who, like Goyen, also project an earth animated by confluent cultures and mythologies. We have seen Willa Cather's *The Song of the Lark*, where in the section entitled "The Ancient People" she dramatizes the presence of indigenous origins and the necessity of heeding ancestral voices that still echo above ground. Cather's description of Mesa Verde in *The Professor's House* (1935) reiterates this point. And her 1925 introduction to Sarah Orne Jewett's short fiction celebrates Jewett's characters "who grew out of the soil and the life of the country near her heart," and her stories, which "melt into the land and the life of the land until they are not stories at all, but life itself."[79] Surely this was Cather's own aim as well. On Cather's gravestone is a phrase from *My Antonia* (1918): "That is happiness; to be dissolved into something complete and great."[80]

There are other U.S. writers who also trace this mythic American topography. Paul Metcalf's virtually unkown *Apalache* (1976) and Ursula K. LeGuin's under appreciated *Always Coming Home* (1985) employ new narrative forms to encompass oral and visual traditions – songs, dances, and pictographs – of the indigenous cultures they both imagine and remember. Meridel LeSueur's short stories, written from the thirties through the forties and fifties and finally collected in *Corn Village* (1970), *Harvest* (1977), and *Song for My Time* (1977), often refer to the animate earth. The inhabitants of her underground are the victims of capitalist exploitation. LeSueur begins her story "The Dark of the Time," with a passage similar to the one that begins Goyen's *The House of Breath*, except that LeSueur's intent is more explicitly political: "Wounded from the city, return – return to the dust of earth . . . all moving underneath, all is anguish and moving and the great culture of the underground common to our people emerging in the night like rich herbal emanations."[81] Coming before these works is William Carlos Williams' remarkable revision of U.S. cultural exclusivity. In my introduction, I cited from Williams' essays to show how his work runs absolutely counter to the cultural exclusivity correctly identified by Octavio Paz in the Puritan foundations of the U.S. Williams' *In the American Grain* (1925) presents the interactions of both Anglo and Hispanic cultures with indigenous American cultures in a book that falls somewhere between literature and history and is rarely included in canonical listings of American literature, in part for this reason.

The U.S. writers I've just named, along with Rulfo, Garro, and many other Latin Americans writers, accomplish what Carlos Fuentes describes in his essay on "eccentric writing." Recall his statement, which I quoted in my introduction to Part One: "The role of the marginal cultures is that of the guardians of memory. A memory of what the West sacrificed in other cultures through imperialist expansion and what it sacrificed within its own culture."[82] The list of Latin American novels and stories that engage memories "of what the West sacrificed" is long and must include Miguel Angel Asturias' *Hombres de maíz* (*Men of Maize*, 1949), Alejo Carpentier's *Los pasos perdidos* (*The Lost Steps*, 1953), José María Argueda's *Los ríos profundos* (*Deep Rivers*, 1958), Rosario Castellanos' *Oficio de tinieblas* (*Rite of Shadows*, 1962), Julio Cortázar's "Axolotl" (1964), Carlos Fuentes' psychological parable "Chac Mool" (1974) and *Una familia lejana* (*Distant Relations*, 1981), Luisa Valenzuela's "El lugar de su quietud" ("The Place of Its Quietude," 1975), Eduardo Galeano's trilogy *Memoria del fuego* (*Memory of Fire*, 1982–86), Mario Vargas Llosa's *El hablador* (*The Storyteller*, 1987), and Isabel Allende's "Walimai" in *Cuentos de Eva Luna* (*The Stories of Eva Luna*, 1990). In these works, ancestral apparitions may be given visible form or make themselves heard or felt in other ways: in the disembodied voices in *Pedro Páramo*, the larval salamander in "Axolotl," the ancient stone figure in "Chac Mool." Or, they may be present in the narrative structure of the work itself: in Galeano's trilogy or Vargas Llosa's *The Storyteller*.

Whether or not ancestral presences are *embodied* by writers is ultimately less crucial than the fact that they engage cultures that are themselves in some sense ghostly, subterranean, and silenced in many parts of the Americas. These writers share the impulse to transcend the constraints of rationalism and realism, an impulse that I will call Ancestral with a capital A. This Ancestral impulse leads them to privilege cultural knowledge other than that which proceeds from European sources – knowledge not gained by empirical or inductive means, knowledge lived rather than learned, transmitted orally and visually and often intuitively rather than in writing. One of Fuentes' characters in *Distant Relations* observes that the

Ancestral impulse engages "la herencia de las orejas y la memoria de la boca"[83] ("the inheritance of the ears and the memory of the lips."[84]) W. S. Merwin, in his poem "Witness,"[85] epitomizes this legacy of what is told, seen, and remembered:

> I want to tell you what the forests
> were like
>
> I will have to speak
> in a forgotten language

The Ancestral impulse, inspired by forgotten languages, must be considered in terms of the another characteristic attributed to Latin American writers: what Roberto González Echevarría calls the Archival impulse. In *Myth and Archive* (1990), González Echevarría develops the metaphor of the Archive (which he also capitalizes) to approach the cultural sources and textual resources of Latin American narrative. The word "archive," as defined by the *Oxford English Dictionary*, refers to "a place in which public records or other important historic documents are kept" – an institution of collective social memory, a repository of written documents not (yet) fully catalogued or indexed. González Echevarría defines Archive as a "repository of stories and myths, one of which is the story about collecting those stories and myths."[86] The second part of this statement implies his consequent analogy: the Latin American writer as anthropologist.

González Echevarría first posits a parallel between the Archival impulse and anthropological assumptions of objective cultural description and then traces what he argues are parallel postmodernist shifts in both anthropology and fiction – from Bronislow Malinowski and Marcel Griaule to Clifford Geertz and James Clifford in anthropology, and from Gallegos to Borges and García Márquez in fiction (151). Whether novelists create an objective narrative perspective with respect to the culture their fiction describes (Gallegos), or whether they situates themselves ironically with respect to their narrative authority (Borges and García Márquez), Latin American novelists are, in González Echevarría's definition, Archivists. The definition is complicated by the assertion that the Archive is itself a form of mythic discourse, but González Echevarría concludes not with myth in any indigenous cultural sense but with the contemporary myth of scientific objectivity. "Archival fictions are narratives that still attempt to find the cipher of Latin American culture and identity, hence they fall within the mediation provided by anthropological discourse" (173).

This analogy suggests that writers, like anthropologists, aim to stand outside the cultures they describe, and that literary and anthropological language are descriptive in similar ways and for similar reasons. While it is true that anthropological assumptions may operate in works that embody ancestral presences, those assumptions do not contain or exhaust their meaning. What would be excluded, were we to read this fiction solely in terms of González Echevarría's metaphoric Archive, are precisely the ancestral presences, the echoes and antiphonies and murmurs of buried belief systems that still resonate in contemporary culture. Whereas González Echevarría's metaphor of the Archive is useful in thinking about intertextual aspects of Latin American fiction, it is not useful when it comes to narrative modes with mythic aspirations. *Pedro Páramo* and *Recollections of Things to Come* dramatize worlds in which originary collective traditions are *not* written and *not* available to anthropological observation precisely because they elude the European assumptions about history and literature that have created the very Archive to which González Echevarría refers. Rulfo and Garro conjure these originary traditions in literary structures, of course, but their aim is to convey elements of Mexican reality that have little to do with writing.

"It is astonishing," comments Octavio Paz in *The Labyrinth of Solitude*, "that a country with such a vivid past – a country so profoundly traditional, so close to its roots, so rich in ancient legends even if poor in modern history – should conceive of itself only as a negation of its origins" (87). But this very negation fuels the anxiety about origins that impels writers to attend to Ancestral presences. Vera Kutzinski recognizes this irony when she suggests that it is not writers but critics – not literature but what she calls the "Library of American Literature" – that has "negated" cultural origins. Paz, too, recognizes this distinction. Kutzinsky notes that Paz is discussing textuality and canonicity in Mexico as it has been defined by European standards and values: he "demonstrates, throughout *The Labyrinth of Solitude*, that this negation of the kinds of origins stored in the texts that compose the Library of American Literature is the only way to make accessible to the imagination those ancient legends and traditions."[87] We have already seen many cases – Fuentes, Cather, Goyen, Garro, Rulfo – where such negation is a dialectical strategy that allows American writers to (re)possess their history imaginatively.

If we were to take the metaphor of the Archive as definitive, we would also have to exclude writers like Manuel Puig and Luis Rafael Sánchez, who use clichés in structural and substantial ways. Though clichés may be written, they are derived from spoken speech or popular visual and auditory media (movies, television, song lyrics); they obey a vernacular imperative, not a bibliographic one. My point is that to select a generalizing metaphor for Latin American fiction that privileges written records over oral or visual modes of remembering, and that itself becomes a metaphor for scientific discourse, is to exclude significant portions of Latin America's usable past.

An adequate interpretive paradigm, then, must include the Ancestral as the necessary complement to the Archival; it must encompass the oral and

visual modes of cultural remembering that exist alongside written traditions. These diverse cultural traditions and media – indigenous and European, ancient and contemporary – coexist in the inclusive narrative structures that are the subject of the following chapters. To conclude this
chapter, I want to quote in full the statement of Fuentes' character in *Distant Relations* about "the inheritance of the ears and the memory of the
lips":

El mexicano decía que la expulsión de los dioses por la ciudad moderna nos con-
dena a un tiempo ilusorio porque es el de nuestra limitación humana; percibimos
parcialmente una secesión lineal y creemos que no hay otro tiempo... . Todos los
pueblos antiguos se niegan a desterrar las formas viejas en beneficio de las nuevas;
unas y otras, en vez de expulsarse sucesivamente, se suman en una acreción per-
manente. Allí, todo está vivo y presente, como entre los pueblos de Madagascar
que resumen la historia posible en dos vertientes: la herencia de las orejas y la
memoria de la boca. (16)

The Mexican was saying that the expulsion of the gods by the modern city has
condemned us to an illusory time, a time imposed by human limitations; we perceive, unclearly, only chronological sequence and we believe there is no other
time. . . . All ancient people refuse to abandon the old ways in favor of the new;
rather than being cast aside one after the other, some realities accumulate in a
permanent accretion. When this happens, all things are living and present, as is
true among the peoples of Madagascar, who conceive of history as two flowing
currents: the inheritance of the ears and the memory of the lips. (11)

This character, you will recall, is an archeologist, but his insistence on history as "permanent accretion" obviates any positivistic scientific stance.
Here, Fuentes proposes that modern science – the archeologist, the anthropologist – may still encompass mythic history, if only they will. The
Ancestral and Archival are not binary oppositions but complementary
structures; one may choose one's ancestors and one's library, one's precursors, or inherit them. In all cases, they must be heeded. The character's reference to Madagascar universalizes Fuentes' proposition.

So ancestral voices "accumulate" in American fiction. In *Sometimes a
Great Notion*, the U.S. novelist Ken Kesey acknowledges this point with
an aural metaphor. His narrator hears the silence of the American ancestral past and describes it by saying that "the reverberation often exceeds
through silence the sound that sets it off; the reaction occasionally outdoes
by way of repose the event that stimulated it; and the past not uncom-
monly takes a while to happen . . . ."[88]

So it does, but happen it will. Ghosts are fierce and instructive, and they
are also very, very patient.

PART TWO

INTERTEXTUALITY
AND TRADITION

As speaking subjects we continue, we take up the same effort, older than ourselves, on which we are implanted onto each other, which is the manifestation, the becoming of truth. We say that the true has always been true, but this is a confused way of saying that all previous expressions live again and receive their place in the expression of the moment, so that one can, if one wishes, read it in them after the fact, find them again in it.

Maurice Merleau-Ponty, *La Prose du monde*[1]

It is the power of mutation which the mind possesses to *re*discover the truth. . . . the continual change without which no symbol remains permanent.

William Carlos Williams[2]

WHETHER THE WRITER self-consciously recuperates or invents usable precursors is, according to Maurice Merleau-Ponty, beside the point. The writer's medium requires it, no matter whether he or she intends it. As a phenomenologist, Merleau-Ponty generalizes about all speaking subjects; as a literary critic, I want to specify particular works and consider *how* they "implant onto each other," *how* they construct the "becoming of truth" that Merleau-Ponty describes. I agree with Merleau-Ponty that all cultural texts are intertexts, but writers and readers respond to their textual traditions in different ways and for different purposes, often according to the importance given by a culture to its own history and the history of its interactions with other cultures. A principal function of the literary critic, especially the literary comparatist, is to attend to the text's dialogue with other texts and to the historical experiences that condition the conversation. Significant differences in attitudes toward cultural authority and literary tradition may be revealed in so doing.

My second epigraph signals the American attitude I am tracing here: William Carlos Williams' statement epitomizes the American impulse to create and include precursors, to recuperate ruptured traditions, to "*rediscover the truth.*" As if to counter the very charge of originality, which in a "new" world may be read as isolation, dissociation, irrelevance, or even sterility, American writers are likely to flaunt their incorporation of previous texts and traditions. The Peruvian critic Julio Ortega was perhaps the first to notice this inclusive intertextuality as a response to historical anxiety. In his 1969 study *La contemplación y la fiesta* (*Contemplation and Fiesta*), he refers generally to this tendency as "una voluntad integrada" and "este impulso integrador":

1) La narrativa latinoamericana actual revela *una voluntad integrada*, que es su núcleo problematizador, su inserción también en una estética más universal;
2) y *este impulso integrador* reclama una perspectiva autocrítica en cuanto el género mismo es cuestionado desde la escritura.

Los narradores latinoamericanos más universales—sobre todo Cortázar y Fuentes – han enfrentado los problemas que la cultura occidental agudizó en el medio siglo: de algún modo *este impulso integrador* es la respuesta latinoamericana a un diálogo cuyos términos de arte y pensamiento—imágenes, pues, del hombre en el mundo – habían sido planteados en *múltiples escisiones*.

1) Contemporary Latin American narrative demonstrates *a desire to be inclusive* that is its problematizing core and its way of inserting itself into a more universal aesthetic;
2) and *this inclusive impulse* reclaims a self-critical perspective to the extent that the genre itself is questioned in the writing.

The most universal Latin American writers – above all Cortázar and Fuentes – have confronted the acute problems of Western culture at mid-century: in some way *this inclusive impulse* is the Latin American response to a dialogue whose terms in art and thought – images, that is, of man in the world – have been proposed in myriad fragments.[3]

Ortega's perception of this inclusive impulse as a response to *múltiples escisiones* (multiple fragments or splinters or shards) anticipates my argument. I, too, find a paradoxical and highly productive tension between inclusive narrative strategies, on the one hand, and the awareness of historical discontinuity, on the other; between universalizing fictions and the competing awareness of historical discontinuity that inspires them.

Take the writers Ortega names. Carlos Fuentes praises what he calls "multivocal" texts[4] and Julio Cortázar describes his own mobile structures as "constellations," "crystallizations," "*figuras*."[5] Julio Ortega does not mention Borges in this essay, but he might well have, for Borges' spare fictions are, of course, parables of the inclusive intertextuality that Ortega describes. Borges revolutionized the way we read, and he did so, ironically, through conservative means, through the affirmation of multiple traditions and tradition itself. So Borges' character Pierre Menard is "original" by virtue of repetition, by virtue of the intertextual recovery of his literary "origins." His *Quixote* is "preposterous" in the etymological sense of the word: "pre" and "post" converge in his intertext, literally dramatizing the simultaneous existence of what Frank Kermode has called "the work as it was and the work as it now is."[6] Borges' narrator delivers a paen to this inclusive historicity of literature. His celebration of its capacity to chart the changing relations of history and truth over time is surely a response to the American need to accommodate diverse cultural traditions in literary form. Menard's (and Borges') intertextuality rejects historical progression and supersession but not historical meaning. Literary tradition is a palimpsest and a palindrome, change is permanent, repetition is linked to creation; in the New World, it seems, history and literature repeat themselves originally, and sometimes verbatim.

So we understand that Menard's activity as writer is utterly tied to his experience as reader. Despite his fictive French nationality, Pierre Menard is the epitome of an American trope: the writer-reading, or the writer-as-reader. We will see that this trope has a great deal to do with American attitudes toward tradition as such. Recall Borges' assertion that Argentine writers have "a great sense of time" because they write in "a new country."[7] He also tells us that he is "an excellent reader":

Qué otros jacten de los libros que les ha sido dado escribir; yo me jacto de aquellos que me fue dado leer. . . . No sé si soy un buen escritor; creo ser un excelente lector, o, en todo caso, un sensible y agradecido lector.

Let others boast of the books that they have been able to write; I boast of those I have been able to read. . . . I do not know if I am a good writer; I believe that I am an excellent reader or, in any case, a sensitive and grateful reader.[8]

Borges' insistence is culturally specific: American writers are "excellent," "sensitive," "grateful" readers because they are necessarily engaged in constructing literary traditions – hence cultural authority, communal identity, political autonomy. Speaking of his own generation of Latin American writers, Carlos Fuentes writes of Borges that he "permitted us to go forward with a sense of possessing more than we had written, which was all that we had read, from Homer to Milton to Joyce. . . ."[9] Fuentes celebrates Borges' "supreme narrative synthesis" of the cultural traditions of Spanish America, including the Arabic and Jewish traditions in Spain: "I certainly would not have had this early, fraternal revelation of my own Arab and Jewish heritage without such stories as 'Averroes' Search,' 'The Zahir,' and 'The Approach to al-Mu'tasim' " (53).

This American experience of repossessing multiple traditions depends, then, upon creative reading. In an essay on the detective novel, Borges writes:

Los géneros literarios dependen, quizá, menos de los textos que del modo en que éstos son leídos. El hecho estético requiere la conjunción del lector y del texto y sólo entonces *existe*. Es absurdo suponer que un volumen sea mucho más que

un volumen. Empieza a *existir* cuando un lector lo abre. Entonces *existe* el feó-
meno estético, que puede parecerse al momento en el cual el libro fue engendra-
do.[10]

Perhaps literature depends less on texts than on the way in which texts are
read. The aesthetic experience requires the conjunction of reader and text and
only then does it *exist*. It is absurd to suppose that a book is much more than a
book. It begins to *exist* when the reader opens it. It is then that the aesthetic phenomenon *exists*; this can be considered the moment in which the book was
engendered.

Literature *exists* (note Borges' repetition) by virtue of its readings, the historical location of its readers, and the contingencies of genre. Literary tradition is the history of readings and expressive forms.

Pierre Menard's achievement is "preposterous" not only in the etymological sense of the word but also in its usual sense: ridiculous, absurd,
incredible. This reinforces my sense that in Pierre Menard Borges dramatizes the historical difficulties of the New World writer-as-reader. He sati-
rizes as well as celebrates American adaptations of previous texts and traditions, for he knows that New World writers run the risk of overvaluing
the past – and worse, overvaluing *others'* pasts, *others'* cultural and literary traditions. Surely Borges' character Menard is guilty of wanting to *be*
Cervantes, of wanting to *be* a seventeenth-century writer – in short, of suc-
cumbing to irrelevance with respect to his own historical present. Another of Borges' stories, "The Gospel According to St. Mark," is even more
explicit in this respect. A family in a rural region of Argentina reads the
biblical account of the crucifixion and literally reenacts it. This is a cau-
tionary tale: in postcolonial contexts, readers must be cunning, creative,
and critical, not merely literal.

Borges' emphasis on the writer-as-reader foresees a central postmodernist position; or, more precisely, postmodernist theorists have lately generalized what has long been the American writer's experience. In this
respect, the critic Jon Thiem calls Borges a "quintessential postmodernist," a "paradigmatic postmodernist": "The great tradition of past writing puts the postmodern writer into the position of a reader, who may be
thrilled by the riches of the past or feel overwhelmed by their authority. In
the reader, the postmodern writer has found an ideal figure through which
to explore the splendors and miseries of belatedness."[11] In fact, this postmodernist sense of belatedness mirrors ironically the New World writer's
intertextual project of establishing a usable past. New World writers are by
definition "belated" with respect to European traditions and practices, but
their awareness of this fact is hardly postmodern, nor is it necessarily negative. Aureliano Babilonia is behind in his reading of Melquíades' manu-
script but catches up in time to see his destiny whole; Pierre Menard is
heaped with praise for his creative belatedness, his achievement made pos-

sible *because* of his historical distance from his essential precursor. Gustavo Pérez Firmat's observation about Cuban writers is to the point: "If, on the one hand, the derivativeness of New World culture locks the writer into certain modes of expression, the distance from the source implicit in the very notion of derivativeness gives him a privileged hermeneutic position with respect to the cultural products of the Old World."[12] Latin American writers are more engaged in creating their own traditions than in lamenting their belatedness with respect to others'.

Whether or not postmodernists emphasize belatedness, they unanimously follow Borges in arguing that texts situate themselves with respect to other texts, that literature is quotation, dialogic exchange, parodic stylization. Umberto Eco's declaration seems designed to describe Pierre Menard as reader and writer: "Between 1965 and today, two ideas have been definitively clarified: that plot could be found also in the form of quotation of other plots, and that the quotation could be less escapist than the plot quoted."[13] Even the anachronism is appropriate; Pierre Menard, master of belatedness, precedes Eco's prescribed time frame by two decades. Preposterous, indeed.

What distinguishes postmodern theorists from New World writers on this point is that the former consider quotations to circulate randomly rather than in any culturally constitutive way. Thus, when the Chilean writer José Donoso is asked whether he considers his novels to be postmodern, he responds that in their "confusion of the telling and the told" and in their use of "loose fragments," they might be. But, he demurs, "they preserve a sort of sociological and, somehow, political meaning."[14] I take Donoso's assumption that postmodernist categories by definition exclude "sociological and political meaning" as an inadvertent sign of the difference between the historicizing intentions of contemporary American writers and most postmodernist theories of quotation, pastiche, and parody. The difference involves the question of how cultural and textual fragments become available (usable) in the present of the writer and reader, how they are used and how (or whether) cultural values may be assigned. The postmodernist emphasis on the derivative nature of the process suggests that quotation merely repeats what antedates it, that everything has been seen, done, and experienced already.[15] To the extent that postmodernist theory rejects the capacity of quotation to modify the "given" – to "*re*discover the truth," in Williams' phrase – it is inapplicable to the literature I discuss here. These writers' intertextual strategies are based on judgments of value designed to influence precursors and foster community. They recognize that fictions are usable only when they are *re*constituted by the combined agency of readers and writers over time.

Whether we take Borges' emphasis on the writer-as-reader to be postmodernist (readings are partial, meanings contingent) or, for that matter, as modernist meta-narrative (*all* readers have partial histories and contingent interpretations) is beside the point. What interests me here is how Borges reflects the situation of the New World writer. Reading comes to symbolize the writer's imperative to adapt previous works of literature to local use, to integrate them into a usable tradition. This emphasis is recognizably American in foregrounding the writer's function as receptor of multiple cultures, histories, and texts, and it is consonant with my argument that New World writers have tended to *seek* precursors and cultural sources rather than avoiding or denying their influence. The American awareness of writers-as-readers – as inheritors of cumulative, communal, contradictory, mutable traditions – is dramatized in the intertextual techniques and transcultural processes that I will discuss in Part Two. My concern is with how received texts and traditions are animated by, and animate the writer's historicizing imagination.

CHAPTER FOUR

Synchronic Structures

Mario Vargas Llosa, *Conversation in The Cathedral*

Julio Cortázar, *62: A Model Kit*

. . . creemos en la ficción del tiempo, en el presente, el pasado y el futuro, pero puede ser también que todo ocurre simultáneamente, como decían las tres hermanas Mora, que eran capaces de ver en el espacio los espíritus de todas las épocas.

> Isabel Allende, *La casa de los espíritus*[1]

. . . we believe in the fiction of past, present, and future, but it may also be true that everything happens simultaneously – just as the Mora sisters said, who could see the spirits of all eras mingled in space.

> Isabel Allende, *The House of the Spirits*[2]

THE SYNCHRONIC STRUCTURES that I discuss in this chapter and the fragmentary structures that I will discuss in the next one are related in their awareness of the multiple and often contradictory traditions they inherit, modify and pass along. In both chapters, I discuss writers who use historical and narrative fragments to challenge the progressive linearity of positivism and positivism's preeminent literary form, the novel. But their narrative strategies allow me to make distinctions among them. Whereas Mario Vargas Llosa and Julio Cortázar create structural and/or metaphoric wholes in which fragments may be endlessly included, Angelina Muñiz-Huberman and Sandra Cisneros resist that possibility, flaunting the fragments as such.

This distinction might lead (deceptively) to the critical commonplace that Muñiz-Huberman's and Cisneros' fragmentary fictions are "postmodernist" in their acceptance of "free play" in a decentered world, whereas Vargas Llosa's and Cortázar's synchronic structures are "modernist" in their hope of an overarching structure. In fact, such a dichotomy would be reductive in the extreme, for none of these writers attempts to mend the fragments; rather, each creates structures in which difference circulates separately, singly, or severally. Whether they use fragments synecdochally to suggest an absent entity, or synchronically to suggest coexisting historical relations, their narrative structures are open, eccentric, multiple, conflictual, and inclusive. They are "totalizing" fictions but *not* in any totalitarian (hierarchical) sense. On the contrary, they self-consciously include narrative mechanisms to deconstruct their own inclusiveness. Without such mechanisms, totalizing structures might indeed risk becoming totalitarian or, at least, unduly appropriative. It is a risk that these writers would be the first to recognize.

I

Synchronic structures abound in contemporary Latin American fiction. Rather than providing a formal definition, I want to offer instances. Here, I will say only that the usual sense of the verb "to synchronize" – as in "synchronize your watches" or "synchronized swimming" – is misleading, because it suggests events and actions that are coincident, and therefore presumably consonant or even identical. The structures that I am calling synchronic indicate the opposite – in their simultaneous, contradictory, and sometimes bewildering array of events, settings, and subjects. García Márquez's narrator Melquíades records the events of one hundred of years of solitude so that they may coexist (we are told) in a single instant – the instant before Macondo is blown away by a biblical hurricane; Carpentier composes a *baroque concerto* in which Satchmo and Vivaldi play at once; Borges' character envisions an infinite *Aleph*, impossible to describe; Cortázar plays surrealist *hopscotch* and constructs a cubist *model kit*; Vargas Llosa overhears a contrapuntal conversation in an ambiguous *cathedral*. Before discussing these last two instances in detail, I will consider how synchronic structures respond variously to Archival and Ancestral cultural sources.

"El Aleph" ("The Aleph") dramatizes what Borges describes in "The Argentine Writer and Tradition."[3] Traditions are multiple and hybrid and often superimposed; native and imported histories circulate in eccentric orbits and ambits. So Borges' narrator laments that he cannot describe in words the "infinite" Aleph that he has beheld with his own eyes because language is "un alfabeto de símbolos cuyo ejercicio presupone un pasado que los interlocutores comparten."[4] (". . . a set of symbols whose use among its speakers assumes a shared past.")[5] This story is usually understood as an ironic parable about the impossibility of expressing the infinite simultaneity of human experience in a literary form that is neither endless nor simultaneous – in words that follow one after another on printed pages. The stubborn incompatibility between synchronic models such as Borges' Aleph and their diachronic verbal medium does create an unspoken sense of rebellion against the formal constraints of literary expression. But my concern is how this rebellion is culturally and historically located: "The

Aleph" must be understood in its Argentine context and read as a parable of the predicament (and potential) of the American writer, who writes (and reads) where a shared past *cannot* be assumed.

This story is much more specifically located than most of Borges' stories – in the "ancestral home," the "old and inveterate Garay Street home" of the narrator's friend, whose name, Carlos Argentino, could hardly be more specific. The narrator's vision of the infinite Aleph occurs where cultural traditions do not unfold diachronically, one after another, but coexist synchronically in local contexts. So the narrator regales us with a list of what he sees in the Aleph – "a limited catalogue of endless things," to use Borges' description of Whitman's poetry and his own story.[6] I will cite only a small part of the passage:

> . . . vi las muchedumbres de América . . . vi en un traspatio de la calle Soler las mismas baldosas que hace treinta años vi en el zaguán de una casa en Fray Bentos . . . vi una quinta de Adrogué, un ejemplar de la primera versión inglesa de Pinio . . . vi un poniente en Querétaro que parecía reflejar el color de una rosa en Bengala; vi mi dormitorio sin nadie . . . vi el Aleph, desde todos los puntos, vi en el Aleph la tierra, y en la tierra otra vez el Aleph y en el Aleph la tierra, vi mi cara . . .[7]

> . . . I saw the multitudes of America . . . I saw in a backyard of Soler Street the same tiles that thirty years before I'd seen in the entrance of a house in Fray Bentos . . . I saw a summer house in Adrogué and a copy of the first English translation of Pliny . . . I saw a sunset in Querétaro that seemed to reflect the color of a rose in Bengal; I saw my empty bedroom . . . in the Aleph I saw the earth and in the earth the Aleph and in the Aleph the earth; I saw my own face . . ."[8]

Borges' Aleph, with its mystical power of universal inclusion, also (necessarily) includes the contradictory claim of individual idiosyncrasy: "I saw my own face. . . ." Borges' narrator, echoing Whitman, discovers that he contains multitudes: the forces of universality and particularity are not opposed; images of infinity are tied to finite American events and locales; "endless things" delimit American spaces.

One is immediately tempted to say that the bookish Borges created metaphors of wholeness in response to the bewildering multiplicity of the Archive; surely his (uncatalogued) library of Babel is the quintessential metaphor for such overwhelming textual synchrony, and his garden of forking paths the metaphor for the infinite narratives contained therein.[9] But the narrator's vision in "The Aleph" is more comprehensive still, for the Aleph synchronizes not only texts and literary traditions but also territories and their ghostly residents ("I saw the delicate bone structure of a hand . . . I saw the rotted dust and bones that had once deliciously been Beatriz Viterbo . . .") and so responds to the mythic impulse I have called Ancestral, as well as to an Archival impulse. That the emphasis is on the narrator's avowed inability to *write* the Aleph (though he does so, of course, in his narrative called "The Aleph") weights the balance of his anxiety toward the Archival; so does his allusion to the English poet Michael Drayton's "topographical epic" *Polyolbion*, a seventeenth-century aleph-like attempt to create a text that literally *contains* the newly self-conscious English nation. But as I have said, Ancestral presences are also strongly felt by Borges' narrator – why wouldn't they be? – in the "ancestral home" of Borges' particularized Argentino.

An essay by Julio Ortega on Alejo Carpentier's synchronic narrative strategies begins with Borges. Ortega notes that "already in Borges an acute critical preoccupation with History is visible: a longing for complete participation. . . ."[10] According to Ortega, Borges appeases this "longing for complete participation" by means of stories about the "destinies of characters that culminate in the impersonal and saving integration of universal History: Borges' longing for participation is, of course, also a critical activity. . ." (191). And a local one: Beret E. Strong points out that the Argentine avant-garde movement *ultraísmo*, in which Borges was a central figure in the twenties and thirties, was actually culturally conservative. In its aim to "expose a national identity thought to be buried under the collective weight of several million immigrants, Borges and his peers were – theoretically, at least – excavating the past, not creating something new."[11] Borges did, of course, create something new by virtue of his reconstitution of the very idea of newness as return, repetition, and recuperation; for Borges, originality is (already) inscribed in "universal History." Aware of his oblique relations to European and American traditions – to "universal History" – the Argentine writer obeyed the impulse, both Archival and Ancestral, to conserve and include it all, magically, at once.

Alejo Carpentier also responded to his American cultural context by developing an aesthetics and an ideology of historical synchrony in which he (more explicitly than Borges) ties Latin America's cultural syncretism to literary form. Carpentier's experience of Surrealism in France during the twenties and thirties opened the way for him to theorize Latin America's discontinuous histories and diverse cultural identities: his formulation of *lo real maravilloso americano* and his related discussion of *lo barroco* – the New World Baroque – is a calculated "territorialization" of literary structure.[12] Carpentier translated the irrational juxtapositions of the European Surrealists from sewing machines and umbrellas to American cultural contexts. Whereas Surrealism was produced in the laboratories of the imagination, according to Carpentier Latin American writers had no need of such laboratories. They had only to look around them to find entire cultures, races, and histories juxtaposed, coexisting and contradictory.

La nueva novela latinoamericana no puede ser diacrónica sino sincrónica, es decir, debe llevar planos paralelos, acciones paralelas, y debe tener al individuo siempre relacionado con la masa que lo circunda, con el mundo en gestación que lo esculpe, le da razón de ser, vigor, savia y los medios de expresión *en todos los dominios de la creación*, sea plástica, sea musical, sea verbal.

The new Latin American novel cannot be diachronic but rather synchronic, that is, it must maintain parallel planes, parallel actions, and it must always relate the individual to what surrounds him, to the gestating world that forms him, gives him meaning, vigor, nourishment, and the means of expression *in all realms of creation*, whether artistic, musical, verbal.[13]

. . . *en todos los dominios de la creación*: the reference is to artistic creation and also to the universe. Again we witness the American impulse to include multiple histories and diverse cultures in synchronic rather than progressive structures, in music and murals as well as words. Structural synchrony and cultural syncretism are indivisible in Carpentier's New World Baroque.

Carpentier's construct has become an overarching metaphor for Latin American cultural heterogeneity. García Márquez, in *De amor y otros demonios* (*Of Love and Other Demons*, 1994), makes the New World Baroque his theme. This novel is set in Baroque colonial Cartegena and describes a character who has amassed a vast library that includes *The Four Books of Amadís of Gaul* and the *Quixote*; furthermore, the Baroque sonnets of Garcilaso de la Vega are woven throughout the text and revised by the characters according to their own amorous needs. Renaissance scientists, Enlightenment rationalists – Galileo, Leibnitz, Voltaire – are also discussed, suggesting that European historical periods and texts accumulate in layers in the New World. But García Márquez is more concerned with Ancestors than Archives. One character, a Spanish bishop, recalls his activities of colonization and conversion in the New World:

Habló de Yucatán, donde habían construido catedrales suntuosas para ocultar las pirámides paganas, sin darse cuenta de que los aborígenes acudían a misa porque debajo de los altares de plata seguían vivos sus santuarios. Habló de batiburrillo de sangre que habían hecho desde la conquista: sangre de español con sangre de indios, de aquellos y estos con negros de toda laya, hasta contubernio cabría en el reino de Dios.[14]

He spoke of Yucatán, where they had constructed sumptuous cathedrals to hide the pagan pyramids, not realizing the natives came to Mass because their sanctuaries still lived beneath the silver altars. He spoke of the chaotic mixing of blood that had gone on since the conquest: Spanish blood with Indian blood, and both these with blacks of every sort, even Mandingo Muslims, and he asked himself whether such miscegenation had a place in the Kingdom of God.[15]

The Spanish bishop wonders and the Colombian author knows. This last phrase echoes intertextually Carpentier's *The Kingdom of This World*; like that novel, this one celebrates cultural and racial *mestizaje*. Another character, when asked if he is Spanish, responds, "At my age, and with so much mixing of bloodlines, I am no longer certain where I come from. Or who I am." To which his interlocutor responds: "No one knows in these kingdoms. And I believe it will be centuries before they find out" (114). García Márquez's novel is an exuberant contribution to this ongoing inquiry.

My epigraph documents another instance of structural synchrony, namely, the decisive moment at the conclusion of Isabel Allende's *La casa de los espíritus* (*The House of the Spirits*, 1982) when Alba understands that she will write one hundred years of Chilean history. As she attempts "to reclaim the past," Alba surrounds herself with piles of documents, texts literally circling around her, including the notebooks of her grandmother, Clara. It is crucial to her character's project, Allende makes clear, that the notebooks *not* be ordered sequentially, for Alba knows that usable history is not based in chronology but in clairvoyance – another order but an order nonetheless, and a more powerful one. Clara has, we are told, *arranged* her notebooks, and Alba will now do so again for her own purposes. The synchrony of their histories is clear: "Escribo, ella escribió, que la memoria es frágil y el transcurso de una vida es muy breve y sucede todo tan de prisa, que no alcanzamos a ver la relación entre los acontecimientos, no podemos medir la consecuencia de los actos . . ." (383; "I write, she wrote, that memory is fragile and the space of a single life is brief, passing so quickly that we never get a chance to see the relationship between events; we cannot gauge the consequences of our acts. . ." 367). The simultaneous accounts of successive generations – "I write, she wrote" – encodes a concept of culture that is cumulative rather than progressive, intermittently available, sometimes invisible, always binding. For Alba Ancestral voices *are* Archival sources.

In fact, we have already seen a synchronic structure earlier in this novel: the mural that Alba paints on her wall. Alba's mural represents her family's history in space rather than time. In the author's memorial to her daughter entitled *Paula* (1994), Allende returns to this metaphor of historical memory as a mural, here explicitly linking structural synchrony to cultural syncretism:

Mi memoria es como un mural mexicano donde todo ocurre simultáneamente: las naves de los conquistadores por una esquina mientras la Inquisición tortura indios en otra, los libertadores galopando con banderas ensangrentadas y la Serpiente Emplumanda frente a un Cristo sufriente entre las chimeneas humeantes de la era industrial. Así es mi vida, un fresco múltiple y variable que sólo yo puedo descifrar y que me pertenece como un secreto.[16]

My memory is like a Mexican mural on which all times are simultaneous: the ships of the Conquistadores in one corner and an Inquisitor torturing Indians in another, galloping Liberators with blood-soaked flags and the Aztecs' Plumed Serpent facing a crucified Christ, all encircled by the billowing smokestacks of the industrial age. So it is with my life, a multilayered and ever-changing fresco that only I can decipher, whose secret is mine alone."[17]

In the context of this heartbreaking account of the death of a beloved daughter, such a view of history is consolatory: the past is present, the dead are with us. Thus Allende, a Chilean writer now living in the U.S., describes a Mexican mural (surely Diego Rivera's mural on the walls of the stairwell at the Palacio Nacional in Mexico City); the mural depicts history synchronically and Mexican culture syncretically; the viewer (Allende) stands before this totalizing history and sees her own life; her reader is directed to the *difference* between this comprehensive mural and the linear structure of her book, and is asked to wonder at the felt history it nonetheless contains.

Such synchronic structures are hardly limited to recent Latin American fiction (or Mexican murals either, for that matter). The great European modernists – Flaubert, Woolf, Joyce, Proust, Huxley, Durrell – devised a brilliant array of narrative strategies to subvert the linearity of the novel. Their efforts were impelled by their growing awareness of the disjunctions between their sequential medium and the psychological interiority they wished to portray. The disjunctions were handled thematically as well as structurally, of course; "words cannot tell" became a trope, and other expressive media – among them music and collage, as we will see – were offered as *more* telling than words. The tension between their diachronic medium (the novel) and their synchronic message (the psyche; society) was variously conveyed by multiple places and perspectives at a single moment (Big Ben repeatedly chiming one o'clock in *Mrs. Dalloway*) or multiple moments in a single place (Durrell's *Alexandria Quartet*). This second strategy had already been perfected in the visual arts by Impressionists and Cubists, who had engaged modulation, montage, transformation, juxtaposition, multiple and/or fractured perspectives to create visual metaphors of synchrony. For example, Monet's twenty-eight canvases of the facade of Rouen cathedral at various times of day, painted between February and April 1892 and again during the same months of 1893, dramatize the tension basic to synchronic structures: identity in difference, difference in identity, perpetual movement (i.e., change) in a perdurable structure. Monet's serial canvases, like Cézanne's repeated renderings of Mont Sainte-Victoire or Van Gogh's multiperspectival rooms, anticipate Borges' Aleph and his garden of forking paths: these artists create structures aimed at distilling time to a single instant and space to a solitary point, so that all may be said to be *present* in both the temporal and the spatial sense of the word.

Consider one more European example. Umberto Eco says that Joyce in *Finnegans Wake* "offers us the entire wisdom of mankind, without determining whether or not it reflects a unique Eternal truth. He is concerned only with the cultural repertoire assembled by the whole of History. . . ."[18] This novel is Joyce's infinite Aleph and also his library of Babel. Eco writes:

. . . Joyce engages a reality composed of all that has been said of it and organizes this world according to rules which are derived, not from the things themselves but from words that express things. He proposes a form of the world in language, a hypothesis offered from within the linguistic format. (84)

Finnegans Wake foregrounds the antipositivism inherent in synchronic structures and the revision of causal sequence that such structures imply.

Roland Barthes describes the "antihero" reader created by such structures:

Imagine someone . . . who abolishes within himself all barriers, all classes, all exclusions, not by syncretism but by simple discard of that old specter: logical contradiction; who mixes every language, even those said to be incompatible; who silently accepts every charge of illogicality, of incongruity; who remains passive in the face of Socratic irony (leading the interlocutor to the supreme disgrace: self-contradiction) and legal terrorism (how much penal evidence is based on a psychology of consistency!) Such a man would be the mockery of our society: court, school, asylum, polite conversation would cast him out: who endures contradiction without shame? Now this antihero exists. . . . Thus the biblical myth is reversed, the confusion of tongues is no longer a punishment, the subject gains access to bliss by the cohabitation of languages working side by side: the text of pleasure is a sanctioned Babel.[19]

What (if any) are the differences between Europe's "sanctioned Babels" and the synchronic structures so widespread in contemporary Latin American fiction? How does the "antihero" reader differ (if he or she does) in the Americas?

II

Both *Conversación en La Catedral* (*Conversation in The Cathedral*, 1969) by Mario Vargas Llosa and *62: modelo para armar* (*62: A Model Kit*, 1968) by Julio Cortázar open with scenes in which the novels' main characters, Santiago Zavala and Juan, respectively, are reading European novels. The novel within each of these novels is placed conspicuously in the opening scene and is clearly of considerable intellectual and emotional importance to its reader. Although neither protagonist comments in detail upon the reasons for his choice of reading material, each nonetheless feels a powerful affinity for the novel he has chosen. Santiago Zavala, in *Conversation in The Cathedral*, is reading *Point Counter Point* by Aldous Huxley, and Juan, in *62: A Model Kit*, is reading *Niagara: A Stereophonic Novel* by Michel Butor.

I have said that New World writers in search of a usable past are likely to emphasize their position as readers, that is, their role as recipients of

multiple texts and traditions.[20] For Vargas Llosa and Cortázar to place novels in the hands of their characters at the very outset of their narratives is
to foreground this American historical awareness, to dramatize what has
been received, and to consider how (whether) it is readable. These issues,
couched in terms of the "belated" reader, have lately been hailed as para-
digmatically postmodern, but they have, in fact, *long* been paradigmatical-
ly Latin American. José Donoso confirms this point in an interview I have
already cited. Speaking about his own intertextual strategies, Donoso
acknowledges that they might be considered postmodernist, but "I did it,
of course, before I ever knew anything about the postmodern."[21] As it happens, he uses Vargas Llosa's *Conversation in The Cathedral* to characterize the Latin American writer-as-reader:

Vargas Llosa's *Conversation in The Cathedral*, the novels by Onetti, or those by
Fuentes, they allude, I think, to an already-made vocabulary of images. They are
explorations into the European and American novel of experimentation. I mean,
it was all of Faulkner again, in many ways in a different guise, a different Faulkner, but nevertheless many things had been taken from Faulkner, as they had
been taken from Virginia Woolf or, as Gabriel García Márquez recognizes in his
own case, the direct influence of *Orlando*, of James Joyce, and so forth. I mean,
they had a vocabulary, a way of looking at things. (13)

In *Conversation in The Cathedral* and *62: A Model Kit*, Vargas Llosa and
Cortázar double the paradigm of the writer-reading by putting books in
their characters' hands, books that also depend upon the "antiheroic" reader's efforts to make formal and substantial connections.

Here the different nature of reading for a Madame Bovary or a Don
Quixote is obvious. Whereas Madame Bovary and Don Quixote read
romances that mediate between their desires and the world, and ultimately cancel the world in favor of their desires, Santiago and Juan are reading
novels that reflect their world and encourage their active engagement in it
(not their withdrawal from it). The literary traditions alluded to in
Madame Bovary and *Don Quixote* are just that, allusions – a means of
describing the characters' personality, education, their social status and
their hearts' desires. On the contrary, Vargas Llosa's and Cortázar's intertextual uses of Huxley and Butor are strategic means by which to include
European precursors who also created synchronic structures and whose
novels now circulate simultaneously with/in their own.

Huxley and Butor used nonverbal models – musical counterpoint and
Cubist collage – to dramatize historical experience as simultaneous rather
than progressive.[22] The title of Aldous Huxley's 1928 novel makes explicit its musical metaphor. Counterpoint is the simultaneous performance of
two sets of musical notation and, when translated into literary performance, becomes for Huxley a means of expressing his satiric vision of the
manifold and simultaneous nature of social interaction. In *Point Counter*

Point, the narrative is divided into relatively short sections that present simultaneously the points of view of many characters, as might the voices of a fugue. In an opening scene, the nature of counterpoint and its analogy to human experience is developed. A character, listening to Bach's Suite in B Minor for flute and strings, revels in the "complex and multitudinous earth" expressed by violin, cello, and flute in the fugal allegro section: "The parts live their separate lives; they touch, their paths cross, they combine for a moment to create a seemingly final and perfected harmony, only to break apart again."[23] So also the "human fugue" that Huxley portrays even as Bach's suite is playing: one character weeps at the sheer beauty of the music, another feels vague sexual longings; and in an adjacent room yet other characters dissect frogs, too busy with their scientific investigation to realize that they are hearing any music at all.[24] This contrapuntal juxtaposition of disparate tones, rhythms, and voices, whether instrumental or human, does not always result in harmony, as Huxley demonstrates. The description of the separate lives of Bach's contrapuntal voices continues, describing the experiential counterpoint as well: "Each is always alone and separate and individual. 'I am I,' asserts the violin; 'the world revolves round me.' 'Round me,' calls the cello. 'Round me,' the flute insists. And all are equally right and equally wrong; and none of them will listen to the others" (23). Irony and satire arise out of this contrapuntal dissonance: individuals see only their own points of view, which, because they are limited, are inevitably distorted. The isolation of the characters within their separate worlds is as central to this kind of novelistic counterpoint as is the multiplicity of those worlds. Huxley's nonlinear narrative allows him to juxtapose non sequiturs and incompatible scenes (using letters, diaries, and notebooks as well as narrated fragments) to produce not only irony and satire but also parody and caricature. It is surely this rendering of multiple perspectives simultaneously and satirically that attracts Vargas Llosa's character and Vargas Llosa himself to Aldous Huxley's fiction.

It is in the ninth chapter of *Point Counter Point* that Huxley realizes the full potential of his contrapuntal technique, and it is here that one senses acutely the link between Vargas Llosa and Huxley, for this chapter takes place in a London bar. The time is one o'clock in the morning and the bar is filled with a variety of people engaged in many simultaneous conversations, fragments of which are juxtaposed to related conversations taking place not only in the bar but elsewhere in London at the same time.[25] This chapter is a vivid intimation of Vargas Llosa's more extended conversations in a bar in Lima called La Catedral.

Like the title of Huxley's novel, Vargas Llosa's title calls attention to the aural metaphor that underlies his novel's structure, in this case conversation rather than musical counterpoint. Vargas Llosa's presentation of his novel as a spoken fiction unmediated by a third-person (i.e., novelistic) narrator allows him to express the digressive, synchronic nature of lived history in a structure that manages to undermine linearity even more thoroughly than does Huxley's. (Vargas Llosa has long been aware of the auditory potential of his medium: in describing an early novella entitled "Los cachorros" ["The Cubs"], he says that he wanted "a story more sung than told and, therefore, each syllable was chosen as much for musical as for narrative reasons.")[26] In *Conversation in The Cathedral*, a polyphony of human voices is orchestrated to suggest the multiplicity of simultaneous cultural and social interactions, as well as the constraints of written narrative to express that simultaneity. The structural devices offered to challenge those constraints – montage of conversational fragments; the volatile shiftings from past to present and from one conversation to another; the ironic interpolation of conflicting spoken accounts of the same event – have been the object of critical scrutiny and do not need detailed analysis here.[27]

The effect of Vargas Llosa's technical virtuosity (as implied in his statement about "The Cubs") is to force our consideration of the nature of the printed word not only semantically but also acoustically. Writing is, in one sense, arrested or frozen speech: the phonetic alphabet, an abstraction of sight from sound, is a highly advanced form of technology that fixes the auditory flux and makes analysis not only possible but inevitable. Vargas Llosa's novel embodies a complex interaction between oral and written media, for it is with the sound of their voices and the voices they recall that his characters invoke the past. Their invocation is ritual and incantatory; their contrapuntal phrases and images, the polysyndeton and parataxis, the antiphonal exchanges and ceaseless echoes of human speech become at points rhapsodic, embodying in synchronic rather than sequential fashion a welter of specific historical and cultural detail. One might even consider the conversations in La Catedral to be rhapsodic in its etymological sense (*rhapsôidia*, literally "stitching together," a term used by the ancient Greeks to describe their epic song). Their conversation recalls an era when verbal art had no fixed text to reproduce, such as we now take for granted, but depended upon the epic singer's improvisational art.[28] The printed text of *Conversation in The Cathedral* is aimed at evoking participation in just such an oral/aural medium; in this sense, the novel predicts *El hablador* (*The Storyteller*, literally *The Speaker*, 1987), Vargas Llosa's brilliant novel about the simultaneity of oral and written (indigenous and Western) traditions in contemporary Peru.

I have stressed the significance of the writer Santiago as reader of Huxley's novel, but this novel also dramatizes the insight that Logos is a matter of listening. Vargas Llosa's "sanctioned Babels" are, in fact, more biblical than Borgesian in their emphasis on spoken speech. Postmodernist claims for the priority of written over spoken language are simply not applicable to *Conversation in The Cathedral*. In *Of Grammatology* and *Writing and Difference*, both published in 1967, Jacques Derrida argues for the primacy of the written or printed word. Spoken speech is relegated to an inferior status by Derrida because it supposedly reinforces an illusory "metaphysics of presence" – the mistaken sense that the world can be known: ". . . the thought of the thing as *what* it *is* has already been confused with the experience of pure speech; and this experience has been confused with experience *itself*. Now, does not pure speech require inscription somewhat in the manner that the Leibnizian essence requires existence and pushes on toward the world, like power toward the act?"[29] Terence Hawkes explains Derrida's opposition to the "metaphysics of presence" that spoken language presumably creates: "Derrida sees this belief in 'presence' as the major factor limiting our apprehension of the world: a distorting insistence that, in spite of our always fragmentary experience, somewhere there must exist a redeeming and justifying *wholeness*, which we can objectify in ourselves as the notion of Man, and beyond ourselves as the notion of Reality."[30] The synchronic structure based in spoken language in *Conversation in The Cathedral* recognizes that wholeness is an illusion, but a necessary one if cultural communities are to survive. It is precisely a self-aware "metaphysics of presence," with a capacity for multiple perspectives and constant correction, that Vargas Llosa both creates and affirms. There are no transcendental signifieds, but there are many ramifying signifiers.

So the dichotomies of postmodernist definition (here, spoken speech versus written speech) are gracefully transcended. Vargas Llosa creates a literary structure that constitutes the reader not only as reader but also as listener, and so orients his audience toward a certain type of collective memory.[31] I have already touched upon these collective sources in my discussion of ancestral voices that animate the earth in the fiction of Goyen, Garro, and Rulfo, and I will do so in subsequent chapters when I discuss the different oral sources of Sandra Cisneros, Manuel Puig, and Luis Rafael Sánchez. In all cases, a variety of voices may be (over)heard in the felt history of these literary fictions.

Point Counter Point and *Conversation in The Cathedral* give us writers-as-readers who are also listening – to Bach in a London drawing room, to a rhapsody of human voices in a Lima bar. So they present the struggle between felt history and literary form thematically as well as structurally. The novelist Phillip Quarles in *Point Counter Point* is constantly aware of the inadequacy of his novelistic medium to express the synchronicities of human experience, and finds an inherent contradiction between his ideal of fidelity to the fluid spontaneity of his perception and the sequential nature of narrative.[32] Quarles' goal is to express his "inner" experience of "outer" phenomena (the goal of the European stream-of-consciousness writers at the time), and to this end he proposes the "musicalization of fiction." Quarles asserts that the artist can, if he chooses, transcend both the single point of view and sequential narrative with contrapuntal plots, variations on themes, modulations among various aspects of reality. The harmonic relations of the auditory medium have neither fixed point of view nor linear axes; when applied to fiction, counterpoint can provide the novelist with the means of breaking down the "watertight compartments" in which people live.[33] The Symbolists – Mallarmé, Rimbaud, Verlaine, Laforgue – had already exploited the potential of music to evoke many spaces and many times in a single poem. Placing music above all other arts, they abandoned the external landscape techniques of the Romantic poets for the acoustic space of the auditory imagination.[34]

For Huxley, the "musicalization of fiction" does not deny temporal movement but allows for a Bergsonian *durée* that is intuitive and indivisible, that conflates the remembered past and the anticipated future in the present of the characters' experience. One character, listening to the ticking of a clock, thinks about time's passage in just such terms: "The moving instant which . . . separates the infinite past from the infinite future advanced inexorably through the dimension of time" (125). Huxley acknowledged that there could be in a verbal medium no exact equivalent to musical counterpoint; whereas several lines of notes may be played simultaneously to make music, two or more lines of words, when read simultaneously, are unintelligible.[35] Nonetheless, the analogy of the dynamic field of counterpoint becomes for Huxley and his alter ego in the novel the conversion factor capable of transforming "the moving instant" into language.

Santiago Zavala, Phillip Quarles' counterpart in *Conversation in The Cathedral*, works for a newspaper called *La Crónica* even as he is absorbed in reading Huxley's unchronological novel *Point Counter Point*. Although Santiago is used to carving slices out of the flow of time as he writes about one event or another for the newspaper, he realizes that such accounts, while necessarily falsified by their linguistic medium, are also necessary fictions by which we order and understand at least one level of our temporal existence. Whereas the individual reporter necessarily dissects temporal reality, the newspaper as a whole perhaps does not. I have already cited Marshall McLuhan on the development of the newspaper during the early nineteenth century, with its mosaic effect of many events on one page: "The format of the book page offers a linear, not a picturesque perspective. It fosters a single tone and attitude between a writer, reader, subject, whereas the newspaper breaks up this linearity and singleness of tone, offering many book pages at the same moment. . . . The newspaper is a space-time landscape of many times, many places, given as single experience."[36] We are given no indication that the journalist Santiago, absorbed in *Point Counter Point*, is conscious of the paradoxical temporal nature of his medium as is, say, Vargas Llosa's journalist in *The War of the End of the*

World or García Márquez's in *Chronicle of a Death Foretold*. Nonetheless, it is clear that Vargas Llosa intends to create the multiple "space-time landscape" of the newspaper in *Conversation in The Cathedral*.[37] Like the presence of the novelist Phillip Quarles in Huxley's *Point Counter Point*, the presence of the journalist Santiago Zavala makes the relationship between felt history and novelistic structure the thematic and structural core of this novel.

I have called *Conversation in The Cathedral* a synchronic narrative structure; even the coincidental meeting of Santiago Zavala and Ambrosio Pardo, the fictional raison d'être of the narrative, may be called synchronic in a broad sense, for coincidence is, of course, the unexpected occurrence of two or more events at the same time. However, Vargas Llosa's fictional structure is not only synchronic but also diachronic, for the author has systematically extended his novel in chronological time, superimposing two time scales, namely, the four hours or so spent in La Catedral and the lifetime – the many lifetimes – contained in the conversation. In his emphasis on the passage of minutes and hours in the bar even as the conversation ebbs and flows synchronically, the author recognizes that the process of recuperating the past in the imagination is not a timeless one but subject to constant modification over time. That he frequents not only a bar called La Catedral but also one called Ultima Hora – literally The Last Hour, figuratively The Last Minute – makes explicit Vargas Llosa's awareness of historical progression as well as the synchronic multiplicity of historical experience.

If Vargas Llosa's intertextuality indicates his attraction to a particular European literary tradition, it also serves to delineate his conscious departure from that mode. Whereas Huxley's contrapuntal structure implies the ultimate resolution of dissonant experience in the ordered work of art, Vargas Llosa's rhapsodic structure is tentative, contradictory, and open-ended. Huxley and his fictional counterpart, Phillip Quarles, perceive reality as fragmented, but both long to counter the fragmentation with the unifying power of their art; the controlled, omniscient narrative voice of *Point Counter Point* seems to offer itself as an antidote to discontinuity. The control of Huxley's narrator becomes apparent when compared to the apparent randomness of Vargas Llosa's, as does the coherence and resolution of Huxley's text when compared to Vargas Llosa's. The experience of dissonance created by Vargas Llosa's rhapsodic structure may be characterized in terms of Barthes' "pleasure of the text," described above. If meaning is to come from the synchronic strains of conversation in La Catedral, it must be the "antihero" reader who creates it by the processes of perception and judgment that such dissonance demands. Whereas Huxley's novelist is a dispassionate observer of life, poised juridically above the chaotic world that he will eventually orchestrate into his own contrapuntal order, Vargas Llosa's journalist is involved in the flux of experience and accepts its disorder and the obstinate triviality of the world. The intertextual relationship makes clear this essential difference: whereas Huxley looks back longingly to Bach, Vargas Llosa looks back ironically at Huxley. For Santiago and his Latin American creator, traditions are discontinuous and precursors must sometimes be created in spite of one's reading.

III

In Julio Cortázar's *62: A Model Kit* (1968), the central character is first seen in the Polidor restaurant in Paris, having just bought a book on the boulevard Saint-Germain. The book is Michel Butor's *6 810 000 litres d'eau par seconde: étude stéréophonique* (1965), a title that has been translated into English as *Niagara: A Stereophonic Novel*.[38] The title suggests that Butor, like Huxley and Vargas Llosa, intends to resist linear narrativity by using an aural metaphor, in this case from the electronic medium of recorded sound. This work was intended for radio broadcast, as were several others of Butor's works written during the same period.[39] Butor, in a note to the reader (whom he casts as radio producer) suggests various orders in which his "monument liquide" may be read and cautions the reader to attend to the dynamic markings indicated in the text. (Cortázar's *Hopscotch* [1963] also provides instructions for the reader that emphasize its synchronic structural aspirations.) In Butor's text, the stereophonic effect results primarily from the interweaving of contemporary descriptions of Niagara Falls with those written by François-René de Chateaubriand after his supposed visit to the Falls in 1791.[40] The Romanticism of Chateaubriand is contrasted with the slice-of-life realism of Butor, and the wild, virgin territory of Chateaubriand with the contemporary domesticated landscape of motels, souvenir shops, and factories. The inane clichés of the contemporary visitors create a dissonant antiphony against which resounds Chateaubriand's oratorical bombast. Man-made noises – car horns and engines, chiming clocks, slamming doors – clash with the sounds of nature, creating the contrapuntal cacophony that serves as background for the sotto voce description of the falls. However distanced by time their visits are, these French literary tourists look at Niagara Falls and see themselves; their descriptions reflect less the falls than their own positions in the history of literary utterance.

Butor uses his venerable countryman's visit to create a synchronic description of his own. By recuperating Chateaubriand's stylized description – based on eighteenth-century Romantic sensational theory, in which mountains and waterfalls were the sine qua non of a sublime response to nature – Butor infuses twentieth-century tourism with Romantic sublimity. The result is comic, ironic, poignant – and historically resonant. Laurent Jenny, in an early discussion of intertextuality, cites Butor's text in

this regard: "... to highlight syntagms ('mythologies') petrified in their formulae, to distance oneself from their banality by opening them up and then
wrest the signified from their atrophy in order to launch a new process of
signification. . . . This is what Butor does to one famous page of
Chauteaubriand in *Niagara: A Stereophonic Novel*."[41] In fact, Butor
evokes an entire literary tradition surrounding the falls. By choosing what
was a compulsory stop for European literary tourists from the mid-eigh-
teenth century on, Butor alludes implicitly to a multitude of texts that resonate with the synchronic density of his own.[42]

In turn, Cortázar embeds Butor's novel in his own *62: A Model Kit* and
adds to it the rich legacy of Latin American literary dicta that also surround Niagara Falls, beginning with the Cuban poet José María de Heredia
and becoming, according to Enrique Anderson Imbert, "una obsesión en la
poesía hispanoamericana."[43] In this way intertextuality itself becomes a
synchronic structural technique, as Laurent Jenny recognizes: "The nature
of intertextuality is to introduce a new kind of reading that explodes the
linearity of the text . . . marking the text with bifurcations that gradually
open its semantic space" (266).

The historical chasm (168 years and cultural eons) separating Butor's
text from Chateaubriand's is both foregrounded and bridged by the simultaneous presentation of the two historical perspectives. The "stereophonic" shifting between these two texts seems at once to emphasize the flow
of time and arrest it. Butor notes this contradiction in an interview: "It is
a book that is completely given over to the theme of acceleration. . . .
Behind the time that accelerates, there is this space of absolute acceleration, of *immobile acceleration*, where the image is formed by the falls
themselves at Niagara."[44] In the "coda" to the work, the speaker interpolates in rapid succession the phrases "l'heure passe," "la nuit passe," "le
mois passe," "les années passent" ("time passes," "the night passes," "the
month passes," "years pass"). The flow of time would seem to simulate the
inexorable flow of water over the falls, and yet the structure of the chapters appears to suggest otherwise. There are twelve chapters, each bearing
the name of a month in calendrical order and each describing characteristics of the appropriate season. While the chapters thus invoke progressive
chronological movement, they also undermine it, for aren't Chateaubriand
and contemporary visitors viewing the falls simultaneously in March,
December, and July? The stylized images and descriptions of the months
are, then, elements of Butor's synchronic structure at the same time that
their names – running across the tops of the pages, repeated as many times
as will fit on the line – suggest the progressive forward movement of time.
So the months become typographic objects, repeated elements in the visual collage of the printed page.[45]

Despite Butor's auditory metaphor (*étude stéréophonique*), then, his
synchrony is not only aural but also visual, his structural inclusiveness

based not only on stereophonic sound but also on Cubist collage. Each of the various voices is set in a different typeface and arranged in various patterns to allow the reader to see them simultaneously; descriptions of sound effects are placed to the right, center, or left of the page so that we may *see* their stereophonic interactions, and the names of the characters are also placed to the right or left of the page so that we may *see* where they stand. From the musical structure that, however contrapuntal or stereophonic, proceeds in time according to internal rhythms and measures, the reader moves into a visual realm where progression and succession are more easily subverted. It is the visual effect – Butor's synchronic structure based on sight as well as sound – that fascinates Cortázar's protagonist Juan as he reads *Niagara* in *62: A Model Kit*. Cortázar is well known, in such stories as "Las babas del diablo" ("Blow-up"), "Axolotl," and "Todos los fuegos el fuego" ("All the Fires the Fire") for his narrative consideration of visual perspective.[46] In *62: A Model Kit*, his character is reading Butor for a reason.

The synchronic structure of *62: A Model Kit* is constructed with visual images that are repeated verbally, modified, multiplied, and rearranged in suggestive conceptual patterns that create not so much a novel as an abstract structure of images with a novelistic ambiance. As Juan sits in the Polidor restaurant in Paris, he hears another diner order "un chateau saignant" (a rare chateaubriand steak) just as he raises his eyes from François-René de Chateaubriand's text, embedded in the novel by Butor that he is reading. He thinks about the odd conjunction of meanings occasioned by Butor's novel and the diner's order:

Y así el hecho de haber abierto el libro y mirado distraídamente el nombre del vizconde de Chateaubriand, ese mero gesto que lleva a un lector crónico a echar una ojeada a cualquier página impresa que entra en su campo visual, había como potenciado lo que inevitablemente había de seguir, y la voz del comensal gordo mutilando como se estilaba en Paris el nombre del autor de *Atala* me había llegado distintamente en un hueco del rumor del restaurante que, sin el encuentro del nombre completo en una página del libro, no se hubiera producido para mi. Habrá sido necesario que mirara vagamente una página del libro (y que comprara el libro media hora antes sin saber bien por qué) para que esa casi horrible nitidez del pedido del comensal gordo en el brusco silencio del restaurante Polidor desencadenase el zarpazo con una fuerza infinitamente más arrasadora que cualquiera de las evidencias tangibles que me rodeaban en la sala.[47]

And so the fact of having opened the book and looked distractedly at the name of the Vicomte de Chateaubriand, that simple gesture which brings a chronic reader to glance at any printed page that comes within his visual range, had in a way given the potential of what inevitably had to follow, and the voice of the fat diner mutilating, as was the style in Paris, the name of the author of *Atala*, had reached me clearly in a hollow in the noise of the restaurant, which, without the encounter with the complete name on a page in the book, wouldn't have been produced for me. It had been necessary for me to look vaguely at a page in the

book (and for me to have bought the book a half-hour before without really knowing why) for that almost horrible neatness of the fat diner's order in the sudden
silence of the Polidor to unchain the clawing with a force infinitely more devas-
tating than any of the tangible evidence that surrounded me in the dining room.[48]

"Chateau saignant" – a rare chateaubriand, literally "castillo sangrien-
to," "bloody castle": these words create a "crystallization" of images, to
use one of Cortázar's metaphors for this process.[49] Leaving Paris and entering a composite European city located in mythic and psychic space,
Cortázar constructs an inclusive model of human experience on a simultaneous plane. Repeating images – a basilisk, a broken doll, the legend of
Erszebet Bathori with its medieval associations of vampirism and blood
(here "chateau saignant" literally becomes a bloody castle) – overlay the
city's geometry of streetcar rails, tunnels, plazas, giving it an aura of time-
lessness and mystery. Shifting "crystallizations" of these images are presented in short, unnumbered prose segments, and become the pieces of
the model kit the reader must construct. Juan knows, as does the reader,
that the pieces are not linked by chronology or causality but by chance
association and momentary conjunction. Cortázar's collage is based upon
the relations of visual images as they "crystallize" in a fluid narrative
present.

Juan is a translator. His stock-in-trade, like that of Phillip Quarles and
Santiago Zavala, are written words, but his primary function is deciphering the "sudden dizzying mass" (as he puts it) of spoken speech. He realizes, as do Phillip and Santiago, that writing orders sequentially what is
neither sequential nor causal. He thinks: "Y no había palabras, porque no
había pensamiento posible para esa fuerza capaz de convertir jirones de
recuerdo, imágenes aisladas y anodinas, en un repentino bloque vertigi-
noso, en una viviente constelación aniquilada en el acto mismo de
mostrarse, una contradicción que parecía ofrecer y negar a la vez . . ." (12;
"And there were no words because there was no thought possible for that
force capable of converting stretches of memory, isolated and anodyne
images, into a sudden dizzying mass, into a living constellation that is
erased with the very act of showing itself, a contradiction that seemed to
offer and deny at the same time . . ." 13). To attempt to prolong the momentary conjunction, the ephemeral model, with words is, Juan thinks, like
"echando paladas de sombra contra la oscuridad" (12; "shoveling shadows
into the darkness" 13).

This sense of the inadequacy of language would seem to echo that of the
European modernists but it does not, for 62: A Model Kit must be considered in terms of Cubist collage. Its "model kit" structure requires that we
visualize its elements as a montage of images and perspectives rather than
a series of events. The Cubist object is portrayed from many angles simultaneously; we see it from the other side of the canvas as well as from the
side where we stand, from the bottom and from the top, a "dynamic colli-

sion of shots taken from different angles," as Wylie Sypher put it in his early, influential study of Cubism in art and literature.[50] Cubist collage can portray multiple perspectives and variable spatial relationships as narrative fiction cannot; in like manner, the words "chateau saignant" multiply and refract visually, creating (Juan insists) a moment in which many cultural and historical perspectives coalesce and then dissolve again into other "constellations." Thus Juan's sense of the inadequacy of language is counterbalanced by the synchronic potential of the novel's structure. The variable visual images that constitute Cortázar's model kit, like the intersecting planes of Cubist collage, represent the world as a set of fluid spatial relationships in which visual perspective, narrative structure, and felt history are inseparable.

IV

Synchronic structures have been created on both sides of the Atlantic to express multiple, simultaneous, conflictual, and even mutually exclusive realities, and they have been called both "modernist" and "postmodernist" as a result. Can differences between Butor and Cortázar, or Huxley and Vargas Llosa be theorized in these terms? Barthes' definition of intertextuality as "re-reading [that] is no longer consumption, but play (that play which is the return of the different)"[51] is clearly applicable to Vargas Llosa and Cortázar. The fact that "play" is specified in both Cortázar's games and Vargas Llosa's music is coincidental, but their structural metaphors nonetheless reinforce Barthes' definition of intertextuality as play, and play as "the return of the different." What differences? Here I would offer several comparative observations.

The European modernists who created synchronic structures did so to communicate psychological difference whereas Latin American writers are currently creating synchronic structures as a way of engaging cultural difference. All are concerned with the nature and experience of duration, but the stream-of-consciousness writers, in their focus on interior duration, take only haphazard account of external events (presumably all that is available to the psyche in any case). In Huxley's novel, intuitive accounts of interior time overshadow the historical time of shared communal contexts; in Butor's novel, questions about the nature of perception take priority, along with related questions of aesthetic modes of expressing perception. Only James Joyce, among European modernists, grappled with issues of cultural difference and historical disjunction comparable to those that concern Vargas Llosa and Cortázar and the other Latin American writers mentioned in this chapter.[52] While Vargas Llosa's and Cortázar's references to Huxley and Butor are indications of *structural* intent, their own novels are designed to serve the different objective of balancing cultural continuity against historical disruption, communal traditions against individual meanings. Synchronic structures are particularly suited to express the felt history of Latin America: the pressure of public events and their subjective interpretations; the shifting interactions of autonomy and solidarity.

It is no coincidence that the Latin American creators of synchronic structures I have mentioned here – Borges, Carpentier, García Márquez, Cortázar, Allende, and I will refer to Fuentes in a moment – are also the reigning masters of magical realism. Synchronic structures admit antinomies, including the magic and the real, and release their creators from the demands of causality and materiality. Fredric Jameson accurately asserts that magical realism relies on synchronic strategies, noting its characteristic "superposition of whole layers of the past within the present."[53] Jameson distinguishes magical realist "breaks and discontinuities" from "an older modernism whose enigmas had less to do with the intricacies of its subject matter than with the peremptory and supremely arbitrary decisions of the high modernist demiurge" (305). Though his radical dichotomizing of modernism and postmodernism is not applicable to contemporary Latin American fiction, he correctly calls attention to the shared cultural conditions impelling both synchronic structures and magical realist strategies. Jameson's discussion includes the layered histories of Faulkner's South.

Southern writers have engaged synchronic narrative strategies for reasons familiar to Latin American writers.[54] Faulkner, acknowledged master of García Márquez and admired contemporary of Borges, created synchronic structures not so much to suggest psychological processes (as European stream-of-consciousness writers did) as to encompass the diverse and discontinuous histories of his cultural community, Yoknapatawpha County. Faulkner referred to his inclusive narrative strategies as "thirteen ways of looking at a blackbird." The phrase is itself an intertext, of course. Faulkner was referring to a poem by Wallace Stevens that consists of thirteen short stanzas, some only two lines long, which show the reader a blackbird from different perspectives and in different settings, situations, and seasons. Faulkner, in his University of Virginia interviews, was asked how he approached historical truth in his fiction. Without referring directly to Stevens, he replied, "I think no one individual looks at truth. It blinds you. You look at it and you see one phase of it. . . . It was . . . thirteen ways of looking at a blackbird. But the truth, I would like to think, comes out when the reader has read all these thirteen ways of looking and has his own fourteenth image of that blackbird which I would like to think of as truth."[55] Note Faulkner's emphasis on the reader, indeed, his implicit identification of himself as reader: a glance is an epiphany, and enough glances will combine to make a usable text, even a tradition.

Faulkner's faith in simultaneous perspectives as a source of truth is shared by Eudora Welty and Carson McCullers. Welty's *The Golden Apples*

(1949) and *The Optimist's Daughter* (1969) and McCullers' *The Heart is a Lonely Hunter* (1954) are instances of synchronic structures that attempt to encompass – metaphorically and structurally – the cultural and historical disjunctions of Faulkner's South. In Welty's autobiography, she names her most basic artistic impulse: "I'm prepared now to use the wonderful word *confluence*, which of itself exists as a reality and a symbol in one. It is the only kind of symbol that for me as a writer has any weight, testifying to the pattern, one of the chief patterns, of human experience."[56]

If Southern writers have long been aware of cultural and historical antinomies, that awareness is now less likely to be focused by regional history than by cultural communities. Of course, the two are often inseparable, as in the work of the African-American writer Albert Murray, whose "blues aesthetic" makes his Georgia musician protagonist in *The Seven League Boots* (1996) an improviser and a self-conscious synthesizer.[57] Jazz, too, is a frequent structural metaphor for textual synchrony and cultural confluence. In fact, Murray does not separate jazz from the blues idiom. He writes of Duke Ellington that his jazz forms are

mostly the result of the extension, elaboration, and refinement of the traditional twelve-bar blues chorus and the standard thirty-two-bar pop song form. *And in doing so he has also fulfilled the ancestral imperative to process folk melodies, and the music of popular entertainment as well as that of church ceremonies into a truly indigenous fine art . . . by using devices of stylization that are as vernacular as the idiomatic particulars of the subject matter itself.* It is not a matter of working folk and pop materials into established or classic European forms but of extending, elaborating, and refining (which is to say ragging, jazzing, and riffing and even jamming) the idiomatic into fine art.[58]

Murray's "ancestral imperative" requires that past forms be integrated into present modes of expression; jazz is synchronic because it obeys the "ancestral imperative" to include those very ancestors. Toni Morrison's *Jazz* (1992) is a recent engagement of this particularly American metaphor. John Edgar Wideman, in his preface to *Fatheralong*, uses quite another metaphor, one drawn from chemistry; he writes of the "compound of immutable elements" that is contemporary African-American culture.[59] The elements may be immutable, but the compound is not. It is volatile, syncretic, synchronic. Like Wideman, Murray, and Morrison, many U.S. "minority" writers are working to dramatize their own cultural "compounds" in inclusive literary structures, an assertion to which I will return in my next chapter.

A contemporary of Faulkner and also an early practitioner of synchronic strategies was the Chicago-born resident of the world, John Dos Passos. Dos Passos created a vast synchronic structure to express the communal complexities of the territory announced in the title of his most famous work, *U.S.A.* (1938).[60] Carlos Fuentes has stated that as he was writing his first novel, *La región más transparente* (*Where the Air Is Clear*, 1958), "Dos Passos was my literary bible,"[61] and Wendy B. Faris has noted that the multiperspectival structure of Fuentes' novel, divided into sections headed by different characters' names, resembles the structure of the U.S.A. trilogy.[62] The resemblance of *The Death of Artemio Cruz* (1962), which is also synchronically structured, to Dos Passos' *Adventures of a Young Man* in his trilogy *District of Columbia* (1952) awaits comparative discussion.

My point is not to multiply examples but to conclude. The experience of writing amid various cultures and histories is perhaps the defining experience of New World writers, and it makes them (recall Borges' self-characterization) "good readers" in the inclusive sense I have explored here. We have seen that New World writers are likely to engage the trope of the writer-as-reader in order to dramatize their own historical positioning as inheritors of multiple traditions. And they are likely to create inclusive narrative structures to reflect their simultaneous participation in all of them.

Terrence Rafferty, in his 1988 *New Yorker* review of *The Art of the Novel*, by Milan Kundera, and *Myself with Others*, by Carlos Fuentes, also notices this tendency. These collections of essays describe their authors' development as writers through their reading. Rafferty finds that "Kundera, serenely European, seems to take the relationship between his reading and his writing entirely for granted."[63] He quotes Kundera on "the spirit of continuity" of the novel: ". . . each work is an answer to preceding ones, each work contains all the previous experience of the novel" (110). Rafferty notes that though Kundera has lived in exile from Czechoslovakia since 1975, his essays reflect the sense of security that comes from belonging to a tradition. He conveys no sense of exile. On the contrary, according to Rafferty, "He's still very much a part of the tradition that shaped him: the literature and philosophy and music of Europe. In terms of the novel, he may even be the Continental culture's greatest current exemplar, its reigning king. He seems to have as little anxiety about his sources as a monarch has about his genes" (111).

Rafferty contrasts Kundera's lack of anxiety of origins to that of Fuentes and American writers generally: "The key problem for writers from the United States and Latin America, though Latin American writers in particular – Cortázar, García Márquez, Cabrera Infante, Puig, Carpentier, Arenas, Donoso" is their status as readers, that is, "how reading and imagination manage somehow to resolve themselves into creation" (115). Rafferty describes Fuentes' search "for his own historical identity, reading promiscuously, trying to fit everything he reads into an already overcrowded self . . ." (114). As I have done, Rafferty connects this inclusive impulse to literary structure: "Fuentes often writes – not just here but also in dense, overreaching fictions like *Terra Nostra* and *The Death of Artemio Cruz*, which try to collapse time, space, and identity into entirely new forms – as if he were struggling to keep everything in view simultaneously . . ." (115). According to Rafferty, in the essays of the final "We" section of *Myself and Others*, it is "as if all difference had been reconciled, the self and others resolved into an all-inclusive unity, an identity so multifarious and complex that it has finally become simple, lapidary" (117). I would question Rafferty's sense of reconciliation ("simple, lapidary"), but I agree with his intuition of the appeal of "all-inclusive" structures in contexts where traditions are multiple and identity multifarious, and where literature must overarch antinomies. Not reconciliation, but recognition and inclusion.

Rafferty clearly sympathizes with Fuentes and devises a collective American persona to say so: "We recognize in his confusion and contradictions and torturous acts of identification more of ourselves than we do in Kundera's splendid precision" (113). Whereas Kundera defends the tradition of the novel against the historical forces that would destroy or supersede it, Fuentes "creates a fable of New World education" (115). Rafferty continues: "We realize that part of the reason Fuentes' novels exasperate us is that they too precisely mirror the dense chaos of our images of ourselves, the ungainly struggles of our readings of the world . . ." (118). Rafferty finds that Fuentes believes in "the spirit of continuity" but that "the tradition he means to be continuous with keeps changing its contours, expanding, ramifying, sprouting heads. . ." (115). I will return to this American hydra in my conclusion.

CHAPTER FIVE

Fragmentary Fictions

Angelina Muñiz-Huberman, *Dulcinea Encantada*
Sandra Cisneros, *Woman Hollering Creek*

A Klee painting named "Angelus Novus" shows an angel looking as though he is about to move away from something he is fixedly contemplating. His eyes are staring, his mouth is open, his wings are spread. This is how one pictures the angel of history. His face is turned toward the past. Where we perceive a chain of events, he sees one single catastrophe which keeps piling wreckage upon wreckage and hurls it in front of his feet. The angel would like to stay, awaken the dead, and make whole what has been smashed. But a storm is blowing from Paradise; it has got caught in his wings with such violence that the angel can no longer close them. This storm irresistibly propels him into the future to which his back is turned, while the pile of debris before him grows skyward. This storm is what we call progress.

Walter Benjamin, "Theses on the Philosophy of History"[1]

THIS PASSAGE IS FROM the ninth of eighteen narrative fragments written by the Jewish-German philosopher Walter Benjamin in 1940, the last year of his life. Benjamin's Angelus Novus refers to a particular angel, created of ink, chalk, and brown wash on paper by the Swiss painter Paul Klee (see frontispiece). The work was acquired by Benjamin in 1921 and bequeathed to his friend Gershom Scholem, the great scholar of Jewish mysticism. Scholem owned the painting until the end of his life; in 1989 his widow gave it to the Israel Museum, where it is today.[2] Scholem wrote an essay in 1972 entitled "Walter Benjamin and His Angel" in which he demonstrated the complex significance of Klee's angel throughout Benjamin's work. He concluded his essay: "If one may speak of Walter Benjamin's genius, then it was concentrated in this angel. In the latter's saturnine light Benjamin's life itself ran its course, also consisting only of 'small-scale victories' and 'large-scale defeats,' as he described it from a deeply melancholy point of view in a letter which he addressed to me on July 26, 1932, one day before his intended, but at the time not executed, suicide."[3]

This "angel of history," its wings uplifted, its feathers (and hair) ruffled, its eyes askew, was painted by Paul Klee in 1920, and described by Ben-

156

jamin in "Theses on the Philosophy of History" in 1940. That Benjamin chooses a *new* angel – Angelus Novus – to preside over the wreckage of history recalls the anxiety surrounding the newness of history in the Americas: I began by proposing Charles Simic's fat old man in faded overalls as a figure of this historical anxiety, and I now propose that Klee's/Benjamin's angel join his company. This new angel is as ethereal as Simic's old man is earthy, a visionary where the old man is myopic; nonetheless, both represent the relations of history and power and suggest the abuses inherent in those relations. Benjamin's angel, itself described in a fragmentary text, hovers over the fragmentary fictions of Angelina Muñiz-Huberman and Sandra Cisneros.

Angelus Novus surveys the "storm of progress," a metaphor signifying for Benjamin the foundations of modernity: rationalism, science, dehumanizing technology, and the triumph of ideologies that privileged an idealized future over a shared past, and ideological abstraction over historical awareness. This storm of progress had by 1940 taken Europe to the point of annihilation. Benjamin's angel "is turned toward the past. Where we perceive a chain of events, he sees one single catastrophe. The angel would like to stay, awaken the dead, and make whole what has been smashed" (257). Muñiz-Huberman and Cisneros create female narrators who, like Benjamin's angel, oversee the fragments of their own histories and the history of their cultures. Unlike Cortázar's and Vargas Llosa's synchronic narrative structures, which metaphorically encompass the disjunctive histories they narrate, these fictions flaunt their fragmentary status. Nonetheless, fragments are only fragmentary with respect to some larger entity; fragmentation can be flaunted only if one intuits or imagines somewhere, sometime, as Benjamin's angel does, a "whole . . . [t]hat has been smashed," even if it never existed; even if it can never be (re)constituted. This is far more than mere nostalgia for a lost past or utopian longing for an unattainable future. In fact, it is a mode of cultural criticism. Benjamin uses fragmentary structures to undercut rationalist notions of progressive history, as do Muñiz-Huberman and Cisneros. Their historical perspective is ironic; they can assess the extent of the "wreckage" because they see it synchronically and spatially rather than sequentially. This inclusive vision represents an opportunity for Cisneros' narrators, and disaster for Muñiz-Huberman's.

Donald Shaw has noted a generalized tendency toward fragmentation in contemporary Latin American fiction, a tendency that he calls "the splintered mirror effect."[4] Unlike Julio Ortega, whom I have quoted on the inclusive impulse ("el impulso integrador") of recent Latin American writers, or Robin Fiddian, who discusses the "totalizing strategies" ("la práctica totalizante o totalizadora") of this fiction, Shaw emphasizes the fragments as such.[5] Referring to a phrase from García Márquez's *Chronicle of a Death Foretold*, Shaw writes: "The very image that García Márquez uses in this novel: 'recomponer con tantas astillas dispersas el espejo roto de la memoria' [13; 'put the broken mirror of memory back together from so many scattered shards' 6] reveals the novelist's awareness that fiction has lost any single viewpoint from which to reflect the world, so that what remains is fragmentary, hard to fit together, even contradictory" (63). Although García Márquez's image also allows the possibility that the shards may be reconstituted in usable form – "recomponer . . . el espejo roto de la memoria" – Shaw nonetheless insists upon the "crisis of confidence in the writer's ability to interpret experience" (64). Shaw's assertion anticipates my discussion of Muñiz-Huberman, Cisneros, and women writers generally, who have long been marginalized or excluded from the processes of historical interpretation. But first, I need to say something more about Klee's angels.

If Klee's Angelus Novus represented for Benjamin an undaunted witness to the disasters of modern history, for Klee himself the angel was a refugee from more private horrors. Klee painted images of angels throughout his long career. In 1939, when the artist was suffering from a incurable illness and felt himself suspended between life and death, he painted twenty-nine winged creatures. These ultimate angels (rare birds, indeed) had become for Klee symbols of his mortal condition. They are always single and solitary: they are never depicted as announcing or witnessing biblical miracles, nor are they accompanied by the consolatory iconography upon which normal Judeo-Christian angels can count. Klee's angels are hybrid, fantastical beings, mixtures of human/animal/spirit. Klee gave them names like "Forgetful," "Ugly," "Unfinished," "Poor," and "Still Female."

Angelina Muñiz-Huberman and Sandra Cisneros, like their women protagonists, are angels of history in the metaphoric terms proposed by Klee and Benjamin: hybrid in a cultural sense and conscious of the need to resist the buffeting winds of modernity. Recall how Benjamin describes Klee's angel: "His eyes are staring, his mouth is open, his wings are spread." Muñiz-Huberman and Cisneros create fictional settings in which histories and cultures collide. Their characters dramatize the difficult (and sometimes disastrous) processes of transculturation – of combining fragmented cultural meanings in order to constitute usable structures of being.

I

Angelina Muñiz-Huberman's novel *Dulcinea encantada* (*Enchanted Dulcinea*) has as its epigraph a phrase by Paul Klee: "The border between interior and exterior is minimal." For the main character of this novel, Dulcinea (or Dulce) even this minimal border no longer exists. She makes no distinction between self and other, past and present; she does not distinguish her own identity from that of other people or from the characters in the books she has read. Her undifferentiated mental state might imply schizophrenia, or at least acute depression. Rather, Dulcinea suffers from what Benjamin diagnosed as the twentieth-century's sickness, the storm of progress. As a girl in Spain, Dulcinea is separated from her parents and her own cultural context by war. She is sent to Russia along with other Spanish children, where the governments of Spain and Russia have agreed to shelter them from the violence of the civil war. The Spanish war ends and World War II begins. Ten years pass before she finally meets her parents again, in Mexico. She does not recognize them in the train station. Her personal history is engulfed by collective horrors, and the self is erased. Dulcinea refers to her own annihilation: "Para mí ya no hay fin de mundo. Mi mundo se destruyó el día que me pusieron en el barco [para Rusia]" ("For me there is no end of the world. My world was destroyed the day that they put me on the ship [to Russia]").[6]

This is not altogether the case. In order to continue to live in history, Dulce replaces her own with imagined ones. If her private history has been reduced or erased – the reader is given to understand that it is too painful *not* to be – her imagined histories are unbounded. She drives around the congested *periférico* (beltway) in Mexico City, an action that circumscribes the narrative present but not the novel's range of historical reference. In her mind, historical and fictional texts and contexts fuse and diffuse and proliferate. Dulce says of herself: "Yo soy tantas historias que a veces me es difícil elegir con cuál me quedo" (26; "I am so many histories that at times it is difficult to choose which one I'll keep"). In fact, Dulcinea keeps them all, superimposing, interweaving, and conflating them. Together they represent this century's storm of progress and comprise the fragmentary structure of the novel itself. The storm is personal, political, and aesthetic.

Clutching the wheel of her car and barely negotiating the hair-raising traffic on the *periférico*, Dulce is simultaneously Don Quixote's enchanting Dulcinea, the lover of Amadís of Gaul, the knight of Spanish chivalric romance, and lady-in-waiting of the nineteenth-century Scottish traveler to Mexico, Fanny Calderón de la Barca.[7] Dulce's imaginary histories are shored up by inserted textual fragments from a great variety of literary, philosophical, and historical sources. Calderón's lyric description of the valley of Mexico as seen from Chapultepec Castle on December 31, 1839, is one of the longest fragments included in *Dulcinea encantada*, and it immediately makes apparent the antinomies of Dulce's simultaneous histories. Even as she is jarred by the congestion and pollution of the world's largest city, she experiences Calderón's text, which describes a mid-nineteenth-century view of Mexico City, where order and beauty are still possible:

Desde la terraza que rodea al castillo, la vista que se ofrece es el más extraordinario panorama que pueda imaginarse. El valle de México se muestra en un mapa; la ciudad, con sus innumerables iglesias y conventos; los dos acueductos cortando la llanura; las avenidas de álamos y olmos que conducen a la ciudad; las aldeas,

lagos y valles que la envuelven. Al norte, la espléndida catedral de Nuestra Señora de Guadalupe. Al sur, los pueblos de San Agustín, San Angel y Tacubaya, que
parecen inmersos en los árboles, como un enorme jardín. Y aunque en las llanuras
de abajo hay muchos campos sin cultivar y muchos edificios en ruinas, el glorioso
marco de las montañas, enseñoreadas por los dos altivos volcanes el Popocatépetl
y el Ixtaccíhuatl, el Gog y el Magog del valle, de cuyos costados gigantescos se
desprenden masas de nubes densas, y con su cielo turquesa siempre sonriendo en
la escena, todo el paisaje, visto desde esta altura, es de belleza sin par.[8]

From the terrace that runs around the castle, the view forms the most magnificent panorama that can be imagined. The whole valley of Mexico lies stretched
out as in a map; the city itself, with its innumerable churches and convents; the
two great aqueducts which cross the plain; the avenues of elms and poplars which
lead to the city; the villages, lakes, and plains, which surround it. To the north,
the magnificent cathedral of Our Lady of Guadalupe – to the south, the villages
of San Augustín, San Angel, and Tacubaya, which seem imbosomed in trees, and
look like an immense garden. And if in the plains below there are many unculti-
vated fields, and many buildings falling to ruin, yet with its glorious enclosure of
mountains, above which tower the two mighty volcanoes, Popocatépetl and
Ixtaccíhuatl, the Gog and Magog of the valley, off whose giant sides great volumes of misty clouds were rolling, and with its turquoise sky forever smiling on
the scene, the whole landscape, as viewed from this height, is one of nearly unpar-
alleled beauty.[9]

Calderón's description recalls the magnificent landscapes by her contemporary José María Velasco, and confirms the cultural complexity of the
landscape she surveys. Popocatépetl and Ixtaccíhuatl, mythic Aztec prince
and princess memorialized as volcanoes side by side forever, become Gog
and Magog, and the Virgin of Guadalupe underscores this cultural syncretism. Her astute outsider's eye encompasses the indigenous and colonial cultures of this earlier postcolonial moment in Mexico. Dulcinea's
habitation of her fellow-traveler's world reiterates the synchronic perspective of Benjamin's angel, who gazes upon the fragments and sees a single
catastrophe.

Other intertexts are interspersed throughout: the twenty qualities
required of a proper chivalric knight, as listed by the Renaissance philosopher Ramón Lull; the thirty-one aspects of the marvelous tale by the Russian formalist Vladimir Propp; passages from the works of Thomas
Browne, San Juan de la Cruz, Fray Luis de León, Ludwig Wittgenstein, and
many others. Textual fragments "pile up" at Dulcinea's feet as wreckage
piles up before Benjamin's angel. The fragments are not integrated into the
present of the narrative nor does any metaphoric structure overarch them:
history accretes in the synchronic, anarchic layers. If the rejection of linear
history is liberating for Borges, Fuentes, and Garro, it is *not* for Muñiz-
Huberman's character. Dulcinea creates her precursors, but she is incapable of distinguishing among them, or herself from them.

Dulcinea makes literal her dissociation:

Claro que sí fui hecha de barro, de ahí mi resquebrajamiento.
   ¿Puede un arqueólogo reconstruir? No, creo que no. Pega las piezas. Las fisuras quedan. Podría volver a salirse el agua por ahí. Pero yo ni siquiera encuentro las piezas. Ni siquiera puedo dar la apariencia de un ser remendado. Soy un ser despedazado. La cabeza se me escapa hacia lo alto. El corazón lo he perdido. Un pie se apoya en la tierra y el otro vacila en el aire. Los brazos, desarmónicos. Los ojos, dando vueltas. La cámara lenta en velocidades dispares. (186)

Of course I was made of clay, so naturally I could break.
   Can an archeologist put me back together. No, I don't think so. Glue the pieces. The cracks remain. Water might run through the cracks. But I can't even find the pieces. I can't even pretend to be mended. I am broken. My head flies off. My heart is lost. One foot is on the ground and the other in the air. My arms unhinge. My eyes roll. Slow motion in different speeds.

The author plays with the contradictory possibilities of *despegar* (literally, to unstick or break; metaphorically, to take off or fly). Bodily fragments attempt to *despegar* in fugitive moments of transcendence. However, they do not fly, but rather fly off. The chaos of Dulce's interior life is isomorphic with the ruins that surround her. The novel ends in this way:

El automóvil se desliza como un trineo en la nieve o un barco en el mar. Las nubes van espaciándose. La luz se vuelve intensa, antes de desaparecer.

· · ·

El Periférico se acaba. El automóvil entra por un camino lateral. Atrás va quedando el asfalto, la tierra apisonada.

Hay árboles: pájaros que están recogiéndose y que cantan su último canto. Ramas inclinadas por el peso de los frutos. Agradable silencio. Claroscuro.

Este lugar sí me gusta, piensa Dulcinea.

Al fondo un castillo. Abruptas rocas hasta llegar a él. La luz en las nubes. El almendrado ojo de Dios.

Se abren las puertas (del cielo). (189–90)

The car slides like a sled on snow or a ship on the sea. The clouds disperse. The light intensifies, then disappears.

· · ·

The beltway ends. The car enters the frontage road. It leaves behind the asphalt, the packed dirt.

There are trees: birds flock and sing their final song. Branches bent with fruit. Pleasant silence. Chiaroscuro.

I like this place, Dulcinea thinks.

In the distance a castle. Steep rocks before arriving there. The light on the clouds. The almond eye of God.

The gates (of heaven) open.

So Dulcinea drives to the end of the vicious circle of progress.

Nevertheless, the last parenthesis of the novel – "del cielo" ("of heaven") – offers a possible reinterpretation of what can otherwise only be understood as the dead end of modern history. There are mitigating textual circumstances in *Dulcinea encantada*: the Benjaminian idea of fragments as a means of opposing the false promise of progressive history and the cabbalistic current that runs through Muñiz-Huberman's fiction.[10] Superimposed on the narrator's fragmentary lists and quotations are the seven seals of the Book of Revelation, each serving as title of a chapter. An apocalyptic historical pattern of crisis and culmination operates in this novel, suggesting that the welter of texts may reflect the fundamental Jewish perception that from the preservation of the collective past arises the possibility of redemption.

Robert Alter addresses this apocalyptic historicism – what he calls "the structure of Jewish tradition" – in the work of Benjamin, Kafka, and Scholem: "Everything originates in the incandescence of revelation, which is then sustained through time in the myriad mirrorings and refractions of exegesis. The whole system is imaginatively focused on the great moment of its origination, however bold and surprising the 'spontaneity' of later interpreters."[11] Alter explores the paradox inherent in this structure, the "Jewish focus on the vista of the *past* [and] the Jewish expectation of a *future* redemption" (106). The final ambiguity of "del cielo" in *Dulcinea encantada* echoes this structure – a tradition that is at once accomplished and potential, remembered and expected, recorded and revealed. So, the messianic kingdom depends upon the remembered ruins.

But what is expected or revealed at the end of *Dulcinea encantada*, and to whom? Alter offers us a possible interpretation in his commentary on the correspondence between Benjamin and Scholem in 1934. They exchanged impassioned letters about the end of Kafka's novel *The Trial* and about the nature of revelation in the works of Kafka generally. Unlike the usual reading of Kafka's novelistic world as devoid of meaning, Scholem wrote to Benjamin:

Kafka's world is the world of revelation, but of revelation seen of course from that perspective in which it is returned to its own nothingness. I cannot accept your disavowal of this aspect. . . . The *nonfulfillability* of what has been revealed is the point where a *correctly* understood theology . . . coincides most perfectly with that which offers the key to Kafka's work. Its problem is not, dear Walter, its *absence* in a pre-animistic world, but the fact that it cannot be *fulfilled*.[12]

A nonfulfillable revelation is a revelation nonetheless. The intervention of God in history – not the human understanding of His revelation – is the foundation of Jewish tradition. Scholem insisted upon this distinction – between the existence of revelation and its intelligibility, between no revelation and indecipherable revelation. In a subsequent letter to Benjamin, Scholem elaborated on his concept of "the nothingness of Revelation":

> . . . a state in which revelation appears to be without meaning, in which it still asserts itself, in which it has *validity* but *no significance*. A state in which the wealth of meaning is lost and what is in the process of appearing (for revelation is such a process) still does not disappear, even though it is reduced to the zero point of its own content, so to speak.[13]

Perhaps, at the end of *Dulcinea encantada*, there is a revelation of nothing – "the nothingness of Revelation." The novel's fragmentary structure suggests that potentiality, rather than progress toward a programmed future, is to be desired. In Hebrew, the word for angel and messenger is the same: *malakh*. Dulcinea is a messenger without a message; her indeterminate revelation is offered, perhaps, as an antidote to the storm of progress.

The openness of Dulcinea's fragmentary history is analogous to what Benjamin labeled *Jetztzeit*, a neologism translated into English as "presence of the now" (and into Spanish as "presencia del ahora" or "tiempo-ahora"). The "presence of the now" is synchronic in its inclusion of cultural precursors, and related to Benjamin's sense of the aura of the work of art. In the fourteenth of his "Theses on the Philosophy of History," Benjamin writes:

> History is the subject of a structure whose site is not homogeneous, empty time, but time filled by the presence of the now [*Jetztzeit*].[14] Thus, to Robespierre ancient Rome was a past charged with the time of the now which he blasted out of the continuum of history. The French Revolution viewed itself as Rome reincarnate. It evoked ancient Rome the way fashion evokes costumes of the past. Fashion has a flair for the topical, no matter where it stirs in the thickets of long ago; it is a tiger's leap into the past. This jump, however, takes place in an arena where the ruling class gives the commands. The same leap in the open air of history is the dialectical one, which is how Marx understood the revolution. (261)

This "tiger's leap" is possible in "the presence of the now": it is the time of revolution and redemption and arises from historical discontinuity. In the "presence of the now," fragments of the past are unexpectedly actualized. Benjamin writes: "Redemption peeps through the narrow crack in the catastrophe of progress."[15] Muñiz-Huberman's fragmentary narrative creates fissures through which disaster glares and through which (rarely) the reader may glimpse the means to redeem the wreckage.

II

A Benjaminian angel of history also hovers over Sandra Cisneros' *Woman Hollering Creek* (1991), in the discontinuous narrative structures of her stories and in their multicultural layers of history and myth. Like Dulcinea, Cisneros' protagonists are engaged in constituting acceptable historical identities from fragmentary cultural sources. Cisneros' stories are situated in Mexico and in Mexican American communities in Texas, literally on the border between cultures, and her narrative structures reflect the cultural and racial *mestizaje* of the world about which she writes.

The title of the story collection is taken from the name of a creek in Texas that runs between San Antonio and Houston; the name sounds odd in English because of its colloquialism ("hollering) but more for its inversion of the usual order of noun and adjective ("woman hollering"). We learn that it is a literal translation of the Spanish name given to the creek by the Spanish colonizers of the region: "La Gritona." The protagonist wonders if the woman hollered in anger or pain. When she asks someone in San Antonio, she receives this answer: "*Pués, allá de los indios, quién sabe* – who knows, the townspeople shrugged, because it was of no concern to their lives how this trickle of water received its curious name."[16] The reference in Spanish to "los indios" confirms the cultural complexities that flow in Woman Hollering Creek.

Cleófilas is Mexican. She has recently come to San Antonio, and the history of this new place interests her. The implication is that she asks her question of a Mexican American who has no sense of history. "How could Cleófilas explain to a woman like this why the name Woman Hollering fascinated her. Well, there was no sense talking. . ." (46). But she eventually finds that there *is* sense in talking: a chicana named Felice helps her to leave her abusive husband in Texas and return to Mexico. Felice has her own pickup truck ("a pickup, mind you. . . . The pickup was hers. She herself had chosen it. She herself was paying for it" 55). She amazes Cleófilas when she drives across the bridge spanning Woman Hollering Creek because she answers "la gritona" for whom the creek was named. Felice hollers like a madwoman. Her holler/grito is the sharpest fragment of memory that Cleófilas retains from her short stay on "el otro lado". Cleófilas thinks back upon this chance acquaintance:

Felice was like no woman she'd ever met. Can you imagine, when we crossed the *arroyo* she just started yelling like a crazy, she would say later to her father and brothers. Just like that. Who would've thought?

Who would've? Pain or rage, perhaps, but not a hoot like the one Felice had just let go. Makes you want to holler like Tarzan, Felice had said.

Then Felice began laughing again, but it wasn't Felice laughing. It was gurgling out of her own throat, a long ribbon of laughter, like water. (56)

There the story ends. In Cleófila's memory, Felice's holler *is* the stream – "a ribbon of laughter, like water" – and the Woman Hollering Creek *is* Felice. So Cleófilas images moments in memory and constructs her own felt history.

The most explicit example of the cultural fragments with which Cisneros' characters construct a usable past is the story "Little Miracles, Kept Promises." In fact, this is not a story in the usual sense, for it consists of a series of *milagros* (miracles) – narrative fragments written on pieces of paper ordinarily pinned to the robes of a saint or a Virgin on an altar or a bulletin board beside it. In a few sentences, signed by people from the scattered towns in south Texas and northern Mexico, whole lives, families, and communities are revealed:

Dear Niño Fidencio,
   I would like for you to help me get a job with good pay, benefits, and retirement plan. I promise you if you help me I will make a pilgrimage to your tomb in Espinoza and bring you flowers. Many thanks.

César Escandón
Pharr, Tejas

Milagroso Cristo Negro,
   Thank you por el milagro de haber graduado de high school. Aquí le regalo mi retrato de graduation.

Fito Moroles
Rockport, Texas

Cristo Negro,
   Venimos desde muy lejos. Infinitas gracias, Señor. Gracias por habernos escuchado.

Familia Armendáriz G.
Matamoros, Tamps. México

Father Almighty,
   Teach me to love my husband again. Forgive me.

s.
Corpus Christi

Saint Jude, patron saint of lost causes,
   Help me pass my English 320, British Restoration Literature class and everything to turn out ok.

Eliberto González
Dallas

Jesus Christ,
   Please keep Deborah Abrego and Ralph S. Urrea together forever.

Love,
Deborah Abrego
Sabinal, Texas
(118, 119, 123, 124)

These fragments are the accumulation of isolated moments, transitory images, and personal histories in a mixed cultural context. Their impressive narrative economy – each *milagro* is plotted and peopled – combines comic and tragic, physical and metaphysical, and catalogues a variety of hopes and possibilities. In their nonliterary language – the spoken quality of these prayers is virtually audible – Cisneros conveys the past as a Benjaminian "time of the now."

In the fifth of his "Theses on the Philosophy of History," Benjamin writes: "The true picture of the past flits by. The past can be seized only as an image which flashes at the instant when it can be recognized. . . " (255). And in his sixth thesis: "To articulate the past historically does not mean to recognize it 'the way it really was' (Ranke). It means to seize hold of a memory as it flashes up at a moment of danger" (255). The relation between Benjamin's commitment to nonprogressive history and his aesthetics of fragmentation is addressed by Richard Wolin:

Benjamin's Kabbalistically influenced conception of the philosophy of history helps to account for his preoccupation with fragmentary works of art as opposed to totality-oriented, classical art – works such as Trauerspiel [German Baroque tragic drama], Baudelaire's Fleurs du mal, and Kafka's parables. For only such "profane" works of art undercut the illusory Enlightenment vision of cumulative historical progress and its concomitant myth of the infinite perfectibility of man. . . . [Fragmentary works] refute the false semblance of reconciliation in fallen, historical life . . . stand in contrast to the semblance of reconciliation fostered by classical works of art; and it is in this sense that they can be said to brush the illusion of historical progress against the grain.[17]

Wolin's final phrase echoes the final sentence of Benjamin's seventh thesis. Referring to the historical materialist (himself), Benjamin writes: "He regards it as his task to brush history against the grain" (257). For Benjamin, temporal discontinuity unmasks the false promise of future perfection, and fragmentary forms are the expressive agent of the unmasking. Fragments will reveal the falsity of the aesthetic unity to which the "classical" work of art pretends. Klaus R. Scherpe attributes to Benjamin the following political/cultural purpose and position: "Benjamin . . . directs all of his energy to activating ideas of heterogeneity and discontinuity in order to preserve, or revive, a revolutionary dynamic within the irreversible process of modernization."[18]

Benjamin has come to epitomize postmodernist concerns, and here, as in Borges' work, we find a central postmodernist attraction: his interrogation of the relation of inherited cultural fragments to present cultural meanings, and his consequent opposition (in Wolin's phrase) to "totality-oriented, classical art." "Totalizing" is anathema to theorists of postmodernism when it implies hegemonic politics, social hierarchies, or unitary truths, but Benjamin distinguishes between "totalitarian" and "totalizing" as postmodernist theorists often do not. Like the New World writers I am discussing, Benjamin responded to historical fragmentation with synchronic structures and images of inclusion: Angelus Novus surveys the wreckage whole, and at once. Benjamin's preference for Baroque art, the *Trauerspiel*, with its nonlinear and unfinished structures, its accommodation of cultural antinomy and historical disjunction, is akin to the New World Baroque as an ideology of cultural inclusion in Latin America in the late forties. Susan Buck-Morse emphasizes Benjamin's engagement of Baroque aesthetics: "Lukács, relying on Hegel's philosophical legacy, was led ultimately to a totalizing conception of metaphysical transcendence, whereas Benjamin, schooled in the very different tradition of the Baroque allegorical poets, remained focused on the fragmentary, transitory object."[19] He used fragments to create an encompassing cultural environment.

Does postmodernism's suspicion of such "totalizing" aesthetics makes it inapplicable to the inclusive intertextual strategies used by New World writers? The answer is yes and no. Surely they coincide with Benjamin, and more recently with Jean-François Lyotard in refusing "Enlightenment narratives of legitimation," "epistemological colonialism," "the mercantilization of knowledge," ills of modernity enumerated in *The Postmodern Condition*.[20] But if, in postmodernist theory, "totalizing" comes to indict *any* signifying structure – if significance itself becomes "totalizing" and the "wholeness" upon which significance necessarily depends becomes horrifying, as it does in Lyotard's influential discussion – then postmodernist theory can no longer be applied to their historicizing use of fragments. To totalize (override difference) in the name of homogeneity is one thing; to totalize (include difference) in the name of heterogeneity, as do the writers I discuss here, is quite another.

To brush history against the grain: Benjamin's image may be applied to Cisneros' narrative procedures and also to some of her characters. Take, for example, Ms. Barbara Ybañez in "Little Miracles, Kept Promises":

Dear San Antonio de Padua,
   Can you please help me find a man who isn't a pain in the nalgas. There aren't any in Texas, I swear. Especially not in San Antonio.
   Can you do something about all the educated Chicanos who have to go to California to find a job. I guess what my sister Irma says is true: "If you didn't get a husband when you were in college, you don't get one."
   I would appreciate it very much if you sent me a man who speaks Spanish, who at least can pronounce his name the way it's supposed to be pronounced. Someone please who never calls himself "Hispanic" unless he's applying for a grant from Washington, D.C.
   Can you send me a man man. I mean someone who's not ashamed to be seen cooking or cleaning or looking after himself. In other words, a man who acts like an adult. Not one who's never lived alone, never bought his own underwear, never ironed his own shirts, never even heated his own tortillas. In other words, don't send me someone like my brothers who my mother ruined with too much chichi, or I'll throw him back.

I'll turn your statue upside down until you send him to me. I've put up with too much too long, and now I'm just too intelligent, too powerful, too beautiful, too sure of who I am finally to deserve anything less.

Ms. Barbara Ybañez
San Antonio, TX
(117–18)

Here the tension is not among texts, as it largely is in *Dulcinea encantada*, but between Mexican and U.S. cultures: the U.S. doctrine of progress is expressed in a Mexican Catholic narrative mode. Ms. Barbara Ybañez accepts the ideology of progress; she believes that she should have what she deserves, and that work and education will be the agents of her satisfaction. Cisneros ironizes her character's belief in her control over her future, and on some level her character understands her own self-deception. This irony is encoded in the narrative structure of the *milagro*: answers to prayers are not based on individual agency or historical control but on divine grace. Ms. Barbara Ybañez has let herself be seduced by the system even as she resists it. She is so sympathetic because her desire reflects the ambiguous power of the myth of progress: the promise of electing an attainable future even as one understands one's impotence to do so. ("I'll turn your statue upside down. . . .")

After the short texts of pinned-on prayers in "Little Miracles, Kept Promises," there is a longer text of some four and a half pages. This one is also in the form of a prayer to – or, rather, a conversation with – the Virgin of Guadalupe. The conversation makes explicit the presence of the past in contemporary Chicano culture.

This longer text is written and signed by Rosario (Chayo) De Leon, from Austin, Tejas. A university student from a Chicano family, Chayo is conscious of her Mexican family heritage and knowledgeable about Mexican cultural traditions. She says to the "Virgencita": "I'm a snake swallowing its tail. I'm my history and my future. All my ancestors' ancestors inside my own belly. All my futures and all my pasts" (126). She knows with certainty that she wants no part of the Virgin as the Virgin is understood by her mother and grandmother, namely, as an image of patience and consolation in the face of her father's drunkenness. "I wasn't going to be my mother or my grandma. All that self-sacrifice, all that silent suffering. Hell no. Not here. Not me" (127). Chayo does, in the end, accept the Virgin, but she does so on her own terms:

I finally understood who you are. No longer Mary the mild, but our mother Tonantzín. Your church at Tepeyac built on the site of her temple. Sacred ground no matter whose goddess claims it.

. . .

When I learned your real name is Coatlaxopeuh, She Who Has Dominion over Serpents, when I recognized you as Tonantzín, and learned your names are

Teteoinnan, Toci, Xochiquetzal, Tlazolteotl, Coatlicue, Chalchiuhtlicue, Co-yolxauhqui, Huixtocihuatl, Chicomecoatl, Cihuacoatl, when I could see you as Nuestra Señora de la Soledad, Nuestra Señora de los Remedios, Nuestra Señora del Perpetuo Socorro, Nuestra Señora de San Juan de los Lagos, Our Lady of Lourdes, Our Lady of Mount Carmel, Our Lady of the Rosary, Our Lady of Sorrows, I wasn't ashamed, then, to be my mother's daughter, my grandmother's granddaughter, my ancestors' child. (128)

Chayo's culture is syncretic in its multiple traditions, and her history synchronic in the simultaneity of those traditions. "Little Miracles, Kept Promises" encodes that history as a garden of forking paths, potential and actual.

"Eyes of Zapata" is one of the few stories in *Woman Hollering Creek* that is not structured in fragmentary form. It is a continuous narrative about Inés Alfaro, common law wife of Emiliano Zapata, and it is from her point of view that we follow the trajectory of Zapata from young horse trader to charismatic leader, and then to heroic martyr of the Mexican Revolution. We see through the eyes of Inés the collective suffering of a community as it is dragged through years of revolutionary violence. Cisneros describes the historical events and the land of Zapata's Mexico – Anenecuilco, Cuautla, Ayala – realistically and in detail. But more than the now-legendary events of the Mexican Revolution, we experience the felt history of Inés as she lives it: as Zapata's lover, then as a woman abandoned but surviving, and finally as a Benjaminian angel of history.

In this story, the metaphor is made actual, for every so often Inés flies. Her perspective leaves its location in time and space, no longer following the historical progression of days and years, and instead presents history as a multidimensional whole. Her flights are not presented as metaphoric (i.e., flights of fancy) but as events. The first time she is swept up, she realizes that she can literally overlook the ruins of the revolution: "From this height, the village looks the same as before the war. As if the roof were still intact, the walls still whitewashed, the cobbled streets swept of rubble and weeds. Nothing blistered and burnt. Our lives smooth and whole" (88). Recollections of things to come: such panoramic history echoes Elena Garro's collective narrator in *Recollections of Things to Come*, who is both the voice of the dead town and its place on earth.

Inés' flights occur unexpectedly and last only briefly, but they give her a synchronic perspective that transcends the chain of events that has led her and Mexico to catastrophe. We might think of an angel's-eye perspective as merely a comforting illusion, but Cisneros does not dehistoricize it in this way. Here is the narrator/angel Inés, now old, abandoned by Zapata, yet still caring for him:

I rise high and higher, the house shutting itself like an eye. I fly farther than I've ever flown before, farther than the clouds, farther than our Lord Sun, husband of the moon. Till all at once I look beneath me and see our lives, clear and still, far away and near. (110)

She sees her son by Zapata, Nicolás, who has sold his name to the PRI (*Partido Revolucionario Institucional*), the political party that grew out of the revolution and is still in power in Mexico. Inés accepts the irony. She sees Zapata as a young man and also sees the scene of his assassination. She sees the day in 1607 when the Spanish viceroy signed the documents, written on *amate* (bark) paper, that confirm the people's right to the land. And on and on, until she concludes: "Nothing better or worse than before, and nothing the same or different" (112). Clearly Cisneros wishes to make explicit the false promise of progress for disenfranchised Mexicans such as those her character is meant to represent.

Inés' flight ends, she again lands in the present but imagines herself once more in the past with Zapata. The story concludes with Inés' words to her beloved Miliano: "My sky, my life, my eyes. Let me look at you. Before you open those eyes of yours. The days to come, the days gone by. Before we go back to what we'll always be" (113). Past, present, and future conjoin in this final sentence to describe a moment that is both remembered and predicted. This vision of historical conjunction recalls García Márquez's retrospective future tense in *One Hundred Years of Solitude* ("Many years later, as he faced the firing squad, Colonel Aureliano Buendía was to remember . . .") and Melquíades' conflation of one hundred years into a single luminous vision of all at once – a kind of Borgesian Aleph. Both authors are self-conscious in their shift from the progress of history to the timeless present of myth. But Cisneros' tone is less tragic than that of García Márquez or Benjamin or Muñiz-Huberman because the historical situations she describes are not apocalyptic. When Cisneros turns her face toward the past, she finds vital cultural fragments, not conflagration. Her characters' pasts eventually complement their present, and in some part explain it. Cisneros' stories rescue her own Mexican past from forgetting, a historical operation that constitutes the imaginary homeland her characters seek.

Cisneros' characters accommodate the antinomies of personal desires and political marginalization by combining communal myths and personal memories. In a 1992 interview in a Mexico City newspaper, Sandra Cisneros stated: "Myths play a big role in my books, and I grew up listening to myths and I am looking for the way to tell Latin American myths. My prince has not yet appeared, but I know that sometime I will see my prince Popocatépetl, and all the Maya and Aztec princes. I want to tell those myths along with the European myths that I heard as a child."[21] Walter Benjamin took Klee's Angelus Novus to represent the totalizing perspective necessary to counter the (totalitarian) storm of progress he was living. So, too, Cisneros understands that an inclusive structure (some mythic or communal totality) is necessary to give meaning to the fragments of her characters' unrecorded histories.

I have referred to the redoubled difficulties of this process for women. Feminist historian Gerda Lerner argues that History has excluded women's history (she uses uppercase to signal the recorded past, lowercase to signal the unrecorded past.) In *The Creation of Patriarchy*, she traces History-making back to the invention of writing in ancient Mesopotamia:

From the time of the king lists of ancient Sumer on, historians, whether priests, royal servants, clerks, clerics, or a professional class of university-trained intellectuals, have selected the events to be recorded and have interpreted them so as to give them meaning and significance. Until the most recent past, these historians have been men, and what they have recorded is what men have done and experienced. They have called this History and claimed universality for it. What women have done and experienced has been left unrecorded, neglected, and ignored in interpretation. . . ."[22]

Writing of the contradiction between women's centrality in creating culture and yet their marginality in the "meaning-giving process of interpretation," Lerner concludes that women's greatest cultural deprivation has been their exclusion from that process: "When . . . at certain historical moments, the contradictions in their relationship to society and to historical process are brought into the consciousness of women, they are then correctly perceived and named as deprivations that women share as a group. This coming-into-consciousness of women becomes the dialectical force moving them into action to change their condition and to enter a new relationship to male-dominated society" (5). My argument throughout this book is that a Heideggerian anxiety in the face of an occluded or negated history is not a problem exclusive to women but familiar to New World writers generally. Nonetheless, it would be absurd not to notice different degrees of "deprivation," to use Lerner's term, or fail to notice that this is a rich moment of women's "coming-into-consciousness," particularly for U.S. women writing from the perspective of marginalized cultural communities.[23]

Does the creation of fragmentary structures by women writers suggest that fragments are all that are available to those excluded from cultural process of History-making? Or that positivist ideologies are even more deceptive for women than for men? Gerda Lerner would say so. In *The Creation of Feminist Consciousness*, she pursues her idea that at certain historical moments women become aware of their marginalization from the "meaning-giving process of interpretation" and enter into that process. She cites approximately twenty examples of women from the twelfth to the late nineteenth century, but notes "the lack of continuity and the absence of collective memory on the part of women thinkers."[24] Women's efforts were so dispersed that across the centuries discussed by Lerner, virtually no continuous traditions could be developed. Ironically, in their lack of shared meta-narratives, women have been "postmodernist" for centuries. Lerner repeatedly laments "the discontinuity in the story of women's intellectual effort. Endlessly, generation after generation of Penelopes rewove the unraveled fabric only to unravel it again" (275). Positivist paradigms of progress are largely irrelevant when applied to women's history.

Who, then, would be more conscious of the need to recuperate historical fragments than women? I made this point earlier with respect to Willa Cather's creation of a usable past for her female character in *The Song of the Lark*. Similarly, the young woman who narrates Cisneros' story "Tepeyac" asks, "Who would've guessed, after all this time, it is me who will remember when everything else is forgotten. . . " (23). Her amazement implies the unexpectedness of her discovery. Who would've guessed that she, a woman, could assert her origins, interpret her history, create her traditions, and pass them along. The same amazement is expressed by Cleófilas in "Woman Hollering Creek" as she remembers Felice's defiant hollering: "Who would've thought? Who would've?" The question confirms this character's intuition that she may participate in the constitution of her own history. She discovers that coherence may be posited, if never fully or finally achieved; that fragments may, in fact, constitute a usable entity – her own (re)constructed past.

The Mexican essayist Carlos Monsiváis has written about the advent of "the first generation of U.S. citizens born in Mexico."[25] Monsiváis refers to the invasion of U.S. consumer culture in Mexico. True, but I would also recognize the cultural presence of Mexico in the U.S. and celebrate literary structures such as Cisneros' that can accommodate multicultural interactions. American cultures are hybrid, and U.S. fiction is currently the richer for processes in our recent history that have led to an increased awareness of cultural difference. Sandra Cisneros knows the history and founding myths of indigenous Mexican culture as well as Mexico's more recent history, and she integrates them in *Woman Hollering Creek* in ways that can hardly be lamented. On the contrary, it is the literary uses of Mexico's traditions, both written and oral, that give Cisneros' work its profound historical resonance, as it does the work of other Chicana writers – Ana Castillo, Cherrie Moraga, Gloria Anzaldúa, Denise Chávez.

In an interview with Sandra Cisneros, Edmundo Magaña had the good idea not to follow the usual interview format of questions and answers but rather to present a series of Cisneros' ideas and opinions in the form of narrative fragments. Among the various subjects about which Cisneros offers opinions are "Rats," "Roses," "Dolls," "The Virgin Mary," "Bulls" ("I would like it if the bulls ate the matadors"), "Maya Prince," "Egypt," "Napoleon," "Ridiculous," "Husbands," "Good Writers," and "Bad Writers." (Good writers include Manuel Puig, Juan Rulfo, Elena Poniatowska, Eduardo Galeano, Mercedes Rodoreda, Marguerite Duras, James Reed,

Jorge Luis Borges; bad writers include Carlos Fuentes, Saul Bellow, Octavio Paz, and "chicano writers.") The content of these opinions is less important than the transcultural energy they embody, the creative drive to reinvent the historical, cultural, and ethnic categories of "Mexican" and "American." She dramatizes the ways in which they have long interacted and overlapped, and the ways in which they continue to do so.

Also interacting and overlapping in *Woman Hollering Creek* are the lines between written and spoken language. Recall the "ribbon of laughter, like water" that issues from Felice's mouth in the title story of the collection. Like the phylacteries that float out of the mouths of saints and angels in Mexican Baroque painting – ribbons upon which are written privileged fragments of biblical or patristic texts – Cisneros' ribbon of laughter registers Cleófilas' awe. It is also a metaphor for the author's own storytelling art. Ribbons issue from mouths as speech, but their truths must be written. So, too, the written prayers in "Little Miracles, Kept Promises" combine oral and written modes. They are prayers in the form of spoken petitions to divine *listeners*, whose answers are sometimes recorded in ex-votos, also called *milagros*: visual images and verbal descriptions of the miracle, painted on small tin rectangles, which the saint or Virgin or Christ (painted in an upper corner) has effected. The conflation of oral and written elements in this story and others reflects the conflation of the words "history" and "story" in the single Spanish word *historia*. Cisneros' creates *historias* from recorded histories and tales that are told. *Woman Hollering Creek* makes present to the reader an array of Archival and Ancestral sources.

III

Walter Benjamin provides the terms to theorize this confluence of the Archival and Ancestral in his consideration of the "counsel" of storytelling and the "aura" of art. Benjamin speaks of the storyteller's counsel and the "usefulness" of stories that are orally transmitted: ". . . 'having counsel' is beginning to have an old-fashioned ring . . . . because the communicability of experience is decreasing" (86). He argues that the printed medium of the novel does not fill the same communal and historical function as stories told to listeners: "The birthplace of the novel is the solitary individual, who is no longer able to express himself by giving examples of his most important concerns, is himself uncounseled, and cannot counsel others" (87). After giving a number of examples, he concludes: "All this points to the nature of every real story. It contains, openly or covertly, something useful. . . . the storyteller is a man who has counsel for his readers."[26] And a woman for hers.

Benjamin's storyteller is a symbol of community, his counsel a cipher for the processes of creating a usable past, i.e., a shared present. Benjamin gives primacy to the aural-oral manifestation of story: to the dialogic wisdom available to interlocutors, and to the communal sound of human voices. Like Cisneros' image of the hollering woman or Vargas Llosa's conversation in The Cathedral, speaking ("old tales and talking," in Faulkner's phrase) structures these written fictions and situates their creators against postmodernism's depreciation of spoken language. The literary work's participation in communal traditions – its counsel – is dialogic and open-ended: "After all, counsel is less an answer to a question than a proposal concerning the continuation of a story that is just unfolding" (86–87). So Benjamin acknowledges the complex relations of the storyteller's history to his or her histories/stories and, by extension, to the listener's and the reader's own.

But the storyteller's counsel is only part of Benjamin's complex meditation on the nature of collective memory. What he famously called the "aura" of art is also relevant here. This aura is the product and index of the historicity of a work of art, the presence of cultural traditions as they are grasped by the *mémoire involuntaire* of the artist.[27] In essays on Baudelaire and Proust, Benjamin argues that a work's aura consists of its power to "recuperate" for the reader (or listener or viewer) an archetypal past – an experience "closer to forgetting than to what is usually called memory."[28] In its emphasis on the aesthetic experience of the reader, his theory is consonant with the Borgesian writer-as-reader's intertextual activity. In the essay on Proust, Benjamin writes that "an experienced event is finite, at any rate, confined to one sphere of experience; a remembered event is infinite, because it is only a key to everything that happened before it and after it" (202). The aura of the work of art is its accumulated cultural meanings as they are understood by the reader or viewer – the "key" to what has "happened before it and after it."

More than the simultaneous "before and after" of a remembered event, the aura of art embodies and transmits the relation of consciousness to history as such. Robert Alter has summarized this near-mythic projection of cultural inclusiveness: "Benjamin associates aura not with memory plain and simple but with involuntary memory, surging from the unconscious. What is remembered, in this fashion, moreover, becomes a kind of inexhaustible semantic wellspring, yielding up endless meanings. . . . the aesthetic experience in general is before all else the most potent and subtle mnemonic that culture has devised."[29] The inclusive capacity of the aesthetic experience – the aura of art as the *cumulative* experience of cultural voices and texts available *synchronically* to the reader – was crucial to Benjamin because he foresaw the disastrous truncation of his own cultural tradition. In "Unpacking my Library," he wrote that "for a true collector the *whole background* of an item adds up to a magic encyclopedia whose quintessence is the fate of his object."[30] The fictions of Cisneros and Muñiz-Huberman are magic encyclopedias in their compulsion to remember and include "the whole background" as an antidote to historical rupture. Benjamin's aura, like his angel, hovers over *Dulcinea encantada* and *Woman Hollering Creek*.

In an essay on the origins of the novel, Carlos Fuentes declares that all great novels are potential novels:

The novel both reflects and creates an unfinished world made by men and women who are also unfinished. Neither the world nor its inhabitants have said their last word. The potential novel is thus the announcement and perhaps even the guarantee of a potential history. Of a potential life. We hope that we are part of an unfinished human presence expressing itself through narrative language.[31]

In his emphasis on potentiality, Fuentes amplifies Benjamin's conception of the aura of the work of art as historically recuperative: traditions motion from the future even as they also emerge from the past. The posthistory of a novel – the voices and texts that it will engender and enrich and with which it will eventually merge or diverge – is as open (and as integral) as its "whole background."

This is so because the writer's intertextual choices will necessarily modify received cultural authority. Hannah Arendt, in her introduction to Benjamin's essays, notes: "Insofar as the past has been transmitted by tradition, it possesses authority; insofar as authority presents itself historically, it becomes tradition."[32] In referring to Benjamin's practice of collecting quotations, Arendt argues that such intertextuality may reflect the literary collector's investment in the tradition or, alternatively, his or her despair at the damage or loss of that tradition. In this latter case, the literary collector – the intertextualist – may obey an impulse to disrupt history rather than conserve it. Arendt argues that Benjamin, writing in the twenties and thirties, "discovered that the transmissibility of the past had been replaced by its citability" (38); she refers to his affinity for Kafka, whose "reaching down to the sea bottom of the past had this peculiar duality of wanting to preserve and wanting to destroy" (41). So, too, Benjamin, who recognized that his own cultural traditions had been irreparably damaged and that he had to devise a new relation to the past, new definitions of cultural authority, new modes of intertextuality.

In *Intellectuals in Power*, Paul Bové makes explicit the abuses that Arendt describes and Benjamin experienced. Traditions can be imperialistic, canons exclusive, and totalitarian regimes the result: ". . . the production of an image of 'tradition' [is] always a necessary tool for the elite to go on 'guiding' the species (or nation or race or class) toward perfection. . . ."[33] Here Bové joins the poststructuralist tradition of anti-traditionalism, equating tradition (*tradere*, to hand over or down) with traducing (*traducere*, to lead over, mislead). Frank Lentricchia, for example, has declared that for artists-intellectuals, "the real problem is how not to be overburdened by the pressures of residual cultures and their traditions. . . ."[34] And again: "Tradition-making is a process of historical repression engineered not by the dead but by the living. . . . all writing, but especially the self-consciously literary sort, with its overdeveloped sense of ancestry, has a marked disposition to suppress its material conditions" (125). Lentricchia and Bové refer to (and, ironically, themselves extend) a hegemonic literary-intellectual tradition, so it is not surprising that, to them, all traditions – tradition as such – would seem to be oppressive.

For writers outside this hegemonic tradition, however, the reverse is likely to be true. Material conditions and oppressive meta-narratives may be foregrounded and questioned by the use of previous texts traditions, rather than unwittingly obscured or suppressed, as Lentricchia assumes. I have already argued this point with respect to women writers and, more generally, writers impelled by the New World anxiety of origins. So the African-American writer Albert Murray, who writes that "each painting . . . is a visual statement that is a reference or allusion to another or other paintings, to which in effect it either says yes and also and also and perhaps also; or it says no or not necessarily or on the other hand or not as far as I for one am concerned."[35] The dynamic and ongoing process of tradition-formation is conveyed by Murray's energetic style. And in Latin American fiction, the proximity of the Spanish words for "tradition" and "betrayal" – *tradición* and *traición* – does not automatically signal political authoritarianism or cultural stagnation. On the contrary, the interactions of *tradere* and *traducere* are often generative – explicitly so in Manuel Puig's novel *La traición de Rita Hayworth* (*Betrayed by Rita Hayworth*, 1968).

Nowhere, then, is poststructuralist theory so inadequate in accounting for the historical operations in/of New World writing as in this tendency to conflate tradition and oppression. I have said that Bové and Lentricchia are writing in and about the context of late European and U.S. modernism, *not* about cultural communities whose traditions have been diverted or destroyed, nor about writers for whom the (re)possession of tradition may be seen as liberating rather than stultifying. Nonetheless, their arguments provide instruction by negative example. They do *not* acknowledge that in such contexts, history may be subversive rather than hegemonic; that the contradictory impulses to destroy and conserve may operate in highly creative tension; and that every record of civilization is, as Benjamin insisted, also a record of barbarism, a record of suppressions and silences. Bové and Lentricchia describe a form of barbarism well known to many New World writers, against which their intertextual engagement of tradition is a strategic instrument.

The intertextuality of these writers thus contains a theory of culture and a political stance vis-à-vis received cultural traditions. They offer constellations of texts designed to convey some part (an aura) of the communal past to its present participants, even as their intertextual activity modifies the traditions they convey. Such constellations (to repeat Cortázar's metaphor) are mobile, decentered, and inclusive. Countless such constellations, evolving over time from the felt histories of individuals and communities, encode a culture's social structures, values, and beliefs, including readers' experience of the texts themselves. Literary works are the *paroles* of their culture's *langue*, the synecdoches and moving symbols of a community and a history. They are conservative – not in a political sense, but in a literal one, for they *conserve* the historical experience of a community in narrative structures such as *Woman Hollering Creek* and *Dulcinea encantada*.[36] But their authors know, as Benjamin did, that cultures are conserved unequally and inconsistently, that traditions are unevenly available and whole histories may be tragically truncated. They know, too, that what *has* been conserved – "things as they really are," to repeat Benjamin's ironic phrase – is always challenged by the potentiality of art, by the not-yet-accomplished conversations among received forms of cultural expression.

CHAPTER SIX

Clichés and Community

Manuel Puig, *The Kiss of the Spider Woman*

Luis Rafael Sánchez, *Macho Camacho's Beat*

. . . la parole humaine est comme un chaudron fêlé où nous battons des mélodies à faire danser les ours, quand on voudrait attendrir les étoiles.
Gustave Flaubert, *Madame Bovary*[1]

. . . human speech is like a cracked kettle on which we tap crude rhythms for bears to dance to, while we long to make music that will melt the stars.
Gustave Flaubert, *Madame Bovary*[2]

I WANT TO DISCUSS a final means by which usable pasts are created in contemporary American literature. Manuel Puig's *El beso de la mujer araña* (*The Kiss of the Spider Woman*, 1976) and Luis Rafael Sánchez's *La guaracha del Macho Camacho*, (*Macho Camacho's Beat*, 1976) demonstrate how communities and traditions may be constructed from the clichés of popular, nonprint media: radio and television, popular music, and the movies. Their intertextuality is less Borgesian than Flaubertian; like Flaubert (and generally unlike Borges) their fiction mixes levels and forms of discourse – musical rhythms and lines, visual forms, spoken languages. In the celebrated phrase from *Madame Bovary* (1856) that I have cited as my epigraph, Flaubert suggests the problem with which he did lifelong battle and the paradox that lies at the core of all literary art: how to transform these common discursive forms into literature. In his homely metaphor of a "chaudron fêlé," a cracked kettle, Flaubert implies that the noise of everyday speech is necessarily opposed to literary language. What, after all, Flaubert asks implicitly, do dancing bears, that symbolic entertainment of unruly street crowds, and their banging culinary accompaniment, have to do with reaching the stellar heights of art? The answer, of course, is a great deal, as Flaubert knew well. Popular languages – whether derived from sentimental fiction, political bombast, animal husbandry, or the cacaphonous sounds of the street – and the tensions among them are basic to the linguistic genius of *Madame Bovary* and become the subject of his unfinished satiric works, *Bouvard et Pécuchet* and *Le Dictionnaire des idées reçues*.

This Flaubertian tendency to use popular phrases and clichés, to couple discordant voices and codes, characterizes the fiction of Manuel Puig and Luis Rafael Sánchez. Flaubert's attitude toward clichés was essentially hostile and his literary use of clichés often satiric and/or ironic. In European modernist fiction, the conventions of which Flaubert largely established, clichés are generally treated as the antithesis of "original," and thus the antithesis of "literary" as well. Flaubert wrote ironic exempla of this position, deprecating clichés and then using them brilliantly to demonstrate their worthlessness. Puig and Sánchez also exploit the varying, often ambiguous, implications of fixed locutions and familiar narrative formulations – not, however, to deprecate them but to demonstrate their social uses.[3] In their novels, clichés become a means of proposing communal values that operate within the texts and reflect outward onto the cultures that contain them.

I have already mentioned the etymological origins of the word *cliché* in the technology of typesetting. Recall that it initially described a ready-made unit of type, a metal plate from which issued unending, standardized reproductions of print or design. The word was derived from the onomatopoeic French verb *clicher*, a variant of *cliquer* (to click) and mimicked the sound of typesetting machines. Now, of course, it has come to figure fragmented, ready-made units of (primarily) spoken speech. In English and Spanish, the word "stereotype" (*estereotipo*) denotes the same device, and the Spanish locution "frase acuñada" (a "coined" or "minted" phrase), also refers to a process of repeated metallic imprinting, with its presumed accompanying din. The French term, however, carries the greatest opprobrium, for French writers of the mid- to late-nineteenth century saw the mechanization of print as pressing literary language into common currency, making it too readily available to undiscriminating bourgeois (mass) consumption. In contemporary literary culture as well, most audiences will deprecate clichés as such: clichés addressed to even relatively unsophisticated audiences tend to be accompanied by signals that downgrade clichés themselves. As Walter Ong has pointed out, contemporary audiences are often encouraged, even assisted, by verbal or visual indicators to reject clichés, to laugh at them, or at least to bracket them as unreliable or ironically intended.[4] Puig and Sánchez create notable exceptions to this tendency; in fact, they use these negative attitudes to heighten the ambiguity that accompanies the literary use of nonliterary language.

My sense of the word "cliché" includes groups of words that convention has solidified into linguistic units, as well as popular narrative structures and phrases that have been repeated often enough to be familiar – or to create the illusion of familiarity – for most readers. I continue here, as in the two preceding chapters, to be interested in idiomatic language that is experienced primarily as spoken rather than written, and in what is considered to be "vernacular."[5] Both Puig and Sánchez present their novels as aural/oral performances; the effective translation of Puig's novel to visual media – on stage and in film, both as drama and musical theatre – confirms my point. *The Kiss of the Spider Woman* is given to the reader as a conversation about movies that establishes community, *Macho Camacho's Beat* as a chorus of popular songs that tells of communal disintegration. Their authors dramatize the enormous potential of electronic media for creativity and communication; they also show their potential to subvert or silence these human capacities and bonds. So they address the problems *and* the possibilities of eliciting meaning from the noise of contemporary mass culture.

The relationship among conventional language, individual expression, and communal identity in Puig and Sánchez is based not on a derisive sense of clichés but on the recognition that all language is grounded in repetition, that there is a residue of formula in all expression, and that novelistic language often artfully intensifies the received linguistic patterns without which communication of any sort is impossible. I use the word "cliché," then, to indicate a range of repeated semiotic patterns that will lead us to consider the nature of literary language and its relation to used (and still-usable) narrative structures. Puig and Sánchez propose that it is upon the operations of such familiar linguistic traditions – upon clichés in this broadest sense – that the coherence of communities depends.

I

The Kiss of the Spider Woman consists largely of dialogue between two men in a prison cell, principal segments of which are movie scenarios told by one man to the other. This ostensibly spoken fiction embodies the rhythms and colloquialisms of conversation unmediated by any narrator – the most recognizable of the conventions of written fiction. Without the usual identifying narrative tags ("said Molina," "said Valentin"), the reader is sometimes in doubt about which of the characters is speaking and must trace the alternating speeches back to a point of reference. So the text reminds the reader that such unmediated conversation is ordinarily the province of film or our own experience of conversation, where *seeing* the speakers or *hearing* the tone of their voices makes clear their identity. The novel's self-presentation as an oral mode rather than a written one is immediately obvious and continually, though implicitly, reiterated.

Molina, a homosexual incarcerated for the corruption of minors, "tells the movies" to Valentin, a political dissident serving time for seditious activities. First to pass the minutes/hours/days, then to nurture the growing bond of communication, both spoken and unspoken, that unexpectedly develops between them, the two inmates share the patently conventional scenarios of movies that Molina has seen in the past. Molina's language is replete with formulae that have become unalterable units through constant use; in the space of a few sentences of movie-telling, he uses phrases like "le da un arranque," "tomar como un desesperado," "una voz de borracho perdido," "pegado a la puerta," "no tiene más remedio," "grita pero como loca," "muerta de miedo," and many more. These fixed phrases contribute to the intimate energy of Molina's movie-telling. Grade B movie scenarios are the clichés that create meaning in the text and project Puig's sense of the popular culture from which they are drawn.

These narrative clichés interspersed in the characters' dialogue are, in Viktor Shklovsky's terms, *stories* rather than *plots*, the difference being that the events in stories are ordered in a temporal-causal sequence, whereas the events in plots are artfully arranged, distorted, or manipulated – that is, "defamiliarized" by/in the literary structure.[6] According to Shklovsky, stories, unlike plots, may extend indefinitely in time and space, one event following sequentially upon another. This is the case with Molina's movie-telling. Events are recounted like beads on a string, with conjunctions – and, but, then, when, eventually, so, later – initiating a large proportion of his sentences and joining clauses within those sentences. As Molina warms to his movie scenario, the written text reiterates the spatial and temporal extension of the telling, the paragraphs extending over several pages, often containing no fewer than forty conjunctions in a single sentence as Molina connects cinematic events one after another. The structure of Molina's stories is what Shklovsky would term automatic (rather than artistic), each element unambiguously predicting the one that follows.

Whatever *plot* Molina's movie-telling may be said to possess results from his intermittent interruptions of the chains of events he strings together. His stories become plots when he abandons the continuous present tense that is the temporal mode of film, occasionally slowing his narration (and hence our perception of it) to ponder an elusive detail, to make an evaluative comment about the events of the film or the nature of time and his own memory, or to interject a literary or structural indicator such as "puntos suspensivos" ("dot, dot, dot") or "este cuento se ha terminado" ("and well . . . that's all . . . folks . . ."). His enthusiastic descriptions of costume and setting also tend to defamiliarize the stories he tells by foregrounding the process of translating a visual medium into a verbal one. These intermittent interpolations and others call attention to the teller and direct the reader to consider his utterance as a structured artifact, an entity to be contemplated in its own right rather than a transparent vehicle through which we "see" the film being told. Nevertheless, these aspects of literariness do not dominate Molina's narration. He may be narrating events that have been "plotted" in their cinematic medium, but his own narration, when judged in novelistic terms, remains largely story rather than plot. Or, to return to the notion of defamiliarization, his is primarily a familiar mode of telling, not an artistic one.

If the film scenarios recounted by Molina are not defamiliarized, their incorporation into the plotted medium of the novel itself does, of course, condition their status as story. Robert Scholes has suggested that any utterance or human gesture can be made literary by someone else's performance of it: "Any trivial or vulgar bit of speech or gesture can function in a literary way in a story or play, for instance, or even in a Joycean 'epiphany,' just as a piece of driftwood or trash can be incorporated in a work of sculpture, or any found object be turned into visual art by an act of selection and display."[7] Any spoken utterance may be given additional intensity – may be defamiliarized – by being translated into print, just as a photograph or a movie of familiar people or locations may remove them from the mundane, heightening their reality by virtue of their translation into a visual medium.[8] More significantly, in *The Kiss of the Spider Woman*, Molina's stories are embedded in a plot that proposes and develops a human relationship between two marginalized characters whom chance and insidious social and political forces have thrown together. Though most of the novel is unmediated dialogue, as I have said, occasional italicized passages of unspoken internal monologue are interspersed in which Molina tells *himself* a movie, making himself an actor who vents his frustration on Valentin. The text also departs from dialogue in Valentin's stream-of-consciousness monologue at the end of the novel – a delirious mixture of the movies he has been told by Molina and his own political experiences, presented in a highly imaged style.

Scholes, following Shklovsky, argues that we sense literariness in an utterance when we sense its "duplicity" (21), when an utterance calls attention to *itself* as well as to what it describes. The "duplicity" of *The Kiss of the Spider Woman* proceeds in part from the tension between the clichéd movie scenarios and the characters' interior monologues; between narrative that is transparently and externally referential, on the one hand, and utterance that points to more complex forms of interiority, on the other. This interplay between spoken and unspoken, public and private discourse has its correlative in the situation of the characters. Molina and Valentin are, after all, in a prison cell, isolated from the public realm for their "antisocial" behavior. (Valentin has, we learn, spent time in solitary confinement.) The antidote to their inhuman isolation is precisely the language they speak together, language that is in its very essence sociable, shared, common. The conventionality of their idiom strengthens rather than dilutes the communication (community) they establish in their cell. Their clichés, precisely because they are clichés, offer a means of social affiliation that neither has attained in society at large. The characters are acutely aware of the difference between the community developing inside their cell and the hostile world outside. Valentin asks Molina, "¿Y estamos tan presionados . . . por el mundo de afuera, que no podemos actuar de forma civilizada? ¿es posible que pueda tanto . . . el enemigo que esta afuera? . . . Es como si estuviéramos en una isla desierta. Una isla en la que tal vez estemos solos años. Porque, sí, fuera de la celda están nuestros opresores, pero adentro no. Aquí nadie oprime a nadie."⁹ ("Then are we so pressured . . . by the outside world, that we can't act civilized? Is it possible . . . that the enemy, out there, has so much power? . . . It's as if we were on some desert island. An island on which we may have to remain alone together for years. Because, well, outside of this cell we may have our oppressors, yes, but not inside. Here no one oppresses the other."¹⁰) But we sense that Valentin protests too much, for language, however common and communal, may also be a vehicle for social prejudice and political injustice, as both characters know well. Molina, hurt by what he imagines to be Valentin's moral censure, withdraws from language, thinking ". . . no le voy a contar más ninguna película de las que más me gustan, esas son para mí solo, en mi recuerdo, que no me las toquen con palabras sucias . . ." (116; ". . . I won't tell him any more of the films I like the most, they're just for me, in my mind's eye, so no filthy words can touch them . . ." 112). Common speech may create a community of two that temporarily staves off the terrors of human isolation, but it cannot stave off the forces outside the cell that will eventually inflict torture and death upon them.

The language of these social and political forces contrasts with that used by the characters in being presented as typographic rather than spoken. Unlike the dialogue of the friends inside their cell, the dialogue between the prison warden and Molina in the warden's office is labeled according to the speaker, a typographic convention of dramatic literature and recorded judiciary proceedings. So Puig suggests that the warden and the inmate are playing roles and, by extension, that a farce of justice is being enacted. Furthermore, long academic footnotes taken from the works of Freud, Marcuse, Norman O. Brown and others treat the relationship of sex to society in a style that bristles with its own specialized linguistic formulae and could only be written. The footnotes would seem to propose an analytical commentary on the relationship between Molina and Valentin, between homosexuality and political commitment. However, the distance between the impersonal logic of the academic jargon and the plotted urgency of sexual contact and political repression undermines that commentary and provides a primary source of irony in the novel.¹¹

Similar ironic disjunction is created between Valentin's final tortuous interior monologue and the impenetrable typographic surface of the chapter immediately preceding it. This penultimate chapter is a starkly written intelligence report in an abbreviated and impassive style replete with bureaucratic clichés. The language is ominously ambiguous, calculated to mask the operations that it describes. Molina's activities after his release from prison are enumerated in calendar form by a government spy who attempts, in a running commentary, to assign causal links to those activities. A sentence appended to the report tells us that it has been typed in quadruplicate and distributed to authorized personnel, with the original to remain permanently on file. In this image of verbal replication (the quadruplicated report) and ideological fixity (permanently on file) Puig presents the antithesis of the creative repetition that goes on between the cellmates. In the rubber stampings of the authoritarian regime, human life is commodified beyond contempt. For Puig, the threat to expressive language lies not in the formulae of popular culture but in something very nearly their opposite: the standardized, sanitized jargon of a dehumanized and dehumanizing political system.

Puig's novelistic practice may usefully be compared to the cinematic theory and practice of the Soviet filmmaker Sergei Eisenstein. Puig, who studied film making at the Centro Sperimental di Cinematografia in Rome, would naturally have been familiar with Eisenstein's theoretical statements as well as with his films. While I do not intend to argue for Eisenstein's influence on Puig, I would point to an unmistakable similarity in their aesthetic strategies. Eisenstein's writings view art as a means of expressing ideas and "amplifying emotions," and his discussion of his own art focuses on the ways in which images are "born" from the subject matter under consideration.[12] He describes one device in particular, that of showing an action or object without naming it: "Audiovisual cinema . . . begins from the instant the boot's creak is detached from the representation of the creaking boot and . . . attached to the human face that listens to the creak with alarm."[13] Puig as cinematographer-turned-novelist exploits this visual technique, most notably in the love scenes between Valentin and Molina, which no narrator names or describes. By withholding description, Puig proposes that the reader of his written text, already constituted as a listener rather than a reader, become a viewer as well. In such moments of textual silence, Puig avoids syntactic and semantic constraints, maintaining instead multiple possible relations between description and vision.

For Eisenstein, this kind of defamiliarization depends upon the appropriation and transformation *within* the artwork of elements taken from *outside* it. He writes that the artist must discover for each topic—each object, fact, scene, locution—the conjunction of elements that preserves the fact itself and also simultaneously projects the author's attitude toward the fact.[14] This simultaneous sense of things in their familiar and defamiliarized states is also relevant to Puig's novelistic practice. I have said that the social and psychological themes of *The Kiss of the Spider Woman* depend upon the opposition between the interior of the prison cell and the exterior world, with its ironic reversal of the meaning of "freedom" and "incarceration." Furthermore, the film clichés within the novel point to an invisible but nonetheless definite locus outside the novel – the movies themselves – which in turn reflect back into the center of the novel to the prison cell where Molina tells them. Like the structural clichés of the movie scenarios, formulaic phrases also oscillate between the interior and the exterior of the novel, between its printed medium and the spoken language of the world that surrounds it. For example, Valentin's cliché of the desert island, cited earlier, invokes a familiar linguistic world outside the novel even as it signifies the isolation of the fictional characters, "alone together" in their prison cell. And the kiss of the spider woman, which in the movie scenario fatally lures men into her web, becomes in Valentin's final interior monologue the symbol of Molina's love for him, not a trap but a liberation. Thus Puig defamiliarizes clichés in the manner that Eisenstein describes, preserving their familiar, nonartistic essence while at the same time integrating them into a literary structure that contests the values of the culture from which they are drawn.

I began by drawing a sharp distinction between the motives for Flaubert's use of clichés and those of the Puig and Sánchez. Here, though, I would propose a *parallel* between Flaubert's characters Bouvard and Pécuchet, in his novel by that name, and Puig's twosome in this novel. Flaubert avowedly created his characters to pillory the popular culture of the bourgeois democracy of his own time. He proposed to make them as foolish as possible (he originally planned to call the novel *The Memoirs of Two Cockroaches*) but the characters nonetheless engage our sympathy because they are good friends, and very human.[15] If they are also foolish, it is because of who they are, as well as their social or intellectual alliances: middle-aged, marginalized, one fat, the other thin, outlandishly dressed, awkward in love. Despite Flaubert's stated intentions, *Bouvard et Pécuchet* is as much about these characters' hearts as it is about their undiscriminating minds or their misuse of language. And despite his despair at the pervasion of their culture, he inadvertently demonstrates, in his characters' dedication to one another, the means of overcoming that despair. Valentin and Molina are Latin American analogues to Flaubert's characters, out of step with society yet necessarily consumers of its cultural modes; victims of its moral, political, and linguistic obfuscations, yet able to hear each other above the noise.

It seems to me that this novel and *Maldición eterna a quien lea estas páginas* (*Eternal Curse on the Reader of These Pages*, 1980) represent a significant departure from Puig's earlier novels. In *La traición de Rita Hayworth* (*Betrayed by Rita Hayworth*, 1968), *Boquitas pintadas* (*Heartbreak Tango*, 1969), and *The Buenos Aires Affair* (1973), Puig's use of clichés is, in fact, quite similar to Flaubert's in intent. In these earlier novels, Puig uses clichés to satirize contemporary culture and suggest the ways in which the individual is betrayed by cultural stereotypes.[16] On the contrary, in *The Kiss of the Spider Woman*, cinematic clichés become a mode of human reconciliation, a bond that forestalls betrayal even if it cannot ultimately prevent it. So Molina rejects the warden's order to inform on his cellmate, drawing strength to withstand such pressure by telling more movies; and Valentin, despite personal and social prejudice, finds love and understanding with Molina. Unlike Puig's earlier fiction, this novel does not insist upon the falsity of the promises made by popular culture. In *Betrayed by Rita Hayworth*, cinematic stereotypes of aggressive men and submissive women betray a young character in his search for love, whereas in *The Kiss of the Spider Woman*, they become the means by which the characters establish theirs. Molina and Valentin use clichés, rather than being used by them.

The relation of conversation to community is, then, in some real sense the subject of this novel. Texts presented *as written* serve to reinforce institutional structures of domination, whereas the on-going dialogue between Valentin and Molina resists and revises these structures. Puig is frequently labeled a postmodernist, but he nonetheless reverses the Derridean privileging of written over spoken language. In this regard, he is closer to Plato than to Derrida.

Plato cast his writings as dialogue in order to imply that only in the flexible give-and-take of spoken communication, in its present interactions and revisions, can truth be approached (if never fully attained). Socrates, speaking to Phaedrus, states that "instruction" about the nature of "the right, the beautiful and the good" is possible only between speakers:

That Lysias or any other writer, past or future, who claims that clear and permanently valid truth is to be found in a written speech, lays himself open to reproach. . . . lucidity and finality and serious importance are to be found only in words spoken by way of instruction or, to use a truer phrase, written on the soul of the hearer to enable him to learn about the right, the beautiful and the good; finally, to realize that such spoken truths are to be reckoned a man's legitimate sons, primarily if they originate within himself, but to a secondary degree if what we may call their children and kindred come to birth, as they should, in the minds of others – to believe this, I say, and to let all else go is to be the sort of man, Phaedrus, that you and I might well pray that we may both become.[17]

In the relation between Valentin and Molina, Puig dramatizes Socrates' assertion that speech may be "written on the soul of the hearer." As in Vargas Llosa's *Conversation in The Cathedral*, the "metaphysics of presence" disclaimed by Derrida as a modernist illusion is affirmed by Puig and demonstrated by his characters.

II

Macho Camacho's Beat, by Puerto Rican novelist Luis Rafael Sánchez, is written to the tune and rhythm of the *guaracha*, a Caribbean dance rhythm in triple meter. A particular *guaracha* entitled "La vida es una cosa fenomenal" ("Life Is a Phenomenal Thing"), played by Macho Camacho and his band, is sweeping the island. It is heard on every radio, and no space is immune to its frenetic, hypnotic rhythms. The music becomes a metaphor for the language of the novel itself; Macho Camacho's beat pulsates in the background as we enter, by means of equally pulsating prose, the lives of the various characters: the proud, pompous and self-indulgent Senator Vicente Reinosa; his cold, aristocratic wife and spoiled son; his expansive, worldly-wise, lower-class mistress. The movement of music and language contrasts with the traffic jam in which much of the novel is set and, Sánchez implies, with congealed class and cultural hierarchies. If the movies are central to Puig's novel, it is the radio that matters to Sánchez; and if spoken speech structures the former, the rhythms of sung speech impel *Macho Camacho's Beat*.

Sánchez's novel, like Puig's, pretends to be heard rather than read. Sánchez asks his audience ("audience" seems more appropriate than "reader") to consider the nature of the printed word not only semantically but also acoustically. With its alliteration, rhyme, repetition, parataxis, anaphora, and repeating rhythms, Sánchez's stylistic energy is auditory. The musicality of the novel is what first strikes the mind's ear, created as much by the broken syntax and brisk rhythms of the phrasing as by particular fixed expressions. The story seems to be improvised in the fluid, episodic manner of oral poetry or jazz, where there is no fixed text or music, only process and performance.

Jurij M. Lotman's theory of linguistic "automism" is more suited to Sánchez's novel than Shklovsky's discussion of "defamiliarization" because Lotman is concerned with poetry and poetic devices *per se*. He explores how automism may be reversed by means of sound devices, and defines poetic language in terms of its departures from the norms of ordinary speech. If ordinary speech is viewed as unordered (apart from the grammatical regularities of its construction), then poetic language shows itself to be ordered in special ways. In poetic discourse, Lotman asserts, certain elements of sound occur more frequently (or less frequently) than the linguistic norm, a norm that is difficult to formulate but that is known intuitively to every native speaker. Those elements of sound may consist of syllabic or syntactic units, accentual patterns, phonetic phenomena such as assonance, consonance, rhyme, or the position of these elements in the text. Unusual frequency, displacement, or suppression of a given element will make it noticeable, structurally active; such usage makes the reader aware of the form of the utterance—in short, de-automizes it. Lotman contends that the poetic text implicitly proposes the rules by which it departs from the linguistic norm, making it simultaneously a realization and a disruption of order. The poetic work can be described "via two modalities: the system of the realization of certain rules and the system of their violation . . . the text can be identified neither with one nor with the other aspect taken separately. Only the relationship between them, only the structural tension, the mixture of incompatible tendencies, creates the reality of the work of art."[18] (Recall Robert Scholes's requirement that to be considered literary, a text must be "duplicitous.") For Lotman, the task of the reader lies not in "overcoming" these incompatible tendencies but in learning how to detect their functionally contradictory mechanisms.

The linguistic and generic norms from which Sánchez's poetic prose departs are, of course, implicit in the novel. From the beginning, the prose is ungrammatical, fragmented, and far more repetitive, rhythmically and phonetically, than most novelistic prose. In the first paragraph of the novel, the scene is set and the characters are described in colloquial diction and repeating rhythms:

Si se vuelven ahora, recatadas la vuelta y la mirada, la verán esperar sentada, una calma o la sombra de una calma atravesándola. Cara de ausente tiene, cara de víveme y tócame, las piernas cruzada en cruz. La verán esperar sentada en un sofá. . . . Cuerpo de desconcierto tiene cuerpo de ay deja eso, ¿ven?, cuerpo que ella sienta, tiende y amontona en un sofá. . . . También sudada, la verán esperar sudada, sudada y apelotonada en un sofá sudado y apelotonado, sofá sudado y apelotonado que se transforma en cama que se transforma en sofá, miembro pulcro el sofá de un elenco hogareño de travesti que hacen de todo. Como hace el Ace.[19]

If you turn around now, a cautious turn, a cautious look, you'll see her, sitting and waiting, calmness or the shadow of calmness passing through her. She's got a dreamer's face, a wake me up and touch me face, her legs crossed in a cross. You'll see her sitting and waiting on a sofa. . . . A restless body, she has a body of oh cut it out, can you see?, a body that she sits down, lays out, and plops onto a sofa.. . . Sweaty too, you'll see her waiting sweaty, sweaty and plopped onto a sweaty ploppy sofa, a sweaty ploppy sofa that changes into a bed that changes into a sofa, an elegant member of a transvestite domestic cast that can do everything. The way her can can.[20]

The repeated elements of sound, too numerous and obvious to discuss in detail, are not merely a series of auditory identities but a system of differences. Both the woman and the sofa are "sudados y apelotonados" (sweaty and ploppy): on one level, the repetition implies identity – the woman is the senator's mistress, and both she and the sofa are meant to be laid (on) – but on another level the repetition reveals the false and dehumanizing character of that identity, and the moral and political corruption on which such imposed identity is based. Far from creating a tiresome sense of sameness, the repetitions and clichés that characterize every page of this novel insist upon the disparities between language and life. Coincidence on one level only highlights noncoincidence on another; repetition may automize the text syntactically or accoustically while de-automizing it semantically (the repeated, hence expected "sudado y apelotonado" applied to unexpected and disparate nouns). The reader is obliged to consider each word in relation to the words around it (the "transvestite" convertible sofa, the "*Ace*" that "*hace*," the "can" that "can"). So Sánchez creates a complex dialectic of functionally contradictory mechanisms – the primary characteristic of belletristic structures, according to Lotman.

The tense in which the novel is written contributes to its contradictions, for Sánchez embeds clichés in an ongoing present tense that seems to deny their long history of over-use and suggests instead that their usage begins with his text. Language appears to mean only what it means now, whether it is spoken or sung. The idea that a cliché can come alive again through repetition independent of remembering recalls Borges' Pierre Menard, whose identical version of Cervantes' work achieves the status of the original because, we are told, Menard has *forgotten* it in order to repeat it. Repetition *with* remembering, it seems, creates clichés; repetition *without* remembering creates masterpieces. Borges' story is deeply ironic, of course, but nonetheless a parable of historical anxiety: in America one must revise/repeat/reinvent cultural sources. Sánchez, too, suggests that creative repetition may be originary/original.

The short, narrative segments of *Macho Camacho's Beat* constitute another synchronic strategy. They are proposed as a succession of simultaneously observed and recorded instants, each occurring at five o'clock on Wednesday afternoon; each segment concludes with the phrase "a las cinco de la tarde" ("at five o'clock in the afternoon"). It is as if time stops, to start at five o'clock once more in the next segment. The traffic jam, like the vicious circles of Muñiz-Huberman's *periférico* and the "accélération immobile" of Butor's Niagara Falls, reinforces this sense of historical suspension. Yet the very phrase – "a las cinco de la tarde" – that would appear to establish the novel's static historicity also proposes its relation to the ongoing history of literary texts. Federico García Lorca's "Llanto por Ignacio Sánchez Mejías" repeats the same phrase to convey the tragic stasis of the bullfighter's death. Textual repetition/intertextual echoes: Sánchez connects his novel ironically to its Spanish precursor as Borges' Pierre Menard connects his text to its.

Structural tensions are intensified by Sánchez's thematization of the referential divide between words and the world. Life is a phenomenal thing, as the lyrics of the *guaracha* assert, not a verbal thing, and language, whether spoken or written, is inadequate to express the characters' experience. With the exception of one section in the novel, the characters' spoken speech is not put in quotation marks but blends into its noisy narrative surroundings, as if to suggest the confusions of consciousness, speech, and phenomena. The absence of quotation marks also indicates that the characters do not listen to each other. If *The Kiss of the Spider Woman* is comprised almost wholly of dialogue, this novel contains almost none. Familiar speech is presented as spoken not because it creates a community of shared expression but because in the noise of contemporary San Juan, the characters need to speak out loud in order to hear themselves think. Each has his or her formulaic tag, and each comments internally on his or her particular style. Senator Reinosa is the establishment personified and petrified, and his language embodies that fact. He contemplates the speeches he has given to Lions, Rotarians, and Catholic Daughters of America in a "vozarrón regulado para que combine con la fuerza bólida de mi bólida personalidad" (99; "modulated boom so that it blends with the meteoric force of my meteoric personality" 18). He contemplates as well the word *corteja* (mistress) and his deformations of it – the several euphemisms that allow it to be included in his senatorial expense account. Because of their use over long periods of time in a multitude of contexts, clichés—in this case, reductive labels for women—are empty signs and thus replete with meanings. Although the senator's manipulation of the word is to be understood as deplorable (he is incapable of distinguishing his manipulation of the word from his manipulation of women), it nonetheless suggests the receptivity to assigned meaning of much familiar language.

Language and sex are often linked in this novel. In one breath, the senator punningly congratulates himself on his sexual and linguistic virtuosity: "Corteja o ceremonias de ilícita mampostería donde reitero mi virilidad y el triunfo de ella: contradicción del idioma que una la sea tan él . . ." (93; "Love affair or ceremonies of illicit masonry where I reiterate my virility and its triumph: a contradiction in the language that a feminine noun should be so masculine . . ." 72). The senator refers to the feminine noun "virility": the spoken Spanish allows the "el" its full ambivalence ("el" and "él") as the printed medium cannot; in the English translation, this pun is lost altogether. However, the senator's lechery is *not* lost but impugned by the structure of the novel. Caught in a traffic jam on his way to his mistress' house in a working-class barrio of San Juan, the senator never makes it. So the traffic jam becomes an extended metaphor for the impotence of this "powerful" and abusive man.

The senator's bombast is counterpointed by the verbal style of his black mistress, a woman who knows herself and knows how to use men like the senator. Her prose fairly sings with street jive, song tags, and clichés; her sensuality, unlike the senator's, combines touch, taste, sight, smell, and sound, providing the basis of her rebellion against the social order. As Sánchez's narrator puts it, she celebrates "words bargainsale" and "the idea of brevity stipulated by the moving mastery of the lower classes": to her Sánchez gives the most explicit comments on the nature of common language. She says, "Cosas hay que no llegan a saberse, el misterio del mundo es un mundo de misterio: cita citable . . . clicés seriados del gentuzo *a mi me importa todo un mojón de puta*: padre-nuestro suyo" (79; "There are things that are never known to be known, the mystery of the world is a world of mystery: a quotable quote . . . clichés made serious by the commonality *I don't give a whore's hard turd for anything*: her Lord's Prayer" 61). The driving rhythms of this woman's language, like her use of her body, are inspired by an instinctive understanding of how best to elicit a response from these instruments. But neither is powerful enough to alter the inalterable facts of her retarded child and her own position of subservience. She concludes wistfully, "Cuando quiero gozar yo gozo y a veces gozo sin querer . . ." (80; "When I want to enjoy, I enjoy, and sometimes I enjoy without wanting to . . ." 62).

The characters' idiomatic styles are embedded in a narrative that is also rhythmic and repetitive, but with its own special tinge of ironic self-mockery. The narrator uses words like "hermeneutic" and "existential," and describes one character as an Ortegan who lunches on Unamuno, another as emulating Proust. Given his obvious sympathy for the "moving mastery of the lower classes," one senses Sánchez's ambivalence toward the European intellectual and literary traditions that such references evoke – traditions that are obviously his own. Against the rhythms of popular culture the silence of the library is small consolation.

The narrator's refinement lacks the resonance of the popular language that his prose celebrates, but there is something inadvertent here, for Sánchez clearly aims to condemn (not celebrate) a culture where the noise of advertising jingles, mindlessly repeated campaign slogans, and buzzwords drown out any thought that does not keep time to the beat. The unstated subplot of this book is the dehumanizing forces of contemporary mass culture; there is no prison cell to filter the noise, no private realm that is impervious to public assault, as there is in Puig's novel. And though the radios playing the *guaracha* in unison might imply the existence of a collective social consciousness, that possibility is undermined by the obvious isolation of the characters even as they listen to the same message. Propaganda grounded in the perceptual biases of one's language is environmental, invisible, and thus unutterably insidious. Sánchez manages to expose this hidden environment by using the very language that produces it and is produced by it. In deploying clichés for literary and political effect, he reverses the accumulated weight of verbal stereotypes, playing familiar languages in a new register.

III

It is instructive to place Puig's and Sánchez's use of clichés in a comparative American context. Contrast their novels to one by Thomas Pynchon, in which the author explicitly engages the formulae of U.S. popular culture. The language and sounds of mass media are the subject of Pynchon's *The Crying of Lot 49*, but unlike Puig's and Sánchez's narratives, they are not the medium of the novel itself. Rather, the novel is written in conventional discursive prose, with fragments of vernacular interspersed to illustrate the decline of coherence, both social and linguistic. Pynchon's protagonist Oedipa attempts to elude incoherence, but she cannot. There is no character except Oedipa who does not have a set of verbal formulae to which he or she subscribes and by which he or she is obviously circumscribed. Pynchon does not seem seriously to investigate the possibility that contemporary idiomatic language might itself be a means of communication, nor is the reader encouraged to entertain that possibility, so insane are the characters who surround Oedipa. Popular languages are consistently discredited by being assigned to characters who have been completely taken in by a media-glutted culture and who cannot be said to be responsible, linguistically or otherwise.

As for Oedipa, she is surprisingly mute. She asks short questions in somewhat colorless standard English as she tracks down clues, rarely speaking at length; she understands the clichés rattling around her but only uses them when she feels that she must do so to be understood. Pynchon's ambivalence toward popular culture, embodied in Oedipa's curious bilingualism and in the novel's conventional narrative style, suggests the author's vacillation between the conviction that serious character must express itself in standard grammatical forms and the suspicion that standard forms are no longer adequate. Ultimately Oedipa and the novel itself appear to move away from language and toward silence as the only remaining possibility for communication.

Here we see current traces of the historical asymmetry of the Hispanic and Anglo literary traditions. Whereas Romanticism flourished in English and American literature, it did not in Spanish and Latin American literature: contemporary Latin American writers do not look back to relatively recent Romantic precursors but rather to their Spanish Baroque precursors – Góngora, Calderón de la Barca, Lope de Vega, Garcilaso de la Vega in Spain, and in New Spain, Sor Juana Inés de la Cruz. The baroque qualities of Puig's and Sánchez's novels – the intricate sonorities and rhythms of Sánchez, the shiny surfaces of the celluloid plots of Puig – contrast with the presumably inexpressible (Romantic) interiority of Pynchon's character. The Spanish Baroque was the product of a multicultural context, and its decentered forms, when transplanted to New Spain, encompassed the diverse relations of self and other in a single (Catholic) community. Contemporary U.S. culture, on the contrary, inherits two anti-communitarian strains of individualism: the Puritan sense of the solitary self in direct communion with God, and the English Romantic sense of the solitary self in direct communion with nature and spirit. In both traditions, community is viewed negatively: the institutional Church as an obstacle to Puritan piety, the cultural collective as an obstacle to individual (original, artistic) expression. Oedipa's comic condition stems in part from this heritage: she is a Puritan, post-Romantic refugee from contemporary U.S. mass culture.

In distinction to Puig's and Sánchez's baroque inclusiveness, Pynchon's literary structure provides her nowhere to hide.

But perhaps the matter is elsewhere: perhaps Pynchon is simply a modernist in his preference for an intelligible order, and Puig and Sánchez postmodernists in their energetic surrender to disorder? The supposed dichotomy between modernist and postmodernist positions has, in recent critical discussions, too often been constituted along just these lines: whether meaning can be posited or not; whether fragments can be made to cohere or not; whether "old certainties have been replaced by new instabilities."[21] The countervailing Baroque and Romantic concepts of individualism, with their very different Catholic and Protestant bases, remind us how reductive it would be simply to weigh Pynchon against Puig and Sánchez on the supposedly opposing scales of modernism and postmodernism. Modernity has developed (and is developing) unevenly in this hemisphere, and what has been called postmodern in New World writing represents neither a radical break with modernism nor a seamless continuity. Indeed, its most recognizable aspect – its inclusive intertextuality – entails a complex balancing of these alternatives. Through the various narrative strategies I have explored, these writers inhabit the modernist structures they wish both to subvert *and* include. These structures (including the novel itself) may be invested with postmodernist meanings by virtue of their *use*, a process epitomized in the defamiliarization of clichés in *The Kiss of the Spider Woman* and *Macho Camacho's Beat*.

If Puig and Sánchez concentrate on the process of literary creation from the noise of contemporary mass culture, Pynchon uses fragments to illustrate the radical inadequacies of contemporary mass culture. Pynchon's character attempts to harmonize the noise, or at least to turn down the volume; Puig's and Sánchez's characters, on the other hand, attempt to encompass it, to understand the world in its terms. Both positions critique modernist assumptions, Pynchon in his opposition to the technological culture of the U.S., Puig and Sánchez in their opposition to the elitism of literature in Latin America. Their novels emerge from the interactions of their characters' felt histories and the raw materials of their different cultures. Puig and Sánchez defamiliarize by embracing familiar language, Pynchon defamiliarizes by rejecting it.

There are, of course, other attitudes toward the inclusion of popular languages in contemporary U.S. fiction. To Pynchon's evident anxiety that the U.S. has become a disposable culture and that nothing lasts longer than Warhol's designated fifteen minutes, we may juxtapose Donald Barthelme's acceptance of that fact. In his parodic novel, *Snow White*, Barthelme writes:

We like books that have a lot of *dreck* in them, matter which presents itself as not wholly relevant (or indeed at all relevant) but which, carefully attended to, can supply a kind of "sense" of what is going on. This "sense" is not to be obtained by reading between the lines (for there is nothing there, in those white spaces) but by reading the lines themselves – looking at them and so arriving at a feeling not of satisfaction exactly, that is too much to expect, but of having read them, of having "completed" them.[22]

Meaning is no longer "between the lines" but in the materiality of the text itself, on its verbal surface. Barthelme's intertextuality has been described as collage and his method as "the fusion of recycled content with a paste of style."[23] Popular formulae are the raw material of his fiction; made-up museums dot his literary landscape.

African-American writers and critics are also aware of the literary potential of popular languages and the political potential of mixing levels of discourse. Public/private and elite/popular are dichotomies specifically rejected by such "public intellectuals" as bell hooks, Derrick Bell, Michael Eric Dyson, and Cornel West. In an essay entitled "Public Academy," Michael Bérubé notes that these critics celebrate (in West's terms) "the culturally hybrid character of black life."[24] Bérubé contrasts the postwar Jewish intelligentsia – which was also committed to rethinking America's progressive tradition – with this group; the former required "a cordon sanitaire protecting 'real' culture from contamination by the kitsch, dreck, schlock pop, and camp that surrounded it. One cannot imagine . . . the new black intelligentsia adopting the same cultural politics. Nor should they" (75).

Toni Morrison's attitude toward clichés is consonant with Bérubé's assertion, but she emphasizes the historical (rather than current) relations of popular languages and cultural identity. She uses clichés to *conserve* communal traditions (against, she implies, the contemporary U.S. culture of forgetting), a strategy that clearly allies her to contemporary Latin American writers like Puig and Sánchez. Morrison knows that writers must conserve familiar stories and linguistic formulae, that such formulae are woven into the fabric of communities and are necessary to their continuance. In a 1981 interview, Morrison said that she likes

to work with, to fret, the cliché, which is a cliché because the experience expressed in it is important: a young man seeks his fortune; a pair of friends, one good, one bad; the perfectly innocent victim. We know thousands of these in literature. I like to dust off these clichés, dust off the language, make them mean whatever they may have meant originally. My genuine criticism of most contemporary books is that they're not *about* anything. Most of the books that are about something – the books that mean something – treat old ideas, old situations.[25]

Morrison goes on to mention stories that were told and retold in her childhood community and that she has engaged in various of her works of literature. Indeed, how a wide range of folk idioms are received and incorporated into written literary structures is often discussed by both African-American writers and their critics.[26]

To return to Bérubé's comparison of postwar intellectual attitudes and contemporary African-American intellectuals, I want to propose a Latin American analogue. In early- to mid-twentieth-century Latin American novels such as *Doña Bárbara, La Vorágine,* and *Don Segundo Sombra,* the vernacular is *popular* in the Spanish (and Latinate) sense of the word: of the people. *Popular* in Spanish means ethnic and/or lower-class, unlike the English use of the same word to mean wide acceptance and favor. ("Populist" is a better translation of the Spanish *popular* than its English cognate "popular.") Characters speaking the vernacular in these novels signify (and reinforce) the cultural and social gulf between readers – literate, hence participants in the structures of public power – and those characters. By virtue of their speaking the "popular" idiom, the reader knows that they are uneducated, hence from cultures and classes by definition excluded from those same structures of power. This is not the same kind of "cordon sanitaire" created by postwar U.S. intellectuals, but it had the similar effect of confirming existing cultural, social and gender hierarchies.

On the contrary, contemporary Latin American fiction, like contemporary African-American literature and criticism, aims at achieving the opposite effect of bridging the gulf between the literary and the *popular*/popular, and subverting systems upon which cultural inequities have traditionally been based. Cornel West's term "kinetic orality," which he defines as "dynamic repetitive and energetic rhetorical styles that form communities, e.g., antiphonal styles and linguistic innovations that accent fluid, improvisational identities and that promote survival at almost any cost," surely describes the orality in the works of Puig and Sánchez as well.[27] If Flaubert's anti-bourgeois aesthetic led him to impugn cultural systems that permitted the incursion of the formulae of mass culture, it is their more democratic aesthetic that moves these contemporary writers and critics to impugn systems that exclude such formulae. Their "kinetic orality" heightens the question of textuality and intertextuality and thus the issue of audience. Again the reader (listener, viewer) is constituted to foreground the New World writer's desire to participate in traditions actual and imagined.

Comparative Conclusions:
Baroque New Worlds

Behind every idea there are a thousand years of literature. I think you have to know as much as possible of where you are and how you are taking it further.

Gabriel García Márquez[1]

WILLIAM CARLOS WILLIAMS, in his 1939 essay "Against the Weather," drew early attention to the American tendency to create inclusive structures. I have already cited his statement on the "power of mutation" required of New World writers to accommodate their multiple traditions. Williams would have understood this need for inclusive structures better than most, his name a literal cipher of his own converging heritages of Hispanic and Anglo-American cultures (his mother was Puerto Rican, his father Anglo-American). Surely his awareness of both traditions explains his fervent interest in the interactions of the New World's cultures and histories.[2] On Europeans immigrating to the New World, Williams wrote: "It was liberty they needed, not so much liberty for freedom's sake but liberty to partake of, to be included in and to conserve. Liberty, in this sense, has the significance of inclusion rather than a breaking away."[3] Here he describes the American anxiety of origins as an appetite for inclusion, and the artist as the agent of its expression. For Williams, "the significance of inclusion" is not homogenization or unification but the countenancing of multiple, coexisting, conflictual, unfinished histories. Not peace but possibility.

In 1918, Williams wrote about Ezra Pound (whose departure for Europe he could neither comprehend nor forgive), "The accordances of which Americans have the parts and the colors but not the completions before them pass beyond the attempts of his thought."[4] The genuine American writer (Williams emphatically excludes Pound) contemplates the "parts and the colors but not the completions." Because of its vastness and variety, the American writer can only whiff what Williams calls "the aroma of the whole":

196

Being an artist I can produce, if I am able, universals of general applicability. If I succeed in keeping myself objective enough, sensual enough, I can produce factors the concretions of material by which others shall understand and so be led to use – that they may the better see, touch, taste, enjoy – their own world *differing as it may* from mine. By mine, they, different, can be discovered to be the same as I, and, thrown into contrast, will see the implications of a general enjoyment through me. . . .

. . .

This is the generosity . . . of art. It closes up the ranks of understanding.[5]

American artists may draw many histories together "without destruction of their particular characteristics; [art] will draw them together because in their disparateness [it] discovers an identity" (199). For Williams, to discover identity by recognizing difference is the *nature* of art: "Every masterwork liberates while it draws the world closer in mutual understanding and tolerance. This is its aroma of the whole" (199).

This "aroma of the whole" wafts thematically and structurally through the American literature I have discussed. Williams anticipates by decades contemporary critics who speak of "identity in difference" and who justifiably condemn the "totalizing" meta-narratives of Western modernity. However, recent theorists use "totalizing" to signal hegemonic and hierarchizing structures, whereas Williams uses it to describe relative, fluid, open, inclusive ones. Consider this statement on the issues of origins and inclusion by Homi K. Bhabha: "The aim of cultural difference is to re-articulate the sum of knowledge from the perspective of the signifying *singularity* of the 'other' that resists totalization – the repetition that will not return as the same, the minus-in-origin that results in political and discursive strategies where adding-*to* does not add-up but serves to disturb the calculation of power and knowledge. . . ."[6] In the negative charge he gives to "totalization," Bhabha engages the poststructuralist critique of coercive histories; but we hear clear echoes of Williams when Bhabha speaks of a "sum of knowledge" that includes difference. Bhabha argues for an awareness of difference within a decentered totality; he implies that such sum-of-knowledge structures enable divergent histories to unsettle dominant ideologies – what Robert Young has called "white mythologies."[7] Williams' "parts and colors but not the completions," like Bhabha's "adding-*to*," opens up historical understanding, because what is inclusive is also inconclusive. This is what I meant at the end of my first chapter, when I suggested that Borges' fragmentary "modest history" might be the most usable past of all.

We have seen this modest history – this disruptive "adding-*to*" – variously enacted in American literature from south to north. That the Baroque was the principal European style imported into Latin America, and that it continues to function as a cipher of Latin American cultural inclusiveness parallels Williams' pluralist intuition that liberty in America consists not in the lack of historical encumbrances but rather in the opportunity to elect and include them. The multiculturalism debate in the U.S. has revitalized (and revised) Williams' sense of inclusion, and parallels earlier debates in Latin America about cultural inclusiveness, notably the *indigenista* movements that developed throughout Latin American in the first half of this century. In the U.S., as in Latin America, to write politically now is to write about the interactions of cultures and cultural forms. I have repeatedly turned to writers who are political in this sense: my examples attest to their shared desire to create and/or include acceptable sources of cultural authority.

The literary energy generated by this New World project has been directed first toward the imperatives of communal self-definition and second toward the urge for individual self-expression. Communal claims are inseparable from individual histories, of course, and the emphasis on one or the other may shift rapidly within a given culture (as it has in the U.S. in the past three decades as the collective awareness of ethnic, racial and gender differences has evolved).[8] The works I have discussed in the previous chapters share the assumption that if usable communal pasts can be identified (or created), individuated histories will be possible. The first task provides grounds for the second: psychological depiction depends upon the novelist's creative historiography.

As we have seen, this priority of communal claims takes literary form in a variety of ways: in a palpable turn away from the narrative devices of psychological fiction toward archetypalized characters driven by collective histories rather than individual personality; in synchronic structures orchestrated for a chorus of voices rather than a solo; in the frequent foregrounding not so much of competing selves as competing semiotic systems (newspapers, novels, the clichés of film and popular music); in an emphasis on the intertextual operations of traditions rather than the particularities of individual talent. The writers I have discussed privilege the construction of communal histories in which representative individuals may function. *One Hundred Years of Solitude* might serve as an allegory of this process. Macondo (a metonymic Latin America) is founded so that the archetypalized Buendías may then exist and operate. So, too, Borges' "Library of Babel," in which the library's accumulated record of history is privileged, not the single "eternal traveler" who wanders there. Historical patterns often upstage historical personages as these writers chart the rhythms of a collective subject.

Alejo Carpentier is the essential precursor of contemporary Latin American writers in this regard. Carlos Fuentes has said of Carpentier that he made "a conscious and concerted attempt to encompass the Latin American experience as a whole, without undue concern for the differences created by regional or national boundaries."[9] Carpentier liberated Latin American writers from the local by insisting upon the multiple and coexisting histories of every locale. As a result of Carpentier's "relentless effort to synthesize history and the self in a form of Latin American writing," Roberto González Echevarría argues, this author inspired "total novels" (he mentions *One Hundred Years of Solitude* and *The Death of Artemio Cruz*).[10] Borges, too, is totalizing in this sense: he cannot praise Juan Moreira without recalling Platonic philosophy, or describe a pink house in the Buenos Aires suburbs without evoking the hanging gardens of Babylon. We may understand Whitman's and Faulkner's perennial appeal to Latin American writers precisely in terms of their own, consonant compulsion to construct fabulously inclusive literary structures to describe their part of the Baroque New World.[11] Whitman's "limited catalogue of endless things," Faulkner's "thirteen ways of looking at a blackbird," Borges' "palimpsest," Carpentier's "lo real maravilloso americano" and "lo barroco," Paz's "tradition as rupture," Williams' "aroma of the whole," García Márquez's symbolic "thousand years of literature," cited in my epigraph: these American constructs encode the simultaneous operations of conflictual origins and influences, and relativize them in their dynamic, decentered conceptions of tradition as such.

This American energy to amplify and include stems from an awareness of the processes of cultural transmission in colonized or seemingly marginalized contexts. Red Cloud/Moonstone, Brooklyn, Patterson, Oxford/Jefferson, La Habana, Buenos Aires, Aracataca/Macondo: American locality is conceived and depicted in relation to larger geographical and cultural structures in order to (in Bhabha's formulation) "re-articulate the sum of knowledge from the perspective of the signifying *singularity* of the 'other'. . . ." Location is always in some sense *dis*location, *re*location, *trans*location: the fluid relations of local parts to (projected) wholes. We have seen these decentered wholes depicted *thematically* as communities, cultures, and histories (Panther Canyon, Xochicalco, Canudos, Charity, Comala, San Juan). We have also seen them modeled *structurally* in intertextual and synchronic metaphors (music, a model kit, a milagro). And we have seen them encoded *formally* in the converging strains of counterrealism that we now regularly refer to as magical realism, in the generic mixing of journalism and novels and the mixing of the discursive levels – movie plots and academic footnotes, popular songs and erudite allusions. Convergence, divergence, fusion, con/fusion: What comparative conclusions can we draw from these inclusive structures and strategies?

Derek Walcott names the European concept of tradition that must be revised in order to be usable in America: T. S. Eliot's "unbroken arc" is a wildly implausible model of "the education of the black in the Western world," where "a sensibility . . . has been broken and recreated."[12] Walcott rejects Eliot's notion of tradition on the grounds that it is "totalizing" in the negative sense of the word: hegemonic, determined, determining. Yet Walcott's work is itself profoundly totalizing in the inclusive cultural and textual sense that *I* intend. His plays, poetry, and essays reflect his vast knowledge and appreciation of Eliot's classical European tradition; indeed, much of his poetic effect depends upon his inclusion of that tradition in a Caribbean setting. Thus Walcott flaunts the paradox of his cultural positioning: his traditions are both deeply related to European traditions and deeply not. His work is characterized by antinomy, by coexisting and contradictory elements that are equally necessary and inextricably intertwined. Clearly, conceptions of cultural tradition based on European ideas of singularity and supersession cannot account for the inclusive historicizing imagination of New World literature, whether Hispanic or Anglo-American.

I cite Walcott in part to complicate this last dualism (Hispanic and Anglo-American). This Caribbean poet and playwright has commented on his cultural and literary affinity for American writers writing in Spanish, even as his own British literary education and attitudes, however ironized, are everywhere apparent in his work. And Walcott's reference to Eliot complicates another dualism: Europe versus America. Eliot left America for Europe but his concern for the nature of tradition (like Walcott's) is recognizably American; his "unbroken arc" is surely one more version of the American historical desire for inclusive structures of significance.[13] Be that as it may, Eliot's strategies are decidedly *not* usable or useful in Walcott's Caribbean, and his indictment of Eliot's "unbroken arc" is consonant with what I have consistently found to be the case: New World writers require dynamic and decentered structures, not unbroken arcs, to model the multiple and coexisting traditions they engage and extend.

Octavio Paz's "tradición de la ruptura" ("tradition of/as rupture") provides an alternative understanding of New World tradition as such. His oxymoronic phrase serves as the title of the first chapter of his *Hijos del limo* (*Children of the Mire*, 1974), a comparative history of European and American poetic traditions. The phrase – unfortunately translated in the published translation as "tradition against itself" – echoes Baudelaire's "tradition of the new," but Paz's project is, predictably, more inclusive. In the word "tradition" Paz acknowledges cultural continuity, but "continuity" involves the simultaneous operations of multiple traditions and heterogeneous expressive forms. Thus, in his first paragraph Paz must, of necessity, question his own metaphor:

¿Puede llamarse tradición a aquello que rompe el vínculo e interrumpe la continuidad? Y hay más: inclusive si se aceptase que la negación de la tradición a la larga podría, por la repetición del acto a través de generaciones de iconoclastas, constituir una tradición, ¿cómo llegaría a serlo realmente sin negarse a sí misma, quiero decir, sin afirmar en un momento dado, no la interrupción, sino la continuidad?[14]

Can something be called a tradition that breaks bonds and interrupts continuity? Moreover, even if we accept that the negation of tradition could, by repeating its negations over generations of iconoclasts, constitute a tradition, how could it really be a tradition without negating itself, that is, without affirming at a given moment not interruption but continuity?[15]

Continuity outweighs interruption, but here continuity implies a process of cultural accumulation and accommodation, not a linear movement in which the past is supplanted by the future: so Paz immediately begins to ironize modernity's love affair with the new, the original, the "interruption."

Paz concludes this first paragraph with another version of the same question:

¿Cómo puede lo moderno ser tradicional? Si tradición significa continuidad del pasado en el presente, ¿cómo puede hablarse de una tradición sin pasado y que consiste en la exaltación de aquello que lo niega: la pura actualidad? (17–18)

How can the modern be traditional? If tradition signifies the continuity of past to present, how can we speak of a tradition without a past that consists in the exaltation of that which it denies: the pure present? (my translation)

Paz admits that he will necessarily respond to his own question from a "biased" point of view, "that of a Spanish American" (121).

La modernidad es una tradición polémica y que desaloja a la tradición imperante, cualquiera que ésta sea; pero la desaloja sólo para, un instante después, ceder el sitio a otra tradición que, a su vez, es otra manifestación momentánea de la actualidad. La modernidad nunca es ella misma: siempre es *otra*. Lo moderno no se caracteriza únicamente por su novedad, sino por su heterogeneidad. Tradición heterogénea o de lo heterogéneo, la modernidad está condenada a la pluralidad: la antigua tradición era siempre la misma, la moderna es siempre distinta. La primera postula la unidad entre el pasado y el hoy; la segunda, no contenta con subrayar las diferencias entre ambos, afirma que ese pasado no es uno sino plural. Tradición de lo moderno: heterogeneidad, pluralidad de pasados, extrañeza radical. . . . (18, Paz's emphasis)

Modernity is a polemical tradition which displaces the tradition of the moment, whatever it happens to be, but an instant later yields its place to still another tradition which in turn is a momentary manifestation of modernity. Modernity is never itself; it is always *the other*. The modern is characterized not only by novelty but by otherness. A bizarre tradition and a tradition of the bizarre, modernity is condemned to pluralism: the old tradition was always the same, the modern is always different. The former postulates unity between past and present; the latter, not content with emphasizing its own differences, affirms that the past is not one but many. The tradition of the modern is thus radical otherness and plurality of pasts. (1–2, Paz's emphasis)

This is no "unbroken arc," no unitary version of modernity: on the contrary, using the same verb as Walcott, Paz undertakes an extended historical examination of "the breaking of the main Western tradition [that] caused many traditions to appear" (123). He discusses conceptions of time and patterns of history ("the relation between past, present, and future differs in each civilization" 9), the persistence of the past in the present ("the most remarkable fact about contemporary Mexico is the persistence of ways of thinking and feeling that belong to the colonial era, or even the pre-Hispanic world" 67), and the asymmetrical development of "modernity" in Spain and the rest of Europe.

If Paz conceives of culture as accumulation, accommodation, intersection, rise and fall – as the asymmetrical and inclusive interactions of heterogeneous traditions – then it follows that he would reject the modern conception of tradition as progressive and, by extension, the meaning of the word "modern" itself. Rather than "new," for Paz "modern" means a complex relation to tradition; so he recuperates the premodern (Shakespearean) significance of "modern" – that which is familiar, commonplace, known. The Mexican cultural anthropologist Néstor García Canclini also notes Paz's contradictory relation to modernism, wondering "why one of the most subtle exponents of the modern in Latin American literature and art is fascinated by a return to the premodern . . . ." He notes that in Paz's work "the simultaneous exaltation of the modernist aesthetic and social premodernity show themselves to be compatible. . . ."[16] García Canclini concludes that this is a recognizable "versión liberal del tradicionalismo" ("liberal version of traditionalism") in Latin America, and he includes Borges along with Paz as modernists who refuse to embrace the new without respect for the known. He might have included Julio Cortázar and Alejo Carpentier as well, both of whom also explicitly contest the modern meaning of "modern."[17] We may think of these writers as revolutionary in the original sense of the word: a repeating historical process, a renewal not by destroying or invalidating past forms but by returning to and revitalizing them.

One final concept – a revolutionary one in this older sense – will suffice to conclude my discussion. "Baroque" as a term describing a particular New World cultural ideology and aesthetic was first developed by Carpentier in the forties and subsequently by Paz, Sarduy, Lezama Lima, Fuentes, and others. Among contemporary Latin American writers and critics, the New World Baroque has become an essential metaphor for the inclusive interactions of cultures and histories in the Americas.

In *Children of the Mire*, Paz's discussion of the Baroque begins in Europe, of course, and is comparative. His argument is this: in Hispanic literature and culture, the tradition of the Baroque is primary, whereas in English, German, and French literature and culture the Romantic is primary. According to Paz, Romanticism emerged as a reaction to the Enlightenment, as "an attempt of the poetic imagination to rekindle souls desolated by critical reason" (81). In Spain, on the other hand, a Romantic movement did not flourish because Enlightenment rationalist paradigms were not established: "In Spain this reaction against the modern age could not appear, because actually Spain did not have a modern age: she had neither critical reason nor bourgeois revolution, neither Kant nor Robespierre" (82). Of course, there *were* Romantic Spanish and Latin American writers, but they were minor ("bombastic and derivative," says Paz) in comparison to the writers of the Baroque period.[18] Historically, then, the Baroque is analogous in importance in Hispanic literary history to Romanticism in the rest of Europe. Contemporary writers in English look to their Romantic precursors, whereas contemporary writers in Spanish look to their Baroque precursors. Paz's own Baroque precursor is the great Mexican poet Sor Juana Inés de la Cruz; his magisterial study of her life and work is integrally a study of the Baroque in its European and New World manifestations.[19]

Alejo Carpentier preceded Paz in theorizing a New World Baroque. Motivated by the same need for historical and cultural definition that subsequently motivated Paz, Carpentier created an aesthetic and ideology of difference specific to Latin America. He insisted upon the continuity of indigenous Latin American and Baroque traditions, arguing that the Baroque is not merely a European art-historical category but the sign of cultural syncretism, symbiosis, *mestizaje*.

¿Y por qué es América Latina la tierra de elección del barroco? Porque toda simbiosis, todo mestizaje, engendra un barroquismo. El barroquismo americano se acrece con . . . la conciencia de ser otra cosa, de ser una cosa nueva, de ser una simbiosis, de ser un criollo; y el espíritu criollo de por sí, es un espíritu barroco.[20]

And why is Latin America the chosen territory of the baroque? Because all symbiosis, all *mestizaje*, engenders the baroque. The American Baroque develops along with . . . the awareness of being Other, of being new, of being symbiotic, of being a *criollo*; and the *criollo* spirit is itself a Baroque spirit.[21]

Contemporary Latin American writers and critics have followed Carpentier in engaging the New World Baroque, or *neobarroco*, as an inclusive historical and cultural category.[22]

In the U.S. and Europe, Carpentier's conceptions of "lo barroco" and "lo real maravilloso americano" have been absorbed (often indiscriminately) into discussions of magical realism, but Latin American writers are well aware of the distinction. García Márquez, for example, has demurred when critics call him a magical realist, but he has absolutely no hesitation in calling his own work Baroque. In a 1969 interview, he paid homage to the "orígenes maravillosos" ("marvelous origins") of the Spanish Baroque, mentioning the novels of chivalry, the *Quixote*, and the theatre and poetry of the Golden Age: "Style, elegance, luxury, and total excess have not been given their due. Young Latin American novelists have known how to be inventive in the best tradition of the Spanish Baroque and, at the same time, engage in social criticism that is no less telling for being colorful."[23] In 1969, García Márquez would surely have included himself among the "young Latin American novelists" who combine Baroque fantasy and social criticism. The Baroque artist's rejection of the opposition between appearance and reality (an opposition upon which rationalism and realism depend) is the model for García Márquez's counterrealistic practice. In *One Hundred Years of Solitude*, such hallucinatory scenes as the banana company massacre or the serial murder of the seventeen Aurelianos are contemporary stagings of the essential Baroque trope, la vida es sueño ("life is a dream").

Other Latin American writers and critics have stressed other aspects of the New World Baroque, but always within the framework of cultural syncretism established by Carpentier and *la tradición de la ruptura* elaborated by Paz. Severo Sarduy speaks of the inclusive intertextuality of the New World Baroque in terms of Bakhtin's concepts of dialogism and heteroglossia; among Sarduy's subtitles indicating these inclusive strategies are "substitution," "citation," "proliferation," "condensation," "parody," and (of course) "intertextuality."[24] Referring to Latin America, Carlos Fuentes has described the volatile shiftings and realignments of Baroque forms as the "culture of the incomplete, of the voracious, of the intertextual that is the Baroque."[25] Then, in Baroque fashion, he amplifies his claim: "The configuration of the new universal culture is Baroque."[26]

Is this tenable? To what extent is the Baroque a usable metaphor for historical interactions in cultures in the rest of the Americas? "Voracious," one might feel, fairly describes the attitudes and behavior of the U.S. during this century, but Fuentes is referring not to politics or economics but to the necessary *mestizaje* of postcolonial forms of expression. Magical realism is a recent flowering of the Baroque in contemporary Latin American fiction and is flourishing worldwide, especially on the peripheries of western culture – presumably the "new universal culture" to which Fuentes refers. But my comparative interest is in contemporary U.S. literature. Can this Latin American model of Baroque inclusiveness – with its ideal of non-Hegelian, heterogeneous, decentered wholes – be related to post-Romantic structures of inclusion in U.S. literature?

Paz is correct, of course, to draw a stark contrast between Romantic and Baroque forms of thought and expression, and to attribute notable differences in the U.S. and Latin America to these different cultural heritages. Romanticism's conception of the unitary self departs diametrically from the more collective institutional ideology of the Baroque. In Latin America, Baroque forms defined ecclesiastical, political and social collectivities, and still do, a fact that partly explains the preference I have noted in contemporary Latin American literature for communal dramas over psychological ones. The Baroque privileges the inclusion of individual differences within a centralized system, whereas Romanticism privileges individual autonomy within a pluralist system. So, beginning in the mid-nineteenth century, U.S. writers interested in imagining coherent communities and usable histories had to dilute inherited Romantic notions of individualism by means of mythic strategies. Transcendentalism was both an American outgrowth of European Romanticism and an antidote to it, preferring to imagine *shared* human features and hence communal and cosmic possibilities. As a result, the nineteenth-century U.S. novel differs distinctly from its English counterpart in its archetypalized characters and mythic underpinnings. One has only to think of Thoreau's *persona* at Walden Pond, Melville's Ahab, and Hawthorne's Wakefield to recognize an American repositioning of European Romantic subjectivity. These characters and their authors displace idiosyncratic feeling with idealizing structures of self and society. For this reason and others, the U.S. romance tradition is comparable to contemporary instances of Latin American magical realism as the nineteenth-century European novel generally is not.

T. S. Eliot's "unbroken arc" must also be understood as a reaction against Romanticism's isolated, idiosyncratic self. We recognize Eliot's intertextual use of myriad precursor texts and traditions as an American way of addressing his historical anxiety of origins. This intertextuality also provided him the means to theorize an "impersonal" art that foregrounds the art object over the artist's singular sensibility. In "Tradition and the Individual Talent" Eliot writes: "Poetry is not a turning loose of emotion . . . it is not the expression of personality, but an escape from personality."[27]   He praises the seventeenth-century Metaphysical poets (Donne, Crashaw, Marvell) – labeled as such by Samuel Johnson who, in the eighteenth century, deprecated their involuted "yoking together by violence" of the "most heterogeneous ideas." But it is precisely this yoking of difference, this metaphoric encompassing of antinomy, that Eliot admires and revalidates for twentieth-century readers. The poet, according to Eliot, "is constantly amalgamating disparate experience; the ordinary man's experience is chaotic, irregular, fragmentary . . . in the mind of the poet these experiences are always forming new wholes."[28] For Eliot the Metaphysicals were paragons of this process. In his reaction against Romanticism (and the English Romantic poets), Eliot resuscitates the English Baroque, though not for the same reasons of cultural inclusiveness that Carpentier and Paz were to resuscitate the Baroque in Latin America.[29] Eliot's purpose in devising what is arguably still the most influential Anglo-American theory of tradition in this century was to show the pressure of the totality of traditions upon the individual work of art. His focus is not on the originality of the poet but on the inclusiveness of the poem.

Eliot's theory of tradition is, then, transindividual and transcultural but as I have said, he does not concern himself with the historical interactions of specific cultural traditions. Nonetheless, his emphasis on the dialectic between tradition and individual talent (while recognizing the greater power of tradition) is not unlike Paz's statement at the beginning of *Children of the Mire*, or Cather's autobiographical character at Panther Canyon, attempting to (re)enter a history "larger than her own," or Williams' historical positioning of individual experience "in the American grain" or, more recently, the protagonist in Cisneros' "Never Marry a Mexican," who fervently wants both to remember and to forget her Mexican heritage. What *is* different, as I have said, is Eliot's blindness to cultural difference as such.

But not all U.S. writers suffer this limitation. Cather includes recently transplanted central European cultures in her plains novels, as well as the vestiges of ancient indigenous cultures; Williams includes Hispanic and Anglo cultural sources, as does Cisneros in her fiction. And certainly the most influential writers in the U.S. today are those exploring and cultivating areas of uncertainty created by cultural contact.[30] Our increasing consciousness of cultural diversity – what Christopher Hitchens has called "the hyphenate principle"[31] – has encouraged (and been encouraged by) writers who foreground multiple and coexisting cultural forms. Of course, cultural differences have always existed in the U.S., but it is undeniable that they have been obscured by the dominant culture's ideological investment in a "color-blind" mainstream.

For obvious reasons, writers from marginalized racial and ethnic communities are impelled to recuperate cultural and historical differences and create inclusive structures to express them. And many of these writers are women. Eliana Ortega and Nancy Saporta Sternbach argue that the central question of identity in the fiction of contemporary U.S. Latina writers, including Cisneros, "arises as a result of the negation, marginalization, and silencing of Latinas' history by official discourse, that is, the dominant culture's version of history."[32] Walter Shear says virtually the same thing about contemporary Asian American writers, noting that Amy Tan's *The Joy Luck Club*, ". . . like other Chinese-American books . . . articulates 'the urge to find a usable past' – it is made up of a series of intense encounters in a kind of cultural lost and found."[33] Nancy J. Peterson, too, makes this point in her discussion of Louise Erdrich's *Tracks* and Native American writing generally: "Writers like Erdrich . . . face a vexing set of issues: unrepresented or misrepresented in traditional historical narratives, they write their own stories of the past only to discover that they must find a new way of making history, a way of 'forging a new historicity.'"[34] Again, Mary O'Connor refers to African-American women writers' relation to their unrepresented history by citing a statement from Alice Walker's novel *The Color Purple*: "You black, you pore, you ugly, you a woman. Goddam, he say, you nothing at all."[35] O'Connor continues: "*This nothingness* – constituted by all that is the negative of society's values in race, class, and gender – *may be seen as a place of origin* for not only Alice Walker's *The Color Purple* but for much black feminist writing. It is a nothingness imposed from without, an entity defined by the patriarchal and white world of power and wealth."[36]

Toni Morrison amplifies this point, lamenting the lack of historical consciousness in the U.S. as a whole: "We live in a land where the past is always erased and America is the innocent future in which immigrants can come and start over, where the slate is clean. The past is absent or it's romanticised. This culture doesn't encourage dwelling on, let alone coming to terms with, the truth about the past. Memory is much more in danger now than it was thirty years ago."[37] The absence of a usable past, Morrison implies, is caused by the generalized amnesia of contemporary U.S. culture. But her sensitivity to that absence is surely conditioned by her experience as an African-American and a woman.

In her essay, "Unspeakable Things Unspoken: The Afro-American Presence in American Literature," Morrison calls for an inclusive theory of texts and traditions "that truly accommodates Afro-American literature: one that is based on its culture, its history, and the artistic strategies the works employ to negotiate the world it inhabits."[38] With this end in view, she offers a reading of *Moby-Dick* as exemplary of such inclusiveness. Her choice is surprising on the surface, but it is what lies beneath the surface of Melville's novel that attracts Morrison's attention. She discusses its "unspoken, unspeakable" meaning, its "hidden course," which is Melville's challenge to whiteness as an "idealized significance" in Anglo-American culture. Morrison does not make a binary distinction between what is spoken and what is not, because what is unspeakable may remain unspoken by a writer but heard nonetheless. Morrison hears many forms of silence and she takes Melville's silence to be an inclusive strategy, citing Chapter 42 of *Moby-Dick*, "The Whiteness of the Whale," in which Melville asserts his desire to find a "comprehensive form" (17). Morrison celebrates the resulting "complex, heaving, disorderly, profound text" (18) for its capacity to include and accommodate otherness. Melville's inclusiveness is unspoken, but it nonetheless conditions his novel.

Morrison does not explicitly describe *Moby-Dick* in terms of the New World Baroque, but her understanding of the novel's inclusive and disruptive aims clearly corresponds to Latin American writers' revalidation of the Baroque aesthetic of difference.[39] The similarities are obvious in Carlos Fuentes' essay on the "Dixie Gongorist" Faulkner, where he explicitly engages the irony that Morrison also encounters in *Moby-Dick*, namely, that verbal abundance may signify collective silence:

El barroco, me decía alguna vez Alejo Carpentier, es el lenguaje de los pueblos que, desconociendo la verdad, la buscan afanosamente. Góngora, como Picasso,

Buñuel, Carpentier o Faulkner, no sabían: encontraban. El barroco, lenguage de la abundancia, es también el lenguaje de la insuficiencia: sólo lo incluyen todo quienes nada poseen. Su horror al vacío no es gratuito; se debe al hecho cierto de que se está en el vacío, de que carece de seguridad; la abundancia verbal, en *El reino de este mundo* o en *¡Absalón, Absalón!*, significa la desesperada invocación de un lenguaje que llene las ausencias de la razón y la fe. No de otra manera acudió el arte barroco post-renacentista a llenar los abismos abiertos por la revolución copernicana.[40]

The Baroque, Alejo Carpentier once told me, is the language of peoples who, not knowing what is true, look fervently for it. Góngora, like Picasso, Buñuel, Carpentier and Faulkner, didn't know: they discovered. The Baroque, language of abundance, is also the language of insufficiency: only those who possess nothing can include everything. [The Baroque] horror of a vacuum is not accidental; it is due to the fact that the vacuum exists, that there is no certainty; the verbal abundance of *The Kingdom of This World* or *Absalom, Absalom!* signifies the desperate invocation of language that fills the absences remaining after the exercise of reason and faith. In this fashion post-Renaissance Baroque art began to fill the abyss opened by the Copernican revolution.

Beyond the antirationalism and antipositivism of the Baroque, Fuentes focuses on the inherent paradox of Baroque form: its inclusive inconclusiveness, its abundant "insufficiency." Baroque works do not provide definitive accounts; they are contingent modes of historical discovery, provisional forms of "filling the abyss."

In his own usable tradition, Fuentes includes Góngora, Carpentier, Buñuel, and Faulkner, as Morrison includes Melville and, in her subsequent critical essay *Playing in the Dark*, Poe, Cather, and Hemingway. In situations of historical discontinuity, Morrison advocates what she calls "this process of entering what one is estranged from."[41] So precursors are created and American traditions (re)constituted.

Postmodernist theory echoes certain aspects of the New World Baroque: its emphasis on historical rupture and hybrid cultures, the fragmentation of the cultural past in contemporary artifacts, the mixing of cultural levels and generic forms. Despite these similarities, postmodernist categories must be adapted to local use. The problem is that theorists have tended to level cultural and historical differences, refusing historically constituted meanings as totalizing (hegemonic).[42] On the contrary, New World writers create totalizing (inclusive) structures on the assumption that usable pasts may still be imagined in literary texts and constituted in/by literary traditions; their fiction dramatizes the possibility that partial positions may still be related to contingent wholes. These writers thematize an anxiety of origins, but they also thematize a New World response: the desire for participation in meaningful histories and communities, and the risks involved in doing so. My point is this: what began in Europe as a salutary "postmodernist" challenge to modern structures of domination has too often become in practice an uncritical identification of tradition with totalitarianism, history with hegemony. The writers I have discussed in this study are engaged in the contrary process of recuperating histories and traditions – "this process of entering what one is estranged from."[43]

The need for cultural specificity in applying postmodernist positions is implicit in García Márquez's critique of theory and theorists: "I think a lot about culture, but about popular culture. And I'm the product of a culture of immediate and burning problems. The French move in a thoroughly glacial sphere of pure ideas. And they don't succumb easily. They are brought up and formed in academic tournaments. I don't like to theorize."[44] In fact, most New World writers (including García Márquez) *do* like to theorize, but their theories emerge from particular historical contexts and address particular cultural conditions.[45] I have attempted to do likewise and have, therefore, intentionally limited my own discussion of postmodernism to three areas of recent American literary practice:

1. Magical realist strategies that revise and amplify modern(ist) conceptions of reason, rationality, and individualism: the particular Latin American confluence of gothic, romance, Surrealist, and indigenous American cultural forms are postmodern in their admission of ontologies banned from the modern(ist) novel.

2. Synchronic and intertextual strategies that respond to an American historical anxiety by revising and amplifying positivist models of progress and causal logic: the mixture of modes, the openness to generic experimentation, and the inclusive intertextuality that link disparate cultures and histories in postmodern ways impossible within modern(ist) conventions of mimesis.

3. Conceptual reconstitutions of tradition that refuse to privilege the new, and require instead that newness (uniqueness, creativity) reside in something more than simply that which is most recent. Such reconstitutions may be said to be postmodern in challenging modern(ist) notions of originality and emphasizing instead the New World writer's urge to return to origins as a means of recovery and renewal.

To the extent that theories of postmodernism privilege inclusive structures of difference and challenge European structures of rationalism and positivism in specified cultural contexts, they are usable in the Americas. That postmodernist theories may themselves be a recent response to historical anxiety, and thus consonant with the American literary responses I have traced here, is a possibility worth exploring. So, too, is the intuition that stories and symbols may articulate postmodernist positions as theory itself cannot. To explore these possibilities is to historicize postmodernist theory in ways that make it useful in American comparative contexts. For the present, critics and readers will do well to turn to theorists who relate Baroque aesthetics and ideology to their consideration of postmodernism in the Americas.[46] The Baroque has had a long and complicated history in the New World as postmodernist theory does not (yet, anyway); to engage the latter in relation to the former will allow the critic to speak of cultures without necessarily speaking of nations, to speak of history without necessarily speaking of progression, succession, or supersession.

These are the beginnings of a flexible model for comparative American cultural criticism. Theorists and writers of the New World Baroque know that the "sum of knowledge" is in process, and that it accumulates according to the multiple interactions of imagined worlds and historical ones. They also recognize their shared obligation to connect those worlds. Usable pasts depend upon such connections, and such connections are arrived at only by struggling to include: cultures and communities, histories and myths, individuals and groups, genres and media. The unfinished nature of the project is obvious.

Notes

PREFACE

1. Although some critics have tended to treat the newness of American culture as a liability, Brooks treats it as a literary opportunity: "The present is a void and the American writer floats in that void because the past that survives in the common mind is a past without living value. But is this the only possible past? If we need another past so badly, is it inconceivable that we might discover one, that we might even invent one?" Quoted in Russell Reising, *The Unusable Past: Theory and the Study of American Literature*, (New York: Methuen, 1986), p. 13. I am indebted to both sources, and refer implicitly to both in my own use of the phrase.

   In *History and Value*, Frank Kermode employs the phrase "usable past" (but does not refer to Brooks), qualifying it as "a past which is not simply past but also always new." He does not concern himself with the American problematics of a "new" history (as Brooks does), but to the extent that his "new" suggests "current" or "present" or "relevant," his qualification is applicable to my discussion. *History and Value* (Oxford: Clarendon Press, 1988), p. 116

2. Seymour Menton, *Latin America's New Historical Novel* (Austin: University of Texas Press, 1993), p. 16.

3. Linda Hutcheon elaborates this concept in "Telling Stories: Fiction and History," in *The Politics of Postmodernism* (London: Routledge, 1989), pp. 47–61.

4. R. B. Kershner, "Dances with Historians," *Georgia Review* 45 (Fall 1991), 591.

PART ONE. ANXIETY OF ORIGINS

1. David Hume, *Letters to William Strahan* (Oxford: Clarendon Press, 1888), p. 155.

2. Hannah Arendt, "The Concept of History," in *Between Past and Future* (1961; rpt. New York: Viking Press, 1969), p. 68.

3. Georg Lukács, *The Historical Novel*, trans. Hannah and Stanley Mitchell (1962; rpt. New York: Penguin, 1981). This study was written in 1936–37, published in Russian shortly thereafter, and first translated into English in 1962. Subsequent page references are cited in the text.

4. Georg Wilhelm Friedrich Hegel, *The Philosophy of History*, trans. J. Sibree (New York: Willey Book Co., 1944), p. 87. The lectures that constitute this book were first delivered in 1822–23, again in 1824–25, and in 1831, the year of his death.

5. A number of studies have explored this question in the Americas. See, for example, David M. Jordan, *New World Regionalism: Literature in the Americas* (Toronto: University of Toronto Press, 1994); Amaryll Chanady, ed., *Latin American Identity and Constructions of Difference* (Minneapolis: University of Minnesota Press, 1994); George Yúdice, Jean Franco, and Juan Flores, eds., *On Edge: The Crisis of Contem-*

porary Latin American Culture (Minneapolis: University of Minnesota Press, 1992); and Silvia Spitta, *Between Two Waters: Narratives of Transculturation in Latin America* (Houston: Rice University Press, 1995).

6. Jorge Luis Borges, "El escritor argentino y la tradición," in *Discusión* (1932); rpt. in *Obras completas* (Buenos Aires: Emecé Editores, 1989), 1, p. 272.

7. Borges, "The Argentine Writer and Tradition," trans. James E. Irby, in *Labyrinths*, ed. Donald A. Yates and James E. Irby (New York: New Directions, 1962), p. 183.

8. The phrase is the Cuban novelist Lezama Lima's. A useful discussion of this theme is Brett Levinson, "Possibility, Ruin, Repetition: Rereading Lezama Lima's 'American Expression,'" *Revista Canadiense de Estudios Hispánicos* 18, no. 1 (1993), 49–66

9. Bloom refers to (but does not cite) Borges' remark that "poets create their precursors." See *The Anxiety of Influence* (London and New York: Oxford University Press, 1973), p. 19. The first three sentences of Bloom's work refer to Shelly, Borges, and Eliot respectively.

   John T. Irwin comments that "Bloom has always acknowledged that one of his own major precursors in the theory of influence was Borges in the Kafka essay." *The Mystery to a Solution: Poe, Borges and the Analytic Detective Story* (Baltimore: Johns Hopkins University Press, 1994), p. 429.

10. See Djelal Kadir, *Questing Fictions: Latin America's Family Romance* (Minneapolis: University of Minnesota Press,1986).

11. The first phrase is Alan Wilde's in *Horizons of Assent: Modernisim, Postmodernism, and the Ironic Imagination* (Baltimore: Johns Hopkins University Press, 1981), p. 44; the second is David Lodge's in "Modernism, Antimodernism and Postmodernism," in *Working with Structuralism* (London: Ark Paperbacks, 1986), p. 14. Both follow Derrida's argument in *Of Grammatology* on this point, as do virtually all postmodernist theorists.

12. Fredric Jameson, "Postmodernism and Consumer Society," in *The Anti-Aesthetic: Essays on Postmodern Culture*, ed. Hall Foster (Port Townsend, Washington: Bay Press, 1983), p. 125.

13. Julio Cortázar, *Rayuela* (Buenos Aires: Editorial Sudamericana, 1963), p. 88 (my translation, my emphasis).

14. For a persuasive discussion by a critic who *does* consider the particular processes of canon formation in Latin America, see Walter D. Mignolo, "Canons A(nd) Cross-Cultural Boundaries (Or, Whose Canon Are We Talking About?)," *Poetics Today*, 12, no. 1 (1991), 1–28.

15. The first quatrain of Sonnet 59 reads: "If there be nothing new, but that which is / Hath been before, how are our brains beguil'd / Which, labouring for invention, bear amiss / The second burden of a former child." *New Cambridge Edition* (New York: Houghton Mifflin, 1944).

16. In fact, Freud's oedipal masterplot is predicated upon this linear, progressive history in which each generation "begets" a new generation that in turn and in time "bests" the former one. In Chapter 3, I discuss a number of non-Freudian notions of the self operating in American traditions of counterrealism and suggest, in my metaphor of the animate earth, that the model of Freudian intergenerational conflict has not been taken up by Latin American writers in part because of their opposition to positivism. In the novels I discuss there, generations do not supersede but circulate. In this context, see Graciela Maturo, *Fenomenología, creación y crítica: sujeto y mundo en la novela latinoamericana* (Buenos Aires: Editorial García Cambeiro, 1989).

17. Martin Heidegger, *Being and Time*, trans. John Macquarrie and Edward Robinson (San Francisco: Harper, 1962), p. 393.

18. Carlos Fuentes, "Central and Eccentric Writing," in *Lives on the Line: The Testimony of Contemporary Latin American Authors*, ed. Doris Meyer (Berkeley: University of California Press, 1988), p. 122.

19. Geoffrey Hartman, also an influential U.S. theorist of tradition- and canon-forma-tion, argues (along with Bloom) that their primary mechanism is conflict, an argu-ment that proceeds, like Bloom's, from European post-Romantic conceptions of orig-inality and individual genius. See "Towards Literary History," in Geoffrey Hartman's collection of essays, *Beyond Formalism: Literary Essays, 1958-1970* (New Haven: Yale University Press, 1971), pp. 356–86.

20. Skepticism about Bloom's Freudian and Nietzschean assumptions is lucidly expressed by Mark Edmundson in his chapter "Under the Influence," in *Literature Against Philosophy, Plato to Derrida* (Cambridge: Cambridge University Press, 1995), pp. 199–239. See also Perry Meisel's discussion of the "myth" of originality in *The Myth of the Modern: A Study in British Literature and Criticism After 1850* (New Haven: Yale University Press, 1987); John Guillory's exploration of the con-ceptual development of the individual (and individuality) in *Poetic Authority: Spenser, Milton, and Literary History* (New York: Columbia University Press, 1983); Raphael Falco's study of the construction of literary genealogy in sixteenth- and sev-enteenth-century England in *Conceived Presences: Literary Genealogy in Renais-sance England* (Amherst: University of Massachusetts Press, 1994); Alicia Ostriker's discussion of the Freudian gender determinations in *Stealing the Language: The Emergence of Women's Poetry in America* (Boston: Beacon Press, 1986); and Eliza-beth Gregory's *Quotation and Modern American Poetry: "Imaginary Gardens with Real Toads"* (Houston: Rice University Press, 1996).

    Influential reconsiderations of the Freudian masterplot of intergenerational rival-ry include Giles Deleuze and Felix Guattari, *Anti-Oedipus: Capitalism and Schizo-phrenia*, trans. Robert Hurley, Mark Seem, and Helen R. Lane (New York: Viking, 1977); Juliet Mitchell, *Psychoanalysis and Feminism* (New York: Penguin, 1974); and Nancy Chodorow, *The Reproduction of Mothering: Psychoanalysis and the Sociolo-gy of Gender* (Berkeley: University of California Press, 1978). The intergenerational model of family psychodynamics is also being called into question as an interpretive model for biblical narratives. See, for example, Yael Feldman, "'And Rebecca Loved Jacob', But Freud Did Not," in *Freud's Forbidden Knowledge*, ed. Peter Rudnytzky and Ellen Spitz (New York: New York University Press, 1994), pp. 7–25. Feldman argues that, unlike Freud's Greek mythic and dramatic sources, biblical narratives channel aggressive instincts outside the child-parent relationship to sibling relation-ships. Here, obviously, synchronic rather than sequential generational interactions obtain.

21. D. Emily Hicks, *Border Writing* (Minneapolis: University of Minnesota Press, 1991), p. xxiii (my emphasis). Hicks also relies on her own term "border writing" to resolve the antinomy of the term "magical realism": ". . . unlike the term 'magic realism,' which maintains the binary opposition of magic/real, the term 'border writing' con-notes a perspective that is no longer dominated by nonborder regions" (xxvii). While it is true that the term "magical realism" places its user outside the ontological sys-tem it describes (in which reality *is* magical and the term is therefore irrelevant), I wonder whether "border" does not also have connotations particular to U.S. critics and readers, whether "border" and "nonborder" countries do not simply invert the binarism that Hicks wishes to displace. The more basic question – whether it is desir-able for the critic to propose a term that mediates (or harmonizes) the interactions of divergent cultures and histories—is insightfully addressed by Amaryll Chanady in *Magical Realism and the Fantastic: Resolved Versus Unresolved Antinomies* (New York: Garland, 1985).

22. Carlos Fuentes, "Gabriel García Márquez and the Invention of America," in *Myself with Others*, (New York: Farrar, Straus & Giroux, 1988), p. 188. Subsequent page ref-erences are cited in the text.

23. William Carlos Williams, *In the American Grain* (1925; rpt. New York: New Direc-tions, 1967), p. 226 (Williams' emphasis).

24. Fuentes, "A Harvard Commencement," in *Myself with Others*, p. 206 (my emphasis).
25. Octavio Paz, *The Labyrinth of Solitude*, trans. Lysander Kemp, rev. ed. (New York: Grove Press, 1985), p. 80.
26. Octavio Paz, "La tradición de la ruptura," in *Hijos del limo* (Barcelona: Seix Barral, 1974), Chapter 1, pp. 17–37; this phrase is (regrettably) translated as "tradition against itself" in *Children of the Mire*, trans. Rachel Phillips (Cambridge, Mass.: Harvard University Press, 1974).
27. In an interview, Fuentes reiterates this point, referring to Latin American writers "who are restoring our civilization, the facts of our civilization, who are creating our cultural identity." That he recognizes this project as deeply political is made explicit by his following comment: reconstructing Latin American history "is not the same as offering ideological ghosts for political consumption." "An Interview with Carlos Fuentes," *Kenyon Review*, n.s., 5, no. 4 (1983), 113.
28. Neruda prefaced this homage with another that celebrates and proclaims influence in what I am arguing is a particularly American way: "Greatness has many faces, but I, a poet who writes in Spanish, learned more from Walt Whitman than from Cervantes." Neruda's inclusionary impulse betrays no Bloomian trace; Cervantes is not superseded or buried because Whitman is included. See Pablo Neruda, "The Murdered Albatross," in *Passions and Impressions*, ed. Matilde Neruda and Miguel Otero Silva, trans. Margaret Sayers Peden (New York: Farrar, Straus & Giroux, 1980), p. 377.

Parallel references to Whitman are Octavio Paz's statement: "Whitman is the grandfather of the Latin American avant-garde." (*Children of the Mire*, p. 118); and Borges' final line of his poem "Camden 1892": "La vida y su esplendor. Yo fui Walt Whitman." ("Life and its splendor. I was Walt Whitman.") *Selected Poems, 1923–1967*, ed. Norman Thomas di Giovanni (New York: Dell, 1968), pp. 174–75.
29. Donald Barthelme, *The Dead Father* (New York: Penguin, 1975), pp. 129, 3.
30. An essay comparing the parallel narratives of communal construction in the works of Morrison and Allende has, in fact, been published. See P. Gabrielle Foreman, "Past-on Stories: History and the Magically Real, Morrison and Allende on Call," in *Magical Realism: Theory, History, Community*, ed. Lois Parkinson Zamora and Wendy B. Faris (Durham: Duke University Press, 1995), pp. 285–303. José Saldívar, also develops a relevant comparative axis: ". . . African American writers such as [Toni] Morrison and [Ntozake] Shange were profoundly engaged in a bold cultural conversation with the Afro-Caribbean and Latin American tradition of magic realism." His discussion of Chicano writing also shows the many routes along which influence has traveled from south to north in the Americas. *The Dialectics of Our America: Genealogy, Cultural Critique, and Literary History* (Durham: Duke University Press, 1991), p. 89.
31. In his 1963 essay "Roots" Barbadian writer Kamau Brathwaite complicates the question by arguing that the West Indian writer is "an eccentric at home and an exile abroad." These writers experience a sense of displacement at home, far from their African and European cultural sources, as well as in Europe or Africa, where they long for home. *Roots* (Ann Arbor: The University of Michigan Press, 1993), p. 37.
32. Pablo Neruda, "With Cortázar and with Arguedas," in *Passions and Impressions*, p. 233.
33. Octavio Paz's comparative assertion reinforces my own: "There is a curious similarity between the history of modern poetry in Spanish and in English. At almost the same time Anglo American and Spanish American poets left their native lands. . . . The oscillations between cosmopolitanism and Americanism display our dual temptation, our common mirage: the land we left behind, Europe, and the land we seek, America. The similarity between the evolution of Anglo American and Spanish American literature results from the fact that both are written in transplanted languages. Between ourselves and the American soil a void opened up which we had to

fill with strange words. Indians and mestizos included, our language is European. The history of our literature is the history of our relations with the place that is America, and also with the place where the words we speak were born and came of age." *Children of the Mire*, pp. 137-38.

34. Vera Kutzinski, *Against the American Grain* (Baltimore: Johns Hopkins University Press, 1987). Kutzinski takes William Carlos Williams as a prime example of her argument.

35. Jorge Luis Borges, "Kafka y sus precursores," in *Otras inquisiciones* (1952); rpt. in *Obras completas*, 2, pp. 89-90 (Borges' emphasis); This insight occurs repeatedly in Borges' work.

36. Borges, "Kafka and His Precursors," in *Other Inquisitions (1937-1952)*, trans. Ruth L. C. Sims (Austin: University of Texas Press, 1964), p. 108 (Borges' emphasis).

37. Borges, "Pierre Menard, Author of the *Quixote*," in *Labyrinths*, p. 44 (Borges' emphasis).

38. Borges, "Pierre Menard, autor del Quijote," in *Ficciones* (1944); rpt. in *Obras completas* (Buenos Aires: Emecé Editores, 1989), 1, p. 449 (Borges' emphasis).

39. Borges, "Pierre Menard," p. 44.

40. John T. Irwin, *The Mystery to a Solution*, p. 429.

CHAPTER ONE. THE USABLE PAST

1. Carlos Fuentes, *Latin America: At War With the Past* (Montreal: CBC Enterprises, 1985), p. 9. This work consists of a series of lectures broadcast by the Canadian Broadcasting Company in 1984. Fuentes explicitly defines the term "North American" as meaning the U.S.; in discussing Fuentes' opposition I, too, refer only to the U.S. I cite passages in Spanish and English from fictional works, whereas only English translation are cited for works of *nonfiction*. Unless otherwise noted, the translations are mine.

2. Octavio Paz embodies the contrasting attitudes toward past and future in contrasting attitudes toward the present: "North Americans consider the world to be something that can be perfected, and . . . . we consider it to be something that can be redeemed." *The Labyrinth of Solitude: Life and Thought in Mexico* (1950), trans. Lysander Kemp, rev.ed. (New York: Grove Press, 1985), p. 24. Paz pursues this opposition in his 1979 essay included in the revised edition of *Labyrinth*: "The reality to which we give the name of civilization does not allow of easy definition. It is each society's vision of the world and also its feeling about time; there are nations that are hurrying toward the future, and others whose eyes are fixed on the past" (pp. 358-59).

3. Carlos Fuentes, "La violenta identidad de José Luis Cuevas, in *Casa con dos puertas* (Mexico City: Joaquin Mortiz, 1970), pp. 239-79; I cite from the bilingual edition, *El mundo de José Luis Cuevas*, trans. Consuelo de Aerenlund (New York: Tudor, 1969), p. 8.

4. For a more complete discussion of Fuentes' work in these terms, see Chapter 7 of my book, *Writing the Apocalypse: Historical Consciousness in Contemporary U.S. and Latin American Fiction* (Cambridge: Cambridge University Press, 1989), pp. 148-75. The Cuban novelist Alejo Carpentier was also influenced by Vico's historiography. According to Roberto González Echevarría, Vico replaced Spengler as the historiographic basis of Carpentier's later work: "If Spengler posited a circular history whose cycles were repeated throughout the universe, Vico offers an idea of return that does not deny historicity but affirms it." *Alejo Carpentier: The Pilgrim at Home* (Ithaca: Cornell University Press, 1977), p. 259.

5. Fuentes to Jonathan Tittler, *Diacritics* 10, no. 3 (1980), 49. The phrase occurs in the context of Fuentes' definition of Mexican temporality:

it is a time which conceives itself in a perpetual present, one that is not alienated by the pursuit of the future, a future that we can never reach. . . . This bastardization of the philosophy of the Enlightenment is common to both the capitalist and the socialist bureaucratic systems – the promise of a future, of the paradise on earth. The mythical time, which as I say is a present, does not admit the past as such. It considers what we call the past – in the Western linear system – as a present which is accreting, which is constantly enriching the moment, the instant. The past is never condemned to the past in a mythical system.

A collection of essays on the historical consciousness of North American Indian groups suggests a radical difference of indigenous and Western concepts of time in North America as well. See *The American Indian and the Problem of History*, ed. Calvin Martin (Oxford: Oxford University Press, 1987).

6. Fuentes to Christopher Sharp in *W*, a supplement to *Women's Wear Daily*, 29 October 1976, p. 9. See also Fuentes' essay "La novela como tragedia: William Faulkner," in *Casa con dos puertas* (Mexico City: Joaquín Mortiz, 1970), pp. 52–78.

7. Fuentes, *Una familia lejana* (Mexico City: Ediciones Era, 1976), pp. 163–64; *Distant Relations*, trans. Margaret Sayers Peden (New York: Farrar, Straus & Giroux, 1982), p. 170. Subsequent references are cited in the text.

8. Nina Baym, "Melodramas of Beset Manhood," in *The New Feminist Criticism*, ed. Carolyn Heilbrun (New York: Pantheon, 1985), p. 71.

9. J. Hillis Miller, "Presidential Address 1986: The Triumph of Theory, the Resistance to Reading, and the Question of the Material Base," *PMLA* 102, no. 3 (1987), 287.

10 Roberto González Echevarría discusses the analogous aspect of Latin American literary theory (what he calls the "concept of culture") in *The Voice of the Masters* (Austin: University of Texas Press, 1985), pp. 36ff.

11. My concern here is with American historiography after Hegel. Before Hegel, that is, before the independence of the American states from Spain and England, it is possible to speak in relatively unified terms of historical understanding in the colonial Americas. Despite enormous differences in the social and institutional patterns of the Catholic and Protestant settlement of the Americas, there nonetheless existed a common historiographic conception based on the linear, teleological, apocalyptic historiography of Judeo-Christianity. John Leddy Phelan discusses the similarity between sixteenth-century Spain's sense of its messianic historical mission in the New World and the Puritans' theological visions of a new heaven and earth, though he notes that the immediate sources of the visions were different. Spain's sense of its historical mission was an extension of the Joachimite Messiah-Emperor myth of the late Middle Ages, whereas the English settlers were impelled primarily by Martin Luther's apocalyptic interpretations of the Reformation. See *The Millennial Kingdom of the Franciscans in the New World* (1956), rev. ed. (Berkeley: University of California Press, 1970), p. 21.

12. George Bancroft, "The Progress of Mankind," in *Literary and Historical Miscellanies* (New York: Harper and Brothers, 1855), p. 517. Bancroft is, of course, following a long American tradition of the *translatio* – the conviction that the best of Old World civilization had been transferred to the New World. Frank Kermode traces this tradition from the Puritans through the neoclassicism of Washington and Jefferson to Hawthorne and James. See Chapter 3 of *The Classic* (1975; rpt. Cambridge, Mass.: Harvard University Press, 1983), pp. 83–114.

13. Geoffrey Hartman, "Towards Literary History," in his *Beyond Formalism: Literary Essays, 1958–1970* (New Haven: Yale University Press, 1971), p. 356.

14. Useful comparative studies of nineteenth-century German and Anglo American historicism are presented by Charles Frederick Harrold, *Carlyle and German Thought: 1819–1834* (Hamden, Conn.: Archon Books, 1963), and Kenneth Marc Harris, *Carlyle*

and Emerson: Their Long Debate (Cambridge, Mass.: Harvard University Press, 1978). Further sources on Carlyle's historiography are books by John D. Rosenberg, *Carlyle and the Burden of History* (Cambridge, Mass.: Harvard University Press, 1985), and Hill Shine, *Carlyle's Fusion of Poetry, History, and Religion by 1834* (1938; rpt. Port Washington, N.Y.: Kennikat Press, 1967).

15. Cather implicitly acknowledges her affinity for the German tradition at the beginning of her essay on Carlyle: "Perhaps no man who has ever stood before the public as an English author was [so] thoroughly un-English as Thomas Carlyle. His life, his habits, and his literature were most decidedly German." "Concerning Thomas Carlyle," in *The Kingdom of Art: Willa Cather's First Principles and Critical Statements, 1893–1896*, ed. Bernice Slote (Lincoln: University of Nebraska Press, 1966), p. 421.

    See Patricia Lee Yongue's discussions of Carlyle and Cather's historiography in *Death Comes for the Archbishop* in "Willa Cather on Heroes and Hero-Worship," *Neuphilologische Mitteilungen* 79, no. 1 (1978), 59–66; see also her "Search and Research: Willa Cather in Quest of History," *Southwestern American Literature*, 5 (1975), 27–39. William M. Curtin discusses William James and Cather in "Willa Cather and *The Varieties of Religious Experience*," *Renascence* 27 (1974), 115–23. Cather's education in English and American Romanticism is documented in Susan J. Rosowski, *The Voyage Perilous: Willa Cather's Romanticism* (Lincoln: University of Nebraska Press, 1986).

16. Although not comparative studies, relevant thematic discussions of U.S. literature that include Cather's fiction are Cecil Robinson, *Mexico and the Hispanic Southwest in American Literature* (Tucson: University of Arizona Press, 1977), and Raymond Arthur Paredes, "The Image of the Mexican in American Literature," Ph.D. Diss., University of Texas, 1973.

17. Cather was writing during the years of Turner's greatest acceptance. Turner's thesis, published in 1893, that U.S. democracy was formed in the crucible of the frontier, provided an easily acceptable explanation for the difference between Americans and Europeans. Like Turner and Whitman (and Crèvecoeur before them), Cather asks the question, "What is an American?" but her novelistic response is more complex than Turner's historical thesis because her concerns are metaphysical as well as territorial. It is also more complex than Whitman's, because she posits the attraction backward to the Old World as well as forward to the New, the repulsion of the West as well as its lure. Cather is often associated with Whitman – the title *O Pioneers!* is of course from Whitman's 1865 poem, "Pioneers, O Pioneers" – but her depiction of the historical problematics of the frontier are considerably more subtle than Whitman's.

18. According to Carlyle, "the history of what man has accomplished in this world, is at bottom the History of Great Men who have worked here." Thomas Carlyle, *On Heroes, Hero-Worship, and the Heroic in History*, ed. Archibald MacMechan (Boston: Ginn, 1901), p. 1.

19. This interaction does not really have a historical analogue in Latin America. Angel Rama compares the two areas of heaviest European immigration in nineteenth-century America, the U.S. and the area of Río de la Plata, stating that the immigrants and their descendants did not stamp the national ideology of Argentina as they did in the U.S. This becomes clear, according to Rama,

> if one evokes the extraordinary diffusion of the myth of the pioneer in the United States . . . and then seeks some equivalent entity in South America. Its absence forces us to realize the constricting force which the oligarchic landowners exercised. The "conquering of the desert" in Argentina follows closely upon the "conquering of the West" in the United States, but the former was achieved by the army and the oligarchy, while the latter is owed in large part to immigrants, who were compensated for their efforts with land.

La ciudad letrada (Hanover, N.H.: Ediciones del Norte, 1984), p. 76. Subsequent page references are cited in the text.

20. Thomas Carlyle, "Characteristics," in *Critical and Miscellaneous Essays* (1839), 4 vols. (New York: Charles Scribner's Sons, 1899), 3, p. 39.

21. The name of Thea's German piano teacher is Wunsch, which means "wish" in German. The name may be connected to Carlyle's description of "The Hero as Divinity" in *Heroes and Hero-Worship*, where he refers to Norse mythology: "But perhaps the notablest god we tell of is one of whom Grimm the German Etymologist finds trace: the God Wunsch, or Wish." (p. 28)

22. Willa Cather, *The Song of the Lark* (1915; rev.ed. 1937; New York: Houghton Mifflin, 1983), p. 251. Subsequent page references are cited in the text.

23. William James, *The Principles of Psychology*, 2 vols. (London: Macmillan, 1890), 1, p. 234. According to a contemporary, Cather was "a devoted disciple" of James. See George Seibel, "Miss Willa Cather from Nebraska," *New Colophon* 2, pt. 7 (1949), 202. William M. Curtin, in "Willa Cather and *The Varieties of Religious Experience*," notes that "the period of Willa Cather's apprenticeship coincided with the dominant influence of William James upon her whole generation, from the publication of *The Principles of Psychology* in 1890 to his death in 1910, when his essay 'The Moral Equivalent of War' appeared in *McClure's Magazine*, of which Cather was then the editor" (115).

24. Leopoldo Zea, "The New Order," *The Latin American Mind* (*Dos etapas de pensamiento en Hispanoamérica*, 1949), trans. James H. Abbott and Lowell Dunham (Norman: University of Oklahoma Press, 1963), pp. 135–289. Other relevant studies by Leopoldo Zea are *El positivismo en México* (1943) and *Apogeo y decadencia del positivismo en México* (1944).

25. See Karl Löwith, *Meaning in History* (Chicago: Phoenix Books, 1949), pp. 67ff.

26. According to Spencer, ". . . always toward perfection is the mighty movement – toward a complete development and a more unmixed good, subordinating in its universality all petty irregularities and falling back, as the curvature of the earth subordinates mountains and valleys." *Social Statistics* (1851; rpt. New York: Robert Schalkenback Foundation, 1954), p. 263.

27. See Zea, *The Latin American Mind*, pp. 269–289. Octavio Paz argues that positivism was politically tainted from its earliest appearance in Latin America: "Positivism in Latin America was not the ideology of a liberal bourgeoisie interested in industrial and social progress, as it was in Europe, but of an oligarchy of big landowners. It was a mystification, a self-deceit as well as a deceit. At the same time it was a radical criticism of religion and of traditional ideology. Positivism did away with Christian mythology as with rationalist philosophy. The result might be called the dismantling of metaphysics and religion. . . . It was not complete modernity but its bitter foretaste: the vision of an uninhabited heaven, the dread of contingency." *Children of the Mire*, trans. Rachel Phillips (Cambridge, Mass.: Harvard University Press, 1974), p. 87.

28. See H. Stuart Hughes, "The Decade of the 1890's: The Revolt Against Positivism," in his *Consciousness and Society: The Reorientation of European Social Thought, 1890–1930* (New York: Knopf, 1958), pp. 33–66. Hughes notes the antipathy toward and yet reliance on European positivism by early-twentieth-century theorists who attempted to free themselves from their nineteenth-century philosophical heritage.

Barbara Foley surveys the philosophical rejections of positivism that shaped representational strategies of the modernist novel in Europe and the U.S., in *Telling the Truth: The Theory and Practice of Documentary Fiction* (Ithaca: Cornell University Press, 1986), pp. 212–21. See also James Longenbach, *Modernist Poetics of History: Pound, Eliot, and the Sense of the Past* (Princeton: Princeton University Press, 1987), for a discussion of the antipositivism or "existential historicism" of Pound and Eliot, which manifested itself not in an interest in communal historical patterns so much as the relationship between the individual interpreter and the past.

29. Michael A. Weinstein, *The Polarity of Mexican Thought: Instrumentalism and Finalism* (University Park: Pennsylvania State University Press, 1976). Subsequent page references are cited in the text. Among Mexican intellectuals, Weinstein discusses José Vasconcelos, Antonio Caso, Samuel Ramos, Lucio Mendieta y Núñez, Emilio Uranga, Agustín Basave Fernández del Valle, Leopoldo Zea, and Octavio Paz.

In this context, see also Abelardo Villegas, *Cultura y política en América Latina* (Mexico City: Editorial Extemporáneos, 1978), especially Chapter 3, "José Gaos y la filosofía hispanoamericana," and Chapter 6, "Idealismo contra materialismo dialéctico en la educación mexicana."

30. Nevertheless, Ortega made extended visits to Argentina (one lasting from 1939 to 1942) and declared that he considered himself "half Argentinian." See Franz Niedermayer, *José Ortega y Gasset*, trans. Peter Tirner (New York: Ungar, 1973), p. 94.

31. At the time of Ortega's death in 1955, Carpentier stated: "The influence of Ortega y Gasset on the thinking and the artistic and literary orientation of the men of my generation was immense." Borges, on the other hand, stated that he hardly knew Ortega's writings, an assertion contradicted by his references to Ortega in his own work: "The stoics declared that the universe forms a single organism; it is quite possible that I, by force of the secret sympathy that unites all of its parts, owe much, something, or everything to Ortega y Gassset, whose works I have barely skimmed." Here Borges' involuted homage to and dismissal of Ortega may be attributed in part to Ortega's problematic attitude toward America, mentioned earlier. Cited in Roberto González Echevarría, "Borges, Carpentier y Ortega: Dos textos olvidados," *Revista Iberoamericana* 43 (1977), 697–704.

Paz has reiterated Carpentier's sense of Ortega's influence: "His influence marked profoundly the cultural life of Spain and Hispanic America. For the first time, after an eclipse of two centuries, Spanish thought was listened to and discussed in Hispanic American countries. They not only renewed and changed our ways of thinking and our information: Ortega y Gasset and his circle also left their mark on literature, the arts, and the sensibility of the period. Between 1920 and 1935, in the enlightened classes, as they said in the nineteenth century, there predominated a *style* which came from the *Revista de Occidente*. I am sure that the thought of Ortega will be rediscovered, and soon, by new generations of Spaniards." "José Ortega y Gasset: El cómo y el para qué," in *Hombres en su siglo y otros ensayos* (Barcelona: Seix Barral, 1984), p. 104 (Paz's emphasis). For a general consideration of Paz's relation to twentieth-century Spanish literature and philosophy, see Peter G. Earle, "Octavio Paz y España," *Revista Iberoamericana*, no. 141 (1987), 945–53.

32. Niedermayer comments, "Around the *Revista* Ortega assembled a group of translators not unlike the famous twelfth-century College of Translators of Toledo" (*José Ortega y Gasset*, p. 45).

33. José Ortega y Gasset, *History as a System and Other Essays toward a Philosophy of History*, trans. Helene Weyl (1941; New York: W.W. Norton, 1962), pp. 216, 217, Ortega's italics.

34. Ortega wrote this phrase many times, beginning with his first full-length book, *Meditaciones del Quijote* (1914): *Obras completas* (Madrid: Revista del Occidente, 1966) I, pp. 51–52. For a discussion of Ortega's relation to Husserl and Heidegger, see Philip W. Silver, *Ortega as Phenomenologist: The Genesis of "Meditations on Quixote"* (New York: Columbia University Press, 1978).

35. Paz, "José Ortega y Gasset: El cómo y el para qué," p. 102.

36. I am indebted to Ewell E. Murphy Jr., for making available to me his unpublished study, "Waiting for the Barbarians: The Future of the West in the Historical Philoso-

phy of José Ortega y Gasset," which was presented to the Houston Philosophical Society on February 16, 1978. See also Harold Raley, *José Ortega y Gasset: Philosopher of European Unity* (University, Ala.: University of Alabama Press, 1971).

37. Karl Marx, afterword to the second German edition of *Das Kapital* (1873), in *The Marx-Engels Reader*, ed. Robert C. Tucker (New York: Norton, 1978), p. 302.

38. Weinstein, *Polarity*, p. 17. Weinstein cites Alejandro Korn's "Bergson en la filosofía contemporánea," in *Filósofos y sistemas* (Buenos Aires: Colección Claridad, n.d.), and Alejandro O. Deústua's "El orden y la libertad," in *La filosofía latinoamericana contemporánea*, ed. Aníbal Sánchez Reulet (Washington, D.C.: Unión Panamericana, n.d.), as important statements of the influence of Bergson on Latin American antipositivism.

39. Bergson's ideas have been far more influential on literature than on politics or psychology; they are rarely (and then only briefly) mentioned in standard histories of modern psychology, whereas their presence in European and American literature has been voluminously documented. See, for example, Shiv Kumar, *Bergson and the Stream-of-Consciousness Novel* (London: Blackie, 1962), and Leon Edel, *The Modern Psychological Novel* (New York: Grosset and Dunlap, l964). Wendy B. Faris discusses the influence of Bergson, by way of Proust, on Carpentier's work: "Alejo Carpentier *A la recherche du temps perdu*," *Comparative Literature Studies* 17, no. 2 (1980), 133–54.

40. Paz, "Crítica de la pirámide," in *Postdata* (Mexico City: Siglo Veintiuno, 1970), pp. 116–17; "Critique of the Pyramid," trans. Rachel Phillips Belash and appended to the expanded edition of *The Labyrinth of Solitude* (New York: Grove Press, 1985), pp. 293–94.

41. Fuentes, "La violenta identidad de José Luis Cuevas," in *El mundo de José Luis Cuevas*, p. 14 (Fuentes' emphasis).

42. Henri Bergson, *Creative Evolution*, trans. Arthur Mitchell (1907; rpt. New York: Modern Library, 1944), p. 45.

43. The relativity of factual and fictional narrative was, by the middle of the eighteenth century, a well-established idea. See Ian Haywood, *The Making of History: A Study of the Literary Forgeries of James Macpherson and Thomas Chatterton in Relation to Eighteenth-Century Ideas of History and Fiction* (Rutherford, N.J.: Farleigh Dickinson University Press,1986), pp. 31-35.

44. Borges' essay "El escritor argentino y la tradición" was collected in *Discusión* (1932); rpt. in *Obras completas* (Buenos Aires: Emecé Editores, 1989), 1, pp. 267–74. That Borges conceived of American literature in profoundly comparative and intertextual terms is once again confirmed in his magazine reviews. See *Textos Cautivos: Ensayos y reseñas en "El Hogar" (1936–1939)* (*Captive Texts: Essays and Reviews in "El Hogar" [1936–1939]*), ed. Enrique Sacerio-Garí y Emir Rodríguez Monegal (Barcelona: Tusquets Editores, 1986). In his reviews, Borges' activity of cultural mediation parallels, and sometimes coincides with, Ortega's work of textual transmission in the *Revista de Occidente*. This parallel makes Borges' avowal of ignorance of Ortega all the more intriguing.

45. Borges, "Prólogo" to *Discusión* (1932); rpt. in *Obras completas*, 1, p. 177 (Borges' emphasis; my translation).

46. Borges, *Otras inquisiciones* (1952); rpt. in *Obras completas* 2, p. 132.

47. Borges, *Other Inquisitions*, trans. Ruth L. C. Simms (Austin: University of Texas Press, 1964), p. 167.

CHAPTER TWO. FOR THE RECORD

1. Michel de Montaigne, "On Vehicles," in *Essays*, trans. J. M. Cohen (New York: Penguin, 1958), p. 275

2. Jorge Luis Borges, "El idioma analítico de John Wilkins,"; rpt. in *Obras completas* (Buenos Aires: Emecé Editores, 1989), 2, p. 86.

3. Borges, "The Analytical Language of John Wilkins," in *Other Inquisitions (1937-1952)*, trans. Ruth L. C. Sims (Austin: University of Texas Press, 1964), p. 104.

4. The Hegelian historicism that grounds the novel as a genre is addressed by J. Hillis Miller in "Narrative and History," *ELH* 41 (1974), 455–73. Whereas Lukács accepts as necessary the novel's formal engagement of the assumptions of Hegelian historicism (teleological plotting, rational causality, continuity of character, homogeneity and linearity of time, etc.), Miller's own historical position leads him to challenge (as do many contemporary U.S. and Latin American writers and literary theorists) the Hegelian model of rational history that is deeply embedded, willy-nilly, in the formal conventions of the genre.

In his introductory chapter, "Hegel, Stendhal, and Posthistorical Existence," Michael Valdez Moses addresses the continuing vitality of Hegelian assumptions, despite vehement contemporary theoretical hostility to those assumptions. See *The Novel and the Globalization of Culture* (New York: Oxford University Press, 1995), pp. 3–25.

5. Nelson Goodman, *Ways of Worldmaking* (Indianapolis: Hackett, 1978). See especially the chapters "The Fabrication of Facts" and "On Rightness of Rendering." Subsequent page references are cited in the text. Also relevant here is Mario J. Valdés, *World-Making: The Literary Truth-Claim and the Interpretation of Texts* (Toronto: University of Toronto Press, 1992).

6. Angel Rama, *La ciudad letrada* (Hanover, N.H.: Ediciones del Norte, 1984), pp. 71, 79, 122–123.

7. Bello's long journalistic career is discussed by Federico Alvarez O. in *Labor periodística de Don Andrés Bello* (Caracas: Universidad Central de Venezuela, 1962). Other examples of nineteenth-century literary statesmen who conceived of journalism as an integral part of their intellectual and political activities are Domingo Faustino Sarmiento, José María Heredia, Juan Montalvo, Justo Sierra, and Enrique José Varona. See the study of literary culture and the press in colonial Latin America by José Torre Revello, *El libro, la imprenta, y el periodismo en América durante la dominación española* (Buenos Aires: Universidad de Buenos Aires, 1940). More recent relations between fiction and journalism are discussed by Mario Castro Arenas in *El periodismo y la novela contemporánea* (Caracas: Monte Avila, 1969) and by Alceu Amoroso Limo in *O jornalismo como gênero literário* (Rio de Janeiro: AGIR Editora, 1960). A study of the Latin American tradition of the novelist/jounalist is by Aníbal González, *Journalism and the Development of Spanish American Narrative* (Cambridge: Cambridge University Press, 1993). The "testimonial" novel, which often mediates between fiction and journalism, is intelligently considered by Elzbieta Sklodowska in her article "The Spanish American Testimonial Novels: Some Afterthoughts," *New Novel Review* 1. no. 2 (1994), 31–47.

8. Circulation statistics of newspapers and other periodicals are available in the *Unesco Statistical Yearbook*. The 1994 volume shows the highest-circulation figures of daily newspapers *per one thousand inhabitants* in 1992 in Latin America as follows: Uruguay (240), Venezuela (208), Argentina (144), Cuba (122), Mexico (116); periodicals other than newspapers show the following: Mexico (318) and Cuba (264 in 1990). The circulation of daily newspapers in other Latin American countries is considerably lower: Bolivia (52); Brazil (55). The daily circulation of newpapers in the U.S. *per one thousand inhabitants* is 240; the figure for periodicals other than daily newspapers is not available. The relatively small circulation of dailies in most Latin American countries does not fully reflect the number of readers (newspapers are often read in communal locations, especially in rural areas) or the importance of the press as a conduit

of public opinion and discussion. Furthermore, it should be noted that the audience and influence of Latin American writer/journalists such as Vargas Llosa and Carlos Fuentes is greater than these statistics might indicate, for they often write about Latin America in U.S. and European newpapers and periodicals with wide circulations.

9. Mario Vargas Llosa, "Social Commitment and the Latin American Writer," in *The Modern Experience*, vol. 2 of *Readings in Latin American History*, ed. John J. Johnson, Peter J. Bakewell, and Meredith D. Dodge (Durham: Duke University Press, 1985), pp. 455–64; Marlise Simmons, "A Talk with Gabriel García Márquez," *New York Times Book Review*, 5 December 1982, p. 7. Vargas Llosa's essay and a number of other essays relevant to the current political situation of writers in Latin America are collected in *Lives on the Line: Testimony of Contemporary Latin American Authors*, ed. Doris Meyer (Berkeley: University of California Press, 1988). ˙

10. The metahistorical concerns of these novels are related to the philosophical discussion of narration and cognition current among historiographers and psychologists. See Hayden White, *Metahistory* (Baltimore: Johns Hopkins University Press, 1973); Donald P. Spence, *Narrative Truth and Historical Truth: Meaning and Interpretation in Psychoanalysis* (New York: W. W. Norton, 1982) and Peter Brooks, "Fictions of the Wolfman: Freud and Narrative Understanding," *Diacritics* 9, no. 1 (March 1979), 72–81.

11. Simmons, "A Talk with Gabriel García Márquez," p. 60.

12. This fiction may even (in the cases of Cortázar and Poniatowska) employ the idiosyncratic typography and visual layout of a newspaper, a format that affects the reader in significantly different ways from the printed medium of the book, as Marshall McLuhan did well to remind us. McLuhan writes: "The format of the book page offers a linear, not a picturesque perspective. It fosters a single tone and attitude between a writer, reader, subject, whereas the newpaper breaks up this linearity and singleness of tone and perspective, offering many book pages at the same moment. . . . The newspaper is a space-time landscape of many times, many places, given as single experience." *Counterblast* (New York: Harcourt, Brace & World, 1969), pp. 112–13.

13. Documentary fiction has been intelligently discussed by Barbara Foley, *Telling the Truth: The Theory and Practice of Documentary Fiction* (Ithaca: Cornell University Press, 1986).

14. See E. L. Doctorow, "False Documents," *American Review* 26 (November 1977), 215–32. Roland Barthes and Jacques Derrida have also taken strongly antigeneric positions. See Roland Barthes, "Historical Discourse," in *Introduction to Structuralism*, ed. Michael Lane (New York: Basic Books, 1970), pp. 145–55; and Jacques Derrida, "Limited Inc abc," in *Glyph: Johns Hopkins Textual Studies* 2 (Baltimore: Johns Hopkins University Press, 1977), pp. 162–254.

15. Carlos Fuentes, *Gringo viejo* (Mexico City: Fondo de Cultura Económica, 1985), p. 60; *The Old Gringo*, trans. Margaret Sayers Peden (New York: Farrar, Straus & Giroux, 1985), p. 56 (my emphasis). Subsequent page references are cited in the text.

16. Norman Mailer, *The Armies of the Night* (New York: New American Library, 1968), p. 65.

17. Carey McWilliams, introduction to *The Devil's Dictionary* (New York: Hill and Wang, 1957), p. x. Bierce's Civil War stories were collected in *Tales of Soldiers and Civilians* (1892); a partial collection of his nonfiction writing on the Civil War is collected in *Battlefields and Ghosts* (1931).

18. Bierce, *The Devil's Dictionary*, p. 75.

19. Carey McWilliams, introduction to *The Devil's Dictionary*, p. v.

20. Gore Vidal, *Empire* (New York: Random House, 1987), p. 485.

21. For general treatments of this subject in U.S. fiction, see Thomas Elliott Berry, *The Newspaper in the American Novel, 1900–1969* (Metuchen, N.J.: Scarecrow Press,

1970); and Howard Good, *Acquainted with the Night: The Image of Journalists in American Fiction* (Metuchen, N.J.: Scarecrow Press, 1986). In William Dean Howells' novel, *A Modern Instance* (1882), the newpaper world that Howells knew from life-long association is used primarily as a backdrop for the moral issues of this novel. Upton Sinclair's denunciations of journalism are found in *Love's Pilgrimage* (1911) and his combination autobiography/reportage in *The Brass Check* (1919). In *An American Tragedy* (1925), Theodore Dreiser condemns the press for obtaining news at any cost and for the irresponsible mixture of facts with sensationalist fictions.

22. Fuentes has acknowledged his debt to Dos Passos in an interview reprinted in Emmanuel Carballo, *Diecinueve protagonistas de la literatura mexicana del siglo XX* (Mexico City: Empresas Editoriales, 1965), p. 434.

23. The exception is Cathy N. Davidson's reconsideration of Bierce's fiction in terms of Borgesian postmodernism. See *The Experimental Fictions of Ambrose Bierce: Structuring the Ineffable* (Lincoln: University of Nebraska Press, 1984). A recent edition of Bierce's political writings has been edited by Lawrence I. Berkove, *Ambrose Bierce: Skepticism and Dissent: Selected Journalism from 1898–1901* (Ann Arbor: Delmas Books, 1980). Still to be written are critical reconsiderations of Bierce's anti-interventionist journalism in terms of subsequent U.S. expansionism, and his historical pieces in terms of recent antiwar writings.

24. In the section of *Walden* entitled, "Where I Lived, and What I Lived For," Thoreau classes newspapers with the post office, both of which he deems expendible, calling news "gossip" and insisting that he "never read any memorable news in a newspaper." *Thoreau: Walden and Other Writings* (New York: Bantam Books, 1962), pp. 175–76.

   Such a declaration suggests that Thoreau's topical references exist only to occasion philosophical speculation. Taxation for the Mexican War occasioned "Civil Disobedience" (1849), but is hardly its subject. Indeed, in the context of his brief direct reference to Mexico in that essay, Thoreau implies that reading the newspaper may even inhibit right-minded action: "There are thousands who . . . quietly read the prices-current along with the latest advices from Mexico, after dinner, and, it may be, fall asleep over them both" (p. 89).

   Hawthorne is less condescending than Thoreau, but he too distinguishes definitively between journalism and literary "genius," deprecating the former by comparison with the latter. In "The Old Manse Sketch," he writes, "It is the age itself that writes newspapers and almanacs, which therefore have a distinct purpose and meaning at that time, and a kind of intelligible truth for all times. . . . Genius, indeed, melts many ages into one, and thus effects something permanent. . . . A work of genius is but the newspaper of a century, or perchance of a hundred centuries." In *Mosses from an Old Manse* (London: Frederick Warner, 1844), p. 20.

25. Henry James, "The Question of Our Speech," in *The Question of Our Speech and The Lesson of Balzac: Two Lectures* (New York: Houghton Mifflin, 1905), p. 42.

26. Names now forgotten once accompanied Twain's bylines. See Walter Blair et al., *American Literature: A Brief History* (New York: Scott Foresman, 1964), pp. 106–7.

27. Cather wrote that the "novel is a form of imaginative art" and consequently "cannot be at the same time a vivid and brilliant form of journalism." "The Novel Demeublé," *The New Republic Supplement*, April 1922. In Cather's novel *My Mortal Enemy* (1926), the young woman narrator rejects the suggestion that she become a journalist, saying that she hates the profession. See also James Woodress, "*McClure's* Magazine: 1906–1912," in *Willa Cather: Her Life and Art* (Lincoln: University of Nebraska Press, 1970), pp.119–49.

28. The excellent coverage of the revolution by the Mexican press is suggested in the collection of reprinted articles, most of them without bylines, from newspapers in the state of Jalisco. See Jaime Olveda, Alma Dorantes, and Agustín Vaca, eds., *La prensa*

jalisciense y la revolución (Mexico City: Instituto Nacional de Antropología e Historia, 1985). The titles of some of the articles may suggest the combination of passion, analysis, and prophecy that characterizes them, and much Latin American journalism besides: "Evolución no debe ser anarquía"; "Después de la Revolución sigue la Revolución"; "¿Cuál es la teoría del poder público revolucionario?" "Babel revolucionaria"; and (on June 19, 1920), "La fiera aún ruge" ("After the Revolution Comes the Revolution"; "What is the Theory of the Public Revolutionary Power?" "Revolutionary Babel"; "The Fiend Still Roars.")

29. See the prefatory information in the catalogue from the 1985 exposition *Tierra y Libertad: Photographs of Mexico, 1900–1935 from the Casasola Archive* (Oxford: Oxford Museum of Modern Art and Mexico's Instituto Nacional de Antropología y Historia, 1985). Another exhibition catalogue is *The World of Agustín Victor Casasola: Mexico, 1900–1938* (Washington, D.C.: The Fondo del Sol Visual Arts and Media Center, 1984). The best reproductions of photographs from the Casasola archive are published in *Jefes, heroes, y caudillos* (Mexico City: Fondo de Cultura Económica, 1986).

30. Carlos Fuentes, *Cristóbal Nonato* (Mexico City: Fondo de Cultura Económica, 1987), p. 120 (my translation).

31. See, for example, my article on Julio Cortázar's use of photographic structures: "Movement and Stasis, Film and Photo: Temporal Structures in the Recent Fiction of Julio Cortázar," *Review of Contemporary Fiction* 3, no. 3 (1983), 51–56.

32. Between 1934 and 1941, there were in fact a number of books combining photographs and text, all of which aimed to document the social problems caused by the natural disasters and the international economic collapse of the period. The democratic and democratizing medium of photography was apposite. Besides *Let Us Now Praise Famous Men*, other photo-textual documentaries that responded to social and political imperatives include Erskine Caldwell and Margaret Bourke-White's *You Have Seen Their Faces* (1937), Archibald MacLeish's *Land of the Free* (1938), Paul S. Taylor and Dorothea Lange's *An American Exodus* (1939), and Richard Wright's *12 Million Black Voices* (1941). Among these works, Agee and Evans' *Let Us Now Praise Famous Men* is perhaps the most explicit record of art's struggle with social reponsibility during the Depression.

In this context, see also John Rogers Puckett, *Five Photo-Textual Documentaries from the Great Depression* (Ann Arbor: UMI Research Press, 1984); Carol Shloss, *In Visible Light: Photography and the American Writer, 1840–1940* (New York: Oxford University Press, 1987); and Jeffery Hunter, *Image and Word: The Interaction of Twentieth-Century Photographs and Texts* (Cambridge: Harvard University Press, 1987).

33. James Agee and Walker Evans, *Let Us Now Praise Famous Men* (Boston: Houghton Mifflin, 1941), p. 13. Subsequent page references are cited in the text.

34. So, too, Latin American authors have used journalistic strategies to write about unimaginable events. See my essay, "Deciphering the Wounds: The Politics of Torture and Julio Cortázar's Literature of Embodiment," in *Postcolonial Literature and the Biblical Call for Justice*, ed. Susan VanZanten Gallagher (Jackson: University Press of Mississippi, 1995), pp. 91–110.

35. Elie Wiesel, "A Plea for the Survivors," in *A Jew Today* (New York: Random House, 1978), p. 200.

36. The connection between García Márquez's journalism and his fiction is discussed by Robert L. Sims in "El laboratorio periodístico de García Márquez: Lo carnavalesco y la creación del espacio novelístico," *Revista Iberoamericana* 52, no. 37 (October 1986), 979–89, and also by Robert L. Sims, *El primer García Márquez: Un estudio de su periodismo de 1948 a 1955* (Potomac, MD: Scripta Humanistica, 1991); Carmen Rabell, *Periodismo y ficción en "Crónica de una muerte anunciada"* (Santiago de Chile: Instituto Profesional del Pacífico, 1985), and Jorge Ruffinelli, "Un periodista

llamado Gabriel García Márquez," in his *Crítica en marcha: Ensayos sobre la literatura latinoamericana* (Mexico City: Premia, 1979), 59–69. Also relevant to the generic consideration of this novel are Jorge Olivares, "García Márquez's *Crónica de una muerte anunciada* as Metafiction," *Contemporary Literature* 28, no. 5 (1987), and David William Foster, "Latin American Documentary Narrative," *PMLA* 99, no. 1 (1984), 49–51.

37. García Márquez's journalistic prose has been collected in two volumes: *Crónicas y reportajes* (Bogotá: Editorial La Oveja Negra, 1978) and *De viaje por los países socialistas* (Bogotá: Editorial La Oveja Negra, 1979).

38. Hayden White, "The Value of Narrativity in the Representation of Reality," *Critical Inquiry* 7, no. 1 (1980), p. 10. Subsequent references are cited in the text.

39. Gabriel García Márquez, *Crónica de una muerte anunciada* (Mexico City: Editorial Diana, 1981), p. 16. Subsequent page references are cited in the text.

40. García Márquez, *Chronicle of a Death Foretold*, trans. Gregory Rabassa (New York: Knopf, 1983), p. 12. Subsequent page references are cited in the text.

41. García Márquez, *Cien años de soledad* (Buenos Aires: Editorial Sudamericana, 1967), p. 334.

42. García Márquez, *One Hundred Years of Solitude* (1967), trans. Gregory Rabassa (New York: Avon, 1971), p. 364.

43. García Márquez, *Relato de un náufrago que estuvo diez días a la deriva en una balsa sin comer ni beber, que fue proclamado héroe de la patria, besado por las reinas de la belleza y hecho rico por la publicidad, y luego aborrecido por el gobierno y olvidado para siempre* (*A Story of a Castaway Who Was Lost at Sea for Ten Days in a Raft with Nothing to Eat or Drink, Who was Proclaimed a National Hero, Kissed by Beauty Queens and Made Rich by Publicity, and Later Spurned by the Government and Forgotten Forever* (Barcelona: Tusquets, 1970), p. 8 (my translation). The story was originally serialized in *El Espectador*, Bogotá, 1955.

44. Simmons, "A Talk with García Márquez," p. 60.

45. In terms that complement mine, Carlos Fuentes addresses the purposes that journalism and fiction serve for him: "I try to [conduct political activity] more as a citizen than as a writer. Or as a writer who loves journalism. Because I love journalism, I love writing in papers, and I love friendship and contact and conversation with journalists. So it is at that level of journalism and teaching and lecturing that I try to have a certain political bearing on things." Jason Weiss, "An Interview with Carlos Fuentes," *Kenyon Review*, 5, no. 4 (1983), 113.

46. Octavio Paz, "Todos santos, día de muertos," in *El laberinto de la soledad* (Mexico City: Fondo de Cultura Económica, 1950), p. 42.

47. Paz, "The Day of the Dead," in *The Labyrinth of Solitude*, trans. Lysander Kemp, rev. ed. (New York: Grove Press, 1985), p. 48.

48. Truman Capote, *Music for Chameleons* (New York: New American Library, 1980), p. xvi (Capote's emphasis).

49. Mario Vargas Llosa, *Tía Julia y el escribidor* (1977; rpt. Mexico City: Biblioteca de Bolsillo, 1991), p. 144.

50. Vargas Llosa, *Aunt Julia and the Scriptwriter*, trans. Helen R. Lane (New York: Avon, 1982), p. 116.

51. Vargas Llosa, *Historia de Mayta* (Barcelona: Seix Barral, 1984), p. 274.

52. Vargas Llosa, *The Real Life of Alejandro Mayta*, trans. Alfred MacAdam (New York: Farrar, Straus & Giroux, 1986), p. 246.

53. Vargas Llosa, *¿Quién mató a Palomino Molero?* (Barcelona: Seix Barral, 1986), p. 107.

54. Vargas Llosa, *Who Killed Palomino Molero?*, trans. Alfred MacAdam (New York: Farrar, Straus & Giroux, 1987), p. 86.

55. Walter Benjamin, "Konvolut N," trans. as "Theoretics of Knowledge: Theory of Progress," *The Philosophical Forum* 15, nos. 1–2 (1983–84), 8–9.

56. Vargas Llosa, *A Writer's Reality* (New York: Houghton Miflin, 1991), p. 137.
57. The titles of his later collections support this point. Besides *A Writer's Reality*, there is *La verdad de las mentiras: Ensayos sobre literatura* (*The Truth of Lies: Essays on Literature*) (Barcelona: Seix Barral, 1990). See also "Latin America: Fiction and Reality," in *On Modern Latin American Fiction*, ed. John King (New York: Farrar, Straus & Giroux, 1987), pp. 1–17; and "Is Fiction the Art of Lying?" *New York Times Book Review*, 7 October 1987, pp. 1, 40.
58. Ed Block, Jr., singles out *The Real Life of Alejandro Mayta* as exemplary of "the isolated individual pursuing his or her vocation for the realization of distributive justice," and finds that "the tale of justice is wiser than its urbane and almost skeptical teller." See "Biblical Ideas of Justice in Postcolonial Fiction," in *Postcolonial Literature and the Biblical Call for Justice*, ed. Susan VanZanten Gallagher, pp. 38, 39.
59. Vargas Llosa, "The Author's Favorite of His Novels: *The War of the End of the World*," in *A Writer's Reality*, p. 139.
60. Euclides da Cunha, *Rebellion in the Backlands*, trans. with an introd. by Samuel Putnam (Chicago: University of Chicago Press, 1944), p. iii.
61. Vargas Llosa, *A Writer's Reality*, p. 131.
62. Vargas Llosa has made this point explicitly in an interview in the Washington *Post*: ". . . something that has been happening in Latin American history over the 19th and 20th centuries—the total lack of communication between two sections of a society which kill each other fighting ghosts, no? Fighting fictional enemies who are invented out of fanaticism, out of religious or political or economic blindness. This kind of reciprocal incapacity of understanding that you have opposing you is probably the main problem we have to overcome in Latin America. . . ." Cited in *In These Times*, 4–10 November 1984, p. 19.
63. Vargas Llosa, *La guerra del fin del mundo* (Barcelona: Editorial Seix Barral, 1981), p. 341.
64. Vargas Llosa, *The War of the End of the World*, trans. Helen R. Lane (New York: Farrar, Straus & Giroux, 1984), p. 358.
65. Boris A. Uspensky, "Historia sub specie semioticae," in *Soviet Semiotics*, ed. and trans. by Daniel P. Lucid (Baltimore: Johns Hopkins University Press, 1977), pp. 107–15
66. See D. M. Segal, "Problems in the Semiotic Study of Mythology," in *Soviet Semiotics*, pp. 59–64.
67. See Renée Ribeiro, "Brazilian Messianic Movements," in *Millennial Dreams in Action: Essays in Comparative Study*, ed. Sylvia L. Thrupp (The Hague: Mouton, 1962), 55–69; Ralph Della Cava, "Brazilian Messianism and National Institutions: A Reappraisal of Canudos and Joaseiro," in *Readings in Latin American History*, ed. John J. Johnson, Peter J. Bakewell, and Meredith D. Dodge (Durham: Duke University Press, 1985), 2, pp. 179–94; and, more generally, Michael Adas, *Prophets of Rebellion: Millenarian Protest Movements Against the European Colonial Order* (Chapel Hill: University of North Carolina Press, 1979).
    Vargas Llosa cites da Cunha's analysis of the millennialist fervor as one more set of imposed and misunderstood ideas: "[Da Cunha] explained the rebellion . . . as a deformation of religious ideas that were imported to Brazil and imposed on this community of peasants. These people were educated by fanatical Catholic *integristas*, monks who preached a kind of intolerance and dogmatic vision that was profoundly assimilated by this isolated community of the *caboclos* in the interior of Bahia. . . ." *A Writer's Reality*, p. 131.
68. Uspensky points out that in his imposition of the language of modern Europe on medieval Russia, Peter the Great knew the languages of both cultures and could thus foretell the effects of his actions. His conduct suggests that Peter deliberately "disregarded his own native 'language' as erroneous and accepted as the sole correct 'lan-

guage' that of imported Western European cultural ideas. In this almost irrational attitude toward 'language,' Peter remains a true son of his own culture, for which adoption of the 'correct' language and rejection of the 'erroneous' one proves subjectively to be a more important factor than the potential consequences of these deeds." "Historia sub specie semioticae," p. 113.

69. Vargas Llosa also refers intertextually to two other important literary precursors, R.B. Cunninghame-Graham, who published a book on the Canudos incident in 1920, and Domingo Faustino Sarmiento, who published *Civilización y barbarie, vida de don Facundo Quiroga* in 1884. See Alfred MacAdam, "Euclides da Cunha y Mario Vargas Llosa: Meditaciones intertextuales," *Revista Iberoamericana*, no. 126 (1984), 157–64, and Sara Castro-Klarén, "Locura y dolor: La elaboración de la historia en *Os sertões* y *La guerra del fin del mundo*," *Revista de Crítica Literaria Latinoamericana*, no. 20 (1984), 207–231.

70. Vargas Llosa, "The Author's Favorite of His Novels," in *A Writer's Reality*, p. 133.

71. John Burt Foster, "Magic Realism, Compensatory Vision and Felt History: Classical Realism Transformed in *The White Hotel*," in *Magical Realism: Theory, History, Community*, ed. Lois Parkinson Zamora and Wendy B. Faris (Durham: Duke University Press, 1995), pp. 267–83.

72. Jorge Luis Borges, "Presencia de Miguel de Unamuno," in *Textos cautivos: ensayos y reseñas en "El hogar" (1936–1939)*, ed. Enrique Sacerio-Garí and Emir Rodríguez Monegal (Barcelona: Tusquets Editores, 1986), p. 81 (my translation).

CHAPTER THREE. ANCESTRAL PRESENCES

1. Flannery O'Connor, "The Grotesque in Southern Fiction," in *Mystery and Manners* (New York: Farrar, Straus, & Giroux, 1961), p. 45.

2. Northrop Frye, *The Anatomy of Criticism* (Princeton: Princeton University Press, 1957), p. 314.

3. Vladimir Nabokov, *Strong Opinions* (New York: Vintage, 1973), p. 115.

4. Isabel Allende, *The House of the Spirits*, trans. Magda Bogin (New York: Knopf, 1985), pp. 108, 218. See my essay on Allende's magical realism, "The Magical Tables of Isabel Allende and Remedios Varo," *Comparative Literature* 44, no. 2 (1992), 113–43.

5. Seymour Menton elaborates the relation of Jung's theories to magical realism in *Magic Realism Rediscovered: 1918–1981* (East Brunswick, N.J.: Associated University Presses, 1983).

6. Gabriel García Márquez, *Cien años de soledad* (Buenos Aires: Editorial Sudamericana, 1967), p. 290.

7. García Márquez, *One Hundred Years of Solitude*, trans. Gregory Rabassa (New York: Avon, 1970), p. 316.

8. O'Connor, "The Grotesque in Southern Fiction," p. 44.

9. Eric Gould, *Mythical Intentions in Modern Literature* (Princeton: Princeton University Press, 1981), p. 19.

10. Jorge Luis Borges, "El escritor Argentino y la tradición," in *Discusión* (1932), rpt. in *Obras completas* (Buenos Aires: Emecé Editores, 1989), 1, p. 273.

11. Borges, "The Argentine Writer and Tradition," in *Labyrinths*, ed. Donald A. Yates and James E. Irby (New York: New Directions, 1962), pp. 184, 185.

12. Jaime Alazraki relates this theme to the cabbalah, which he convincingly locates as a source of Borges' mystical investitations. See *Borges and the Kabbalah* (Cambridge: Cambridge University Press, 1988).

13. Borges, "La otra muerte," in *El aleph* (1949); rpt. in *Obras completas*, 1, p. 575.

14. Borges, "The Other Death," in *The Aleph and Other Stories*, trans. Norman Thomas di Giovanni (New York: Dutton, 1968), pp. 110–11.

15. Borges, "Epílogo" to *El hacedor* (1960); rpt. in *Obras completas* (1989), 2, p. 232.

16. Borges, Epilogue to *Dreamtigers*, trans. Mildred Boyer and Harold Morland (Austin: University of Texas Press, 1978), p. 93

17. Borges, "La biblioteca de Babel," in *Ficciones* (1944); rpt. in *Obras competas*, 1, p. 470.

18. Borges, "The Library of Babel," in *Labyrinths*, p. 58.

19. Borges, "La flor de Coleridge," in *Otras inquisiciones* (1952); rpt. in *Obras completas*, 2, p. 17.

20. Borges, "The Flower of Coleridge," in *Other Inquisitions: 1937–52*, trans. Ruth L. C. Simms (Austin: University of Texas Press, 1965), p. 10.

21. Borges, "The Flower of Coleridge," p. 10. Borges quotes from Ralph Waldo Emerson's essay "Nominalist and Realist," *Essays: Second Series*, 1844.

22. Borges' ambivalent relation to Emerson's ideas is notable elsewhere as well. In "The Other Death," a story to which I have referred only briefly, Borges appears to indict Emerson's historical vision as rigidly linear, and oppose it to his own historiography of repetition and recurrence. This story dramatizes the imaginative potential for revising and reliving life, hence multiplying one's lives. It begins with a reference to Emerson's poem "The Past." The reference is clearly ironic because Emerson's poem describes the impossibility of revising the monolithic past – just the opposite of the multiple pasts that Borges' story dramatizes. "La otra muerte," in *El aleph* (1949); rpt. in *Obras competas*, 2, p. 571.

    Borges' poem "Emerson" ends with an imaginative revision of Emerson's life: he makes his "tall New Englander" dissatisfied with his progressive, unrepeatable history: "No he vivido. Quisiera ser otro hombre" ("I have not lived. I want to be someone else"). See *Selected Poems, 1932–67*, ed. Norman Thomas di Giovanni (New York: Delta, 1979), pp. 170–71.

23. Borges, "La esfera de Pascal," *Otras inquisiciones* (1952); rpt. in *Obras completas*, 2, p. 16.

24. Borges, "The Fearful Sphere of Pascal," in *Labyrinths*, p. 189.

25. Borges' sense of these multiple confluences of Romanticism led him to link Whitman and Valéry, an unexpected pairing but, as Borges shows, a justifiable one based on their shared impulse (with Borges') to archetypalize the subject: "Uno de los propósitos de las composiciones de Whitman es definir a un hombre posible – Walt Whitman – de ilimitada y negligente felicidad; no menos hiperbólico, no menos ilusorio, es el hombre que definen las composiciones de Valéry." "Valéry como símbolo," in *Otras inquisiciones* (1952); rpt. in *Obras completas*, 2, p. 64. ("One of the purposes of Whitman's compositions is to define a possible man – Walt Whitman – of unlimited and negligent felicity; no less hyperbolic, no less illusory, is the man defined by Valéry's compositions." "Valéry as Symbol," in *Labyrinths*, p. 188).

26. Leon Chai, *The Romantic Foundations of the American Renaissance* (Ithaca: Cornell University Press, 1987), p. 39. For a discussion of the characteristics of the romance genre beginning with medieval romance, see Fredric Jameson, "Magical Narratives: Romance as Genre," *NLH* 7, no. 1 (1975), 135–163; and Edgar A. Dryden, *The Form of American Romance* (Baltimore: Johns Hopkins University Press, 1988), who extends the U.S. romance tradition to contemporary writers, from Hawthorne through Faulkner to John Barth.

27. Borges, "From Allegories to Novels," in *Borges: A Reader*, ed. Emir Rodríguez Monegal and Alastair Reid (New York: Dutton, 1981), p. 232.

28. Borges, "Nathaniel Hawthorne," in *Borges: A Reader*, p. 219. The essay first appeared in *Otras inquisiciones* (1952); rpt. in *Obras completas*, 2, pp. 48–63.

29. Nathaniel Hawthorne, *The Scarlet Letter* (New York: W. W. Norton, 1978), p. 31. Subsequent page references are cited in the text.

30. Fredric Jameson, "Third-World Literature in the Era of Multinational Capitalism," *Social Text* 15 (Fall 1986), 65–88.

31. Paul de Man, *Allegories of Reading: Figural Language in Rousseau, Nietzsche, Rilke, and Proust* (New Haven: Yale University Press, 1979), p. 191.
32. Borges, "Nathaniel Hawthorne," p. 228.
33. Larry J. Reynolds places Hawthorne's work in broad political perspective in *European Revolutions and the American Literary Renaissance* (New Haven: Yale University Press, 1988). A more narrowly focused study of Hawthorne's political ambiguity is Sacvan Bercovitch, "The A-politics of Ambiguity in *The Scarlet Letter*," *NLH* 19 (1988), 1–27.
34. Borges, *Textos cautivos: Ensayos y reseñas en "El hogar" (1936–1939)*, ed. Enrique Sacerio-Garí and Emir Rodríguez Monegal (Barcelona: Tusquets Editores, 1986).
35. Borges appreciated Poe's sleuth Dupin because of Dupin's deep distrust of analytical rationality, and his preference instead for the intuitive and metaphoric processes of poetry. See John T. Irwin's study of Borges and Poe, *The Mystery to the Solution: Poe, Borges and the Analytic Detective Story* (Baltimore: Johns Hopkins University Press, 1994).

     Besides Borges' ironic rewritings of Poe's mystery stories, he read Poe's *The Narrative of Arthur Gordon Pym of Nantucket* (1838) for its descriptions of fantastic fauna and flora, and included one of them in his *Manual de zoología fantástica* (*The Book of Imaginary Beings*, 1957) under the title "El animal soñado por Poe" ("The Animal Dreamed by Poe").
36. In discussing Borges' magical realism, critics have uniformly focused on Borges' essay "Narrative Art and Magic" (1932). As interesting as this essay is, it reveals less of Borges' own literary preferences and practice than *An Introduction to American Literature* and his essays on U.S. romance writers.
37. Borges, *An Introduction to American Literature*, trans. L. Clark Keating and Robert O. Evans (Lexington: University Press of Kentucky, 1971), p. 7. Subsequent page references are cited in the the the text. The original Spanish edition is *Introducción a la literatura norteamericana* (with the collaboration of María Esther Vásquez) (Buenos Aires: Editorial Columba, 1967). My policy is to provide dual-language citations only for works of fiction; this is a difficult distinction with respect to Borges' work, but here, as in my subsequent citations from his Hawthorne essay, I will give only the English translation.

     Following Borges in spirit is an essay on Mather's fantastical imagination in *Magnalia Christi Americana* and its influence on Harriet Beecher Stowe; see Dorothy Z. Baker, "Puritan Providences in Stowe's *The Pearl of Orr's Island*; The Legacy of Cotton Mather," *Studies in American Fiction* 22, no. 1 (1994), 61–79.
38. There are, of course, critics who emphasize the counterrealistic aspects of mid-nineteenth-century literature. For a useful summary and critique of the romance theorists (Lionel Trilling, Richard Chase, Joel Porte), see Russell Reising, *The Unusable Past: Theory and the Study of American Literature* (London: Methuen, 1986). See also Emily Miller Budick, "Sacvan Bercovitch, Stanley Cavell, and the Romance Theory of American Fiction," *PMLA* 107, no. 1 (1992), 78–91.

     In this context, I recommend Allan Gardner Lloyd-Smith's *Uncanny American Fiction* (New York: St. Martin's Press, 1989). He discusses the "romantic uncanny" of Poe, the "transcendental uncanny" of Hawthorne, the "psychological uncanny" of Bierce and Jack London, and the "symbolic uncanny" of James in ways that correspond to and complement Borges' understanding of these writers.
39. Borges, "Valery as Symbol," p. 197.
40. My purpose here is not to explore in detail the nature of Transcendentalist thought as such but to trace Borges' understanding of it. General studies are Roger Asselineau, *The Transcendentalist Constant in American Literature* (New York: New York University Press, 1980), and William Ellis, *The Theory of American Romance: An Ideology in American Intellectual History* (Ann Arbor: UMI Research Press, 1989).

41. Again, this aspect of Transcendentalism has been amply explored. Lawrence Buell calls the Transcendentalists "children of the Puritans." See *Literary Transcendentalism: Style and Vision in the American Renaissance* (Ithaca: Cornell University Press, 1973), pp.146 ff.

42. Borges, "Nathaniel Hawthorne," pp. 223–24.

   Borges links another nineteenth-century U.S. writer to Kafka: Of Henry James, Borges says, "From the perplexities of the American in Europe James went on to the theme of the perplexity of man in the universe. He had no faith in an ethical, philosophical, or religious solution to essential problems; his world is already the inexplicable world of Kafka. Despite the scruples and delicate complexities of James, his work suffers from a major defect: the absence of life." *An Introduction to American Literature*, p. 55.

   Given this conclusion, it is no wonder that Borges excludes James altogether from his discussion of U.S. literature as dream or hallucination. Still, Borges might have cited James' critical preface to the seventeenth volume of the New York edition, "The Altar of the Dead," a volume that includes "The Jolly Corner" and several other fantastic stories by James. In this preface, James states that he "is prepared with the confession that the 'ghost-story,' as we for convenience call it, has ever been for me the most possible form of the fairy-tale. It enjoys, to my eyes, this honour by being so much the neatest – neat with that neatness without which *representation*, and therewith beauty, drops." *The Art of the Novel: Critical Prefaces* (Boston: Northeastern University Press, 1984), p. 254.

43. Alejo Carpentier, preface to *El reino de este mundo* (*The Kingdom of this World*) (Mexico City: Fondo de Cultura Económica, 1949); reprinted as part of "De lo real maravilloso americano," in *Tientos y diferencias* (Montevideo: Editorial Arca, 1967), pp. 96–132; and translated as "On the Magical Real in America," trans. Tanya Huntington and Lois Parkinson Zamora, in *Magical Realism: Theory, History, Community*, ed. Lois Parkinson Zamora and Wendy B. Faris (Durham: Duke University Press, 1995), pp. 75–88.

44. This phrase is from Borges' introduction to the short fiction of Kafka, in which he again (though here implicitly) aligns Kafka with Hawthorne by arguing for the centrality of "situation" in Kafka's works as well, and the consequent superiority of his short fiction: "Plot and atmosphere are the essential characteristics of Kafka's work, not the convolutions of the story or the psychological portrait of the hero. This is what makes Kafka's stories superior to his novels. . . ." Foreword to *Stories, 1904–1924*, trans. J. A. Underwood (New York: Futura, 1981), p. 8.

45. Nathaniel Hawthorne, "Wakefield," in *Hawthorne's Short Stories*, ed. Newton Arvin (New York: Vintage Books, 1946), p. 41. Subsequent page references are cited in the text.

46. Budick, "Sacvan Bercovitch, Stanley Cavell, and the Romance Theory of American Fiction," p. 80.

47. Lois Parkinson Zamora, "'A Garden Enclosed': Fuentes' *Aura*, Hawthorne's and Paz's 'Rappaccini's Daughter,' and Uyeda's *Ugetsu Monogatari*," *Revista Canadiense de Estudios Hispánicos* 8, no. 3 (1984), 23–40. In this essay, too, I argue that magical realism represents a confluence of counterrealistic literary conventions and modes, including gothic, romance, surrealist, and indigenous American cultural forms.

48. John T. Irwin, *The Mystery to the Solution: Poe, Borges and the Analytic Detective Story* (Baltimore: Johns Hopkins University Press, 1994).

49. William Goyen, *The House of Breath* (New York: Random House, 1950), p. 9.

50. Ixtepec is the name of a town on the isthmus of Tehuantepec with a long history of popular political resistance. Garro's novel, however, is set in north central Mexico, as is clear from her description of political events and the landscape.

51. Elena Garro, *Recuerdos del porvenir* (Mexico City: Joaquín Mortiz, 1963), p. 9.

52. Garro, *Recollections of Things to Come*, trans. Ruth L. C. Simms (Austin: University of Texas Press, 1969), p. 3.

53. Octavio Paz, *Alternating Current* (1967), trans. Helen R. Lane (New York: Richard Seaver Books, 1983), p. 15.

54. Juan Rulfo, *Pedro Páramo* (Mexico City: Fondo de Cultura Económica, 1955), pp. 7–8 (Rulfo's emphasis).

55. Rulfo, *Pedro Páramo*, trans. Lysander Kemp (New York: Grove Press, 1959), pp. 1–2.

56. See Frye, *The Anatomy of Criticism*, pp. 187–88.

57. Clendinnen writes: "The flesh-and-earth identifications are clear in the early account of the composition of the human body inscribed in the Florentine Codex. Blood vessels are likened to reeds, moving the blood through the flesh as water moves through the earth. . . . Quetzalcóatl's theft of human bones from the Lord of the Underworld, along with other indicators, suggests that bone was understood as seed." *Aztecs: An Interpretation* (New York: Cambridge University Press, 1991), pp. 182–83.

58. Octavio Paz, "The Power of Ancient Mexican Art," *New York Review of Books*, 6 December 1990, p. 21.

59. Hugo G. Nutini, *Todos Santos in Rural Tlaxcala: A Syncretic, Expressive, and Symbolic Analysis of the Cult of the Dead* (Princeton: Princeton University Press, 1988), p. 69 (my emphasis).

60. Keith Carter, *The Blue Man* (Houston: Rice University Press, 1990); interview with Anne W. Tucker, p. 124. Subsequent page references are cited in the text.

61. William Goyen, *The Collected Stories of William Goyen* (Garden City, N.Y.: Doubleday, 1975), p. xi.

62. Octavio Paz, "Mexico and the United States," trans. Rachel Phillips Belash, in *The Labyrinth of Solitude* rev. ed. (New York: Grove Press, 1985), pp. 362–63. This essay first appeared in *The New Yorker*, 17 September 1979, pp. 137–53.

63. See W. W. Newcomb, Jr., *The Indians of Texas: From Prehistoric to Modern Times* (Austin: University of Texas Press, 1961). Subsequent page references are cited in the text.

64. Newcomb, "Harmony with Nature, People, and the Supernatural," in *Texas Myths*, ed. Robert F. O'Connor (College Station: Texas A & M University Press, 1986), p. 47.
    Elizabeth York Enstam confirms this point, referring to "a cohesiveness within the villages that went much beyond the support systems provided even by an extended family." She speaks of "a sense of family that was virtually tribal in extent; they knew a kind of community long vanished among peoples of European descent and culture. Of all nineteenth-century inhabitants of Texas, only Afro-Americans had anything like the Indian familial organization." See "The Family," in *Texas Myths*, p. 146. See also Sidner Larson, "Native American Aesthetics: An Attitude of Relationship," *MELUS* 17, no. 3 (Fall 1991–92) 53–67.

65. Newcomb, *The Indians of Texas*, p. 280.

66. Fray Francisco Casañas, *Description of the Tejas or Asinai Indians, 1691–1722*, trans. Mattie Austin Hatcher, *Southwestern Historical Quarterly* vol. 30 (1927), 206–18, 283–304; cited in Newcomb, *The Indians of Texas*, pp. 303–5. Newcomb also cites Fray Gaspar José de Solís' "Diary of a Visit of Inspection of the Texas Missions Made by Fray Gaspar José de Solís in the Year 1767–1768," trans. Margaret K. Kress, *Southwestern Historical Quarterly* 35 (1931), 28–76. See also J. Alden Mason, "The Place of Texas in Pre-Columbian Relationships Between the United States and Mexico," *Texas Archeological and Paleontological Society Bulletin*, Vol. 7 (1935), 29–46.

67. *Caddoan Mounds: Temples and Tombs of an Ancient People* (Austin: Texas Parks and Wildlife Department, May 1984).

68. Relevant to the nature of the Mexican/Texan animate earth is Alfred Avila, *Mexican Ghost Tales of the Southwest*, ed. Kat Avila (Houston: Arte Público Press, 1994).

69. Recall Octavio Paz's metaphoric formulation of this "universal sympathy" characteristic of pre-Hispanic Mesoamerican cultures: a "vital fluid that unites all animate beings – humans, animals, plants – with the elements, the planets, and the stars." See "The Power of Ancient Mexican Art," p. 20.

70. Wayne Ude also relates indigenous and romance traditions in "Forging an American Style: The Romance-Novel and Magical Realism as Response to the Frontier and Wilderness Experiences," in *The Frontier Experience and the American Dream*, ed. David Mogen, Mark Busby, and Paul Bryant (College Station: Texas A & M University Press, 1989), pp. 50–64.

71. William Goyen, *The Collected Stories of William Goyen* (New York: Doubleday, 1975), p. 51. Subsequent page references are cited in the text.

72. Fredric Jameson, "Magical Narratives: Romance as Genre," *NLH* 7, no. 1 (1975), p. 158. Reprinted in slightly different form as "Magical Narratives: On the Dialectical Use of Genre Criticism," in *The Political Unconscious: Narrative as a Socially Symbolic Act* (Ithaca: Cornell University Press, 1981), pp. 103–50.

73. I address this difference in the concluding chapter of my *Writing the Apocalypse: Historical Vision in Contemporary U.S. and Latin American Fiction* (Cambridge: Cambridge University Press, 1989), pp. 176–92.

74. In an interview, García Márquez described the moment when, as a young journalist in Barranquilla, Colombia, he first read William Faulkner: "I discovered that he was writing about a world exactly like the one I had lived . . . a world of heat and slow-moving rivers, small towns and farming country, where storytellers spun long and fantastic tales." García Márquez says that reading southern writers made him realize that "what I had to do was create a reality that would make people uncomfortable, transmit this sense of uneasiness and pain that I encountered. And that is what I found in the southern writers from the United States. I returned to Barranquilla twenty-four hours later, tore up half a novel I had written and started over. Since then I haven't changed my concept of literature." Anthony Day and Marjorie Miller, "Gabo Talks," *Los Angeles Times Magazine*, 2 September 1990, p. 33.

75. See my *Writing the Apocalypse*, pp. 25–51, 123–24.

76. William Faulkner, *Go Down, Moses* (1942; rpt. New York: Vintage, 1990), p. 165 (my emphasis).

77. Susan Power, *The Grass Dancer* (New York: G. P. Putnam's Sons, 1994), p. 26.

78. Louise Erdrich, *Tracks* (New York: Harper and Row, 1988), p. 1. Subsequent page references are cited in the text.

79. Willa Cather, preface to *The Country of the Pointed Firs and Other Stories*, by Sarah Orne Jewett (New York: Doubleday, 1956), pp. 9, 6.

80. Cited by Doris Grumbach, foreword to *The Song of the Lark* (New York: Harcourt Brace Jovanovich, 1988), p. xxix.

81. Meridel LeSueur, "The Dark of the Time," in *Song for My Time* (Minneapolis: Haymarket Press, 1977), p. 50

82. Carlos Fuentes, "Central and Eccentric Writing," in *Lives on the Line: The Testimony of Contemporary Latin American Authors*, ed. Doris Meyer (Berkeley: University of California Press, 1988), p. 122.

83. Fuentes, *Una familia lejana* (Mexico City: Ediciones Era, 1980), p. 16.

84. Fuentes, *Distant Relations*, trans Margaret Sayers Peden (New York: Farrar, Straus & Giroux, 1982), p. 11.

85. W.S. Merwin, "Witness," in *The Rain in the Trees* (New York: Knopf, 1988), p. 65. I have cited the poem in its entirety; it is without punctuation.

86. Roberto González Echevarría, *Myth and Archive: A Theory of Latin American Narrative* (Cambridge: Cambridge University Press, 1990), p. 144. Subsequent page numbers are cited in the text.

87. Vera M. Kutzinski, *Against the American Grain: Myth and History in William Carlos Williams, Jay Wright, and Nicolás Guillén* (Baltimore: Johns Hopkins University Press, 1987), pp. 44–45.
88. Ken Kesey, *Sometimes a Great Notion* (New York: Penguin, 1964), p. 529.

PART TWO. INTERTEXTUALITY AND TRADITION

1. Maurice Merleau-Ponty, *La Prose du monde* (Paris: Gallimard, 1969), pp. 200–1 (my translation).
2. William Carlos Williams, "Against the Weather: A Study of the Artist" (1939), in *Selected Essays* (New York: New Directions, 1969), pp. 213, 208 (my emphasis).
3. Julio Ortega, *La contemplación y la fiesta* (Caracas: Monte Avila Editores, 1969), p. 8 (my translation and emphasis).
4. Carlos Fuentes elaborates this structure in *Cervantes o la crítica de la lectura* (Mexico City: Joaquín Mórtiz, 1976); partially translated as "Cervantes, or The Critique of Reading" in *Myself With Others* (New York: Farrar, Straus & Giroux, 1988), pp. 49–71. See Wendy B. Faris, "'Desyoización': Joyce/Cixous/Fuentes and the Multivocal Text," *Latin American Literary Review* 9, no. 19 (1981), 31–39.
5. In his novel *Rayuela* (*Hopscotch*, 1963), Cortázar uses these spatial metaphors to describe the inclusive artistic process whereby the description of fragmentary phenomena may coalesce into an *imago mundi*. A verbal, visual, or musical "constellation," "crystallization," or "*figura*" suggests a complex interaction of fragments and the artist's synthesizing imagination.

    Morelli, the novelist in *Hopscotch*, spells out Cortázar's inclusive aesthetic. Morelli insists upon the word *figura* rather than *imagen* (image) in order to privilege synchrony over progression, saying that he aspires to write a novel that "acede a la condición de *figura* . . . una obra que puede parecer ajena o antagónica a su tiempo y a su historia circundantes, y que sin embargo los incluye . . . ." *Rayuela* (Buenos Aires: Editorial Sudamericana, 1963), p. 545 (Cortázar's emphasis); (a work that "conforms to the condition of a *figure* . . . a work which may seem alien or antagonistic to the time and history surrounding [the artist], and which nonetheless includes it. . . ." *Hopscotch*, trans. Gregory Rabassa [New York: Avon, 1966], p. 489 (Cortázar's emphasis).

    Using the metaphor of crystallization, Cortázar describes the totalizing impulse of his alter ego: "Morelli había esperado que la acumulación de fragmentos cristalizara bruscamente en una realidad total. . . . una cristalización que, sin alterar el desorden en que circulaban los cuerpos de su pequeño sistema planetario, permitiera la comprensión ubicua y total de sus razones de ser, fueran éstas el desorden mismo, la inanidad o la gratuidad" (533; "Morelli had hoped that the accumulation of fragments would quickly crystalize into a total reality . . . a crystalization which, without altering the disorder in which the bodies of his little planetary system circulated, would permit a ubiquitous and total comprehension of all of its reasons for being, whether they were disorder itself, inanity, or gratuity" 478).
6. Frank Kermode, *History and Value* (Oxford: Clarendon Press, 1988), p. 108. See Kermode's extended consideration of "how the works of the past may retain identity in change" (16), in *The Classic: Literary Images of Permanence and Change* (1975) 2d ed. (Cambridge, Mass.: Harvard University Press, 1983), especially Chapter 1.
7. ". . . he observado que en nuestro país, precisamente por ser un país nuevo, hay un gran sentido del tiempo." (". . . I have observed that in our country, precisely because it is a new country, we have a great sense of time.") See Borges, "El escritor argentino y la tradición," in *Discusión* (1932); rpt. in *Obras completas* (Buenos Aires: Emecé Editores, 1989), 1, p. 272; "The Argentine Writer and Tradition," trans. James E. Irby,

in *Labyrinths*, ed. James E. Irby and Donald A. Yates (New York: New Directions, 1962), p. 183.

8. Jorge Luis Borges, *Textos cautivos: Ensayos y reseñas en "El Hogar" (1936–1939)*, ed. Enrique Sacerio-Garí and Emir Rodríguez Monegal (Barcelona: Tusquets Editores, 1986), cited on the flyleaf.

9. Carlos Fuentes, "The Accidents of Time," in *The Borges Tradition*, ed. Norman Thomas di Giovanni (London: Constable, 1995), p. 53.

10. Borges, "El cuento policial," in *Borges oral* (1979), cited in *Borges*, catalogue of an exhibition at the Biblioteca Nacional in Madrid, 1986, p. 81 (my emphasis; my translation).

11. Jon Thiem, "The Textualization of the Reader in Magical Realist Fiction," in *Magical Realism: Theory, History, Community*, ed. Lois Parkinson Zamora and Wendy B. Faris (Durham: Duke University Press, 1995), p. 242.

12. Gustavo Pérez Firmat, *The Cuban Condition* (Cambridge: Cambridge University Press, 1989), p. 11.

13. *Postscript to "The Name of the Rose"* (New York: Harcourt, Brace, Jovanovich, 1984), p. 65. For a discussion of Eco's theory of intertextuality and his own practice of it (including his intertextual use of Borges in *The Name of the Rose* and *Foucault's Pendulum*), see my essay "Eco's Pendulum Swings," in *Reading Eco: A Pretext to Literary Semiotics*, ed. Rocco Capozzi (Bloomington: Indiana University Press, 1997), pp. 328–47.

14. Nivia Montenegro and Enrico Mario Santí, "A Conversation with José Donoso," *New Novel Review* 1, no. 2 (1994), 13.

15. Norman Bryson discusses quotations as structures of permutation and multiplication, indicting postmodernist theories that preclude "modification of the semiotic field" by assuming that the quoted image can only "dispose or rearrange within the steady state of the system." *Vision and Painting: The Logic of the Gaze* (New Haven: Yale University Press, 1983), p. 141.

CHAPTER FOUR. SYNCHRONIC STRUCTURES

1. Isabel Allende, *La casa de los espíritus* (Mexico City: Editorial Diana, 1982), p. 383.

2. Allende, *The House of the Spirits*, trans. Magda Bogin (New York: Alfred A. Knopf, 1985), p. 367.

3. Jorge Luis Borges, "El escritor argentino y la tradición," in *Discusión* (1932); rpt. in *Obras completas* (Buenos Aires: Emecé Editores, 1989), 1, pp. 267–74; "The Argentine Writer and Tradition," trans. James E. Irby, in *Labyrinths*, ed. Donald A. Yates and James E. Irby (New York: New Directions, 1962), pp. 177–85.

4. Borges, "El Aleph," in *El Aleph* (1949); rpt. in *Obras completas* (Buenos Aires: Emecé Editores, 1989), 1, p. 624.

5. Borges, "The Aleph," in *The Aleph and Other Stories*, trans. Norman Thomas di Giovanni, (New York: E. P. Dutton, 1970), p. 26.

6. Borges, "Commentary on 'The Aleph,'" in *The Aleph*, p. 264.

7. Borges, "El Aleph," pp. 625–26.

8. Borges, "The Aleph," pp. 27–28.

9. The narrator describes the garden as an "infinite series of times, in a growing, dizzying net of divergent, convergent and parallel times. This network of times, which approached one another, forked, broke off, or were unaware of one another for centuries, embraces *all* possibilities of time." Jorge Luis Borges, "The Garden of Forking Paths," in *Labyrinths*, p. 28 (Borges' emphasis).

10. Julio Ortega, "Sobre *El siglo de las luces*," in *Asedios a Carpentier*, ed. Klaus Müller-Bergh (Santiago: Editorial Universitaria, 1972), p. 191 (my translation).

11. Strong states the point more forcefully: "The Argentine *vanguardia* was avant-garde in name only, capitalizing on a European concept appropriate to an entirely different set of social and cultural circumstances. Far from rebelling against the status quo of the literary establishment, it helped strengthen that establishment. The avant-garde's project – apart from popularizing free verse and the metaphor – had little apparent innovative content." Beret E. Strong, *The Poetic Avant-Garde: The Groups of Auden, Borges and Breton* (Evanston: Northwestern University Press, forthcoming.) This statement once again reminds us that Borgesian ideas now routinely declared "postmodern" must instead be understood in their New World historical and cultural context.

12. Carpentier's basic statements of this position are found in his essays entitled "Lo real maravilloso americano" (1949) and "Lo barroco y lo real maravilloso" (1975), trans. Tanya Huntington and Lois Parkinson Zamora, in *Magical Realism: Theory, History, Community*, ed. Lois Parkinson Zamora and Wendy B. Faris (Durham: Duke University Press, 1995), pp. 75–108. See also Amaryll Chanady's discussion of these essays: "The Territorialization of the Imaginary in Latin America: Self-Affirmation and Resistance to Metropolitan Paradigms," in *Magical Realism: Theory, History, Community*, pp. 125–44.

13. Alejo Carpentier, "Problemática del tiempo y el idioma en la moderna novela latinoamericana" ("The Problematics of Time and Language in the Modern Latin American Novel"), in *La novela latinoamericana en vísperas de un nuevo siglo y otros ensayos* (Mexico City: Siglo Veintiuno Editores, 1981), p. 157 (my emphasis, my translation).

14. Gabriel García Márquez, *De amor y otros demonios* (Mexico City: Editorial Diaña, 1994), pp. 140–41.

15. García Márquez, *Of Love and Other Demons*, trans. Edith Grossman (New York; Knopf, 1995), p. 102. Subsequent page references are cited in the text.

16. Isabel Allende, *Paula* (Barcelona: Plaza & Janés, 1994), p. 31.

17. Allende, *Paula*, trans. Margaret Sayers Peden (New York: Harper/Collins, 1994), p. 23. In his study of the "new historical novel" in Latin America, Seymour Menton concurs with Allende's metaphor and my argument; he notes the "panoramic, muralistic, or encyclopedic" aspirations of many contemporary Latin American novels, and links them to Bakhtin's concepts of the dialogic and the carnivalesque. See *The New Historical Novel* (Austin: University of Texas Press, 1993), p. 25.

18. Umberto Eco, *The Aesthetics of Chaosmos: The Middle Ages of James Joyce*, trans. Ellen J. Esrock (Tulsa: University of Tulsa Press, 1982), p. 83.

19. Roland Barthes, *The Pleasure of the Text* (1973), trans. Richard Miller (New York: Farrar, Straus, & Giroux, 1975), pp. 3–4. Barthes' text is itself a "sanctioned Babel" – a collection of critical fragments on a number of writers who create fragmentary and synchronic structures.

20. In a review of the English translation of Vargas Llosa's early short stories, *The Cubs and Other Stories*, Michael Wood comments that this book evokes other books, "not because it makes allusions or seems derivative, but because it aspires so transparently to literature, conjures up so clearly the decorous company of sensitive, intelligent, well-written texts it wishes to join." Generalizing about contemporary Latin American writers, he continues: "These novelists were in the first generation on their continent, I think, to have read so voraciously in so thoroughly international a manner. . . ." "The Claims of Mischief," *New York Review of Books*, 24 January 1980, p. 45. Wood's point needs refining: Latin American writers have always read widely and well, but not until this generation have they *flaunted* their reading in the ways I am discussing here. .

21. Nivia Montenegro and Enrico Mario Santí, "A Conversation with José Donoso," *New Novel Review* 1, no. 2 (1994), 13.

22. Early theoretical writings on "spatial structure," that is, fictions that supplant linear narrative structure with alternative structural models include Joseph Frank's "Spatial Form in Modern Literature" (1945), reprinted in *The Widening Gyre: Crisis and Mastery in Modern Literature* (New Brunswick, N. J.: Rutgers University Press, 1963), and Walter Sutton's "The Literary Image and the Reader: A Consideration of the Theory of Spatial Form," *Journal of Aesthetics and Art Criticism* 16 (1957–58), 112–123.

23. Aldous Huxley, *Point Counter Point* (Garden City, N. Y.: Doubleday, Doran & Co., 1928), p. 23.

24. In his essay "And Wanton Optics Roll the Melting Eye," Huxley refers specifically to this scene as an example of his contrapuntal ideal: "Juxtapose two accounts of the same human event, one in terms of pure science, the other in terms of religion, aesthetics, passion, even common sense; their discord will set up the most disquieting reverberations in the mind. . . . Juxtapose acoustics and the music of Bach (perhaps I may be permitted to refer to the simultaneous scientific and aesthetic account of a concert in my novel, *Point Counter Point*). . . ." *Music at Night* (Garden City, N. Y.: Doubleday, Doran, 1931), p. 40.

25. Another obvious precursor is Flaubert. Given Vargas Llosa's critical study of Flaubert entitled *La orgía perpetua* (*The Perpetual Orgy*, 1975) it would be a fruitful comparative project to consider Vargas Llosa's synchronic strategies in terms of Flaubert's. In *The Pleasure of the Text* Barthes writes: "Flaubert: a way of cutting, of perforating discourse *without rendering it meaningless*. . . . narrativity is dismantled yet the story is still readable . . ." (8–9, Barthes' emphasis). *Conversation in The Cathedral* and the other contemporary synchronic structures I mention "perforate" and "dismantle" discourse in the sense Barthes intends, but for purposes that differ significantly from those of the European modernists, as I will show.

26. Mario Vargas Llosa, preface to the translation of "Los cachorros." *The Cubs and Other Stories*, trans. Gregory Kolovakos and Ronald Christ (New York: Harper and Row, 1979).

27. See Ronald Christ's "Novel Form, Novel Sense," *Review* (Spring 1975), 30–36, for a discussion of cinematic montage in *Conversación en La Catedral*. Also relevant is Jean Franco's "Conversations and Confessions: Self and Character in *The Fall* and *Conversation in The Cathedral*," in *Mario Vargas Llosa: A Collection of Critical Essays*, ed. Charles Rossman and Alan Warren Friedman (Austin: University of Texas Press, 1978), pp. 59–75.

28. Walter Ong discusses "rhapsodic" structure in *Rhetoric, Romance, and Technology: Studies in the Interaction of Expression and Culture* (Ithaca: Cornell University Press, 1971), and *InterFaces of the Word: Studies in the Evolution of Consciousness and Culture* (Ithaca: Cornell University Press, 1977).

29. Jacques Derrida, "Force and Signification," in *Writing and Difference*, trans. Alan Bass (Chicago: University of Chicago Press, 1978), p. 9 (Derrida's emphasis).

30. Terence Hawkes, *Structuralism and Semiotics* (Berkeley: University of California Press, 1977), p. 146 (Hawkes' emphasis).

31. In his essay "Text and the Structure of Its Audience," Jurij M. Lotman emphasizes the *constitution* of the audience in the literary text: "In the literary text, orientation toward *a certain type of collective memory, and consequently toward a structure of the audience*, acquires a character that is different in principle (from that of texts addressed to a personally known addressee, for example, letters or, for that matter, conversation.) The audience of these novels ceases to be automatically implied in the text and becomes a signified (i.e., free) element which can enter the text as part of the game." *NLH* 14, no. 1 (1982), 84 (my emphasis).

32. Huxley's last works attest to his preoccupation with this contradiction: as he became increasingly interested in mysticism and intuitive perception, he increasingly felt the inadequacy of words to express "the primary fact of experience." In *Doors of Perception*, he wrote, "Literary or scientific, liberal or specialist, all our education is pre-

dominantly verbal and therefore fails to accomplish what it is supposed to do." (New York: Harper, 1954), p. 73. And after an experiment with mind-altering drugs, he stated: "To be shaken out of the ruts of ordinary perception, to be shown for a few timeless hours the outer and inner world, not as they appear to . . . a human being obsessed with words, but as they are apprehended, directly and unconditionally, by the Mind at Large. . . ." (73)

33. Huxley often referred to life as a set of relationships among incompatible roles. Here is his complete statement: "We live in a world of non sequiturs. Or rather, we would live in such a world, if we were always conscious of all the aspects under which any event can be considered. But in practice we are almost never aware of more than one aspect at a time. Our life is spent first in one water-tight compartment of experience, then in another. The artist can, if he so desires, break down the bulkheads between the compartments and so give us a simultaneous view of two or more of them at a time. So seen, reality looks exceedingly queer" (*Music at Night*, 40–41). Huxley's character Phillip Quarles uses similar language to describe his projected synchronic narrative, adding "However queer the picture is, it can never be half as odd as the original reality" (*Point Counter Point*, 192).

34. Stéphane Mallarmé affirmed this shift in "La musique et les lettres" (1894) rpt. in *Oeuvres complètes de Stéphane Mallarmé* (Paris: Gallimard, 1945), pp. 635–657. Bernard Weinberg notes Mallarmé's reference to his poem "Un Coup de dés . . ." as an orchestral score and argues that Mallarmé used the musical analogy to suggest the synchronic structure that he wanted to create. *The Limits of Symbolism: Studies of Five Modern French Poets* (Chicago: University of Chicago Press, 1966), pp. 242–243.

What Weinberg doesn't specify is that, unlike most Symbolist poems, the synchronicity of "Un Coup de dés . . ." results from the typography rather than from the auditory devices of the poem. Thus, in this particular poem Mallarmé's synchronic strategies resemble collage more than counterpoint, despite the poet's musical analogy. So, too, Michel Butor's synchronicity in *Niagara: A Stereophonic Novel*, as I will demonstrate shortly.

35. See Huxley's preface to *Art and Artists*, ed. Morris Phillipson (New York: Harper, 1960), pp. 7–8.

36. Marshall McLuhan, *Counterblast* (New York: Harcourt, Brace and World, 1969), pp. 112–13.

37. Vargas Llosa writes regularly for newspapers. Reference to Vargas Llosa's early journalistic career is found in José Miguel Oviedo's "Chronology," *Review* (Spring 1975), 8.

38. Michel Butor, *6 810 000 litres d'eau par seconde: étude stéréophonique* (Paris: Gallimard, 1965); *Niagara: A Stereophonic Novel*, trans. Elinor S. Miller (Chicago: Henry Regnery, 1969). For a more extensive discussion of the musical metaphor in this work, see Michael Spencer, *Michel Butor* (New York: Twayne, 1974), pp. 128–132; and Elinor S. Miller, "Approaches to the Cataract: Butor's Niagara," *Studies in Twentieth Century Literature* 2, no. 1 (1977), 33–54.

39. *Réseau aérien, Description de San Marco, Votre Faust*, and *Illustrations* are examples of Butor's resistence to linear narrative through the use of other media. His essay "La Littérature, l'oreille et l'oeil" ("Literature, the Ear and the Eye") describes his interest in the collaboration of all art forms. See his book *Répertoire III* (Paris: Editions de Minuit, 1968), pp. 391–403.

40. Chateaubriand's description is found in the 1797 "Essai historique, politique et moral sur les révolutions anciennes et modernes considérées dans leurs rapports avec la révolution francaise" ("Historical, Political and Moral Essay on Ancient and Modern Revolutions Considered in Relation to the French Revolution"), and taken up again in the 1801 "Atala, ou les amours des deux sauvages dans le desert" ("Atala, or the Love of Two Savages in the Desert"), in *Mémoires d'outre-tombe* (*Memoirs from Beyond the Grave*). Butor cites the latter version at the end of his novel.

41. Laurent Jenny, "La Stratégie de la forme," *Poétique: revue de théorie et d'analyse littéraires* 7, no. 27 (1976), 279 (my emphasis added, my translation). Subsequent page references are cited in the text.

42. See Peter Conrad's discussion of the literary pilgrimages to Niagara Falls of major nineteenth- and early twentieth-century British writers (among them Trollope, Dickens, Wilde, and Wells) in "Versions of Niagara," *Imagining America* (New York: Oxford University Press, 1980), pp. 3–29.

43. According to Anderson Imbert, "El Niágara, desde Heredia, ha sido una obsesión en la poesía hispanoamericana; cuando [Rafael] Pombo 'En el Niágara' se puso a describir ese 'museo de cataratas', 'fábrica de nubes', 'mar desfondado al peso de sus ondas', manifestó una fuerza visional más poderosa que nadie. Lo que él vió ahí está en el verso: el lector vuelve a ver el Niágara, porque está a la vista Poesía torrencial, como el Niágara mismo." ("Niagara, since Heredia, has been an obsession in Hispanic American poetry; when [Rafael] Pombo 'At Niagara' began to describe that 'museum of falls,' 'factory of clouds,' 'sea without bottom because of the weight of its waves,' he exhibited a visionary power stronger than anyone else's. What he saw there is in the poem: the reader is brought back to Niagara because this is visible, torrential Poetry, like Niagara itself" (my translation). *Historia de la literature hispanoamericana* (Mexico City: Fondo de Cultura Económica, 1954), pp. 203–204. Anderson Imbert explicitly connects Pombo (1833–1913) to the Romanticism of Chateaubriand and Hugo.

44. Georges Charbonnier, *Entretiens avec Michel Butor* (Paris: Gallimard, 1967), pp. 135, 140 (my emphasis, my translation). Butor's comment on his selection of the title of his work is also instructive in this regard: "6,810,000 liters of water per second is the average amount of water that goes over Niagara Falls, and clearly it was important for me to put this amount in my title, that is, *the constant of something mobile*, something very mobile, the constant of a movement" (p. 135, my emphasis, my translation).

45. Butor referred to the physical properties of the printed word in an essay called "Le Livre comme objet" ("The Book as Object") in *Répertoire II* (Paris: Editions de Minuit, 1968), p. 92. Here he criticizes writers for accepting the rigid linear nature of print, arguing in favor of more thoughtful and elaborate layouts of the printed page, and of the replacement of the narrative line with a "surface." This essay and three others – "Philosophie de l'ameublement" ("Philosophy of Furnishings"), "Recherche sur la technique du roman" ("Research on the Technique of the Novel"), and "L'Espace du roman" ("The Space of the Novel") – constitute a statement of Butor's spatial aesthetic.

46. See Marcy Schwartz's discussion of Cortázar's stories "Lejana" and "El otro cielo" in these terms: "Cortázar's Plural Parole: Multilingual Shifts in the Short Fiction," *Romance Notes* 36, no. 2 (1995), 131–37.

47. Julio Cortázar, *62: modelo para armar* (Buenos Aires: Editorial Sudamericana, 1968), pp. 25–26. Subsequent page references are cited in the text.

48. Cortázar, *62: A Model Kit*, trans. Gregory Rabassa (New York: Avon, 1972), pp. 27–28.

49. In *Rayuela* (*Hopscotch*), Cortázar's character Morelli defines "crystallization" as his own aesthetic goal:

> ... una cristalización que, sin alterar el desorden en que circulaban los cuerpos de sus pequeño sistema planetario, permitiera la compresión ubicua y total de sus razones de ser. ... Una cristalización en la que nada quedara subsumido, pero donde un ojo lúcido pudiese asomarse al calidoscopio y entender la gran rosa polícromo, entenderla como una figura, *imago mundis* que por fuera del calidoscopio se resolvía en living room de estilo provenzal, o concierto de tías tomando té con alletitas Bagley. *Rayuela* (Buenos Aires: Editorial Sudamericana, 1963), p. 533 (Cortázar's emphasis).

... a crystallization which, without altering the disorder in which the bodies of his little planetary system circulated, would permit a ubiquitous and total comprehension of all of its reasons for being. . . . A crystallization in which nothing would remain subsumed, but where a lucid eye might peep into the kaleidoscope and understand the great polychromatic rose, understand it as a figure, an *imago mundi* that outside the kaleidoscope would be dissolved into a provincial living room or a concert of aunts having tea and Bagley biscuits." *Hopscotch*, trans. Gregory Rabassa (New York: Avon, 1966), p. 478 (Cortázar's emphasis).

On Cortázar's synchronic metaphors and the narrative strategies, see my essay "Voyeur/Voyant: Julio Cortázar's Spatial Esthetic," *Mosaic* 14, no. 4 (1981), 45–68.

50. Wylie Sypher, *Rococo to Cubism in Art and Literature* (New York: Random House, 1960), p. 276.

51. Roland Barthes, *S/Z*, trans. Richard Miller (New York: Hill and Wang, 1974), pp. 15–16.

52. See Robin William Fiddian's study of cultural affinities and literary influence in "James Joyce and Spanish-American Fiction: A Study of Origins and Transmission of Literary Influence," *Bulletin of Hispanic Studies* 66 (1989), 23–39.

53. Fredric Jameson, "On Magic Realism in Film," *Critical Inquiry* 12, no. 2 (1986), 311; rpt. in Jameson, *Signatures of the Visible* (New York: Routledge, 1990), pp. 128–52. See also Steven Slemon's 1988 essay, "Magical Realism as Postcolonial Discourse," reprinted with revisions in *Magical Realism: Theory, History, Community*, pp. 407–26; and John Erickson, "*Metoikoi* and Magical Realism in the Maghrebian Narratives of Tahar ben Jelloun and Abdelkebir Khatibi," pp. 427–50, in the same volume.

54. Carlos Fuentes' discussion of the shared historical imperatives of Faulkner's South and contemporary Latin America concludes, "La historia del Sur nos da, en cierto sentido, la clave de la literaturea norteamericana" ("The history of the South gives us, in some sense, the key to North American literature"). See "La novela como tragedia: William Faulkner," in *Casa con dos puertas* (Mexico City: Joaquín Mortiz, 1970), p. 64 (my translation).

55. See Frederick L. Gwynn and Joseph L. Blotner, eds., *Faulkner in the University* (Charlottesville: University of Virginia Press, 1959), pp. 173–74.

56. Eudora Welty, *One Writer's Beginnings* (Cambridge, Mass.: Harvard University Press, 1984), p. 102 (Welty's emphasis).

57. With respect to Murray's "blues aesthetic," see his essays "The Visual Equivalent to Blues Composition" and "The Storyteller as Blues Singer," in *The Blue Devils of Nada: A Contemporary American Approach to Aesthetic Statement* (New York: Pantheon, 1996), pp. 117–221.

58. Albert Murray, "The Ellington Synthesis," in *The Blue Devils of Nada*, p. 93.

59. John Edgar Wideman, *Fatheralong: A Meditation on Fathers and Sons, Race and Society* (New York: Pantheon, 1994), p. xv.

60. Dos Passos' trilogy consists of *The 42nd Parallel* (1930), *Nineteen Nineteen* (1932), and *The Big Money* (1936).

61. Quoted in Emanuel Carballo, *Diecinueve protagonistas de la literatura mexicana del siglo XX* (Mexico City: Empresas Editoriales, 1965), p. 434.

62. Wendy B. Faris, *Carlos Fuentes* (New York: Frederick Ungar, 1983), p. 38.

63. Terrence Rafferty, "Articles of Faith," *The New Yorker*, 16 May 1988, p. 110. Subsequent page references are cited in the text.

CHAPTER FIVE. FRAGMENTARY FICTIONS

1. Walter Benjamin, "Theses on the Philosophy of History," in *Illuminations*, ed. Hannah Arendt, trans. Harry Zohn (New York: Schocken Books, 1955), p. 257. In the context of my comparative discussion, Carlos Fuentes' invocation of Benjamin's angel in

a review of the Hungarian writer György Konrád is relevant. Fuentes speaks of fiction in which

> la grandeza y miseria de vivir en la 'polis' (vivir 'politicamente') debe contemplarse en términos poéticos y fatídicos, casi como el Angelus Novus de Walter Benjamín que se yergue, despliega las alas y vuelve la mirada a la irónica perfección de la historia: la meditación del Angel sobre el pasado redime a la ciudad al verla en ruinas; y estar en ruinas significa haber sobrevivido y poder mostrarnos sus huesos despojados; su ruina es su eternidad y, por tanto, su perfección.

> the grandeur and misery of living in the "polis" (living "politically") must be contemplated in poetic and vatic terms, almost like the Angelus Novus of Walter Benjamin, which rises, unfolds its wings and casts its gaze upon the ironic perfection of history: the Angel's gaze redeems the city in ruins; the ruins signify survival; it can show us its bare bones; its ruin is its eternity and therefore its perfection.

Fuentes goes on to suggest that a Mexican and a Hungarian, a Latin American and a Central European, may share this vision because they have experienced the disruptions of colonization and the consequent struggle to establish a coherent communal identity from the historical fragments. See Carlos Fuentes, "La ciudad en guerra: Notas sobre György Konrád," *nexos*, no. 138 (June 1989), 39–40 (my translation).

2. See Robert Alter, *Necessary Angels: Tradition and Modernity in Kafka, Benjamin, and Scholem* (Cambridge, Mass.: Harvard University Press, 1991), pp. 113–16. Subsequent page references are cited in the text.

3. Gershom Scholem, "Walter Benjamin and His Angel," in *On Walter Benjamin: Critical Essays and Recollections*, ed. Gary Smith, trans. Werner Dannhauser (Cambridge, Mass.: MIT Press, 1988), p. 86.

4. Donald Shaw, "On the New Novel in Spanish America," *New Novel Review* 1, no. 1 (1993), 59–73. Subsequent page references are cited in the text.

5. Julio Ortega, *La contemplación y la fiesta* (Caracas: Monte Avila Editores, 1969), p. 8; Robin William Fiddian, "James Joyce and Spanish-American Fiction: A Study of Origins and Transmission of Literary Influence," *Bulletin of Hispanic Studies* 66 (1989), 33.

6. Angelina Muñiz-Huberman, *Dulcinea encantada* (Mexico City: Joaquín Mortiz, 1992), p. 85. Subsequent page references are cited in the text. Translations are mine.

7. This brilliant chronicler of mid-nineteenth-century Mexico, a Scotswoman, arrived in Mexico with her husband, the Spanish ambassador to Mexico, in 1839. During her two-year stay, she wrote detailed letters to her daughter, which were collected in 1842 and published as *Life in Mexico*.

8. Muñiz-Huberman does not use the standard Spanish translation of this work, which is Frances Calderón de la Barca, *La vida en México durante una residencia de dos años en ese país*, trans. Felipe Teixidor (Mexico City: Editorial Porrúa, 1959). Teixidor's translation is closer to the original English original than Muñiz-Huberman's, but I nonetheless cite from *Dulcinea encantada*, p. 27.

9. Frances Calderón de la Barca, *Life in Mexico* (New York: Doubleday, 1963), p. 82.

10. See Angelina Muñiz-Huberman's study of the Hispano-Hebraic cabbalistic tradition in *Las raíces y las ramas: fuentes y derivaciones de la cábala hispanohebreo* (Mexico City: Fondo de Cultura Económica, 1993).

11. Alter, *Necessary Angels*, p. 100. See also the discussion of this eschatological element in Benjamin's work by Klaus R. Scherpe, "Dramatización y des-dramatización de 'el Fin': la conciencia apocalíptica de la modernidad y la posmodernidad," in *Modernidad y posmodernidad*, ed. Josep Pico (Madrid: Alianza Editorial, 1988), pp. 349–85.

12. See *The Correspondence of Walter Benjamin and Gershom Scholem, 1932–1940*, trans. Gary Smith and Andre Lefevere (New York, Shocken, 1989), pp. 126–27 (Scholem's emphasis); cited by Alter, p. 107.

13. Scholem, *Correspondence*, p. 142 (Scholem's emphasis); cited by Alter, p. 109.
14. An editorial footnote states: "Benjamin says *'Jetztzeit'* and indicates by the quotation marks that he does not simply mean an equivalent to *Gegenwart*, that is, present. He clearly is thinking of the mystical *nunc stans.*" *Illuminations*, p. 261.
15. Cited by Scherpe, "Dramatización y des-dramatización de 'el Fin'," p. 359 (my translation).
16. Sandra Cisneros, *Woman Hollering Creek* (New York: Random House, 1991), p. 46.
17. Richard Wolin, *Walter Benjamin: An Aesthetic of Redemption* (New York: Columbia University Press, 1982), p. 59.
18. Scherpe, "Dramatización y des-dramatización de 'el Fin'," p. 359 (my translation).
19. Susan Buck-Morse, *The Dialectics of Seeing: Walter Benjamin and the Arcades Project* (Cambridge, Mass.: MIT Press, 1991). p. 160.
20. Jean-François Lyotard, *The Postmodern Condition: A Report on Knowledge*, trans. Bennington and Brian Massumi (Minneapolis: University of Minnesota Press, 1984), pp. 20–35. Lyotard's argument is well known: the logocentric tradition of universal philosophic categories descended from Plato to Hegel and Lukács are based on the Western "project of totalization" (34).

    The willingness of Lyotard to "totalize" about the Western "project of totalization" (34) is remarkable: "We have paid a high enough price for the nostalgia of the whole and the one, for the reconciliation of the concept and the sensible, of the transparent and communicable experience. . . . Let us wage a war on totality; let us witness to the unpresentable, let us activate the differences and save the honor of the name." "Answering the Question: What is Postmodernism?" trans. Régis Durand (appendix to *The Postmodern Condition*) p. 82.
21. Edmundo Magaña, "Entrevista con Sandra Cisneros" ("Interview with Sandra Cisneros"), *Semanal*, in *La Jornada*, 20 December 1992, p. 22 (my translation).
22. Gerda Lerner, *The Creation of Patriarchy* (New York: Oxford University Press, 1986), p. 4. Subsequent page references are cited in the text.
23. That this need to create and foster historical continuity is the shared province of women writers is widely agreed upon. Diana Fuss reiterates Lerner's point: ". . . since women as historical subjects are rarely included in 'History' to begin with, the strong feminist interest in forging a new historicity that moves across and against 'his story' is not surprising." See "Getting into History," *Arizona Quarterly* 45, no. 4 (1989), 95.

    More specifically, Rose Kamel writes about the tradition-making impulse of Tillie Olsen: "If *not* to find an audience is always a kind of death, discovering the responsive reader valorizes the obscured artists' suffering and strength, giving them the power to formulate riddles we have never addressed, let alone redressed. As Harold Bloom has explained, literary forefathers have always influenced their writing sons, often causing them the 'anxiety of "this" influence.' For Tillie Olsen, literary foremothers help engender and empower otherwise silenced women writers." See "Literary Foremothers and Writers' Silences: Tillie Olsen's Autobiographical Fiction," *MELUS* 12, no. 3 (1985), 71.
24. Gerda Lerner, *The Creation of Feminist Consciousness: From the Middle Ages to Eighteen-seventy* (New York: Oxford University Press, 1993), p. 139.
25. Cited by Victor Flores Olea, "Identidad nacional: Los rostros en movimiento," *Semanal*, in *La Jornada*, 3 January 1993, p. 24.
26. Walter Benjamin, "The Storyteller," in *Illuminations*, p. 86.
27. Benjamin, "On Some Motifs in Baudelaire," in *Illuminations*, p. 186.
28. Benjamin, "The Image of Proust," in *Illuminations*, p. 202.
29. Robert Alter, *Necessary Angels*, p. 104.
30. Benjamin, "Unpacking My Library," in *Illuminations*, p. 61 (my emphasis).
31. Carlos Fuentes, "Two Centuries of Diderot," in *Myself with Others: Selected Essays* (New York: Farrar, Straus & Giroux, 1988), p. 88.

32. Hannah Arendt, "Introduction: Walter Benjamin: 1892–1940," in *Illuminations*, p. 38.
33. Paul Bové, *Intellectuals in Power: A Genealogy of Critical Humanism* (New York: Columbia University Press, 1986), p. 239.
34. Frank Lentriccia, *Criticism and Social Change* (Chicago: University of Chicago Press, 1983), p. 119.
35. Albert Murray, "Bearden Plays Bearden," *The Blue Devils of Nada: A Contemporary American Approach to Aesthetic Statement* (New York: Pantheon, 1996), p. 124.
36. Semiotic theories of culture inform my conclusion: Jurij M. Lotman theorizes culture as "non-hereditary information acquired, preserved and transmitted by the various groups of human society." "Problems in the Typology of Culture," in *Soviet Semiotics*, ed. and trans. Daniel P. Lucid (Baltimore: Johns Hopkins University Press, 1977), p. 213. C. S. Peirce also insists on this point: "The real . . . is that which, sooner or later, information and reasoning would finally result in, and which is therefore independent of the vagaries of me and you. Thus the very origin of the conception of reality shows that this conception essentially involves the notion of a community, without definite limits, and capable of a definite increase of knowledge." *The Collected Papers of Charles Sanders Peirce*, ed. Charles Hartshorne and Paul Weiss (Cambridge, Mass.: Harvard University Press, 1931), 5, pp. 186–87.

CHAPTER SIX. CLICHÉS AND COMMUNITY

1. Gustave Flaubert, *Madame Bovary* (Paris: Flammarion, 1986), p. 259.
2. Flaubert, *Madame Bovary*, trans. Francis Steegmuller (New York: Modern Library, 1957), p. 216.
3. The French hostility to commonplace expression continues in contemporary critical thinking. Roland Barthes states his distrust of linguistic and cultural stereotypes in *Le Plaisir du texte* (Paris: Editions du Seuil, 1973); Michel Riffaterre concurs in his essay "Fonction du cliché dans la prose littéraire," in *Essais de stylistique structurale* (Paris: Flammarion, 1971); Jacques Derrida's general philosophical suspicions of spoken language are cited in subsequent notes. Margery Sabin contrasts the use of clichés and idiomatic language in the English and French novelistic traditions in a two-part article entitled "The Life of English Idiom, The Laws of French Cliché," *Raritan* 1, nos. 2–3 (1981), 54–72, 70–89.
4. Walter Ong, "Literacy and Orality in Our Times," *Profession* 79 (1979), 6. Ong's example is the U.S. television character Archie Bunker, whose clichés are systematically debased by his malaprops, his prejudices, and his comic incompetence. Ong's point is that in this degradation of oral formulae we witness popular culture under the influence of literacy. My point is the obverse: in the uses of oral formulae in contemporary Latin American fiction, we are witnessing literacy under the increasing influence of popular culture.
5. Norman Page distinguishes among types of popular speech according to the kind and degree of convention adopted. Dialect and idiolect represent the opposite ends of the spectrum, dialect referring to all the characteristics of speech that *unite* the individual to some recognizable social, regional, or other group, idiolect referring to the idiosyncrasies of individual speech that *distinguish* the individual from the group. *Speech in the English Novel* (London: Longman Publishers, 1973).
6. Viktor Shklovsky, "Tristram Shandy," in *Russian Formalist Criticism*, ed. and trans. Lee T. Lemon and Marion J. Reis (Lincoln: University of Nebraska Press, 1965), pp. 25–57. In the same volume, see also Shklovsky's essay "Art as Technique," pp. 3–24.
7. Robert Scholes, *Semiotics and Interpretation* (New Haven: Yale University Press, 1982), p. 18. Subsequent page references are cited in the text.

8. Marshall McLuhan argues that clichés become archetypes as they recede in time from the user; clearly, repetition is fundamental to both. See Marshall McLuhan with Wilfred Watson, *From Cliché to Archetype* (New York: Viking, 1970), p. 198.

9. Manuel Puig, *El beso de la mujer araña* (Barcelona: Seix Barral, 1976), p. 206.

10. Puig, *The Kiss of the Spider Woman*, trans. Thomas Colchie (New York: Avon, 1980), p. 202.

11. Although I do not pursue gender questions here, others have done so most helpfully. See, for example, Elías Miguel Muñoz, "El discurso utópico de la sexualidad en *El beso de la mujer araña* de Manuel Puig," *Revista Iberoamericana* 52 (1986), 361–78. I subsequently cite the discussion of gender in Puig's novels in Julian Paul Smith's book *The Body Hispanic*.

12. See the essays by Sergei Eisenstein collected in *Film Forum: Essays in Film Theory*, ed. and trans. Jay Leyda (New York: Harcourt Brace, 1949), and in *Film Sense*, ed. and trans. Jay Leyda (New York: Harcourt Brace, 1970).

13. Cited by A. K. Zolkovskij and Ju. K. Sceglov, "Structural Poetics is a Generative Poetics," in *Soviet Semiotics*, ed. and trans. Daniel P. Lucid (Baltimore: Johns Hopkins University Press, 1977), p. 190, n. 13.

14. Cited by Zolkovskij and Sceglov, "Structural Poetics," p. 179.

15. Jorge Luis Borges points to characteristics of the copyists that, he argues, their creator may not have set out to demonstrate, characteristics that ultimately mirror Flaubert himself. "Vindicación de 'Bouvard et Pécuchet,'" in *Discusión* (1932), rpt. in *Obras completas* (Buenos Aires: Editorial Emecé, 1989), 1, pp. 259–62.

16. See my comparative discussion of Puig's earlier fiction in "The Reader at the Movies: Semiotic Systems in Walker Percy's *The Moviegoer* and Manuel Puig's *Betrayed by Rita Hayworth*," *American Journal of Semiotics* 3, no. 1 (1984), 49–67.

17. Plato, *Phaedrus and the Seventh and Eighth Letters*, trans. Walter Hamilton (New York: Penguin, 1973), pp. 100–1.

18. Jurij M. Lotman, *Analysis of the Poetic Text*, ed. and trans. D. Barton Johnson (Ann Arbor: Ardis, 1976), p. 40.

19. Luis Rafael Sánchez, *La guaracha del Macho Camacho* (Buenos Aires: Ediciones de la Flor, 1976), pp. 13–14. Subsequent page references are cited in the text.

20. Sánchez, *Macho Camacho's Beat*, trans. Gregory Rabassa (New York: Pantheon, 1980), p. 5. Subsequent page references are cited in the text.

21. The phrase is taken from Paul Julian Smith's essay on Fuentes, Puig, and Lyotard in *The Body Hispanic: Gender and Sexuality in Spanish and Spanish American Literature* (Oxford: Oxford University Press, 1989), p. 204. Here Smith offers an application of Lyotard's definition of postmodernism to these writers' works. In an otherwise useful essay, Smith sets up a dichotomy between modernism and postmodernism and finds Fuentes to be modernist and Puig postmodernist on the grounds that the latter does not perceive "order, harmony, or deep structure in the plural text" (184, n.11), whereas the former presumably does. In his discussion of *The Death of Artemio Cruz*, Smith pursues this point. Fuentes "puts his faith in the ability of the novel to say the 'unsayable.' For Lyotard such a position would remain modernist in spite of its denial of the master discourses" (204, n. 25). On the contrary, according to Smith, in *The Kiss of the Spider Woman* Puig does not put his faith in the "unsayable" and is therefore a postmodernist. In my view, such determinations belie the complex indeterminacy of both works, and eclipse cultural and literary distinctions with theoretical ones.

22. Donald Barthelme, *Snow White* (New York: Atheneum, 1967), p. 106.

23. John M. Ditsky, "'With Ingenuity and Hard Work, Distracted': The Narrative Style of Donald Barthelme," *Style* 9, no. 3 (1975), 393.

24. Michael Bérubé, "Public Academy," *The New Yorker*, 9 January 1995, p. 76.

25. Toni Morrison in an interview with Thomas LeClair, "The Language Must Not Sweat," *The New Republic*, 21 March 1981, p. 26. In this context, see also Deborah

L. Clarke, "What There Was Before Language": Preliteracy in Toni Morrison's *Song of Solomon*," in *Anxious Power: Reading, Writing, and Ambivalence in Narrative by Women*, ed. Carol J. Singley and Susan Elizabeth Sweeney (Albany: SUNY Press, 1993), pp. 265–78.

26. See, for example, the volume dedicated to this theme entitled *Language and Literature in the African American Imagination*, ed. Carol Aisha Blackshire-Belay (Westport, Conn: Greenwood Press, 1992); and John F. Callahan, *In the African-American Grain: The Pursuit of Voice in Twentieth-Century Black Fiction* (Urbana: University of Illinois Press, 1988).

27. Cornel West, "Black Culture and Postmodernism," in *Remaking History*, ed. Barbara Kruger and Phil Mariani (Seattle: Bay Press, 1989), p. 93.

COMPARATIVE CONCLUSIONS

1. Gabriel García Márquez, interview with Marlise Simmons, "García Márquez on Love, Plagues, and Politics," *New York Times Book Review*, 21 February 1988, p. 23.

2. *In the American Grain* (1925) takes as a given the hemispheric definition of America; see also Julio Marzán, *The Spanish-American Roots of William Carlos Williams* (Austin: University of Texas Press, 1994).

3. William Carlos Williams, "Against the Weather: A Study of the Artist" (1939), in *Selected Essays* (1954; rpt. New York: New Directions, 1969), p. 208.

4. Williams, *Kora in Hell* (1918), in *Imaginations* (New York: New Directions, 1970), p. 26. Williams no longer considered Pound or Eliot to be American writers, even though he should have; they are, of course, primary examples of his thesis.

5. Williams, "Against the Weather," pp. 197–98 (Williams' emphasis).

6. Homi K. Bhabha, "DissemiNation: time, narrative, and the margins of the modern nation," in *Nation and Narration*, ed. Homi K. Bhabha (London: Routledge, 1990), p. 312.

7. See Robert Young's study of European historiography from Hegel to Bhabha and Spivak: *White Mythologies: Writing History and the West* (London: Routledge, 1990).

8. Thomas MacFarland develops this point: "The claims are rarely in equipoise. At times the social voice will historically become more insistent, as for instance in Marxist ideology, and at other times the call of the individual, as in Rousseau's *Confessions*, will seem of overwhelming importance." *Originality and Imagination* (Baltimore: Johns Hopkins University Press, 1985), p. 31.

9. Luis Harss and Barbara Dohmann, *Into the Mainstream: Conversations with Latin American Writers* (New York: Harper and Row, 1966), p. 38.

10. Roberto González Echevarría, *Alejo Carpentier: The Pilgrim at Home* (Ithaca: Cornell University Press, 1977), p. 273.

11. Cleanth Brooks' description of Faulkner as a "Dixie Gongorist" is not lost on Fuentes, who celebrates the appellation as the sign of their shared worldviews. He writes in his essay on Faulkner, "It is no accident, then, that the language of Faulkner, deprecated as "Dixie Gongorism" by some North American critic, is the Baroque language of our great literary tradition." "La novela como tragedia: William Faulkner," in *Casa con dos puertas* (Mexico City: Joaquín Mortiz, 1970), p. 66 (my translation).

12. Walcott's statements were made in an interview with Sharon Ciccarelli in *Chant of Saints*, ed. Michael Harper and Robert Stepto (Urbana: University of Illinois Press, 1979), p. 303. David Mikics discusses Walcott's sense of the New World's "fractured or mediated" relation to European traditions and his rejection of "the sterile, confining alternative between affiliating himself with and reacting against European tradition. . . . Walcott identifies Whitman, Neruda, Borges and St. John Perse as New World

writers who overcome this restricive dualism." David Mikics, "Derek Walcott and Alejo Carpentier: Nature, History and the Caribbean Writer," in *Magic Realism: Theory, History, Community*, ed. Lois Parkinson Zamora and Wendy B. Faris (Durham: Duke University Press, 1995), p. 381.

13. Eliot's concern with the dialectic between tradition and the individual talent follows this recognition, and it is characteristically American. Octavio Paz has said of both Eliot and Pound: "They went off to Europe not as expatriates, but in search of their origins; their journey was not one of exile but a return to the source. It was a movement in the opposite direction from Whitman's: not the exploration of unknown spaces, the American beyond, but the return to England. However, England, separated from Europe since the Reformation, was only one link in the broken chain. Eliot's Anglicism was a European trait; Pound, more of an extremist, jumped from England to France and from France to Italy." *Children of the Mire: Modern Poetry from Romanticism to the Avant-Garde*, trans. Rachel Phillips (Cambridge, Mass.: Harvard University Press, 1974), p. 123.

Adriana Méndez Rodenas has compared Eliot and Paz from a feminist position, showing how both conceptions of tradition impede women's access to, and entry into the tradition. Nonetheless, there are relative differences between the two: Paz is far more open to cultural difference than Eliot. See "Tradition and Women's Writing: Toward a Poetics of Difference," in *Engendering the Word: Feminist Essays in Psychosexual Poetics*, ed. Temma F. Berg (Urbana: University of Illinois Press, 1989), pp. 29–50.

14. Octavio Paz, *Hijos del limo: Del romanticismo a la vanguardia* (Barcelona: Seix Barral, 1974), p. 17.

15. The English-language version of *Hijos del limo* was first presented as the Charles Eliot Norton lectures at Harvard University. The English text of the lectures differs somewhat from the text published subsequently in Spanish. In fact, this first paragraph appears fully *only* in the Spanish version, so this translation and the following one are, of necessity, mine. I have, however, used the published English translation, *Children of the Mire*, for subsequent citations from Paz's text.

16. Néstor García Canclini, *Culturas híbridas: Estrategias para entrar y salir del modernismo* (Mexico City: Grijalbo, 1989), p. 98 (my translation). Subsequent page references are cited in the text.

17. In *Hopscotch*, Cortázar's character Morelli argues that different historical periods "coincide" synchronically; he refers to ". . . pintores y escritores que rehúsan apoyarse en la circunstancia, ser 'modernos' en el sentido en que lo entienden los contemporáneos, lo que no significa que opten por ser anacrónicos; sencillamente están al margen del tiempo superficial de su época. . . ." *Rayuela* (Buenos Aires: Editorial Sudamericana, 1963), p. 545; (". . . painters and writers who refuse to seek support in what surrounds them, to be 'modern' in the sense that their contemporaries understand it, which does not mean that they choose to be anachronistic; they are simply on the margin of the superficial time of their period. . . ." *Hopscotch*, trans. Gregory Rabassa [New York: Avon, 1966], p. 489).

Similarly, Carpentier writes: "Me apasiono por los temas históricos . . . para mí no existe la modernidad en el sentido que se le otorga; el hombre es, a veces, el mismo en diferentes edades, y situarlo en su pasado puede ser también situarlo en su presente" ("I am passionate about historical themes . . . to me, modernity does not exist in the sense given to it today. Humans are, sometimes, the same in different ages, and placing them in the past may be the same as placing them in the present"). Cited on the cover of *Guerra del tiempo y otros cuentos* (Madrid: Ediciones Alfaguara, 1963).

18. Luiz Costa Lima discusses Latin American Romanticism, emphasizing its greater objectivity when compared to other European conceptions of Romantic subjectivity: "Observation did not find its ground, so to speak, in a subject who would convert

nature into a means of stimulating and ordering the reading of himself or herself; its ground resided instead in the object observed, in the land that was to be replaced on the written page." *The Control of the Imaginary: Reason and Imagination in Modern Times*, trans. Ronald W. Sousa (Minneapolis: University of Minnesota Press, 1988), pp. 162–63.

19. Octavio Paz, *Sor Juana Inés de la Cruz o las trampas de la fe* (Mexico City: Fondo de Cultura Económica, 1982); Paz, *Sor Juana or The Traps of Faith*, trans. Margaret Sayers Peden, (Cambridge, Mass.: Harvard University Press, 1988); see also Paz's "Introducción a la historia de la poesía mexicana," in *Las peras del olmo* (Mexico City: UNAM, 1957), pp. 11–48.

20. Alejo Carpentier, "Lo barroco y lo real maravilloso," in *La novela latinoamericana en vísperas de un nuevo siglo* (Mexico City: Siglo Veintiuno Editores, 1981), p. 126.

21. Carpentier, "The Baroque and the Marvelous Real," trans. Tanya Huntington and Lois Parkinson Zamora, in *Magical Realism*, p. 100.

22. Among the most important considerations of this category by novelists are: José Lezama Lima, *La expresión americana* (Santiago: Editorial Universitaria, 1969); Severo Sarduy, "El barroco y el neobarroco," *América Latina en su literatura*, ed. César Fernández Moreno (Mexico City: Siglo Veintiuno Editores, 1972), pp. 167–84; Carlos Fuentes, "La violenta identidad de José Luis Cuevas," in *Casa con dos puertas* (Mexico City: Joaquín Mortiz, 1970), pp. 239–79 (see the bilingual edition of this essay, *El mundo de José Luis Cuevas*, trans. Consuelo de Aerenlund [New York: Tudor Publishing Co, 1969]); Fuentes, "The Baroque Culture of the New World," in *The Buried Mirror: Reflections on Spain and the New World* (New York: Houghton Mifflin, 1992), pp. 194–213.

Useful critical definitions of the New World Baroque may be found in the following: Julio Ortega, *La estética neobarroca en la narrativa hispanoamericana* (Madrid: José Porrúa Turanzas, 1984); Ortega, "El Inca Garcilaso y el discurso de la abundancia," *Revista Chilena de Literatura* 32 (1988), 31–43; Georgina Sabat-Rivers, "El barroco de la contraconquista: primicias de conciencia criolla en Balbuena y Domínguez Camargo," *Relecturas del barroco de indias* (Hanover, N.H.: Ediciones del Norte, 1994), pp. 59–95; Roberto González Echevarría, "Guillén as Baroque: Meaning in *Motivos de son*," *Calaloo* 10, no. 2 (1987), 302–17 (rpt. in González Echevarría, *Celestina's Brood* [Durham: Duke University Press, 1993], pp. 194–211); and my own essay, "Alejo Carpentier, François de Nomé, and the New World Baroque," in *Poetics of the Americas*, ed. Jefferson Humphries and Bainard Cowan (Baton Rouge: Louisiana State University Press, 1997).

A special issue of *Revista de crítica literaria latinoamericana* (no. 28, 1988) presents a number of essays that address the Baroque as a New World category. See John Beverley, "Nuevas vacilaciones sobre el Barroco," pp. 215–27; Mabel Moraña, "Barroco y conciencia criolla en Hispanoamérica," pp. 229–51; Julio Ortega, "Para una teoría del texto latinoamericano: Colón, Garcilaso, y el discurso de la abundancia," pp. 101–25.

23. Cited in Miguel Fernández-Brazo, *Gabriel García Márquez: Una conversación infinita* (Madrid: Editorial Azur, 1969), p. 75 (my translation). Elsewhere in the interview, García Márquez refers again to the Baroque tradition that contemporary Latin American novelists draw upon and extend: "Nosotros arrancamos, estamos muy fundados en el Siglo de Oro español" (78; "Our point of departure, our roots, are in the Spanish Golden Age").

24. Severo Sarduy, "El barroco y el neobarroco," passim.

25. Carlos Fuentes, Interview with Alfred MacAdam and Charles Ruas, *Paris Review* 23, no. 82 (1981), 153.

26. Fuentes, *El mundo de José Luis Cuevas*, p. 39.

27. T. S. Eliot, *Selected Essays: 1917–1932* (New York: Harcourt, Brace, 1932), p. 10.

28. Eliot, *Selected Essays*, p. 247.
29. In his seminal essay, "The Concept of Baroque in Literary Scholarship," René Wellek notes that in literary critical discussion of English and U.S. literature, the term "Baroque" came late, "much later than [Eliot's] revival of interest in Donne and the metaphysicals. . . . Grierson and T. S. Eliot do not use it, though Eliot apparently spoke of a baroque period in his unpublished Clark lectures on the metaphysical poets." "The Concept of Baroque in Literary Scholarship," in *Concepts of Criticism* (New Haven: Yale University Press, 1963), pp. 85–86.

   The term "Baroque" is still virtually unused in English literary history, a detail that explains in part the rarity of comparative studies of English and Spanish literature of this period. An admirable exception is L. Elaine Hooper, *John Donne and Francisco de Quevedo: Poets of Love and Death* (Chapel Hill: University of North Carolina Press, 1978).
30. This exploration reflects the "ethnocultural nation" that the U.S. has now become – a multiculturalist society approaching the diversity of Latin American cultural contexts such as those of Mexico and the Caribbean. The term is quoted from Michael Lind's study, *The Next American Nation: The New Nationalism and the Fourth American Revolution* (New York: The Free Press, 1995). Lind's distinctions among the stages of U.S. demographic structures are useful; he proposes Anglo-America (1789–1861), Euro-America (1875–1957), and Multicultural America (1972–present). He also distinguishes between cultural pluralists and multiculturalists, in terms of their attitudes toward difference. Lind's comparative assertions are particularly suggestive in my own comparative literary context. For example: "We Americans are more like our neighbors the Mexicans – a racially diverse cultural nation – than like our neighbors the Canadians – a collection of two or more nationalities lacking any common Canadian culture or identity that would survive the breakup of Canada into several states. We Americans . . . are defined by a common language and culture; and as long as these unite us, we will constitute an ethnocultural nation" (259).
31. Hitchens defines this principle as the preference of old and new minorities "to emphasize their micro-diversities, while many among the majority regard that very stress as un-American. . . ." *New York Times Book Review*, 25 June 1995, p. 7.
32. Eliana Ortega and Nancy Saporta Sternbach, "At the Threshold of the Unnamed: Latina Literary Discourse in the Eighties," in *Breaking Boundaries*, ed. Asunción Horno-Delgado et al. (Amherst: University of Massachusetts Press, 1989), p. 3. Virtually all critics writing about chicana fiction agree on this point. See especially Yvonne Yarbro-Bejarano's study of the construction of an inclusive, multiple subject from ruptured indigenous and European traditions in "Gloria Anzaldúa's *Borderlands/La Frontera*: Cultural Studies, 'Difference,' and the Non-Unitary Subject," *Cultural Critique* 28 (Fall 1994), 5–28.
33. Walter Shear, "Generational Differences and the Diaspora in *The Joy Luck Club*," *Critique* 34, no. 3 (1993), 193. Shear quotes Shirley Geok-lin Lim's "Twelve Asian American Writers in Search of Definition," *MELUS* 13 (1986), 57.
34. Nancy J. Peterson, "History, Postmodernism, and Louise Erdrich's *Tracks*," *PMLA* 109, no. 5 (1994), pp. 982–94. The final quoted phrase is from Diana Fuss' "Getting into History," *Arizona Quarterly* 45, no. 4 (1989), 95.
35. Alice Walker, *The Color Purple* (New York: Pocket Books, 1982), p. 187.
36. Mary O'Connor, "Subject, Voice, and Women in Some Contemporary Black American Women's Writing," in *Feminism, Bakhtin and the Dialogic*, ed. Dale M. Bauer and S. Jaret McKinstry (Albany: SUNY Press, 1991), pp. 199–217 (my emphasis).
37. Toni Morrison, "Living Memory," in *City Limits* 31 March–7 April 1988), 10–11; see also her essay, "Rootedness: The Ancestor as Foundation," in *Black Women Writers*, ed. Mari Evans (New York: Anchor, 1984), pp. 339–45.

38. Morrison, "Unspeakable Things Unspoken: The Afro-American Presence in American Literature," *Michigan Quarterly Review* 28, no. 1 (1989), 11.

39. Morrison cites Terrence Rafferty's comparison of Kundera and Fuentes (as I do at the end of Chapter 4) and identifies with what Rafferty describes as Fuentes' New World need to invent cultural values:

> I was refreshed by Rafferty's comments. With the substitution of certain phrases, his observations and the justifiable umbrage he takes [with respect to Kundera's exclusion of American literature] can be appropriated entirely by Afro-American writers regarding their own exclusion from the "transcendent 'idea of the novel.'"
>
> For the present turbulence seems not to be about the flexibility of a canon, its range among and between Western countries, but about its miscegenation. The word is informative here and I do mean its use. A powerful ingredient in this debate concerns the incursion of third-world or so-called minority literature into a Eurocentric stronghold. (6)

Like Carpentier's use of *mestizaje*, Morrison's "miscegenation" celebrates the interactions of heterogenous traditions and also calls attention to racial injustice that has usually accompanied it in the Americas.

40. Carlos Fuentes, "La novela como tragedia: William Faulkner," p. 67 (my translation follows).

41. Morrison, *Playing in the Dark: Whiteness and the Literary Imagination* (New York: Vintage, 1993), p. 4.

42. In any case, as Robert Young has pointed out, totalization will always remain metaphoric: "We have seen the ways in which Sartre's *Critique* shows how totalization cannot work without a movement of self-transcendence, a repeated interpolation of an excess beyond the totality which paradoxically then means that the totality can no longer be a totality." *White Mythologies*, p. 84.

43. Morrison, *Playing in the Dark*, p. 4.

44. Interview with Marlise Simmons, "García Márquez on Love, Plagues, and Politics," p. 24. García Márquez's "popular culture" is probably a literal translation of *cultural popular*, meaning indigenous and lower-class cultures rather than mass culture, as it does in English.

45. Unlike most applications of postmodernist *literary critical theory*, the discussion of postmodernist *social formations* in Latin America has achieved a useful level of specificity. See, for example, the essays included in *The Postmodernism Debate in Latin America*, ed. John Beverley, José Oviedo, and Michael Aronna (Durham: Duke University Press, 1995); also useful is George Yúdice, "Postmodernity and Transnational Capitalism in Latin America," in *On Edge: The Crisis of Contemporary Latin American Culture*, ed. George Yúdice, Jean Franco, and Juan Flores (Minneapolis: University of Minnesota Press, 1992), pp. 1–28. Yúdice begins his essay by noting the recent "attempt to endow [Latin American] heterogeneous formations with the cachet of mainstream postmodern rhetoric" (1). My own sense (at least in literary studies) is the opposite: the indiscriminate application of postmodernist categories to contemporary Latin American fiction is an attempt to endow "mainstream postmodernist rhetoric" with the cachet of writers like Borges, Puig, Vargas Llosa.

46. Besides the Latin American literary sources I have cited, see the sociological elaboration of the Baroque as a metaphor for contemporary culture by Boaventura de Sousa Santos, *Toward a New Common Sense: Law, Science and Politics in the Paradigmatic Transition* (New York: Routlege, 1995). For a philosophical application of the Baroque as metaphor, see Gilles Deleuze, *The Fold: Leibniz and the Baroque* (1988), trans. Tom Conley (Minneapolis: University of Minnesota Press, 1993). Both scholars stress Baroque "multiplicity that makes for inclusion" (Deleuze, p. 31), and its suspended forms, which "impede closure and completion" (de Sousa Santos, p. 501).

Index

Adams, Henry, 11, 18
The Education of Henry Adams, 25
Adorno, Theodor, 25
Agee, James, 57–9, 62
Let Us Now Praise Famous Men, 37,
52, 56–8, 224n32
allegory, 87–8
Allende, Isabel, 11, 138, 152
The House of the Spirits, 16, 18, 118,
133; 138–9
Of Love and Shadows, 43
murals as metaphors in, 138, 235n17
Paula, 138
"Walimai," 123
Alter, Robert, 162
on Benjamin's "aura," 174
Ancestral vs. Archival impulse
in Allende, 138
in Borges, 135
in Cisneros, 173
in Fuentes, 124
and González Echevarría, 124–6
in Latin American literature, 135–6
antipositivism, 12, *see also* positivism
of Baroque, 208
of Borges, 13–14
influence of Bergson on, 220n38
Latin American, 39
Mexican, 27–8
in modern U.S. and European literature, 218–19n28
anxiety of origins, 176, 196
vs. anxiety of influence, 5–8
defined, 5
as historical anxiety in American literature, 14, 17–19, 27, 189, 206–8,
214n31, 214n33
postmodernism as response to, 209
apocalypse
in Benjamin, 162–3
as colonizing ideology, 216n11
in García Márquez, 118
in Jewish tradition, 162–3
in Kafka, 162

in Muñiz-Huberman, 162
in Scholem, 162
as theme of Vargas Llosa's *The War of
the End of the World*, 72–3
archetypes, 83
Borges' use of, 82–7, 198
García Márquez's use of, 81, 198
in magical realism, 78
in New World writing, 198
in Romanticism, 228n25
Arenas, Reynaldo, *The Ill-Fated Peregrinations of Fray Servando*, 16
Arendt, Hannah
on Benjamin, 175
on Hegel, 2
Arguedas, José María, 11, 12
Deep Rivers, 123
Asian American writers, 206
Asturias, Miguel Angel, *Men of Maize*,
123

Bakhtin, Mikhail, 204, 235n19
Baldwin, James, 11
Baroque, 160, 197, 208, 248n46
American, 203–4, 207–10, 245n11
Golden Age, Spanish, 204, 247n23
as model of Latin American inclusiveness, 204
and postmodernism, 209–10
Spanish, vs. English Romanticism,
192–3, 202–5, 247n29
Baroque, New World, 5, 167, 193, 202–4,
246n22
and Carpentier, 136, 202, 203–4
and Faulkner, 199, 207–8, 246n11
according to Fuentes, 204, 207–8
as inclusive form, 207–8
inclusive structures and strategies in,
199, 202
and magical realism, 203, 204
as metaphor for interaction of American histories and cultures, 204–10
as model for comparative criticism,
209–10

DATE DUE

Demco, Inc. 38-293